LATIN AMERICA
YESTERDAY AND TODAY

LATIN AMERICA
YESTERDAY AND TODAY

EDITED BY JOHN ROTHCHILD

THE GEORGE SCHOOL READINGS
ON DEVELOPING LANDS

Clark D. Moore, Series Editor

PRAEGER PUBLISHERS

New York • Washington

Published in the United States of America in 1974
by Praeger Publishers, Inc.
111 Fourth Avenue, New York, N.Y. 10003

Library of Congress Catalog Card Number: 73-1914

Contents

LATIN AMERICA
YESTERDAY AND TODAY

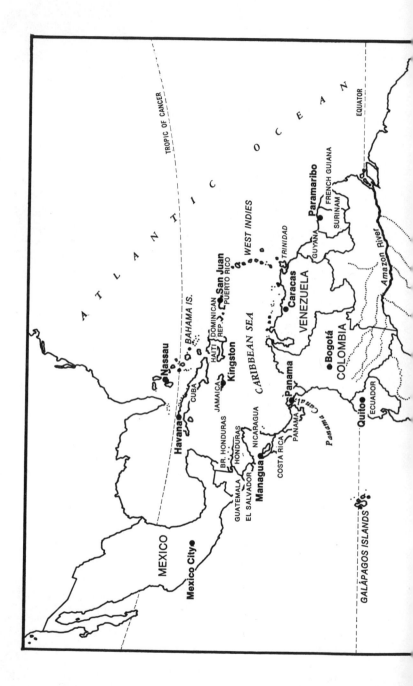

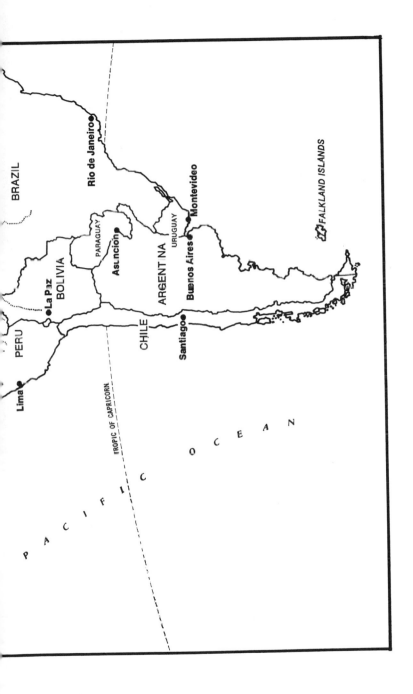

General Introduction

This book is an attempt to understand Latin Americans by describing how they see themselves. I have relied mostly on Latin American writers: putting Latin American actions into North American thoughts would probably reveal more about us than about them. At the same time, I have tried to emphasize the Latin American reasons for why things happen, which often have little to do with the reasons that we ascribe. As onlookers from the United States, we use numbers to calculate Latin America's economic growth, while the Latin American person tends to distrust numbers. We seek facts to explain his palace revolts—and are swamped by the chaos of names and dates spewed back at us—whereas the Latin American writer has little faith in facts. We perceive a disorderly world in Latin America, full of senseless coups and surprise revolutions, while the Latin American finds his world predictable, and, if anything, unchanging. It makes more sense to see Latin America through the eyes of its own inhabitants, and that is what this book is mostly about.

In making the selections, I have neglected to cover the major products, rivers, mountains, capitals, politicians, and countries in any systematic way. Readers who are reassured by such facts can find them in Appendix 2 of the book. But a comprehensive treatment of Latin America (including South America, Central America, Mexico, and the Caribbean islands) is both impossible in a book that covers everything from the year zero to the present, and misleading for a continent that changes its appearance so abruptly. While the rivers and mountains stay pretty much the same, the political parties, major exports, forms of government, and individual leaders appear and disappear so quickly that to list the most current ones would be to tempt fate and to insult tomorrow (from the Latin American point of view).

1

The Latin American character that makes up the continent is a mixture of fiction, fantasy, politics, history, and daily life. This book includes all of these. A page of fiction may be preceded or followed by a page of history—the real, the mysterious, and the make-believe are part of this book, because all of them are a part of the collective mind of Latin America.

The Latin American, of course, is of no single personality. Some people doubt that anything can be said that would apply to twenty countries and tens of islands—that no words could possibly surround both Indians who spend their lives hoeing a few feet of ground with small sticks, and also *hacendados* with fleets of Mercedes Benzes; raucous coastal dock workers and ascetic mountain farmers; pure blacks and pure whites and every shade between; sea-level life and life in places like La Paz, 15,000 feet up; Spanish-speaking people, Portuguese-speaking people, French Haitians, Aymará Indians, and revolutionary Cubans. There is some validity to this doubt, as anybody who has ever mistakenly called a Chilean a Puerto Rican can attest. But there is also something—something recognized by Latin Americans themselves—that ties the continent together. It is the common thread that the book seeks to follow.

The book jumps around a lot from century to century and from place to place, especially in the early selections. The general drift of the book is to build a composite picture of the modern Latin American by treating in separate chapters each of the important influences that make up that picture. The book begins with a geographical setting, with an emphasis on the special ways that Latin Americans view their environment. Then there are parts that deal with different historical and cultural influences—the Indians who populated the continent first, the Spaniards who conquered it, the European immigrants who helped build the modern cities. The last half of the book deals with how the contemporary Latin American, the product of all these separate heritages, is coping with life and with politics.

The history of Latin America is not as dry and distant as the history of the United States, both because the Latin American does not so quickly reject his past and because his past tends to repeat itself. The Latin American is not the product of the hard sorting and melting that

produced the North American middle class. Studying
Polish customs and history would not help anybody
understand the modern North Americans, probably not
even those of Polish extraction. But in Latin America, the
Inca Indian, for instance, has found his way into the soul
of a Lima businessman or a Quito politician. So, for the
Latin American, Indian history can be an expression of his
own character: it is still present and has not been dissolved into something else. This book takes us back
through the Indian legacy, through the Spanish and black
influences, and connects them to the mind of the Latin
American that you meet on the street today.

Hopefully, this book will help people who are confused by the news from Latin America, but it is also for
people who want to meet up with the neighboring culture face-to-face. I have in Part XI tried to deal with some
of the tensions that made it hard for North Americans to
understand Latin America—on either a political or a personal level. The fact that we happen to share a hemisphere seems to lead to the notion that we also share a
philosophy, that we are potential allies in an otherwise
untrustworthy world, and that we must merge. We are
supposed to feel more friendship and solidarity with
Latin America than with other parts of the world, and
yet our relations with the bottom half of the hemisphere
always seem strained. While we continue to call ourselves good neighbors and to create alliances, there is
an undercurrent of fear, distrust, and misunderstanding.
Part of this schism derives from the North American posture of paternalism toward Latin America, from our habit
of sending the marines when things don't go as we think
they should, from the endless development and other
U.S.-concocted schemes to ensure that Latin America
changes for the better (that is, to be more like us). But
part of the misunderstanding comes from more personal
sources, from the myths about Latin America that we
harbor and would like to believe—stories about bandits
and fat generals and lazy peasants.

There is plenty of evidence that laziness, violence,
emotionalism, and fatalism are part of the Latin American
character. But it also seems to be more than coincidence
that we repeatedly find in Latin Americans all of the
goblins of our Protestant ethic culture, precisely the qualities that we reject as a nation. Is it possible that as we

extract raw materials from the southern part of the hemisphere, we also dump our psychological refuse there, creating an image of Latin America that is a composite of our own fantasy fears? When we invade and attempt to solve the "problem" of Latin America, who are we really attacking? (Latin Americans may do it to us in reverse, chiding the United States for its racism and its materialism while it continues to mistreat Indians and buy television sets.)

Finding out about Latin America is not a simple discovery, because all of us already live with an imaginary Latin America in our heads. In sifting through all my own reactions, I found a great tension and also the potential for a great understanding with Latin Americans. But this understanding can come only after we realize that we are not good neighbors, but simply strangers who naïvely think they know each other.

PART I.

THE MYTHS OF GEOGRAPHY

Introduction

Geography is important to Latin Americans, but not so much in the practical sense. We capture mountains by knowing their height, or distance by knowing the miles, but these notions of geography mock the Latin American sense of the world. If you ask how far it is to a certain place in Peru, you are likely to be told that it is just over the next hill, only to be told the same thing two miles later. If you ask when something will arrive in Ecuador, you will undoubtedly be answered with *"ya mismo"* (literally, "already the same," or "right away"). It doesn't matter that the thing isn't getting there for four days. The Latin American does not believe that space or time can easily be controlled or dominated by mathematics. The businessman, of course, is forced into being punctual and accurate on occasion; but the culture around him is full of lazy stretches and quick bursts, politenesses, surprises, and chaos. The selections on geography, for this reason, are not devoted to measuring sticks.

Suffice it to say that the twenty countries from Mexico to Chile include every kind of topography imaginable—from big mountains in some places to big deserts in others, forests, lakes, plains, coasts, ice caps, jungles, islands, snow and swelter, cities and villages. All this diversity is often crammed into a very small space—going from the mountains of Peru to the coast (from 10,000 feet to sea level in a matter of hours) takes you vertically through more changes than you would get traveling across the entire North American continent.

What is different about Latin American geography or environment is the way its people perceive it. This part of the book, then, is about the interchange between the Latin American surroundings and the Latin American character—what a person sees in his world and what

6

makes him see it that way. The North American viewed his own frontier as an invitation, as manifest destiny, while the Latin American in Argentina, confronting virtually the same landscape, saw emptiness, aloneness, and despair. The two excerpts on Argentina show how the Latin American feared the power that the pampas and the rolling plains held over him.

Other geographic regions of Latin America are viewed with equal awe and respect. The Amazon is still impregnable, still full of snakes and legendary creatures. The mountains are still impassive and inert, the rivers are full and untamed, and in most countries, movement from city to city is carried on one-lane dirt roads. Latin American geography is a gigantic obstacle course. Its cities are modern, polluted, crowded, and hurried. The terrain beyond invites people to enjoy and respect their natural surroundings, but not to try too hard to change them.

Since the Latin American terrain is generally rougher than that found in North America, some people have used the environment as an explanation for the relative lack of progress of the southern part of the hemisphere. Others have said that the tropical climate found along the coasts and in Brazil and the Caribbean is responsible for a more listless, decadent, floating group of people. The excerpt by Gilberto Freyre, a Brazilian writer, describes how climate may have affected the Portuguese settler in Brazil differently from, say, the English settler in Jamestown. But terrain and climate in themselves are not enough to encompass the Latin American's reticence, his wariness of coming up against nature. Inhabit Latin America with our own *gringo* population, and there would be schemes to blow out the jungle, to pave the pampas, to melt the mountains: our fetish for dominance, for control, would change the geography. It takes only some exaggeration and a sense of humor to imagine what would happen if North America were populated entirely by Latin Americans: the middle of the country would break out in vines.

In spite of (or perhaps because of) the geographic difficulties, Latin America has always been a continent of illusions. A good example of what this means is found in the Latin American gold rush. During the sixteenth century and beyond, the Spaniards embarked on a frantic search for gold based on the El Dorado legend—vague rumors of a lost Indian kingdom where gold was supposedly thrown into a lake during religious ceremonies. The legend exploded across the continent, and El Dorado was rumored to be everywhere. Hundreds of colonists spent frustrated years or even their entire lives in pursuit of the lost kingdom that was never found. The North American gold rush, by comparison, was a hard-cash bargain. There was real gold in the rivers, washed out from the mud, worked over and somehow stripped of any fantasy, except economic fantasy. The North American mind knew how to find gold and how to use gold, while the Latin American believed in the magic of gold, protected by vines and fears and mythical creatures. El Dorado was a flaky quest, but it still lingers: something in the gold myth is reflected in most Latin American enterprise, driving people to attempt the impossible and then to be destroyed by the impossible. Latin American geography, like El Dorado, is full of surreality.

Victor Alba, in the first article of this part, runs through the list of flora and fauna and mineral riches and animals, and concludes with Von Humboldt's observation that Latin America is a beggar sitting on a bench of gold. Some geologists doubt even the bench; they say that the continent is not that rich, that the supposed oil lakes and fat mineral seams are not as extensive, or as accessible, as people have presumed. Latin America would understand this skepticism: the potential riches have always meant betrayal, have been siphoned off into a few pockets or into U.S. corporate profits; the promise of industrial utopia, like El Dorado, remains to be fulfilled.

It is hard to tell how heavy the bench of riches under the Latin American "beggar" actually is, since most of it is still hidden. Latin American man has not triumphed over geography or nature or chaos; he has not, like North American man, forced nature to submit to him. The core of the United States was a beckoning to supersede, to progress, while the core of Latin America, inside of everything, is the Amazon jungle, an impossible tangle of vines. The Amazon is a symbol of the Latin American spirit, much as the railroad across the plains expressed the essence of North America. The jungle is a trackless, violent, unsure, passionate, fantastic surprise. Teodoro Sampaio, in an excerpt included in this part, describes the pull of the interior on the Brazilian *bandeirantes,* the pathfinders who roamed and even populated the Amazon during the sixteenth through eighteenth centuries. Something of the *bandeirante* still exists in the Latin American personality: a few years ago, in recognition of it, Brazil moved its capital from the coast to the interior.

Many of the Latin American myths of geography, about the fantasy jungle and the shimmering El Dorado, have outlived their time, as the continent is covered with great cities—Rio de Janeiro, Buenos Aires, Mexico City, São Paulo—each with several million inhabitants. Latin America is becoming an urban continent: a third of its people now live in the cities. There are similarities among city people everywhere. But as the frontier and rural farm and cowboy myths followed North Americans into the metropolis, so the pampas, El Dorado, and the jungle have their lingering effect on the way Latin Americans see their daily lives. Their emotional map has not changed as much as their physical one.

How the Latin American views his surroundings, of course, depends on who he is and where he lives. The Indian on the Andean *hacienda* and the black piece laborer in the seaport do not think alike, nor do their environments look alike to them. There are great schisms all over the continent, but the most obvious difference is between the mountain people living down the spine of the Andes, and the coastal people living on the hot fringes of the sea. As one of the excerpts points out, an Ecuadorian from mountainous Quito has more in common with a Bolivian than with another Ecuadorian from a coastal town.

There is an ongoing debate whether Latin America is a continent of vast, untapped resources or whether it is poor in land and mineral deposits. In this selection, Victor Alba, a contemporary Latin American writer, examines Latin America's natural resources—its plant and animal life, its soil and minerals. Alba sides with those who see a potentially rich continent that because of geographic barriers and primitive technology has not realized its potential. The selection is taken from Alba's book *The Latin Americans,* published in 1968.

A Beggar on a Bench of Gold

By Victor Alba

The flora and fauna of Latin America are abundant: the task of classifying them has only just begun. This abundance is reflected in the national coats of arms, many of which display an animal or plant characteristic of the country: Guatemala shows the brilliant quetzal bird (which also gives its name to the unit of currency); Peru, the llama; Uruguay, the sheep.

Indian corn (maize), the potato, the tomato, tobacco, and many tropical fruits are native to America. The Mayas smoked tobacco through their noses. For the Aymará Indians in what is now Bolivia, potatoes were like bread; they dried and preserved them for winter—as they still do. Corn is still the basic food of many Latin Americans.

Columbus took to Cuba the seeds of the sugarcane, which the Arabs had introduced into Spain. The Spaniards also brought with them from the Old World rice, wheat, and oranges, among many other plants. They also introduced into the New World the banana from Africa and the mango from the Philippines.

The Indians were familiar with rubber, which they used to make balls with which they played a kind of basketball. Until 1870 rubber was produced only in Brazil, Peru, and Colombia, but in that year an Englishman, Sir Henry Wickham, took with him several thousand seeds, which, planted in London, produced nurseries for the plantations soon to be established in Ceylon, Indonesia, and throughout Southeast Asia. The quinine of Peru, Ecuador, and Colombia was also taken out by the Dutch, French, and English, who cultivated it in their colonies. In 1727 a Portuguese ambassador stole coffee beans from the Dutch in Surinam, who were cultivating it secretly; carried to Brazil, coffee became that country's principal product.

Today there are great harvests of bananas and other tropical fruits, coffee, sugar, and cotton. Brazil produces nearly half the world's supply of coffee, and the Caribbean islands account for almost one-third of its sugar. Chile has excellent wines; Ecuador's cocoa is famous. Corn, the staple food of the people, is grown everywhere, and so to a lesser degree is wheat. But only very recently has there been an attempt to introduce new crops or improve existing ones, or to satisfy the needs of the domestic market.

Scarcely one-third of the surface of Latin America is arable; scarcely half of that is cultivated; a quarter of that half is used for grazing. The richest farmland is concentrated in a few regions, like the Bajío in Mexico; the 300-mile semicircle of pampas around Buenos Aires (where the black soil reaches a depth of twelve feet); the Colombian and Venezuelan *llanos* (the latter used almost wholly for cattle-raising); and the lowlands of southern Brazil. Near the Pacific coast, plantations make good use of the land, but in general the agricultural yield is low, the land is wasted, and only the indispensable minimum is cultivated—again as a result of social causes. Still, in some parts of Latin America it is not unusual to harvest two and even three crops a year.

The animals that are the basis of modern agricultural wealth in Latin America were brought in by the conquistadors: the horse, cattle, and sheep. The Spaniards also brought with them chickens, asses, pigs, dogs, and cats. (The only animal that did not acclimate was the camel, either in colonial times or in the nineteenth century, when it was tried as a means of transporting immigrants across the Isthmus of Panama.) The horse had existed in a wild state in Latin America, but had disappeared by the time the Spaniards arrived. Today it is essential for farming and above all in cattle-raising, which is a major industry in Argentina, Uruguay, Venezuela, and Colombia. The *llaneros* (in Colombia and Venezuela), the gauchos (in Argentina, Brazil, and Uruguay), and the *guasos* (in Chile) are—like the cowboys of the American West—excellent horsemen. (For a gaucho, the worst conceivable fate is the loss of his horse. In the Argentine army, during the last century, gauchos who received the death penalty were sentenced instead to serve in the infantry.)

The lumber industry, although little developed, has caused significant deforestation in the regions around Latin America's cities. Moreover, the scarcity of coal has made it necessary to use wood for cooking, which has increased the deforestation. But there are still more than two million square miles of rare woods and more than 1,500 varieties of hardwood growing in Latin America. The quebracho of Chile and Argentina is much in demand for making railroad ties, and Peruvian balsa is used in ship-building. Cinchona bark yields quinine. Tropical woods are still much used by cabinetmakers. But at the time when the lumber industry might have thrived, lack of transportation facilities hampered it, and today, with the appearance of plastics, wood is losing its usefulness.

The subsoil of Latin America is much richer than the topsoil, but it has been little and poorly exploited. The Spaniards concentrated on gold and silver, which served to finance their wars in Europe (and, indirectly, to ruin their country). Available techniques did not make possible the discovery of Latin America's huge deposits of other minerals; even if these had been discovered, they could not have been used, since Europe had plenty of minerals and its industry at that time was well supplied with raw materials. The growing industries of the eighteenth century opened up new markets for minerals, but Latin American society was exclusively oriented to exploitation of the land, and its leaders were not interested in extending the sources of wealth. Exploitation of the existing mines, however, was continued. The needs of the industrial countries induced foreign entrepreneurs to explore Latin America further and to exploit new sources of wealth. Being foreigners, they were interested in making the greatest possible profit without concerning themselves with the future or the interests of the Latin American countries—an attitude that, in certain cases, has had serious economic consequences and ended by producing extreme nationalistic reactions among Latin Americans.

More than 10 percent of the world's tin now comes from Bolivia. Venezuela provides the greater part of the United States' imports of iron, Chile of copper. Caribbean bauxite represents more than half of the world's supply. Mexico, Bolivia, and Peru supply the greater portion of the world's silver. (Two mines in Mexico alone—in Guanajuato and Pachuca—yield one-third of the silver used in the world today.) In the last fifty years Mexico and Venezuela have developed a mighty oil industry; oil has also been found in Colombia, Peru, Brazil, Argentina, Chile, Ecuador, and Bolivia, although still not in quantities sufficient to meet the needs of these countries. There is also little coal in Latin America; it is found only in Mexico, Colombia, Brazil, and Chile.

Latin Ameria's potential wealth is far greater than its actual riches. Venezuela is the world's second largest producer of oil, but experts say that there is more oil under Bolivia than in all the rest of South America. Chile's copper reserves account for about one-third of the world's supply. There are known to be iron reserves of about 5 billion tons, in addition to 80 billion tons of available potential reserves, nearly all of high quality; these represent one-third of the world's reserves. The most important deposits are those of Minas Gerais and Matto Grosso in Brazil, which represent more than 80 per cent of the Latin American reserve. The salt deposits of Zipaquira, in Colombia, extend over several thousand square miles and are several hundred feet deep.

Alexander von Humboldt, the German scholar and writer who traveled throughout Latin America in the early nineteenth century and wrote about its geography, flora, and fauna, said that Latin America was like "a beggar sitting on a bench of gold."

As this account by a contemporary Latin American historian illustrates, the Spaniards were interested in geography for one principal reason—to find the quickest route to the gold. Quesada was one of the first explorers to endure unbelievable hardships in search of El Dorado (the mythical kingdom of gold that the Spanish heard about from the Indians). But hundreds of others followed behind him, and Quesada's journey is symbolic of how the Spaniards populated the entire continent. They were disappointed at not discovering easy riches, but their quest led them to beautiful lands and sites for colonies. Without El Dorado, Quesada would never have found the city of Bogotá, and his followers probably would not have populated New Granada, which later became Colombia. This account is taken from Germán Arciniegas' book *Latin America: A Cultural History.*

The Legend of El Dorado
By Germán Arciniegas

. . . El Dorado was on every tongue and its capital in many places from the Río de la Plata to Coro, Venezuela, and Santa Marta on the Colombian beaches. And everywhere, with malice aforethought, the Indians directed the Spaniards to distant provinces where they said gold might be found. The object was to get the white men off their land.

The most famous of the conquistadors who explored for El Dorado was Don Gonzalo Jiménez de Quesada (1500–79), the Knight of El Dorado. . . .

. . . Unlike Cortés, who advanced from the Gulf Coast to the Aztec capital in a few months through territory peopled by great nations, Quesada spent two years fighting his way from the coast of the Caribbean to the presumptive capital of El Dorado on the crest of the Andes. He crossed the rawest, hottest, and loneliest jungles by forced marches, and his story, as reported by his historian, Fray Pedro Aguado (who died after 1589), can stand comparison with the most dramatic passages in certain novels of our own time.

. . . When Quesada and his soldiers reached the summit of the Andes, they found nothing but a high green plateau dotted with lakes, not even a llama. The trees were dwarfed. The Indians dealt in salt, which they mined from the entrails of a mountain. El Dorado's gold was found only in some little lizards and toads and miniature chieftains made of gold which passed from hand to hand. The natives themselves had obtained them by bartering salt. Those amulets, or *tunjos*, were tossed into the sacred lake on days of important ceremonies. The Indians were savages who cherished their gold frogs as coin that pleased the gods of rain and the harvest. Unlike the Aztecs, they had no intention of cutting out their prisoners' hearts with obsidian knives.

Yet Jiménez de Quesada founded the New Kingdom of Granada upon the fugitive image of El Dorado. Before returning to Spain to converse with the emperor about his conquests, he made Santa Fe de Bogotá the capital. . . .

This selection, written by a Brazilian named Sampaio in 1900, describes the geography of Brazil as perceived by its seventeenth-century inhabitants. Sampaio shows how the three great geographic regions of Brazil—the jungles, the northern deserts, and the mountainous coastal areas affected the thoughts and actions of the Brazilian colonizers. He identifies the northern backlands (or *sertão*) as the source of wild myths, passionate urges to explore, and hidden surprises; the desert as a monotonous labyrinth that promises oblivion and despair; and the coast as the smooth, easy place that attracts the settled populations. The Sampaio excerpt shows how the Latin American mythologizes his surroundings, making them into sanctuaries of fantasy, how he tends to live on the ocean fringes of the continent, but is continually obsessed by the unknown jungle at the core of his environment. Notice the powers that the Latin American ascribes to his geography. Although he was writing about the past, Sampaio's actual descriptions, and his awareness of the interplay between geography and the Latin American imagination, are still applicable today. His conclusions hold true not only for Brazil but also for the desert, jungle, and coastal regions of the other countries. The selection is taken from *The Bandeirantes*, an anthology of articles depicting the lives of the Brazilian pioneers of that name.

An Environmental Fantasy

By Teodoro Sampaio

... The historians [of the time] speak enthusiastically of the land's inexhaustible fish and game. They describe the great resources with which bountiful nature surrounded enraptured man on all sides. They tell of the abundance of the manatee in almost all the estuaries and rivers of the coast, of the large and numerous whales, and also of the sea lions and porpoises which bred on both land and sea. Frei Vicente do Salvador reports that in the seas of Brazil there even appeared men known as Hipupiaras who had been seen on land pursuing the Indians, whose eyes and noses they were fond of eating. This same historian tells us with the disarming simplicity and credulity of Herodotus that there were snakes in this country that came at night to suckle the breasts of ladies, as gently and softly as if they were their own children. The historian Gandavo relates the wonders of the *giboiuçu* (boa constrictor), which would swallow a whole deer and then burst open from glutting itself, whereupon all the meat on its body rotted, leaving only the spine, the head, and the end of the tail intact; and, the historian goes on, "after it has remained for a time in this condition, little by little the flesh begins to grow again, until it is covered anew with flesh, as completely as before."*

Of the country's interior, contemporary historians leave us the most mysterious and fantastic accounts. The same Gandavo writes that some men assured him that in this land they had seen serpents with large and terrifying wings (although they were rather rare monsters) and also enormous lizards whose testicles smelled sweeter than musk. Another contemporary historian cites among the many riches of the vegetable kingdom the "soap tree" and the "glass tree"....

* Pero Magalhães de Gandavo, *The Histories of Brazil* (2 vols.; New York, 1922), II, 176.

The strangest legends circulated about the multitude of heathen who lived in the *sertões*. The Guaiasi of the far west were so dwarfish that they seemed a parody of men. The Matuiú had their feet reversed. The Corugueana were fifteen-foot giants who decorated their lips and nostrils with pieces of gold. A tribe in Ceará was reported to devour its aged to save them the travail of living. A tribe of the southern pampas had legs like those of birds. Most of these outlandish heathen were indescribably ferocious. No one dared enter their domains without a large and competent following.

The great treasures of the *sertão* were thus guarded by the highest mountains, by immense and unfordable torrents, by ferocious tribes, and by monsters of terrifying aspect. That there might exist treasures unprotected by creatures of dread never occurred to men's imagination. In America as in Colchis, the golden fleece or El Dorado is guarded by mosnters—three-tongued dragons or winged serpents—but always monsters. It was a popular belief among the settlers that a mysterious "something" impeded the discovery of the riches of the *sertão,* and that death was the inevitable punishment for anyone so imprudent as to dare reveal the secret. . . .

Toward the north the relief of the country is much less rugged. The land, less varied in its geological composition, rises without large or abrupt differences in level. . . . The landscape is generally dry and monotonous. Over a vast region the vegetation has always the same rachitic, spiny, twisted form, characteristically accentuated in the species that constitute the type of *catinga* [desert plain] where acacias, jujubes, and a great variety of cacti flourish in hot, rocky soil. The rains are sparse in their annual season, and sometimes they stop completely for successive years. On the moistureless earth, under a burning sky, the vegetation then seems to die. Stripped of their foliage the trees seem scorched by fire. The springs go dry; the rivers are mere gullies where signs of the water which once ran there are barely perceptible. The large rivers which come from afar and whose sources are found in other climates flow across this parched land as strangers, announcing their passage by long rows of greener vegetation like an oasis in the desert plain. Here and there the salt marshes, mantled by carnaubas in handsome arrangement, break the wearisome monotony of the landscape and mark the site of a small settlement under the arching shade of the palms.

The *catinga*, however, is not an impenetrable barrier. Its unique vegetation makes it more like a labyrinth, with a multitude of paths and clearings, always alike, and transformed as if by magic, to revive for a day, only when a chance rain fills the merciless sky. If the peril of virgin forest is solitude without trails or egress, the terror of the *catinga* is the bewilderment which their multiplicity never fails to cause. The beast, led by instinct, can range to the uttermost parts and reach his destination without straying; but once a man enters the *catinga* and his memory falters in choosing a trail, he is a victim whom only a miracle will save. . . .

The southern region is quite different. Here the coastal forest narrows. The mountains come down to meet the ocean, and more than once their steep cliffs project into its waters as promontories. The topography is more varied and therefore more beautiful. The mountain ranges multiply, and some raise their summits more than two thousand meters above the sea. . . .

Here the bare fields, whose mournful tranquility is broken only by the woodlands of araucaria, are open regions leading deep into the continental interior. Here in fact are the gateways to the western *sertões*. The rivers have their source almost in sight of the sea, then plunge into the unknown to serve the insatiable ambition of the conquerors through endless plains whose level, sweeping horizons suggest the mute surrender of the unknown before the audacity of the newcomers. . . .

The following two selections (one from a book, the other from an epic poem) together can be taken as a general description of the Argentine countryside and of the forests and plains regions throughout Latin America. Note how Sarmiento, the author in the first selection, relates the pampas of Argentina to the erratic politics and prevalent violence of that country. Note, too, the sense of how diminished man appears here—a small blot on the plain, suspended in nothingness, driven by futility and fatalism. As Sampaio did with the jungle, both authors here give almost psychic powers to the plains and forests.

The prose selection is taken from *Life in the Argentine Republic in the Days of the Tyrants,* a classic nineteenth-century political work by Domingo Sarmiento, a foremost educator and statesman of his time. The poetry is excerpted from *Martin Fierro,* most famous of the Latin American epics, dealing with the life of the nineteenth-century gaucho, or Argentine cowboy.

The Empty Pampas

By Domingo Sarmiento

... Immensity is the universal characteristic of the country: the plains, the woods, the rivers, are all immense; and the horizon is always undefined, always lost in haze and delicate vapors which forbid the eye to mark the point in the distant perspective, where the land ends and the sky begins. On the south and on the north are savages ever on the watch, who take advantage of the moonlight nights to fall like packs of hyenas upon the herds in their pastures, and upon the defenseless settlements....

... This constant insecurity of life outside the towns, in my opinion, stamps upon the Argentine character a certain stoical resignation to death by violence, which is regarded as one of the inevitable probabilities of existence. Perhaps this is the reason why they inflict death or submit to it with so much indifference, and why such events make no deep or lasting impression upon the survivors.

The inhabited portion of this country—a country unusually favored by nature, and embracing all varieties of climes—may be divided into three sections possessing distinct characteristics, which cause differ-

ences of character among the inhabitants, growing out
of the necessity of their adapting themselves to the
physical conditions which surround them.

In the north, an extensive forest, reaching to the
Chaco, covers with its impenetrable mass of boughs a
space whose extent would seem incredible if there
could be any marvel too great for the colossal types of
Nature in America.

In the central zone, lying parallel to the former, the
plain and the forest long contend with each other for
the possession of the soil; the trees prevail for some
distance, but gradually dwindle into stunted and
thorny bushes, only reappearing in belts of forest
along the banks of the streams, until finally in the
south, the victory remains with the plain, which displays its smooth, velvet-like surface unbounded and
unbroken. It is the image of the sea upon the land;
the earth as it appears upon the map—the earth yet
waiting for the command to bring forth every herb
yielding seed after its kind. We may indicate, as a
noteworthy feature in the configuration of this country, the aggregation of navigable rivers, which come
together in the east, from all points of the horizon, to
form the Plata by their union, and thus worthily to
present their mighty tribute to the Ocean, which receives it, not without visible marks of disturbance and
respect. But these immense canals, excavated by the
careful hand of Nature, introduce no change into the
national customs. The sons of the Spanish adventurers
who colonized the country hate to travel by water,
feeling themselves imprisoned when within the narrow limits of a boat or a pinnace. When their path is
crossed by a great river, they strip themselves uncon-
cernedly, prepare their horses for swimming, and
plunging in, make for some island visible in the distance, where horse and horseman take breath, and by
thus continuing their course from isle to isle, finally
effect their crossing. . . .

But above all the peculiarities of special portions of
the country, there predominates one general, uniform,
and constant character. Whether the soil is covered
with the luxuriant and colossal vegetation of the

tropics, or stunted, thorny, and unsightly shrubs bear
witness to the scanty moisture which sustains them; or
whether finally the pampa displays its open and
monotonous level, the surface of the country is generally flat and unbroken—the mountain groups of San
Luis and Cordova in the center, and some projecting
spurs of the Andes toward the north, being scarcely an
interruption to this boundless continuity. . . .

A Gaucho's Lament, from *Martín Fierro*
By José Hernández

. . . . . .

I mounted, and trusting to God,
I made for another district—
because a gaucho they call a vagrant
can have no place of his own,
and so he lives from one trouble to the next
lamenting what he has lost.

He's always on the run,
always poor and hounded,
he has neither a hole nor a nest
as if there were a curse on him,
because being a gaucho . . . curse it,
being a gaucho is a crime.

He's like the Government post-horses,
one leaves him, another takes him on—
there's no end to this sport—
from his childhood he's like
a young tree growing
without shelter on a hill.

His home is the wild grassland,
his shelter is the desert plain;
and when he's half starving,
if he lassos a yearling calf
they hound him to the end
because he's a "gaucho thief."

. . . . . .

And at that hour of the evening
when everything is falling asleep,
and the world seems to enter into
a life of pure calm,
he makes his way to the grasslands
with sorrow in his soul.

The little lamb bleats
by the side of the white ewe,
and the tethered calf calls out
to the cow as she moves away—
but a gaucho in his misfortune
has no one to hear him cry.

. . . . . .

With no aim or fixed course
in that immensity,
with that great darkness round him,
a gaucho roams like a ghost—
out there, the authorities
will never catch him asleep.

Courage is his hope—
caution is his protection—
his horse means safety . . .
and you live in watchfulness
with no help except from heaven
and no friend except your knife.

. . . . . .

And so one night, I was out there
gazing at the stars,
which it seems are more beautiful
the more unhappy you are,
and that God must have created them
for us to find comfort in them.

A man feels love for them,

and it's always with joy
that he sees the Three Marys coming out—
because when there's rain,
as soon as it clears, on the pampa,
the stars are a gaucho's guide.

Your Professors are no good here,
experience is all that counts;
here, those people who know everything
would see how little they know—
because this has another key
and a gaucho knows what it is.

It's a sad thing to spend whole nights
out in the midst of the plain,
gazing at the stars
that God created, in their course,
without any company except
the wild beasts, and your loneliness.

One of the frequent explanations given by those who describe Latin America as "underdeveloped" is that its tropical environment produces lazy and sluggish people, in contrast to the rugged, prodding people created in the United States or Western Europe. This selection, by Brazilian sociologist Gilberto Freyre, discusses the Portuguese explorers to tropical Brazil in the 1500's, but many Latin Americans of other eras share its viewpoint—holding their environment responsible for their condition. Only part of the continent is actually tropical, but arguments similar to Freyre's are applied to the frigid, barren Andes Mountains, to the impassable giant rivers, and to the arid deserts. Latin Americans often view their geography as hostile and impossible to work with. In contrast to Alba's thesis in the first selection of the book, Freyre does not completely accept the beggar-on-a-bench-of-gold theory, choosing to emphasize the cussedness of the land and its resources. Many believe Latin America to be more like a beggar sitting on a rough bench of fool's gold.

This excerpt comes from Freyre's classic, *Masters and Slaves*, an extended look at Brazil's history and character.

A Rude Climate

By Gilberto Freyre

. . . In this essay . . . climate is to be looked upon as the rude and practically all-powerful agent that it was for the Portuguese in 1500: an irregular, swampy climate, leading to disturbances of the digestive tract; a climate that, in its relation to the soil, was unfavorable to agriculture, especially of the European variety, since it permitted neither a traditional form of labor regulated by the four seasons of the year nor the profitable cultivation of those alimentary plants to which the European had been accustomed for so many centuries.

The Portuguese colonist in Brazil had to alter quite radically his system of alimentation, whose base now had to be changed, with a perceptible deficit, from wheat to manihot flour; and this was true also of his system of labor, which, in view of the physical and chemical conditions of the soil, as well as the meteorological conditions, could not be the same as the easy-going mode of tillage in the Portuguese homeland. In this respect the English colonizer in the United States had a decided advantage over the Portuguese in Brazil, for the former in America met with physical conditions of life and sources of nutrition similar to those in the mother country. In Brazil there was necessarily a certain lack of balance that affected the morphology as well as the efficiency of the European, owing to the lack, immediately felt, of those chemical means of alimentation that he had known in his own country. This lack, along with the difference in the meteorological conditions under which agricultural labor, performed by Negroes but directed by him, had to be performed, gave to the colonizing activities of the Portuguese an original, creative character such as neither the English in North America nor the Spaniards in Argentina could claim for their efforts.

Although the Portuguese came nearer than any other European colonizer of the Americas to being familiar with the climate and conditions of the tropics, it was, all the same, a rude change that he underwent in removing to Brazil. Within the new circumstances of his physical life he found his economic and social life also compromised.

Everything here in this new land was in a state of disequilibrium, marked by great excesses and great deficiencies. The soil, leaving aside certain patches of black or reddish earth of exceptional fertility, was far from being suited to the planting of everything one might desire, as the earliest chronicler had pictured it in his enthusiasm. Rugged, intractable, impermeable, it was in good part rebellious to the discipline of agriculture. The rivers were another enemy of regularized agricultural effort and a stable family life. Death-dealing floods and sterilizing droughts—that was what the waters brought with them. And in addition to the land and jungles that were so difficult to cultivate, in addition to the rivers which it was impossible to utilize for the purposes of an agricultural or industrial economy or even for the regular transport of products—in addition to all this, there were the swarms of larvae, the multitude of insects and worms, harmful to man. Especially to the one engaged in agriculture, who, the moment he began setting out his plantations, was afflicted on all sides by "ants that do much damage" (to his crops) and by the "caterpillar of the fields"—curses that the Indian witch-doctors defied the padres to exorcise with their prayers and the ringing of their bells. . . .

The varied geography of Latin America, where the contrasts are much more severe than in the United States, does not produce identical types of people, or even people who can live comfortably side-by-side. In a small country, for example, that contains both 20,000-foot mountains and a Pacific coastline, the differences in geography create a schism between the inhabitants of the two regions. All along the Andes, you can feel an obvious antagonism between the coastline people and the mountain people, a fact that makes real political unity in any of the Andean countries (Peru, Colombia, Ecuador, and to some extent Chile) that much more difficult. The same rivalry between coasts and mountains—in Ecuador in this selection—can be felt in Central America and parts of Mexico.

Up Against the Mountains

By John Rothchild

Like all Latin American countries with mountains and a coastline, Ecuador is cut between the spirit and the flesh. Quito, the capital city, is wrapped around mountains at 9,000 feet above sea level. Quito is all churches and white adobe and small streets; the mountains are uplifting but confining, and the streets imitate the confinement. The bodies of the people of Quito are hidden in stiff and thick clothes, often too thick even for the weather, and people can be seen with white handkerchiefs to their mouths to protect themselves from the imagined impurities of the air. The Quito houses, open to the outside by a small, distrustful square in the door, seem forbidding. Like a Chinese puzzle, there are walls within walls, walls two feet thick that separate the street from the casual visitor, more walls separating the casual from the intimate part of the houses, protected in the center.

The people of Quito, like the mountains, seem stocky, impenetrable, impassive, and stoic; they talk in the slow, high lilt of a choirboy. Their eyes are upwards or sideways, they do not look at you, they are enshrouded. The skin of the Quito people is white, anemic, even bleached, the parties are formal, the houses are orderly. If there is an image of Quito, it is of the bleeding Christ, suffering, resigned—black-clad ladies in mourning, occasional laughter, occasional drops of red.

The people of Quito, like the people all down the Andean spine through Colombia, Bolivia, Peru, and even through the mountains of Mexico and Central America, share certain traits. They distrust the coastal

people, as a convert might distrust his instincts, and
for that reason there is little unity. In Ecuador, when
you get tired of the mountains, with their monasteries,
their Catholicism, their immutability, their purity, and
their martyrdom, you can take a bus down to Guayaquil, the coastal port city, which is like most cities on
the Latin American Pacific side. The first thing you
discover as you go from 9,000 feet to zero is your
body: there is an unwrapping as clothes get thinner
and the air gets thicker, and even breathing becomes
sensual. As you move downward, the Spanish gets
faster and more slurred, the volume of talk is increased, the air is filled with talk, the people slouch,
the neckties are removed, the bodies melt. The coastal
towns are slapdash smears, the huts are like the first
little pig's reed house, and there are gaping cracks in
the walls, bodies in the cracks, heads out the windows,
naked children in the streets. You can look from the
street into the most intimate of encounters; the coastal
people are loud, bawdy, mocking, unabashed. There
are pigs rooting, laundry flopping, and when the bus
stops on the coast, the hot dog and banana sellers
approach not in a cautious line, but in a wave of
screaming, toothless women and plates of chicklets.

The work of Quito is introspection, drudgery, and
ecstasy, the heart; the work of Guayaquil is commerce, the flesh, and the wallet. Spiritual or idealistic
thoughts do not travel far through the turgid air of a
Guayaquil night; everything is dissolved to a sweaty
denominator. You think cynical thoughts in Guayaquil,
mercenary, sexual thoughts. There are, of course,
prostitutes in Quito and priests in Guayaquil, but
neither seems at home: Guayaquil is the comfort of
the prostitute, where love is the transfer of meat and
money; Quito is the comfort of the priest, where love
is the transfer of suffering and redemption. No wonder
the coastal people are called monkeys by those looking down from the mountains. No wonder that Ecuador, like most Latin American countries, is trapped
between the mountains (with tradition, landed oligarchs, European culture, heavy velvet draperies) and
the coast (with flick-knives, orange colors, newness,

winding streets, chameleonlike passion). The mountains are prearranged, dressed in Roman squares like colonial towns; beauty is a beauty of granite. The coast is spontaneous, sloppy; beauty is a ripped cloth with skin showing through.

Ecuador is caught in this schizophrenia. There is little intercourse between the coast and the mountains; the country does its business in Guayaquil, its praying in Quito, its sex in Guayaquil, its love in Quito, its sin in Guayaquil, its salvation in Quito. For every person selling his body on the coast, there is a person praying for his soul in the sierra. The coast is straw, the mountain is clay, the coast is airy, the mountains are heavy, the coast is chance, the mountains are planned, the coast dances, the mountain trudges, the coast is naked, the mountain is masked, the coast is blacks and drums, the mountain is Indians and flutes. The countries of Latin America are divided across the hemisphere in horizontal stripes, but they should have been divided, people say, by ripping the coast all the way from Mexico to the tip of Chile, and making that one country—by leaving the remaining mountaintops as another country. As it is, there is a constant tension between the heart and the pocketbook, the profane and the sacred, that makes for unsettled governments and unresolved national identities. But then, the same division exists in the Latin American soul.

PART II.

THE INDIAN LEGACY

Introduction

The Spanish "conquered" South America, conquered the Indians, while the English "discovered" North America, denying that Indians already lived there. The attitudes behind these two words have a lot to do with why the North American Indian was shunted aside, killed, and ignored; whereas the South American Indian, who served the Spanish as mistress, slave, or convert, became the backbone of the Latin American culture.

Latin American whites are often surprised at the outrage expressed by North American tourists on seeing an Indian beggar kicked from the door of a restaurant in some Andean town. "Why do you care?" they ask. "Didn't you kill yours off instead?" The Indians in their society were not eliminated, although they generally receive brutal treatment at the hands of whites and mestizos (mixed Indian and white blood). But something of the early Indian civilizations in Latin America has survived the enslavement and oppression of the Spanish, and the twentieth-century Latin American writers have turned to the Indian as the source of their cultural identity.

There are hundreds of Indian tribes in Latin America, different enough so that they seem as strange to each other as they do to non-Indians—reformed Auca headhunters at the fringes of the Amazon oil lands; primitive wooden-hook fishing tribes on the coastal rivers and Central American islands; stoic, distrustful, mournful Andean sheepherders who scratch-cultivate small plots of land with a stick; tamed descendants of the Arucanians in Chile who now live in isolation much like Indians on U.S. reservations.

The ancestors of these tribes populated Latin America long before the arrival of the Spaniards. Most historians and archaeologists accept the view that they came from

30

Asia, across the Bering Strait, and southward through Mexico and Central America, probably between 10,000 and 20,000 years before Christ. They fanned out across the continent, forming fishing communities in coastal areas, jungle cultures, and highly developed civilizations in the valleys and highlands of Central and South America.

There are many small Indian tribes still flourishing in Latin America, living in inaccessible and rough jungle and mountain terrain. These tribes are so numerous and diverse that it would be impossible to include them in this book; and also, they exert only a minor influence on general Latin American life. On the other hand, the descendants of the three major Indian cultures—the Aztecs, Mayas, and Incas—have had a tremendous effect on the personality of Latin America, and they are usually the center of political controversy in the countries that they occupy.

This part deals with these Indians. They make up a large percentage, perhaps as much as a third, of the populations of Bolivia, Peru, Ecuador, Colombia, and Mexico. They cover the mountains and arid stretches of these countries with small, impossible parcels of land—broken off from the large *haciendas* where they once served as virtual slaves. Some of them are still slaves on the *haciendas*, working the masters' lands most of the year in return for the right to work a small plot for themselves. Sometimes the Indians come to the cities in search of a little extra money, and huddle in the stick shacks that are famous in almost every Latin American urban center— the rings of poverty around the cities.

Most of the mountain Indians wear ponchos and open sandals made from reeds or from old tires. Most speak two languages—Spanish, which they learn crudely and speak with a halting embarrassment, and the language of their ancestors, either a Mayan dialect (Mexico), or the Inca Quechua (Ecuador, Peru), or Aymará (Bolivia). Their native language is not the only communion with the past, for Indians have retained many of the customs and beliefs of their ancestors, filling them in around the Spanish colonial and now the modern forms of living. For instance, Indians have merged their own deities and beliefs into the Spanish Catholic religion, sneaking their own gods into saint's clothing as best they could. Their culture has survived through such delicate assimilation.

The role of today's Indian is a complicated one. There is some Indian blood in almost everybody in Latin America, but exactly how much is still a crucial question in placing people along a color and prestige scale that spans many gradations. It is actually difficult to define an Indian, because many people who look and live like Indians prefer to think of themselves as whites. Often these mestizos who are actually closest to the Indian way of life are responsible for the most brutal treatment of the Indians. Perhaps the best way to describe a Latin American Indian is as a person who either does not or cannot claim to be white. In any case, the pure Indian stands at the bottom of the blood pyramid. He is generally undernourished, lives in a hut made from straw, and works interminably at tilling the soil for some white *hacienda* owner, or, if he has been the benefactor of agrarian reform, for his own family. The life of an Indian is not valued very highly by non-Indians in Latin America, especially in countries like Ecuador, Peru, and Bolivia, where the majority of the people are mestizos. Chile and Argentina have largely white, European populations; the Indians in Chile were wiped out in the North American style. Brazil and the Caribbean areas have a more complicated cultural mixture that includes a lot of blacks as well as Indians and Europeans.

The Aztecs, Incas, and Mayas (notwithstanding the prejudice faced by their descendants) evolved a culture far superior to the one that the Spanish brought them, and this heritage is the source of both pride and resentment in Latin America. A good illustration of the ingeniousness of life under the Incas is provided in the excerpt from William Prescott's classic, *The Conquest of the Incas,* written in the nineteenth century. The Incas had just begun to solidify their conquest of most of the Andean region of South America when the Spaniards arrived about 1500. The Incas had conquered many tribes in Bolivia and Peru, and had just established bases in Ecuador when they got the news of the Spanish landing. They were not always kind to tribes they conquered, but their treatment often proved to be more humane than the way the Spaniards treated their conquered subjects. The

Aztec civilization, more brutal than the Inca in its sub-jugation of neighboring tribes, was in other ways as advanced as that of the Inca. The Mayas, who seemed to vanish mysteriously from their cities sometime before the Spanish conquest, were also highly advanced in architecture, astronomy, and mathematical concepts during the height of their civilization as much as fifteen hundred years ago.

Notwithstanding their superiority both in numbers and perhaps in social organization, the Indians were quickly conquered and reduced to objects of slavery and potential conversion—first to Catholicism and then to feudalism. (How they were conquered so easily, we will discuss in the next part.) Their role as packhorses for the white man and marginal soil tillers has not changed that much since the sixteenth century, at least not in the Andean countries. A group of Indians in Ecuador were given the chance, a couple of years ago, to film their own lives, and the script of the film, included as a selection here, is the most accurate expression I have seen of the way the Indian views his daily life in most Latin American countries.

Of course, the position of the Indian has shifted in some places: he has gained political power through various bloody clashes in Bolivia, and he has taken over land through massive agrarian reform in Mexico. But in most countries, the results of agrarian reform—splitting up the old *haciendas* and turning them over to the Indians—have been generally disappointing. The old wealthy agricultural elite has moved to the cities, because farming no longer pays, and it has sold off the dusty *hacienda* shells at fat profits to the former slaves. In many places there are just too many Indians for the parcelization of land to offer any real sustenance; and where the land is very good, owners have been reluctant to sell. The excerpt on agrarian reform follows events in Bolivia, but the same story could be told about Peru, Ecuador, Colombia, and to some extent Mexico.

Ironically enough, while the real Indian is subjected to dire poverty, unflinching prejudice, and subjugation, the abstract Indian of literature and art is praised as the soul of the continent, the source of all its virtues. The concluding selection in this part, by historian Mariano Picón-

Salas, explains the Indian contribution to the Latin American character—the profound Indian nature that has seeped through the Spanish domination into the modern *latino* psyche.

The purpose of this selection is to show the level of civilization attained by the Incas before the arrival of the Spaniards—a level that many believe has not been reached in Latin America since that time. The Incas were a conglomeration of various Indian groups along the spine of the Andes, their culture centered around Peru and Bolivia, where many of their ruins can be seen today. The Inca empire may extend back to 1200 A.D., but the culture reached its height about 1500, or just before the Spaniards landed in Peru. The Incas did not have a democracy—the ruling priesthood class was hereditary—but as the selection points out, they had an elaborate social-security and welfare system to ensure the health of their subjects. The Incas expanded their empire by conquering other tribes, but once pacified, the tribes were treated with a good deal more kindness than the British or North Americans have exhibited toward their empires. While the details of daily life explained here differ substantially from what was happening with the Aztecs in Mexico or the Mayans in Central America (the Aztecs were known to be more brutal and warlike, the Mayans to have more fully developed mathematical and scientific concepts), both of these cultures to the north were, like the Incas, highly organized. These three Indian cultures are looked on by Latin Americans as the source of their special identity as a people, even more than the Spanish culture. This selection comes from *The Conquest of Peru,* the classic work on the subject by William Prescott, a nineteenth-century American historian.

The Culture of the Incas

By William Prescott

... But the Peruvian institutions [Prescott uses "Peru" to describe the Inca empire] must be regarded from a different point of view from that in which we

study those of other nations. The laws emanated from
the sovereign, and that sovereign held a divine commission, and was possessed of a divine nature. To
violate the law was not only to insult the majesty of
the throne, but it was sacrilege. The slightest offense,
viewed in this light, merited death; and the gravest
could incur no heavier penalty. Yet, in the infliction of
their punishments, they showed no unnecessary cruelty;
and the sufferings of the victim were not prolonged by
the ingenious torments so frequent among barbarous
nations. . . .

The fiscal regulations of the Incas, and the laws
respecting property, are the most remarkable features
in the Peruvian policy. The whole territory of the empire was divided into three parts, one for the Sun,
another for the Inca [the ruling class], and the last for
the people. Which of the three was the largest is
doubtful. The proportions differed materially in different provinces. . . .

The lands assigned to the Sun furnished a revenue
to support the temples, and maintain the costly ceremonial of the Peruvian worship and the multitudinous
priesthood. Those reserved for the Inca went to support the royal state, as well as the numerous members
of his household and his kindred, and supplied the
various exigencies of government. The remainder of
the lands was divided, *per capita,* in equal shares
among the people. It was provided by law, as we shall
see hereafter, that every Peruvian should marry at a
certain age. When this event took place, the community or district in which he lived furnished him with a
dwelling, which, as it was constructed of humble
materials, was done at little cost. A lot of land was
then assigned to him sufficient for his own maintenance and that of his wife. An additional portion was
granted for every child, the amount allowed for a son
being the double of that for a daughter. The division
of the soil was renewed every year, and the possessions
of the tenant were increased or diminished according
to the numbers in his family. . . .

A more thorough and effectual agrarian law than
this cannot be imagined. In other countries where

such a law has been introduced, its operation, after a time, has given way to the natural order of events, and, under the superior intelligence and thrift of some and the prodigality of others, the usual vicissitudes of fortune have been allowed to take their course, and restore things to their natural inequality. . . . The nearest approach to the Peruvian constitution was probably in Judea, where, on the recurrence of the great national jubilee, at the close of every half-century, estates reverted to their original proprietors. . . .

A part of the agricultural produce and manufacturers was transported to Cuzco, to minister to the immediate demands of the Inca and his Court. But far the greater part was stored in magazines scattered over the different provinces. These spacious buildings, constructed of stone, were divided between the Sun and the Inca, though the greater share seems to have been appropriated by the monarch. By a wise regulation, any deficiency in the contributions of the Inca might be supplied from the granaries of the Sun. But such a necessity could rarely have happened; and the providence of the government usually left a large surplus in the royal depositories, which was removed to a third class of magazines, whose design was to supply the people in seasons of scarcity, and, occasionally, to furnish relief to individuals, whom sickness or misfortune had reduced to poverty; thus, in a manner, justifying the assertion of a Castilian document, that a large portion of the revenues of the Inca found its way back again, through one channel or another, into the hands of the people. These magazines were found by the Spaniards, on their arrival, stored with all the various products and manufactures of the country— with maize, coca, *quinoa,* woolen and cotton stuffs of the finest quality, with vases and utensils of gold, silver, and copper, in short, with every article of luxury or use within the compass of Peruvian skill. . . .

The impositions on the Peruvian people seem to have been sufficiently heavy. On them rested the whole burden of maintaining, not only their own order, but every other order in the state. The members of the royal house, the great nobles, even the public functionaries, and the numerous body of the priesthood, were all exempt from taxation. The whole duty of defraying the expenses of the government belonged to the people. Yet this was not materially different from the condition of things formerly existing in most parts of Europe, where the various privileged classes claimed exemption—not always with success, indeed—from bearing part of the public burdens. The great hardship in the case of the Peruvian was, that he could not better his condition. His labors were for others, rather than for himself. However industrious, he could not add a rood to his own possessions, nor advance himself one hair's breadth in the social scale. The great and universal motive to honest industry, that of bettering one's lot, was lost upon him. The great law of human progress was not for him. As he was born, so he was to die. Even his time he could not properly call his own. Without money, with little property of any kind, he paid his taxes in labor. No wonder that the government should have dealt with sloth as a crime. It was a crime against the state, and to be wasteful of time was, in a manner, to rob the exchequer. The Peruvian, laboring all his life for others, might be compared to the convict in a treadmill, going the same dull round of incessant toil, with the consciousness, that, however profitable the results to the state, they were nothing to him.

But this is the dark side of the picture. If no man could become rich in Peru, no man could become poor. No spendthrift could waste his substance in riotous luxury. No adventurous schemer could impoverish his family by the spirit of speculation. The law was constantly directed to enforce a steady industry and a sober management of his affairs. No mendicant was tolerated in Peru. When a man was reduced by poverty or misfortune (it could hardly be by fault) the arm of the law was stretched out to minister relief; not the stinted relief of private charity, nor that which is doled out, drop by drop, as it were, from the frozen reservoirs of "the parish," but in generous measure, bringing no humiliation to the object of it, and placing him on a level with the rest of his countrymen.

No man could be rich, no man could be poor, in Peru; but all might enjoy, and did enjoy, a competence. Ambition, avarice, the love of change, the morbid spirit of discontent, those passions which most agitate the minds of men, found no place in the bosom of the Peruvian. The very condition of his being seemed to be at war with change. He moved on in the same unbroken circle in which his fathers had moved before him, and in which his children were to follow. It was the object of the Incas to infuse into their subjects a spirit of passive obedience and tranquility—a perfect acquiescence in the established order of things. In this they fully succeeded. The Spaniards who first visited the country are emphatic in their testimony, that no government could have been better suited to the genius of the people; and no people could have appeared more contented with their lot, or more devoted to their government.

Those who may distrust the accounts of Peruvian industry will find their doubts removed on a visit to the country. The traveler still meets, especially in the central regions of the table-land, with memorials of the past, remains of temples, palaces, fortresses, terraced mountains, great military roads, aqueducts, and other public works, which, whatever degree of science they may display in their execution, astonish him by their number, the massive character of the materials, and the grandeur of the design. Among them, perhaps the most remarkable are the great roads, the broken remains of which are still in sufficient preservation to attest their former magnificence. There were many of these roads, traversing different parts of the kingdom; but the most considerable were the two which extended from Quito to Cuzco, and, again diverging from the capital, continued in a southern direction towards Chili. . . .

The system of communication through their dominions was still further improved by the Peruvian sovereigns, by the introduction of posts, in the same manner as was done by the Aztecs. The Peruvian posts, however, established on all the great routes that conducted to the capital, were on a much more extended plan than those in Mexico. All along these routes, small buildings were erected, at the distance of less than five miles asunder, in each of which a number of runners, or *chasquis*, as they were called, were stationed to carry forward the despatches of government. These despatches were either verbal, or conveyed by means of *quipus* [knotted ropes used as a counting device], and sometimes accompanied by a thread of the crimson fringe worn round the temples of the Inca, which was regarded with the same implicit deference as the signet ring of an Oriental despot.

The *chasquis* were dressed in a peculiar livery, intimating their profession. They were all trained to the employment, and selected for their speed and fidelity. As the distance each courier had to perform was small, and as he had ample time to refresh himself at the stations, they ran over the ground with great swiftness, and messages were carried through the whole extent of the long routes, at the rate of a hundred and fifty miles a day. The office of the *chasquis* was not limited to carrying despatches. They frequently brought various articles for the use of the Court; and in this way, fish from the distant ocean, fruits, game, and different commodities from the hot regions on the coast, were taken to the capital in good condition, and served fresh at the royal table. It is remarkable that this important institution should have been known to both the Mexicans and the Peruvians without any correspondence with one another; and that it should have been found among two barbarian nations of the New World, long before it was introduced among the civilized nations of Europe.

By these wise contrivances of the Incas, the most distant parts of the long-extended empire of Peru were brought into intimate relations with each other. And while the capitals of Christendom, but a few hundred miles apart, remained as far asunder as if seas had rolled between them, the great capitals Cuzco and

Quito were placed by the high roads of the Incas in immediate correspondence. Intelligence from the numerous provinces was transmitted on the wings of the wind to the Peruvian metropolis, the great focus to which all the lines of communication converged. Not an insurrectionary movement could occur, not an invasion on the remotest frontier, before the tidings were conveyed to the capital, and the imperial armies were on their march across the magnificent roads of the country to suppress it. So admirable was the machinery contrived by the American despots for maintaining tranquillity throughout their dominions! It may remind us of the similar institutions of ancient Rome, when, under the Caesars, she was mistress of half the world. . . .

It is true, their fanaticism—or their policy—showed itself in a milder form than was found in the descendants of the Prophet. Like the great luminary which they adored, they operated by gentleness more potent than violence. They sought to soften the hearts of the rude tribes around them, and melt them by acts of condescension and kindness. Far from provoking hostilities, they allowed time for the salutary example of their own institutions to work its effect, trusting that their less civilized neighbors would submit to their scepter, from a conviction of the blessings it would secure to them. When this course failed, they employed other measures, but still of a pacific character; and endeavored by negotiation, by conciliatory treatment, and by presents to the leading men, to win them over to their dominion. In short, they practiced all the arts familiar to the most subtle politician of a civilized land to secure the acquisition of empire. When all these expedients failed, they prepared for war. . . .

Yet, once in the field the Inca did not usually show any disposition to push his advantages to the utmost, and urge his foe to extremity. In every stage of the war, he was open to propositions for peace; and although he sought to reduce his enemies by carrying off their harvests and distressing them by famine, he allowed his troops to commit no unnecessary outrage on person or property. "We must spare our enemies," one of the Peruvian princes is quoted as saying, "or it will be our loss, since they and all that belong to them must soon be ours." It was a wise maxim, and, like most other wise maxims, founded equally on benevolence and prudence. The Incas adopted the policy claimed for the Romans by their countryman, who tells us that they gained more by clemency to the vanquished than by their victories. . . .

The first step of the government, after the reduction of a country, was to introduce there the worship of the Sun. Temples were erected, and placed under the care of a numerous priesthood, who expounded to the conquered people the mysteries of their new faith, and dazzled them by the display of its rich and stately ceremonial. Yet the religion of the conquered was not treated with dishonor. The Sun was to be worshiped above all; but the images of their gods were removed to Cuzco and established in one of the temples, to hold their rank among the inferior deities of the Peruvian Pantheon. Here they remained as hostages, in some sort, for the conquered nation, which would be the less inclined to forsake its allegiance, when by doing so it must leave its own gods in the hands of its enemies. . . .

Yet the Peruvian sovereigns did not trust altogether to this show of obedience in their new vassals; and, to secure it more effectually, they adopted some expedients too remarkable to be passed by in silence.—Immediately after a recent conquest, the *curacas* and their families were removed for a time to Cuzco. Here they learned the language of the capital, became familiar with the manners and usages of the court, as well as with the general policy of government, and experienced such marks of favor from the sovereign as would be most grateful to their feelings, and might attach them most warmly to his person. Under the influence of these sentiments, they were again sent to rule over their vassals, but still leaving their eldest sons in the capital, to remain there as a guaranty for their own fidelity, as well as to grace the court of the Inca. . . .

Yet little less remarkable was another device of the Incas for securing the loyalty of their subjects. When any portion of the recent conquests showed a pertinacious spirit of disaffection, it was not uncommon to cause a part of the population, amounting, it might be, to ten thousand inhabitants or more, to remove to a distant quarter of the kingdom, occupied by ancient vassals of undoubted fidelity to the crown. A like number of these was transplanted to the territory left vacant by the emigrants. By this exchange, the population was composed of two distinct races, who regarded each other with an eye of jealousy, that served as an effectual check on any mutinous proceeding. In time, the influence of the well-affected prevailed, supported, as they were, by royal authority, and by the silent working of the national institutions, to which the strange races became gradually accustomed.

The Peruvian institutions, though they may have been modified and matured under successive sovereigns, all bear the stamp of the same original—were all cast in the same mold. The empire, strengthening and enlarging at every successive epoch of its history, was, in its latter days, but the development, on a great scale, of what it was in miniature at its commencement, as the infant germ is said to contain within itself all the ramifications of the future monarch of the forest. Each succeeding Inca seemed desirous only to tread in the path, and carry out the plans, of his predecessor. Great enterprises, commenced under one, were continued by another, and completed by a third. Thus, while all acted on a regular plan, without any of the eccentric or retrograde movements which betray the agency of different individuals, the state seemed to be under the direction of a single hand, and steadily pursued, as if through one long reign, its great career of civilization and of conquest.

The ultimate aim of its institutions was domestic quiet. But it seemed as if this were to be obtained only by foreign war. Tranquillity in the heart of the

monarchy, and war on its borders, was the condition
of Peru. By this war it gave occupation to part of its
people, and, by the reduction and civilization of its
barbarous neighbors, gave security to all. Every Inca
sovereign, however mild and benevolent in his domestic rule, was a warrior, and led his armies in person.
Each successive reign extended still wider the boundaries of the empire. . . .

. . . The life of an Inca was one long crusade against
the infidel, to spread wide the worship of the Sun, to
reclaim the benighted nations from their brutish super-
stitions, and impart to them the blessings of a well-
regulated government. This, in the favorite phrase of
our day, was the "mission" of the Inca. It was also the
mission of the Christian conqueror who invaded the
empire of this same Indian potentate. Which of the
two executed his mission most faithfully, history must
decide.

Yet the Peruvian monarchs did not show a childish
impatience in the acquisition of empire. They paused
after a campaign, and allowed time for the settlement
of one conquest before they undertook another; and,
in this interval, occupied themselves with the quiet
administration of their kingdom, and with the long
progresses, which brought them into nearer intercourse
with their people. During this interval, also, their new
vassals had begun to accommodate themselves to the
strange institutions of their masters. They learned to
appreciate the value of a government which raised
them above the physical evils of a state of barbarism,
secured them protection of person, and a full participation in all the privileges enjoyed by their conquerors;
and, as they became more familiar with the peculiar
institutions of the country, habit, that second nature,
attached them the more strongly to these institutions,
from their very peculiarity. Thus, by degrees, and
without violence, arose the great fabric of the Peruvian empire, composed of numerous independent and
even hostile tribes, yet, under the influence of a common religion, common language, and common government, knit together as one nation, animated by a

spirit of love for its institutions and devoted loyalty to its sovereign. What a contrast to the condition of the Aztec monarchy, on the neighboring continent, which, composed of the like heterogeneous materials, without any internal principle of cohesion, was only held together by the stern pressure, from without, of physical force! . . .

This selection jumps us ahead several centuries, from the culture of the Incas, to take a look at the modern-day descendant of the Incas, at how he views his daily life. It is the English translation of the Quechua soundtrack of the film *Chashnami Nucanchijpaj Causai,* produced by Ecuadorian Indians a few years ago, to depict a typical day in an Indian community. The setting of the story is Ecuadorian, but the general tone of futility, disappointment, and rage, and the treatment received by the Indians, applies to the rest of Latin America as well. It should be pointed out that white people in the Ecuadorian capital, Quito, were shocked by this "revolutionary" film, while Indians saw it as just another day at the market. The selection uses several Spanish words, which are translated in order of appearance:

Campos—fields, or lands

Cantón—a province

Patrón—the bossman, any authority figure

Blancos—white people (used for almost any non-Indian)

Quinoa—quinine

Campesinos—Indians, or peasants

Cholos—mestizo merchants, people who look and actually live pretty much like Indians, but think of themselves as non-Indians. The *cholos* are often the most brutal toward the Indians.

Chichería—the bar where *chicha* (or white-lightning liquor) is sold to Indians. On any market day, you can see the drunken results of the *chicería* lying along the highway. (Some Indian groups, like the Otavalos of Ecuador, have a system whereby the wife gets drunk one week and the husband the next; you can see a fallen Indian with his or her sober spouse standing by to assist.)

Our Lives

By Manuel Bagua, Vicente Lema, Federico Muñoz, Manuel Naula, Scott Robinson, and Michael Scott

This dark room is where we live. We have nothing but a reed door between two mud walls. It is a poor little house.

Here are our crops and our animals. This is all that we have. We have no pasture for our burro, for our cow, for our sheep.

Our house is the same as the houses of our neighbors, with a roof made of grass. Here we live with our families and form our community.

The community where we live in our small huts is surrounded by mud walls to protect our crops and animals. In all the *campos* of our Ecuador, we speak only our language Quechua.

All of these communities are far from the city, from the capital of the *cantón*. Around our houses are only our little plots of land. The large fields belong to the *patrón*.

Here is another community, also of Indian people. We Indians are the majority in the *cantón* and in the entire country. Majority means that there are more Indians than *blancos*.

Large fields of barley grow, but little of it is ours.

These are beautiful heads of barley, our food and the food of our children, which we grow with great care.

The most delicious food is prepared from the *quinoa*. It is the plant of our ancestors, the Incas, who lived here before the Spaniards came. Over these paths we walk barefoot, carrying animals and grain long distances.

The footpaths lead to the road. On it men and women go to the town, to the market to sell our animals and crops. *Campesinos* who have no money cannot go in the bus; most of us go on foot.

On the road run the buses. Many of the drivers are not responsible. They run over people and animals. They carry many people, even on top and hanging to the back, at the risk of their lives. Those who have money go by bus. It is in the bus that the mistreatment of the *campesino* begins.

We go to the market. The *cholos* and hucksters start taking advantage of us. They buy our products at low prices.

Many people of the *campo* go to buy and sell. We are cheated by a few cunning merchants. The *cholos* abuse the *campesinos*. This is the place, the people, the market, where illegal taxes are collected.

We have no way to entertain ourselves. We have no movies. We don't know how to play ball. We have only the *chichería* to enjoy ourselves with our friends, where we spend our money and enrich the owner.

We are all kinds of people, from all parts of the country. We are poor. We have no power in the government. The government is not of the *campesino*.

We live in misery and sorrow.

Many people sell their grain at the market. The buyers rob us with unfair measures and weights. The hucksters are those who get all of our grain and then sell it back at raised prices when we don't have any.

This is the animal market where also there is no lack of cheaters. Where many taxes are unfairly collected from the *campesino* because he doesn't know the laws. Because of this we have to learn the laws and how to defend ourselves.

Many buyers, *cholos,* and traders abuse the *campesinos* by taking their money against their will.

Has this happened to you? . . . When they pay us less than our animals are worth, what can we do?

Our women sell their little handworks, like sashes and braidings, but they don't bring in anything, nobody pays much. Why aren't our products worth anything? But the *blancos* sell many things at high prices. They sell ponchos, shirts, pants, cloth, thread, and other things. Why can't we, too, sell the same things at our own markets?

Why don't we have money to buy things that we

don't have, like this water pond? They make us leave, dirty and unwashed.

In the *cantón* capital they have plenty of water. They have public health service. We don't even have light. All we have is a little candle, this weak little flame. The *blancos* have electric light which works in the night. The *campesino* doesn't have any, we live in the dark at night.

In the *cantón* are services of the center of public health. There are drugstores, there are schools, there are decorated plazas and the large buildings of the municipality. The *campesinos* don't have services like drugstores, like the people in the *cantón* capital have.

The *campesino* has no money. He goes to the money-lenders to borrow. The *campesinos* don't know the laws. They go to the lawyers to get justice. But the lawyers cheat him and don't work for justice, but rather for money. They don't make justice for the *campesinos*.

Our church ought to teach love, charity and justice, but it doesn't. The people are dying of their hunger for these things. They are sad because they're not taught.

The municipality has many employees. But they don't care about the *campesinos*. The employees know how to collect taxes without authority, even though they get their own salaries.

Brothers, why don't we too have the things that the *cholos* and *blancos* have? This is our land, we were Ecuadorians before anyone else. From now on we must all get together and talk about how we can work united to get what we want.

I include this selection on agrarian reform, because in Latin America the battle for Indian rights revolves around ownership of the land. Since the Spanish conquest, the rural Indian has been tied to the large *haciendas* (plantation farms) doing backbreaking work in return for the use of a small plot of land for his family, or perhaps a meager salary. While outright slavery has been abolished, the Indian usually feels tied to the white landowner for life; he has no options, and it takes all his energy just to keep alive.

In their attempts to change this condition, most Latin American countries have tried to carry out some sort of agrarian reform plan. Mexico instituted one after the Revolution of 1910; other countries have begun to re-divide land as recently as ten years ago. The plans vary, but in most cases the Indians are expected to buy the land away from their former masters.

Agrarian reform, for various political reasons, has languished, and many groups of Indians have rebelled on a local scale, forcibly taking over the *haciendas,* resulting in skirmishes with the police or the army.

This selection deals with agrarian reform in Bolivia, where Indians have more political power than anywhere else in Latin America, due to a series of revolutionary movements in the early 1950's. But the fate of Bolivian land reform, and the resistance of the non-Indians to carrying it out, also applies to the other countries—even to Mexico. Pay special attention to the arguments against agrarian reform; they are heard throughout Latin America.

In general, the Indian has not yet lost his peasant status, although in countries like Bolivia, Peru, and Colombia, where Indians comprise more than one-third of the population, he is pushing hard.

Revolution and Land Reform
By William E. Carter

Because Bolivia has had a chronic deficit of food-stuffs, agrarian reform was looked upon by many—particularly in the country's urban centers—as a grave threat to the very physical survival of the populace. The consensus among urban dwellers was that peasants were either too ignorant to manage land without direction or, were they to attain sufficient know-how, would be interested only in providing subsistence for themselves and would not make the needed effort to feed the rest of the population.

Correlations between Bolivia's agrarian reform and its level of production have been the subject of much

debate, partly because the difficulty of measuring subsistence production on a wide and representative scale
has always made statistics on Bolivian agriculture
questionable. There is no doubt that the *latifundia*
[large *haciendas*] were inefficient as productive units.
Yet, in spite of their antiquated tools and techniques,
they *were* self-supporting and *had* for many years
succeeded in supplying urban markets with the major
portion of their food needs. Their destruction left an
organizational vacuum, which, through the emerging
rural *sindicato* [farm union] network, the Bolivian
government exerted considerable effort to have filled.
But in the months immediately preceding and following the issuance of the Agrarian Reform Decree, the
situation in vast stretches of the countryside was truly
chaotic.

Bolivia's five basic foodstuffs have traditionally
been: potatoes, wheat, maize, rice, and sugar. There
seems to be a general consensus that urban supplies
of all these products, except rice and sugar, fell substantially in the years immediately following the decree. Yet by the end of the 1950s, through a reorgani-
zation of the productive and marketing systems,
supplies of potatoes and maize began to surpass pre-
reform levels, and rice and sugar supplies increased
so dramatically that, in terms of value, they alone
more than made up for all other alleged production
declines. . . .

Bolivia in general is an underpopulated country,
its rate of demographic growth being one of the
lowest in Latin America. Yet many pockets of the
country have population as dense as that of Puerto
Rico and Haiti, and in these places, even after land
redistribution, newly married couples are finding
that they must either leave their community or else
satisfy themselves with a very small land parcel—
often no more than a quarter of a hectare [a hectare
is 2.47 acres]. They are thus forced to supplement
their income with either cottage industry or outside
employment. Under such circumstances even moderate demographic increase looms as a threat.

It is not surprising, then, that the major cities of

Bolivia—particularly La Paz—are being overwhelmed by young rural migrants. The unfortunate fact is that industrial and urban services are not growing rapidly enough to absorb them. Downtown streets are packed with the unemployed and the underemployed. In keeping with such limited urban opportunities, the countryside, in spite of the scarcity of land, continues to hold many, and the problem of *minifundia* ("very small subsistence land plots") will probably continue for generations to come.

Yet the Bolivian Indian today experiences a freedom and power never before known, freedom that derives from not one but a series of measures related both directly and indirectly to the reform. These include: 1) the abolition of labor tribute and cash rent obligations, 2) the creation of a strong peasant *sindicato* movement, 3) the granting of universal suffrage, 4) the massive extension of educational facilities, and 5) the distribution, with titles, of million of hectares of cultivable land to hundreds of thousands of peasant families. There has been much indirect spinoff from these measures. Institutions set up for implementing them, while sometimes falling far short of primary goals, have been extremely fruitful in fulfilling the latent functions of providing new organization and direction to rural communities.

For the peasant, direct control over one's own labor and increased access to land has not only brought about an enormous expansion of opportunities to earn cash, but it has also contributed significantly to the opening up of direct linkages with the national market and, thus, resulted in a new nationwide distributional system. . . .

The 1952 revolution has shaken Bolivian society in an unprecedented way. [The Indians rose up in a major revolt in 1952, resulting in political concessions and some land reforms.] The landed elite, deprived of their traditional manorial base, have either emigrated or else been forced to adjust and reorient their claim to power. Kachitu [a Bolivian town] stands as an example of their changing destiny—very few of the original *vecino* [neighborhood] families remain in that

town today. Of these, some have adjusted and function well as wholesalers or middlemen, while others
seem to have lost all hope. To a man, they are in a
far weaker economic position than they were in 1952,
in spite of the fact that Kachitu is busier than ever. . . .

The Kachitu case represents only one point along a
continuum of responses to agrarian reform. What happened there, however, does demonstrate the importance of the reform for Bolivian society. Elimination
of tribute labor freed the Indian from the monolithic
hold of the country's small, landed elite, and evidence
of this fact may be seen in the thousands of abandoned manor houses and tens of thousands of greatly
improved peasant huts that can be found throughout
the country today. The psychological dimension of
the change has been tremendous, charged with the
euphoria of entering into a great new adventure.

In spite of this euphoria, agrarian reform has not
raised Bolivia's peasants far above the paleotechnic
level of production that prevailed before the revolution, and the likelihood is that they will remain there
for a long time to come. There will be gradual expansion into new lands of the Oriente, but this will in-
volve only a small minority of the country's over-
crowded highlanders. Rather, the prospect for most
peasants today is a slightly improved standard of
living combined with gradual cultural homogeniza-
tion. Rural communities will become more involved
in national politics and possibly more effective as
major political pressure groups. As this happens,
regional differences will become blurred and the
peasant will be caught up in a growing proletariza-
tion or national popular culture. Deeply rooted in
Amerindian tradition, it will be unique in the
Americas.

Cultural patterns and prejudices die slowly, and
former elites will defend their privileges as long as
they possibly can. . . . In the 1960s [an] official
attached to the Bolivian National Planning Board
[told] me that Bolivia's only hope was to pile all the
campesinos together and set fire to them. In spite of
revolution and reform, then, *campesinos* continue to

occupy the bottom of Bolivia's social heap. The ideals of the revolution revolved around the concept of an open society with equal opportunity for all. But, to cite only one example of how these ideals have been diverted, the school system set up by the revolutionary government to implement universal education became dichotomized between urban and rural and thus tended to institutionalize traditional caste boundaries. Even at their best, rural schools today tend to prepare individuals for provincial rather than urban leadership.

With all the changes that have occurred, either success in regional politics and commerce or absorption into the semiskilled urban labor pool, is about as high as a peasant can presently hope to climb. If he aspires for more, the fruits of change can be bitter indeed. Because this is so, the euphoria of reform may eventually give way to widespread and corrosive frustration. Should that ever happen, Boliva will not have seen the last of violent revolution.

The descendants of the great Indian cultures share some traits in common—especially their humility, stoicism, melancholy, and fatalism. These qualities still surround the mountain tribes (the Aymará in Bolivia; Incas, or Quechuas—as they are now named by the language they speak—in Peru and Ecuador; Aztecs, Toltecs, and Mayas in Central America and Mexico) and can be felt in their sad, dirgelike music, in their belief that they are helpless to change the universe, in their silent acceptance of white cruelty. Picón-Salas describes a collective mentality of Latin American Indians (which does not, by the way, apply to jungle or coastal tribes), and much of what he sees has also been integrated into the general culture of whites and mestizos. Latin America's distrust of material progress, its reliance on God's will ("Si Dios quiere"— if God wills it—is a part of the vocabulary in every country), and its resignation to hardship are all traits inherited from the Indian soul. The selection is taken from Picón-Salas' excellent book A Cultural History of Spanish America.

The Fate of the Indians
By Mariano Picón-Salas

What does the aboriginal mind tell us? Although there are native differences as remarkable as those separating the Aztec from the distant world of the Inca—the blood-drunk fierceness of the former, for example, in contrast to the peaceful, orderly collectivism of the latter—the modern observer, even at this distance in time, can distinguish a subtle Indian atmosphere, an intangible something that profoundly divides the psychology and forms of ideation of the aborigine from those of his conqueror. . . .

First and foremost, the Indian peoples conceived history as destiny and catastrophe, in marked contrast to the dynamic optimism of the Renaissance which the Spanish conquistador embodied in his own fashion. No concept was farther from the Indian mentality than the Western idea of progress. According to the awesome legend of the suns in Aztec theogony the universe has already been destroyed four times: by tigers, winds, showers of fire, and water. Each successive destruction has engendered a new race of men that inherits nothing from its predecessor and is equally helpless in the face of destiny. The crude giants that fed on wild acorns perished along with the first sun; they were the useless and foolish inventions of the god Tezcatlipoca. The people surviving the destruction of the second world by hurricanes were changed into monkeys as an example of the willfulness of the gods. To create a new sun after the end of the fourth world, the lords of heaven, assembled at Teotihuacán, were obliged to institute the first sacrifices. Two of the gods—the valiant poor deity and the timid rich one—were consumed in a vast bonfire; from the ashes of one emerged the new sun, and from the ashes of the other the moon. "Essential to the Aztec religion," writes Alfonso Caso, "is human sacrifice, for if men could not exist without the creation of gods, the latter in turn must be supported by sacrificial offerings of the magic substance, the vital essence contained in the human blood and heart." In Aztec theogony even life in heaven was continual warfare and sacrifice. For the sun to shine each morning, Huitzilopochtli—the fierce young god who, in the course of each day, journeys from the dwelling place of the living to the chill domain of the dead—must eternally engage in renewed battle with the stars and the moon. He is helped in this daily strife—symbolized by the fiery serpent—by the souls of the warriors who have died in the *guerras floridas* or on the sacrificial stone. To be reborn the next day, however, he must be gathered into the belly of the earth mother at sunset. But all this cosmic struggle would be inadequate if mankind did not give the sun the *chalchiuatl*—warm human blood, the beverage that nurtures divinity best and enables it to confront so many perils with energy. Nourished by the red liquor of sacrifice, the sun boldly faces the squadrons of warriors—the southern stars—which seek to block his path across the sky.

The idea of immolation indicates how life forever feeds upon death. Coatlicue—the mother goddess who symbolizes the earth and into the womb of whom the sun sinks each evening so as to be born again the next day—is also called the "devourer of offal" because she feeds upon human cadavers. Her feet and hands are claws with which she grasps death and putrescence in order to beget life anew. In Maya mythology this essential pessimism is no less somberly expressed. When the builder and the maker spirits decide to destroy by flood one of the many worlds they have created, and when Digger of Faces, Death Bat, Wizard Turkey, and Wizard Owl come to finish off mankind, the drama of the universe occurs with the same unexpectedness and the same merciless terror. In the *Popol Vuh* [a Mayan legend], "Men try to climb into their abodes, but their collapsing abodes make them fall. They try to climb trees, but the trees cast them far off. They try to crawl into holes, but the holes scornfully reject their faces." The account ends: "Such was the destruction of a people fated to be destroyed, fated to be annihilated. Their mouths, their faces, all were destroyed, all were annihilated." Another mythical tale in the *Popol Vuh,* explaining the preordained circle in which life revolves, tells the story of the animals that went to carry a message to the gallant young ballplayers who had not returned from the country of Xibalba, the land of death. The first creature to start was a louse. On the way the louse meets a toad, which devours the louse. The toad takes up its journey until it meets a viper. The viper eats the toad, and a hawk eats the viper. Thus a fateful chain continues until the last creature falls before the unerring blowgun of the gods. . . .

But perhaps this very feeling of inexorable fate gave the native cultures their stoicism and their indifference to pain, for both the Aztec and the Inca—though for differing social and political ends—trained their people in such mute, ascetic calisthenics. Among the Inca the well-ordered, collectivist society lent itself to such institutions as the *mitimaes,* which permitted, at the mere whim of the state, the transfer of families and whole villages far from their native region. Among the Aztec this stoicism led to the support of such a cruel caste as the Knight Eagles and Tigers, who as servants of the sun were charged with providing food for the sun and waging *la guerra florida.* The impressive Aztec sculpture called the "Knight Eagle," which at first view calls to mind a twelfth-century European Crusader, embodies the native ideal of a stern, rigidly controlled fortitude. Reserve, restraint, a wrapt absorption in duty—these are the qualities that this block of andesite, which registers neither wrath nor the faintest glimmer of a smile, seems to communicate to us. The terrible discipline of *Calmecac*—a kind of institute for nobles that subjected them to severe fasting and purification exercises to overcome sleep and cold—shaped the ruling caste.

The stoic acceptance of suffering and the exalted impassiveness of the Indian in the face of torture and death were to be the earliest themes of Spanish American epics. . . . Aztec mythology promised the gallant warrior who died in battle the most beautiful transformation: to be changed into a hummingbird, the delicate, glittering bird that feeds on flowers.

There is no inconsistency between this stoicism and two other traits apparently general in the aboriginal world: humility and melancholy. In the *Popol Vuh*, for instance, the older brothers of the Master Wizard Magician, who were "very great musicians, singers, and all-knowing wisemen," were punished by the gods because they had humiliated their younger companions. They climbed a tree to catch birds, but the tree grew so fast that they could not get down. Each tried to remove his loincloth to use as a rope, but it changed into a tail and each brother turned into a monkey. Earlier the offended Wizard Magician and his younger brothers had said: "In their hearts they have debased us to the level of servants; we shall humble them accordingly." The sadness of the Indian —so well interpreted by the Inca Garcilaso de la Vega in his sensitively written *Royal Commentaries of the Inca*—is one of the psychological traits of the natives that impressed the Spaniards from the outset. About Aztec songs Friar Diego Durán wrote in the sixteenth century: "They were so plaintive that the mere sound and the dance brought a feeling of sadness. I have seen dancing accompanied by lovely songs that were sometimes so plaintive that it filled me with sorrow and I listened with a heavy heart." Commenting on a native dance surviving in the Jauja region of Peru, a modern historian—José de la Riva Agüero—wrote about the Quechua Indians: "Theirs is tender, gentle, doleful poetry of naïve charm and pastoral softness, suddenly darkened by fits of the most tragic despair. More reserved and bound by tradition than any other people, this race possesses the gift of tears and the cult of memory. Guardians of mysterious tombs and forever mourning among these cyclopean ruins, their favorite diversion and bitter consolation are to sing about the woes of their history and the poignant grief that lies in their hearts. Near Juaja the Indian maidens, who represent the chorus of princesses in the popular pageant of the Inca, still intone the words as they bow with infinite piety before Huáscar, the vanquished monarch: 'Let us wipe away his tears and, to relieve his distress, let us take him to the country where he may breathe the fragrance of the flowers—*Huaytaninta musquichipa-huay.*'"

PART III

THE SPANIARDS AND THE SPIRIT OF THE CONQUEST

Introduction

An absurd menagerie of Spaniards, dragging horses, blunderbusses, and heavy armor, penetrated the Indian civilizations at the beginning of the sixteenth century, just a few years after Columbus' discovery. Hernán Cortés took off from Cuba toward Mexico after double-crossing the Cuban governor who presumably would have directed the expedition; Pizarro hit Peru a few years later with only one hundred men and a few horses. With this kind of modest support, and with almost no knowledge of terrain, Indian languages, food, climate, or the people they were fighting, the Spaniards made two great civilizations, and several second-rate ones, heel before their mastery in a matter of a decade. These conquerors were not the frugal English settlers, escaping to a new beginning in North America with their small plots of woodland; these were rapacious *hidalgos*,* fired by the myths of knight-errantry, embarrassed by their low social status at home, and determined to do something great for the Cross.

The roving armored circus splashed to the shores and baffled the Aztecs in Mexico and the Incas in Peru, who saw in the Spaniards a mixture of gods, buffoons, despoilers, vagabonds, and men from another planet. The confrontations faced by Pizarro in Peru, Cortés in Mexico, and lesser conquistadors elsewhere, are remarkably similar. There was early cautious exploring, trying to befriend the local tribes antagonistic to the main rulers, followed by fierce battles. The best description of what happened

---

* *Hidalgo*, which literally means "son-of-something," was a term of derision applied to Spanish adventurers of the lower class, who had aristocratic pretensions but no worthy family name.

comes from Bernal Díaz del Castillo, a rather irreverent sidekick of Cortés' who went along for the conquest of Mexico and kept a diary. The scenes repeated here from his book could also have taken place in Peru, where Pizarro was fighting and conning the Inca chief Atahualpa. Atahualpa was told by Pizarro that his life would be spared if he would give his weight in gold to the Spaniards. But after the gold was counted out, Pizarro had Atahualpa killed anyway.

The Spaniards' victory over the Indians had a lot to do with such double-crossing all over the continent, but it had more to do with Indian fatalism and the belief that the Spaniards were gods. In Mexico, the legend of Quetzalcoatl, the white bearded god who would someday return to take over the land, was in large part responsible for thousands of Indians permitting themselves to be defeated by a handful of sick Spaniards. In some sense, the Indians wanted to lose, an emotion ensured, as Díaz explains it, by the Spaniards hiding their dead and lighting off cannons at opportune moments with godlike timing to prove their connection with the thunderous heavens.

The first part of the Díaz selection describes the fierceness of the interminable battles that the Spaniards spent long months fighting. The second part deals with the motivations of Spaniards to endure such hardships and dangers. As Díaz somewhat naïvely tells it here, the conquerors' hearts were set on God, while their eyes were fixated on the gold that Montezuma (the Aztec supreme ruler whom they held captive) was doling out to them. Perhaps one can see in the Díaz book the beginnings of the conflict that still exists in Latin America between the great romantic gesture and noble sacrifice and the willingness to be bought off.

The gold was represented by the conqueror and his band, whereas God came with the friars and priests and missionaries that poured into Latin America. The religious conversion was much more difficult than the gold-hustling, because the priests had to deal with the Indians as converts, at the same time that they often took actions that denied Indians their humanity. The whole episode was about as controversial as Vietnam, and for the same reasons: how can you destroy those you are trying to save? The priest often had to resort to silly rituals to justify the actions of his fellow conquerors. One such ritual was the *requerimiento,* an ornate document that the priest would read, in Spanish, to Indians before a battle or enslavement was about to begin. The *requerimiento* exhorted the Indians to accept Jesus and the Virgin and the teachings of the Bible and to throw off their evil false gods—or else the Spaniards would justifiably attack. The Indians, who didn't understand a word of it, were dumbfounded—but it made the Spaniards feel better.

The role of the friar, or priest, in the conquest is described here by Salvador de Madariaga. That description is followed by Madariaga's explanation of how the character of both the conqueror and the friar evolved into the modern Latin American personality.

At the same time the Spaniards were encircling most of the hemisphere with their rigidity, their morality, and their strict Scriptures, the Portuguese were easing themselves into Brazil. (The English, French, and Dutch also colonized small sections of Latin America, mostly Caribbean islands. But none of these countries could create settlements powerful enough to rival the predominance of the Portuguese and the Spanish.) The incredible contrast in the styles of conquest, explained here by Brazilian historian Gilberto Freyre, have survived to the present time, where the balmy, sexual, dancing Brazil is set apart from the plodding formality of the Spanish-speaking part of the continent. You can see how this difference occurred by looking at how Brazil was colonized in the first place.

The untrustworthy, rapacious types of people who came along for the Spanish conquest have always been unfavorably contrasted with the pious, upright, and uptight English Puritans who settled New England. Oviedo, a Spanish historian of the sixteenth century, warns the would-be conqueror about to sail for Latin America to beware of the people who are eager to sign up in his army—the double-crossers, throat-cutters, and vagabonds. To judge by the conquest itself, the warnings went largely unheeded.

Advice to a Would-be Conqueror
By Gonzalo Fernández de Oviedo y Valdés

SIR CAPTAIN: Understand me and understand yourself. When you make up a company to go to the Indies, and especially in Seville (for it is there, on the steps of the cathedral, that the soldiers are wont to gather), you should first examine the face of each; having scrutinized the face, you will see part of the evil beneath. But because the outward aspect may deceive you in the choice of a soldier, you should make secret inquiry concerning his habits, his mode of life, his skills, and his nationality; for even in that sacred place there are some who will lie about their countries and even their own names for the sake of going to the Indies. And do not attach much importance to his height and his well-combed beard, but rather try to find out whether he is of good character and family, and a frank and modest man. And if he tells you that he was in the battle of Ravenna, dismiss him, if he is a Spaniard, since he remained alive or was not taken prisoner; and do the same if he speaks of the battle of Pavia; and dismiss him if he tells you that he was in the sack of Genoa or Rome, since he did not get rich; and if he was there, and gambled his wealth away or lost it, do not trust him. Those slashed hose and shoes will not do at all for such lands as the Indies, full of ambushes and thick with trees and hawthorns, where there are so many rivers to swim and so many swamps and bogs to cross.

The dress and the person should conform to your needs; above all do not take a man whose faith is suspect, or one less than twenty-five or more than fifty years old. And do not take such fine-feathered birds and great talkers as those I mentioned above, for in the many years that I have seen them in the Indies, and before that in Europe, I have found that few turn out well. As long as there is gold, or they suspect that they will get it through your hands, they will serve you diligently; but be careful, for the minute that things do not go their way they will either slay you or sell you or forsake you, when they find that you promised them more in Spain than you can produce. . . .

And before you begin this examination, examine yourself, and make sure that your aim is to serve God and your king by converting the Indians and treating them well, and by finding a way to lead them to the Republic of Christ. Do not enslave them without cause, or stain your hands with blood without cause or justice, or rob them or remove them from the lands where God created them; he gave them life and humanity not to help you carry out any evil design but in order to save them. . . . And do not say that you are going to the Indies to serve the king and to employ your time as a brave man and an *hidalgo* should; for you know that the truth is just the opposite; you are going solely because you want to have a larger fortune than your father and your neighbors. However, you can do everything you want to do without hurting others or jeopardizing your soul. And do not seek any estate or treasure that might cost you such a price, if in so doing you lose that invaluable treasure by which you were redeemed and God freed you from Hell. . . .

COMRADE AND FRIEND: If you decide to go to the Indies, when you are in Seville ascertain first of all whether the captain with whom you are going is a man who will fulfill what he promises, and learn on the basis of what word or guaranty you are entrusting your life and person to his will—because many of these captains promise what they do not have, know, or understand; and they pay for your person with words that are worth less than feathers; because feathers, though the wind bear them away, at least have some substance and you know their purpose, which is to float in the air aimlessly; but the words of a liar are without substance and, having been said, are invisible and vanish like air. . . . Do you not see that he speaks of what is yet to come, and promises what he neither has nor understands? And once you are free of the perils of the sea and the land, which are innumerable, and come to the Indies, if he should succeed, he neither knows nor rewards you; and if you fall ill, he does not heal you; and if you should die, he will not bury you. . . . And if he gives you an allotment of Indians, he does not care to ascertain whether you are competent to teach them or whether you yourself have more need of a teacher than of governing others, in order that both your consciences may be at rest. And since these estates are acquired unjustly, God permits them to be lost, and you with them. . . .

I observe that for every man who has made his fortune in these parts and has returned to Castile with or without it, an incomparably larger number have lost both their fortunes and their lives. You will say: What should I do? Shall I hold back from going to the Indies, where so many go and return rich—men who were formerly poor and do not measure up to me in ability, merit, or capacity for work? Is it fitting that for lack of courage I should fail to do what so many have done who are older than I and not of such good health and presence? I do not counsel you not to go to the Indies, nor to go there; but I do counsel you, whether you come or not, first to justify yourself with God and to commend yourself to Him. I am aware that it is proper and necessary to seek one's fortune, especially for men of good family who were not reared behind the plow; but let the undertaking be well thought out, and once you have determined upon it, never let greed turn you aside from the loyalty that you owe, and never let necessity give occasion for you to be considered an ingrate or to tarnish your good name; for if you only set your mind to it, in the Indies as elsewhere you can live without offense to your fellow-men.

The following narrative is taken from a diary of the Spanish conquest of the Aztecs in Mexico. It was written in the sixteenth century by Bernal Díaz del Castillo, an aide to the conqueror Hernán Cortés. Note the fierceness of the battles, the unbelievable hardships endured by the Spaniards, and how strange the Indians appeared to the invaders (and vice versa). The conquest proceeded in this fashion all over Latin America.

What motivated the Spaniards to take these risks? How did a few hundred of them manage to subjugate thousands of organized Indians? These excerpts from Díaz's diary provide some clues, which also apply to Pizarro's victories over the Incas in Peru and to the exploits of various second-string conquerors. In the opening paragraphs, we find Díaz on foot, underscoring the importance of the horses that the Spanish brought with them from Europe. The horses were doubly useful in battles, because aside from their maneuverability, the Indians believed them to be mythological creatures.

Simultaneously, as Díaz points out, the Spaniards believed in their own other-wordly creatures, the apostolic apparitions that accompanied them in battles. Although Díaz, considered to be a humorist, pokes some fun at those who said they saw apostles in the sky, it is undeniable that you fight harder if you think apostles are on your side.

And while the Spaniards could believe they had been sent to Mexico by God, which gave them a certain swaggering confidence, the Indians continued to think of the Spaniards as gods, which might have caused them to resist less fiercely. (As Díaz shows, the Spaniards tried not to shake the Indians' faith in their immortality and quickly buried their dead.)

The final two parts in this excerpt, which do not follow chronologically from the first two, show the constant interplay between God and gold that impelled the Spaniards through the conquest. On one day, the Spaniards are sacrificing everything to the glory of God, and on the next they are bickering over the treasure presented them by the Aztec king, Montezuma. (The Spaniards were guests at Montezuma's palace for a time. Later they captured the Aztec king and imprisoned him, the cause of renewed warfare.)

The main reason for the Spaniards' victory, however, was the hatred of many of the local Indian tribes for their Aztec or Inca masters. Without these tribes fighting on their side (both in Mexico and in Peru), the Spaniards would never have had sufficient manpower to survive the wars.

In "The Grace of God" part, Díaz talks about "destroying the ships." He is referring to the original landing in Mexico, when Cortés had the ships burned so that no chickenhearted conquerors would be tempted to mutiny or return to Spanish territory.

The Conquest of Mexico
By Bernal Díaz del Castillo

A Day of Battle

Just at this moment we caught sight of our horsemen. But the great host of Indians was so crazed by their attack that they did not at once see them approaching behind their backs. As the plain was bare and the horsemen were good riders, and some of the horses were very swift and nimble, they came quickly upon them and speared them as they chose. As soon as we saw the horsemen we fell on the enemy so vigorously that, caught between the horsemen and ourselves, they soon turned tail. The Indians thought at that time that the horse and rider were one creature, for they had never seen a horse before.

The savannah and fields were now full of Indians, running to take refuge in some thick woods near by, and as they fled Cortés explained to us that he had been unable to come sooner because there was a swamp in the way, and he had had to fight his way through another host of warriors before he could reach us. Three horsemen and five horses had been wounded.

After the horsemen had dismounted beneath some trees beside which some houses stood, we returned thanks to God for granting us so complete a victory. Then, as it was Lady Day, we named the town which was afterwards founded here Santa María de la Victoria, on account of the fact that this great victory was won on her day. This was the first battle that we fought under Cortés in New Spain.

When it was over, we bandaged our wounded with

cloths, for this was all we had, and sealed the wounds of our horses with fat from the corpse of an Indian that we had cut up for this purpose. We then went to look at the dead that were lying about the field, and found more than eight hundred, most of whom had been killed by sword-thrusts, and the rest by cannon, muskets, or crossbows. And many lay groaning on the ground, half dead. For wherever the horsemen had passed there were great numbers of dead and wounded. The battle had lasted over an hour; it was now late, and we had eaten nothing. So we returned to camp, weary with fighting, bringing five prisoners whom we had taken, two of whom were captains. Then, after burying our two dead, one of whom had been fatally struck in the throat, the other in the ear, and attending to the wounds of the rest, we posted sentinels and guards, took our supper, and rested.

It is here, according to Gomara [another Spanish writer, contemporary of Bernal Díaz], that Francisco de Morla arrived on a dapple-grey horse in advance of Cortés and the rest of the cavalry, and the blessed apostles St. James and St. Peter appeared. I say that all our deeds and victories were the work of Our Lord Jesus Christ, and that in this battle there were so many Indians to every one of us that the dust they made would have blinded us, had not God of His unfailing mercy come to our aid. It may be, as Gómara says, that those glorious apostles did appear, and that I, a sinner, was unworthy to see them. However, I did see Francisco de Morla arrive on a chestnut horse at the same time as Cortés; and I seem to see that whole battle again with my sinful eyes, even as I write, with every detail as it took place. It may be I was not worthy to see either of the two apostles. But if so, since there were more than four hundred soldiers in our company, as well as Cortés himself and many other gentlemen, the miracle would have been discussed and evidence taken, and a church would have been built in their honour when the town was founded. Also the town would not have been called as it was Santa María de la Victoria, but Santiago or San Pedro instead. . . .

Playing Up to God

One of our men was killed in the fighting, and sixty were wounded. All our horses were wounded also. I too was hit twice, once on the head by a stone, and once in the thigh by an arrow. But this did not prevent me from fighting, performing my watch, and helping our men. And all our wounded did the same. For unless our wounds were very dangerous, we had to fight and watch despite them, for the unwounded would not have been able to perform these duties alone.

Having returned to our camp, well contented and giving thanks to God, we buried the dead in one of the Indians' underground houses, so that they should not see we were mortal but believe that we were indeed *Teules,* as they called us. We piled a great deal of earth over this house so that they should not smell the corpses. . . . It was a poor comfort to be without even oil and salt to dress our wounds. And there was another thing we lacked—a severe hardship. We had no clothes to protect us from the cold wind that blew off the snowy mountains and made us shiver. Our lances, muskets, and crossbows made a poor covering. Still, we slept more peacefully than on the previous night, when so many of us had been on guard or patrol. . . .

The Grace of God

Those readers who are interested by this history must wonder at the great deeds we did in those days: first in destroying our ships; then in daring to enter that strong city despite many warnings that they would kill us once they had us inside; then in having the temerity to seize the great Montezuma, king of that country, in his own city and inside his very palace, and to throw him in chains while the execution was carried out. Now that I am old, I often pause to consider the heroic actions of that time. I seem to see them present before my eyes; and I believe that we performed them not of our own volition but by the guidance of God. For what soldiers in the world, numbering only four hundred—and we were even fewer—would have dared to enter a city as strong as Mexico, which is larger than Venice and more than four thousand five hundred miles away from our own Castile and, having seized so great a prince, execute his captains before his eyes? There is much here to ponder on, and not in the matter-of-fact way in which I presented it. . . .

The Grace of the Pocketbook

When Diego de Ordaz and the other soldiers arrived with samples of gold and reports that the whole land was rich, Cortés, on the advice of Ordaz and others, decided to demand from Montezuma that all the *Caciques* and people of the land should pay tribute to His Majesty, and that he himself, as the greatest chieftain, should also give some of his treasures. Montezuma replied that he would send to all his towns to ask for gold, but that many of them possessed nothing more than some jewels of small value that they had inherited from their ancestors. He at once dispatched chieftains to the places where there were mines and ordered each town to give so many ingots of fine gold of the same size and thickness as they usually paid in tribute, and the messengers carried two ingots as samples. Some places, however, only contributed jewels of small value.

. . . Within twenty days all the chieftains whom Montezuma had dispatched to collect the gold tribute returned, and as soon as they arrived Montezuma sent for Cortés and our captains, also for certain of us soldiers whom he knew, because we belonged to his guard, and made us a formal address in words like these:

"I wish you to know, my lord Malinche [his word for Cortés] and my lords Captains and soldiers, that I am indebted to your great King and bear him good will, both for being such a great king, and for having sent from such distant lands to make inquiries about me. But what impresses me most is the thought that he must be the one who is destined to rule over us, as

our ancestors have told us and even our gods have
indicated in the answers they have given us. Take this
gold which has been collected; only haste prevents
there being more. What I myself have got ready for
the Emperor is the whole of the treasure I received
from my father, which is under your hand in your
own apartments. I know very well that as soon as you
came here you opened the door and inspected it all,
and then sealed it up again as it was before. When
you send it to him, tell him in your papers and letter:
'This is sent by your loyal vassal Montezuma.' I will
also give you some very precious stones to be sent to
him in my name. They are *chalchihuites* and must not
be given to anyone else but your great prince, for each
one of them is worth two loads of gold. I also wish to
send him three blowpipes with their pellet-bags and
moulds, since they have such beautiful jewel-work
that he will be pleased to see them. And I should also
like to give him some of my own possessions, though
they are small. For all the gold and jewels I had I
have given you at one time or another."

On hearing this speech we were all amazed at the
great Montezuma's goodness and liberality. Doffing
our helmets most respectfully, we expressed our deep
thanks, and in a most cordial speech Cortés promised
that we would write to His Majesty of the magnificence and liberality with which he had given us this
gold in his own royal name. After a further exchange
of compliments Montezuma dispatched his stewards
to hand over all the gold and treasure in the sealed
chamber. It took us three days to examine it and
remove all the embellishments with which it was
decorated; and to help us take it to pieces Montezuma sent us silversmiths from Atzcapotzalco. There
was so much of it that after it was broken up it made
three heaps of gold weighing over six hundred
thousand pesos. . . .

After the weight was taken the King's officers said
that the bars and grains and ingots and jewels, all
together, came to more than six hundred thousand
pesos, and this did not include the silver and the
many other jewels which were not yet valued. Some

soldiers said there was more. All that remained to be done was to take out the royal fifth, and then give each captain and soldier his share, preserving their shares for those who had remained at Villa Rica. It seems, however, that Cortés attempted to postpone the division until we had more gold, good weights, and a proper account of the total. But most of us said that the division must be made at once. For we had noticed that when the pieces taken from Montezuma's treasury were broken up there had been much more gold in the piles, and that a third of it was now missing, having been taken away and hidden for the benefit of Cortés, the captains, and the Mercedarian friar. We also saw that the gold was still diminishing. After a good deal of argument what was left was weighed out. It amounted to six hundred thousand pesos without the jewels and bars, and it was agreed that the division should be made next day.

First of all the royal fifth was taken. Then Cortés said that another fifth must be taken for him, a share equal to His Majesty's, which we had promised him in the sand-dunes when we made him Captain-General. After that he said that he had been put to certain expenses in Cuba and that what he had spent on the fleet should be deducted from the pile, and in addition the cost to Diego Velázquez of the ships we had destroyed. We all agreed to this and also to pay the expenses of the advocates we had sent to Spain. Then there were the shares of the seventy settlers who had remained at Villa Rica, and the cost of the horse that died, and of Juan Sedeño's mare, which the Tlascalans had killed with a knife-thrust. Then there were double shares for the Mercedarian friar and the priest Juan Díaz and the captains and those who had brought horses, and the same for the musketeers and crossbowmen, and other trickeries, so that in the end very little was left, so little indeed that many of us soldiers did not want to touch it, and Cortés was left with it all. At that time we could do nothing but hold our tongues; to demand justice in the matter was useless. There were other soldiers who took their shares of a hundred pesos and clamoured for the rest. To satisfy them, Cortés secretly gave a bit to one and another as a kind of favour and by means of smooth speeches made them accept the situation. . . .

. . . Some soldiers too had laid hands on so much that ingots marked and unmarked and a great variety of jewels were in public circulation. Heavy gambling was always going on with some cards which Pedro Valenciano had manufactured out of drum-skins, and which were as well made and painted as the real thing. Such was the state we were in.

It reached Cortés' ears, however, that many of the soldiers were dissatisfied with their share of the gold and said that the heaps had been robbed, so he decided to make them a speech that was all honeyed words. He said that what he had was for us, and that he did not want his fifth but only the share that came to him as Captain-General, and that if anyone needed anything he would give it to him. He said that the gold we had got so far was only a trifle, and that they could see what great cities there were, and what rich mines, and that we should be lords of them all and very rich and prosperous. He used other arguments too, well couched in the manner of which he was a master. In addition he secretly gave golden jewels to some soldiers and made great promises to others, and he ordered that the food brought by Montezuma's stewards should be divided equally among all the soldiers, receiving no greater share himself than the rest.

Now all men alike covet gold, and the more we have the more we want, and several recognizable pieces were missing from the heaps. At the same time Juan Velázquez de León was employing the Atzcapotzalco goldsmiths to make him some large gold chains and pieces of plate for his table. Gonzalo Mejía, the treasurer, privately requested him to deliver this gold to him, since it had not paid the royal fifth and was known to belong to the treasure Montezuma had given us. Juan Velázquez, being Cortés' favourite, refused to give up anything, on the plea that he had not taken any share of what had been collected or anything else, but only what Cortés had given him before the bars were cast.

Gonzalo Mejía answered that what Cortés himself had taken and hidden from his companions was enough, and that as treasurer he demanded all the gold that had not paid the royal fifth. One thing followed another, till both men lost their tempers and drew their swords. Indeed if we had not quickly separated them they would have killed one another, for they were men of great character and brave fighters. As it was they emerged from the battle with two wounds apiece. . . .

Along with the soldiers and scavengers, the conquest also brought religious orders to Latin America—legions of friars and priests who converted the Indians to Catholicism either by force or by persuasion. The friars, who knew the Indian from the other side of the sword, often became more involved in the Indian life than the conqueror, and friars sometimes fought for Indian rights against the self-interests of their Spanish countrymen. Salvador de Madariaga, a contemporary Latin American historian, introduces the friars.

Conquerors of the Cross
By Salvador de Madariaga

The religious side of the mighty adventure was kept alive by the wonderful activity of the friar. The friars were the second prototype of the White strain in the Indies. They were not, of course, fundamentally different from the conquerors. They were in fact conquerors *a lo divino*, as the phrase went in Spain in those days. They stood more for the universal than for the individual pole of Spanish psychology, but this was a matter of degree and of stress rather than of nature; and the two types merged easily into each other. Many conquerors became friars. Las Casas [famous priest who opposed the mistreatment of the Indians] was first a conqueror, later a settler, finally a friar. He is a case in point, for no one ever espoused the cause of the universal spirit with more ardour and zeal; and yet, no one put into his crusade a stronger individual and opinionated stubbornness. The sense of daring, of sacrifice, of achievement, which we found in the conquerors also animates the friars. While the conquerors strove hard to rise and acquire honour and greatness, the friars strove hard to humble themselves. "The Indians marvelled at the fortitude of the preachers, and more so at seeing them so averse to gold and silver of which the secular Spaniards made so much"—writes a contemporary author. This example was at first the only language in which the friars could convey their faith to the natives, and they spoke it even to the risk of death. "And so we lost Fr. Martín de Valencia, out of sheer penitence," writes Juan de Samano in 1537; while the Viceroy Velasco reports to Philip II (1554): "And as the friars of this order of St. Dominic eat no meat and always go on foot, their hardships are intolerable and they do not live long." They made a point of living as modestly as the humblest Indians, "they go about poor and barefoot as we do"—said the Indians of them—"they eat what we do, sit down among us, speak to us mildly." There were several cases of martyrdom, and one perhaps more significant than martyrdom, the case of Fr. Antonio de Roa, who, not content with imitating the poverty of the Indians the better to win their confidence, and finding they did not yet realize the horror of sin, used to have himself lashed during his sermon, and, to demonstrate that the body is a slave, he branded himself with a torch. One day, to prove to his native flock how unbearable Hell must be, he threw himself on a bed of burning coals and stayed on it for a while, showing that it could not be borne for long by men alive, though infinitely milder than the fire of Hell.

Such were the methods whereby the spiritual conquest of the Indies was achieved, or at any rate attempted.

The friar and conqueror are not just museum pieces; something of their way of thinking and of their spirit has survived four hundred years to become part of modern Latin American man. Madariaga skips us ahead a few hundred years, to see how the passion of the conquerors, their distaste for boredom and repetition, and their fascination with sporadic and glorious events are re-created in the contemporary life of Latin Americans. Why build a log cabin, board by board, when you can dream of an empire? Latin Americans tend to work in quick bursts of energy, rather than the slow, plodding way favored in North American tortoise-and-hare stories. Does this difference have something to do with the conquest? Madariaga thinks so, and Latin Americans generally see their distant past as having direct bearing on their own lives; history is much more personal than it is for North Americans.

The Friar and the Conquistador
By Salvador de Madariaga

This friar and this conqueror are the roots of what was later to be known as the "Spaniard," the "Creole," or the "American Spaniard." The prototypes and these other forms evolved from them present a number of common features which are the framework of American-Spanish psychology. The chief of them is a certain "vertical" attitude which strives at the utmost by the self, and is therefore unwilling to bend to daily tasks and weave itself into social patterns with others. A feature, of course, transplanted from Spain. It gives to the Spanish collective tissue—whether in Spain or in America—that grating and rasping consistence which makes it both so tough and so difficult to handle, as well as so static. These men, when the urge to conquer or to convert died down in them, were apt to feel somewhat helpless, and they relaxed into mere being, leaving the doing to others. Next to conquest and conversion, no action seemed worth while in their eyes. The middle stretches of life had no hold on them, and for the most part, they let them lie fallow, waiting for more stimulating tasks and days. Some found this stimulus in commerce, perhaps because in those days storm and pirates turned commerce into something so near gambling. Others found it more straightforward, and simpler also, to gamble at the green table, and it was even possible to come across blends of commerce and gambling. . . . Nearly all gave themselves to the even more hazardous gamble of love, then highly spiced with death. And then, of course, there was civil war.

This feature, deeply ingrained in the Spanish character, had been duly noted down by Bodin, though with that awkward way of interpreting Spanish psychology often to be found in French observers: "The Spaniard is marvellously lazy, outside arms and commerce." It was exacerbated by the conquest. . . .

No laziness in all this. A different tendency of the human spirit. That is all. But the effects of climate and wealth must be taken into account. "Those who are born over here"—writes Father Vetancurt in 1698—"are shrewd and profound in every kind of science, although most of them when they reach the age of forty flag in their studies, and only work while young." We have heard this before. We shall hear it again. And every time with a different explanation. That given by [a] Mexican friar is worth noting: "because the various amusements lead them astray, and as there are not always rewards for so many, they get discouraged, and what makes thoughtful people wonder most is that the capacity for reasoning should dawn so soon in children, and that they should all have such high-spirited souls that few are those who incline towards the mechanical arts and crafts of their elders, the reason being that the climate, abundance and wealth of the land raises their spirit and ennobles their thoughts." The trend upward should be observed. But it would be absurd to read it in our present-day, class-war context. The ambition to rise to knightly leisure warmed every breast with democratic equality. . . .

All this has nothing to do with laziness. In a way, it is universal. The skilled worker of Mexico under the Spanish rule was prosperous enough to wear a ruff and ride a horse, just as his Californian comrade of our days is prosperous enough to wear a white collar and to drive a car. In essence also there was in it something more specifically Spanish: an instinct which seeks to defend the person of the individual from the collective gear. The machinery is the insidious master which, under the disguise of a slave, takes hold of men and makes them its own, reducing them to wheels and levers in a huge world factory. Technique is the no less insidious power of the new tyrant. Hence the true nature of the disinclination of the Spaniard towards technique, and of his love of leisure, which other peoples, less aware of these states of mind and moods, mistake for laziness. A tendency to be rather than to do; to live to-day, and as a tree which gives forth fruit and lets it fall regardless of whether it rots or fructifies, rather than as a bridge between yesterday and tomorrow trodden by the traffic of humdrum life. This disharmony between the upward, static tendency of the Spanish soul, and the onward, dynamic tendency which western affairs took on gradually, was in later days to be one of the deepest causes of the wars of secession.

Brazilians have always been considered to be different from other Latin Americans. Their language is Portuguese, a more lyrical tongue than Spanish, and their music and body movements seem more graceful, flowing, and subtle than the music and movements of Spanish descendants. There are many reasons for Brazil's divergences, but the style of the original Portuguese colonizer is one of the most important. Freyre, the Brazilian sociologist, describes the "unbridled stallions" who entered Brazil in the sixteenth century, and the more informal way they approached sex, the Church, colonial politics, and life in general.

The Portuguese Colonizer

By Gilberto Freyre

It is possible that, with the genetic interests of the population in view, certain individuals were deliberately sent to Brazil whom we know to have been expatriated for irregularities or excesses in their sexual life: for hugging and kissing, for employing witchcraft to induce love or hatred, for bestiality, effeminacy, procuring, and the like. To the wilderness, so under-populated, with a bare sprinkling of whites, came these oversexed ones, there to give extraordinarily free rein to their passions; and the results, it may be, were advantageous to the interests of Portugal in Brazil. Attracted by the possibilities of a free and untram-meled life, with a host of nude women all around them, many Europeans . . . proceeded to settle here out of predilection or of their own free will. Unbridled stal-lions is what they were. Others, like the cabin-boys that fled Cabral's fleet, going up into the jungles, may have remained there out of a taste for adventure or "youthful audacity." And the unions that many of these exiles entered into—unions of Norman "inter-preters," shipwrecked mariners, and new-Christians, Europeans all of them, in the prime of life and the best of health, young and full of masculine vigor, "adventurous and ardent youths, brimming with strength"—the unions that they formed with native women, who were possibly equally clean and phys-ically wholesome, need not always have belonged to the category of those "unhygienic matings" of which Azevedo Amaral speaks. Quite the contrary. Such unions may have served as a "true process of sexual selection" if one takes into account the liberty that the European had of choosing a mate from among dozens of Indian women. Sexual intercourse under such conditions could only have resulted in good healthy animals, even though bad Christians or in-dividuals of unprepossessing character.

To the advantages already pointed out that the Portuguese of the fifteenth century enjoyed over con-temporary peoples who were also engaged in coloniz-ing activity may be added their sexual morality, which was Mozarabic in character: Catholic morality rendered supple by contact with the Mohammedan, and more easy-going, more relaxed, than among the northern peoples. Nor was their religion the hard and rigid system of the Reformed countries of the north, or even the dramatic Catholicism of Castile itself; theirs was a liturgy social rather than religious, a softened, lyric Christianity with many phallic and animistic reminiscences of the pagan cults. The only thing that was lacking was for the saints and angels to take on fleshly form and step down from the altars on feast-days to disport themselves with the populace. As it was, one might have seen oxen entering the churches to be blessed by the priests; mothers lulling their little ones with the same hymns of praise that were addressed to the Infant Jesus; sterile women with upraised petticoats rubbing themselves against the legs of São Gonçalo do Amarante; married men, fearful of infidelity on the part of their wives, going to interrogate the "cuckold rocks," while marriageable young girls addressed themselves to the "marriage rocks"; and finally our Lady of Expectancy being worshipped in the guise of a pregnant woman. . . .

As for the mechanism of colonial administration, marked by feudal tendencies in the beginning, it was lacking in the severity displayed by the Spaniards; it was slack and weak, leaving the colonies and in many respects the proprietors to their own free will. . . . Later it was rendered more rigid through the creation of the office of governor-general. . . . The object in view was to prevent a national consciousness (which would inevitably arise out of a uniformity of treatment and administrative regime) from overshadowing the regional one; but this prophylactic measure against the peril of nationalism in the colony was not carried to the point of sacrificing to it the colony's essential unity, assured by the catechism and by the Ordinances, by the Catholic liturgy, and by the Portuguese language. . . .

All of these elements, beginning with a Christianity that was lyrically social, a cult of the family rather than a religion of the church or cathedral—and the Portuguese, incidentally, never erected great and dominant church edifices of the type to be found at Toledo or at Burgos, just as in Brazil such structures were never to attain the importance and prestige that they had in Spanish America—all these elements and advantages, to repeat, were to favor a colonization that in Portuguese America, as in the "proprietary colonies" of the English in North America, was to rest upon the institution of the slave-holding family, the Big House, the patriarchal family, the only difference being that in our country the family was to be enlarged by a far greater number of bastards and dependents, gathered round the patriarchs, who were more given to women and possibly a little more loose in their sexual code than the North Americans were.

The true formative process of our society, as has been said, is to be viewed from 1532 on, with the rural or semi-rural family as the unit, whether it was a matter of married couples who had come from the homeland or of families that had been set up here through the union of colonists with Indian women, with orphan girls, or even with women whom matchmaking fathers had sent over at random from Portugal. . . .

The formation of Brazil went forward without the colonizers being concerned with racial unity or racial purity. Throughout practically the whole of the sixteenth century the gates of the colony were open to foreigners; the only thing that mattered to the colonial authorities was that the newcomers be of the Catholic faith or religion. Handelmann notes that, in order to be admitted to Brazil as a colonist during that era, the principal requirement was that one profess the Christian religion: "only Christians"—and in Portugal this meant Catholics—"might acquire allotments." "No restriction, however," the German historian continues, "was laid down as to nationality; and Catholics from foreign countries might accordingly emigrate to Brazil and settle there. . . ." Oliveira Lima emphasizes the fact that during the century in question Portugal tolerated within its possessions many foreigners, the Portuguese policy with regard to colonization and settlement not being one of "rigorous exclusion, as later adopted by Spain."

PART IV.

THE SPANISH LEGACY

Introduction

Once the Spaniards took off their armor and settled down, they created a more corseted and rigid society than the one they had escaped in search of fame and adventure. Perhaps they were tired of getting lost in the mountains, confused by Indian dialects, and frustrated over reading the *requerimiento* to incredulous Indian faces. In any case, they began to protect themselves, both from imagined enemies and from the chaos of the conquest, inside the reassuring patterns of colonial cities. This part deals with how the Spaniards constructed their society in the New World—how they formed the governments, the laws, the towns, and the Church.

The new colonies, of course, belonged to the Spanish king or queen, but the problem back at the royal court was how to convince the conquerors of that fact. A whole series of institutions was devised to run the New World, and mostly to counter the authority and power of the Spaniards who had been sent to claim it for the crown. But running Latin America from Spain was a little like Washington trying to govern California through cryptic, handwritten notes delivered on foot.

Nevertheless, Spain was able to hold on to the territories for three hundred years, even if there was an incredible amount of bureaucracy, confusion, intrigue, and murderous plotting. The most important institution established back home was the Council of the Indies, a legislative body appointed by the king which met each day to draw up the laws and regulations for the Indies. The decrees of the Council of the Indies were transmitted to the New World through an elaborate administrative mechanism, all under the direct or indirect power of the royal court. The highest official in Latin America was the viceroy, a kind of governor appointed by the king to run a large expanse of territory. The first viceroy, Antonio de

84

Mendoza, arrived in Mexico in 1535, and at that time he had control over most of the empire. Later in the sixteenth century the viceroyalty of Peru was added, and two additional viceroyalties were established in the eighteenth century—that of New Granada (Panama, Colombia, Ecuador, and Venezuela) in 1717 and La Plata (Argentina, Bolivia, Paraguay, and Uruguay) in 1776. Of course, these countries did not exist as such until independence; during the Spanish rule they were known only as viceroyalties.

Viceroys came and went, dozens of them, and they had mixed success and widely differing intentions. Other institutions were created both to aid and to check the power of the viceroys, as the selection by Victor Alba explains. The most noteworthy of these were the *audiencias*, ruling councils comprising several people, that ruled the territory in the absence of the viceroy or opposed him when he wanted to betray the king. Beyond the *audiencias*, there were also the *corregidores*, who roamed the colony spying on errant or disloyal subjects; the notetakers and counternotetakers and roving ambassadors; the intendants and captains and minor-league viceroys. While all this Spanish authority was being handed down, the Creoles (or Spaniards born in the New World) were building an independent power base through two institutions of local government—the *consulados* and the *cabildos*. As the selection shows, these were the beginnings of self-government and would later provide the impetus for the final break from Spain.

Along with the Spanish officials, the new towns, described here through one serious account and also through the satirical impressions of Concolorcorvo, an eighteenth-century Spanish wit, sprang up methodically across the empire—the rich bazaar of Potosí, Bolivia, where tin was mined; the grand designs of Lima and Mexico City and Quito. The new towns seemed to freeze the passion of the conquest inside their compulsive Roman squares: everything was laid out according to checkerboard plan. The social life took the order of the town and turned it on its side; people clawed and scrambled their way up an equally taut and formal prestige chain. A person's status could be fixed by the intensity of a royal glance, the duration of a curtsy, or the location of his placemat at the table; even pastel shadings of skin color were a measure of worth, as the colonial upper class pirouetted through opulence, decadence, and intrigue.

The Spaniards were not about to abandon the luxury that they had suffered for, and they proved it in their reaction to the new laws. The conscience of the mother country, unsettled at the barbarity and mistreatment of Indians, began to work its way into the royal decrees governing the conduct of Spaniards in the New World. These laws were supposed to prohibit the conquerors and their descendants from harming or exploiting the Indians, but the force of these regulations died out somewhere in the crossing. As one of the excerpts explains, the new laws were scoffed at, ignored, and otherwise fell on the deaf ears of Spaniards who could still count their wounds and repaid themselves for their trouble in Indian slave labor. During this epoch, the servitude was called encomienda—a Spaniard's right to Indian slaves to till the expropriated Indian land. The encomienda relationship did not change drastically for four centuries, although the word used to describe the Indian servitude was modified several times.

If there was a softening in the treatment of Indians during the colonial period, it was not so much because of the new laws as because so many Indians died that there was a dwindling labor force to support the conquerors. Hundreds of thousands of Indians died, and entire populations were wiped out (particularly in the Caribbean area) by diseases transmitted from Europe by the Spanish. The Indians may have introduced the Spaniards to syphilis, their revenge on the conquerors, and Montezuma may have bequeathed diarrhea to the Cortés troups, but it wasn't enough to equal what the Spaniards gave them. The rampant epidemics, and the general brutality of the time, formed the basis for the Black Legend—the notion that Spain was a guilty barbarian, a murderer of innocents, an evil colonizer. As Indians died, the Spaniards could choose among treating the survivors more kindly, importing Negro slaves to take their place (a practice carried out in large scale in Brazil and the Caribbean), or doing the work themselves. The latter was an unacceptable alternative.

The most powerful institution of the time, and the one

that demanded obedience to a higher authority than the Spanish crown, was the Church. The Catholic hierarchy was responsible for some of the worst treatment of Indians, but at the same time, religion and compassion for the newly converted heathen played a part in preventing more rampant brutality. While most Church people turned to the pleasures of position, lust, and opulence, like the rest of the settlers, there was also a strong reform movement. The colonies were exposed to fiery sermons from Bartolomé de las Casas or Father Montesino (like the one presented in this part) that lashed out against enslavement of Indians. But the pleasures of life were too much at hand, and most colonists ignored Las Casas and Montesino.

The Church was not paralayzed by the moral dilemmas of the conquest—at least not enough to stop it from becoming the largest landholder in the empire. (In some viceroyalties, the Church owned a fifth of the territory, a position that it held in some Andean countries until recent times.) Picón-Salas describes the mood and intention of the Church at the time, and also how the Inquisition was transplanted to the colony, gaining moderate popularity in the New World. There were a few Protestants and Jews to torture, and to some extent Indians were the victims of the Inquisition—although it was hard to punish people still in the process of being convinced.

At the same time that the Church was solidifying its more sedentary, ritualistic role in the cities, the Jesuit missionaries were carrying on perhaps the most far-reaching utopian experiment ever attempted. In the wilderness of what is now Paraguay and Brazil, the Jesuits set up model communities of indigenous people, as explained here by Germán Arciniegas.

The Jesuit communities were the object of interest and even envy among other colonists, and they were frequently under armed attack by groups that wanted to take advantage of another Indian labor pool. The Jesuits were finally expelled from Latin America, but before that happened in the eighteenth century, they had managed to have a lasting effect on some of the Indian groups in Paraguay, and on the social ethic of the entire continent.

During most of the events discussed in this part, the Spaniards and their descendants were solidifying their power, drawing their boundaries, and waltzing for position on a social scale of intricate division. The Indians were working.

———————

The next two selections describe the system of government imposed on the new colony by the mother country, Spain. The laws for the colony were drawn up by the Council of the Indies, a legislative body located in Spain and comprising representatives appointed by the king. The Alba excerpt explains the duties of the council; the important thing to remember is that it was closely controlled by the Spanish rulers.

The real problem was how to enforce the laws in the colonies—several weeks away from direct Spanish authority. To organize their colony, the Spanish divided Latin America into what were called viceroyalties, great expanses of territory controlled by a viceroy—appointed by the king and mandated to carry out the laws of the Council of the Indies. There were two original viceroyalties—New Spain, which comprised what is now modern Mexico; and Peru, which included most of the Andes, as well as Argentina. Later, two additional viceroyalties were added.

Along with these major divisions, areas of lesser importance were organized under governors or captains-general, also appointed by the Spanish king.

Down from the viceroys, an elaborate bureaucratic maze of officialdom was established, to ensure that nobody in the colonies could gain enough power to challenge the authority of the mother country. These minor officials—*adelantados, corregidores,* and others that Alba describes—were mostly glorified spies who reported to the king or the Council of the Indies. They were often locked into bitter feuds. At best, it was hard for the council to glean from the various reports any consistent notion of what was going on.

Aside from the political and judicial institutions that Alba discusses, Spain was most interested in finding ways to solidify its control over trade and commerce. It accomplished this through an entrenched state-run economy, and as Alba points out, Latin America has known a much longer tradition of socialism, of state-dominated capitalism, than the United States. Does this have any-

thing to do with the Latins' general desire to "let government do it," rather than to rely on individual action?

Most of these Spanish institutions were hierarchical
and bureaucratic, leading many observers to conclude
that this early experience made Latin America unsuited
to the democratic process. Latin America is famous for
its bureaucracies, as anyone who has tried to cross the
Mexican border can attest. The Madariaga selection, however, describes two important organs of self-government
that developed during colonial times. The *cabildo* and the
consulado, as they were called, were admittedly controlled by the rich and powerful descendants of the
conquerors, but at least they were operated autonomously
and locally. These institutions, which have been compared with the New England town meetings, later became
the first source of opposition to government from Spain.
When Latin America became independent in the nineteenth century, the *cabildos* and *consulados* played an
indispensable part in the rebellion.

Puppet Strings from Spain

By Victor Alba

The principal body governing the Indies was the
Council of the Indies, which had its seat in Seville.
The council, created in 1518 and given definitive form
in 1534, was modeled upon a similar body that, together with the king, made the laws for Castile. The
Council of the Indies made laws for the Indies; proposed candidates for administrative posts in America,
both civil and ecclesiastical; organized fleets and
armadas; sat in judgment on matters of *residencia*
(that is, heard the complaints of subjects against the
viceroy when his term had ended); directed military
affairs; and was the final court of appeals. It was
customary to appoint several members of the council
from among former officials who had served in
America, and inspectors were regularly sent out to
study the situation in the Indies. The legislative activity of the Council was enormous; several compila-

tions of its laws were made, the best known of which was published in 1681.

In America, the king was represented by the viceroy. The viceroy supervised the execution of laws drawn up by the Council of the Indies and appointed local civil and ecclesiastical officials. Although he was supposed to hold office for only three years, his term was often longer. At the end of it, he was answerable for his stewardship before the Council of the Indies.

New Spain (Mexico) and Peru were the first viceroyalties. Later, New Granada (Colombia) and the Río de la Plata became viceroyalties. Other regions— Guatemala, Venezuela, Cuba, Puerto Rico, Santo Domingo, Chile, Louisiana, and, for a time, Florida— were governed by captains generals or by governors. The frontier areas were under *adelantados*.

The judicial system in America was based on a court known as the *audiencia*. The first *audiencias* consisted of three or four judges, but over the years the number steadily grew. There was an *audiencia* in every viceroyalty, captaincy general, or governorship. In addition to their judicial functions, the *audiencias* were also responsible for military, religious, and financial inspections, and served as advisors to the viceroys. There were frequent jurisdictional disputes between the *audiencias* and the viceroys, however, especially since the *audiencia* communicated directly with the royal *audiencia* in Spain, which in turn communicated directly with the Crown.

There were also, in the New World, special tribunals of the army, the treasury, the Church, and the Inquisition (which was of much less importance in the New World than in the Old).

Most of the officials were sent from Spain. This in time gave rise to rivalry between the *gachupines* (Spaniards born in Spain) and the Creoles (Spaniards born in America), because the latter resented having administrative careers closed to them. However, the fact that the officials did not settle permanently but had a limited stay in America, at the end of which they had to give an account of their stewardship, contributed a certain degree of independence to their authority.

Moreover, the Court understood that not all Spanish laws and customs could be applied to the New World. It therefore decreed that while the laws of Spain should serve as models for those made for the Indies, the laws and customs of the Indians should be respected, wherever they were not contrary to the Catholic religion. The Court also took into account the differences among the regions of the Indies, realizing that the same type of government was not suitable for savage peoples and those who were highly organized. Thus the authority of the viceroys was made flexible, and a court of appeals was established so that there should be mutual checks and controls. This system did not always work, for its corruption paralleled that of the Court itself. . . .

To protect its economic interests in the New World, Castile established a monopoly on trade with its lands in America. All Indies trade was regulated by a Board of Trade (Casa de Contratación), founded in 1503. Trade could be carried on only through the ports of Seville and Cádiz in Spain, and through a few ports in America. Two expeditions a year went to America: one to New Spain (Mexico) and the other to Tierra Firme (South America). Both were protected against pirates by an armada. In the eighteenth century, Charles III extended the privileges of trading to eleven Spanish and twenty-four American ports, but did not lift the monopoly.

The Court also imposed many and varied taxes on the new lands. There were taxes on imports (the *almojarifazgo*, the ancient Arab name); on foodstuffs (the *sisa*, so unpopular that the word came to mean what servants kept for themselves when they did the marketing); on metals and precious stones (the *quinto real*, or royal fifth, 20 per cent on all products extracted from the ground); the tax on agricultural products (the *diezmo*, or tithe; in theory, nine-tenths of this went to the Crown and one-tenth to the Church, but in reality, much more often went to the

Church); and on sales (the *alcabala*). Indians were exempted from paying the *diezmo,* but they did pay a tribute.

There were also state monopolies on such goods as playing cards, salt, spices, mercury, and tobacco.

The revenue from all these taxes was sent to the Board of Trade in Seville. Once a week, the Council of the Indies met to examine the accounts, make fiscal decisions, and assign the use of that part of the revenues that went back to America to pay administrative and military expenses. After 1526, every viceroyalty, governorship, and captaincy general had its own budget; any surplus was earmarked for the aid of colonies that showed a deficit. As we shall see, these taxes were the cause of a long series of rebellions by colonizers and Indians alike.

Obviously, this fiscal system had extensive control of the economy. This is significant, for it created in Latin America the tradition of relying on state intervention in business; the planned or directed economy is a Spanish heritage so deeply rooted as today to be considered natural and even essential. No small contribution to this was made by some colonial corporations, like the Guipuzcoana company, to which Charles III granted the economic control of Venezuela.

Yet it should also be said that the colonial administration tried harder to exploit riches that were already known than to discover new ones. There was considerable development in mining, especially in the silver mines, which were more "modern" than European mines of the time. Progress was also made in metallurgy. But in general, the natural wealth—as it was understood in that era—was so great, the fertility of the soil so astonishing to people accustomed to the tired soils of Europe, that there was little interest in seeking new sources of wealth or in modernizing the utilization of those that already existed.

In Brazil, too, the administrative system was based on the concept of the colony as a property of the Crown, which was represented by a viceroy resident in Bahia, the capital until 1763, and subsequently Rio de Janeiro. Brazil was divided into eight captaincies general and eight governorships. The Church was administered by an archbishop and five bishops. The municipal assemblies, similar to the *cabildos,* were democratic in origin, but they lost this character even more rapidly than the Spanish ones and became mere bureaucratic mechanisms. We must also remember that until the nineteenth century, Brazil consisted essentially of a fringe of settlements along the coast and that there were scarcely any Portuguese in the interior. The principal problem of the Portuguese authorities was to combat the incursions of the Dutch, French, and British into Brazil.

Self-Government of Sorts
By Salvador de Madariaga

It is a commonplace that the Spanish American communities suffer to this day from the fact that they were not trained and practised in the art of self-government. As if, in one way or another, countries as far away from the motherland as the Indies were from Spain in the days of the mule and the sail could be governed otherwise than by themselves. Those who write from this standpoint refer their readers, tacitly or expressly, to the superior political wisdom of England, who from her earliest days, it is suggested, accustomed her little ones to walk on the true path of parliamentary institutions. As if, whether in England or in Spain, imperial ways had been laid down out of textbooks of political "science," and not just grown in the blissful and vigorous incoherence of nature. . . .

When the Spanish rule in the Indies is described as centralistic, what is meant is that there were no representative institutions. But even this is only true in the light of Anglo-Saxon habits and should be carefully qualified. There were in the Indies two representative institutions: the *cabildos* and the *consulados.* The *cabildos* were to a considerable extent aristocratic bodies in that a number of their magistrates purchased their mandate from the Crown, or held them as a privilege granted to a family. But there are a number of points to bear in mind. The first is that in every country in those days a considerable number of so-called representative mandates were also infeodated in certain families. Even to this day, the son succeeds the father and the wife the husband in not a few British constituencies. The second point is that this partimonial aspect which representative bodies tended to take on did not make the *cabildos* any less representative. Precisely because of it, the *cabildos* reflected better the actual structure of the society which they were meant to govern, a structure founded on aristocracy and ownership of land. The chief point is that the *cabildos*, powerful as they were, almost independent in law and practically independent in fact, embodied the local spirit and were manned by local men with local roots and interests. . . .

As for the *consulados*, they were home rule institutions for the commercial community; a kind of chamber of commerce with considerable powers of taxation, justice, administration and public initiative. They could appoint deputies to administer commercial justice in other cities than that in which the chief body resided. No appeal against their decisions was allowed other than to the Council of the Indies. . . .

Such a combination of *cabildos* and *consulados* was typical of the political tendencies of the Spanish people when left to themselves. Empirical, local, not well co-ordinated on a national plane, bound by the interests of their province and profession, by no stretch of imagination can it be described as lacking in freedom. It contained all the elements of freedom which the aristocratic nature of the times and the relations between the castes allowed. . . .

Such were the limitations of the almost unlimited power the white upper classes enjoyed. . . . In the course of time, though the royal authorities kept alive their tradition as protectors of the Indians, and as general administrators of justice with an equal solicitude for all, the power of the Whites increased every-

where in the Indies, and particularly in Peru. Ulloa
and Jorge Juan are most convincing in their description of the local omnipotence of the Creole landed
aristocracy. "Every private person"—they write—"es-
teems himself so much owing to what he owns that he
considers himself as a petty king in his own lands,
since he is an absolute lord in them, and almost with
no other subjection than that of his own free will
[...] so that the *corregidores* wield no more authority than that which the most prominent settlers are
willing to grant them." Neither of the two preroga-
tives of authority—taxation and the enforcement of
the law—meant anything for the rich Creoles. They
paid what they wished, as they wished, when they
wished, allowed the main burden of the tax to be
borne by Indians and mongrels, and as for the law,
there was none but their will.

This selection concerns the settling down of the Spaniards after the conquest, the manner in which they built
their colonial towns, cities, and life styles. James Scobie
is writing about Argentina, which differed from other
Spanish colonies of the time because there were few
Indians in Argentina to support feudal agriculture, because the Church was less powerful, and because a
merchant class emerged very early. But the patterns of
laying out the cities of Argentina, the style of life, the
philosophy of political administration, and the rigidity of
social classes were the same all over Latin America.
Scobie teaches Latin American history at Indiana University. The word *vecino* in the selection refers to the original Spanish settlers.

The Spanish Towns

By James Scobie

The Spanish conquistadors were not frontiersmen or
farmers, but rather soldiers, administrators, and masters. Therefore, they turned to the institution of the

city, so deeply rooted in their own history, for the means to settle and control these new lands and peoples. The estimated three hundred thousand Indians in the Argentine area hardly provided the incentive for conquest offered by the millions in the mountain valleys of Mexico or the highlands of Peru. Yet the conquistadors of this area used much the same methods of colonization as in Mexico and Peru, establishing towns that could administer and control the Indian cultures already tied to the cultivation of the land. In the last analysis, the location of Spanish towns and the success of Spanish colonization were determined by the presence of agrarian Indian cultures. . . .

As these Spaniards sought more permanent exploitation than that of mere marauding bands, they founded urban settlements, or, in the contemporary language, cities, always in strict accord with Spanish tradition. The conquistador carefully chose a site with an eye to its defense, its water supply, and the presence of friendly Indians. He laid out a rectangular gridwork of streets and a central plaza on which faced lots for a church and a municipal building. Then, in a ceremony invoking the names of the Holy Trinity, the Virgin Mary, several saints, the king, and the local governor and setting forth the convenience and desirability of colonizing this location, the conquistador officially named and founded the city. The formalities included the creation of a *cabildo,* or town council, composed of several magistrates and councilors, the erection of a pillory and a stake in the center of the principal plaza, the definition of municipal boundaries and jurisdictions, and the survey and assignment of city lots and surrounding garden plots to all *vecinos,* or settlers. At this stage, relations with the native population assumed vital importance to the settlement's survival. The Spaniards needed Indian labor, but the crown and Church refused to recognize enslavement of the natives. The solution, in part inherited from Spain's reconquest of the Iberian peninsula from the Moors, had already evolved in the

Caribbean, Mexico, and Peru—the *encomienda,* or
royal grant of Indians to the tutelage, protection, and
Christianizing influence of the conquistador, in return
for which the *encomendero* was entitled to a certain
portion of their labor. Thus, upon establishment of a
city, Indians were assigned to the principal Spanish
leaders.

On this basis the towns of the Argentine interior
took shape during the second half of the sixteenth
century. Those that were fortunately situated endured to become capitals of present-day provinces
whose boundaries outline the extensive jurisdictions of
the colonial cities. It was in these widely scattered
towns that the society and economy which would
dominate the interior of colonial Argentina began to
emerge.

These were small towns with clearly divided social
classes and modest tastes. The original *vecinos* and
their descendants formed the upper class. Indian
blood ran in some of their veins, for the first conquistadors occasionally recognized their mestizo offspring and endowed them with wealth, power, and
position. But as a group they ... prided themselves
on their pure origins, and increasingly married only
within their own circle. In their hands they held the
control of land and labor. The town lots and garden
lots had been divided among the *vecinos,* and, although
the crown strictly forbade hereditary *encomiendas,* in
practice an Indian village continued to supply laborers
for sons and even grandsons of the same family. The
vecinos also occupied the principal commercial, municipal, and Church positions. In the eighteenth century
Spain would send peninsular officials to fill administrative posts, but the sixteenth-century Argentine towns
were still too unimportant to need such supervision.
On the shoulders of the creole families, therefore,
rested the administration, defense, and welfare not
only of the town but also of a vaguely defined area
sometimes extending as much as two hundred miles
beyond the urban limits. Yet numerically this upper
class was small, in 1600 ranging from twenty-four

vecinos in San Juan and forty in Mendoza to four hundred in Santiago del Estero and five hundred in Córdoba.

Below the creole group extended the masses of the population, of many racial shades and economic levels. As the towns expanded, an urbanized laboring class developed, distinct from the Christianized, or "tamed," Indians of the surrounding villages. Negro slaves, imported by way of the coast, began to appear in the interior during the last decade of the sixteenth century. Slaves, along with Negroes who had purchased their freedom, mestizos, mulattoes, and all imaginable combinations thereof, performed household chores and all manual labor. By 1600 this laboring class probably outnumbered the creole element two to one and was rapidly expanding. . . .

Almost invariably, as has been pointed out, the town reflected the form of a Spanish city—a rectangular gridiron dominated by a central plaza with an imposing church, a municipal hall, and sometimes a building for the crown official. This and a few shops and warehouses near the plaza comprised the central district. Beyond stretched the residences of the creoles, substantial houses made of stone or adobe and built around patios. Frequently a single home, with its fruit trees and gardens, occupied an entire town block. Servants usually formed part of these creole households, while others of the lower class built their mud and straw shacks on the town's outskirts. . . .

Spanish colonial life imitated the courtly fashion of Europe, with heavy emphasis on protocol, petty intrigue, wealth, blue blood, and plumage. Like any imitators, the New World colonialists probably exaggerated the rituals and pretentions observed back at the royal court in Spain. There was much to satirize in Latin American city life of the seventeenth and eighteenth centuries, and Concolorcorvo, one of the most famous Latin American humorists of his day, wrote this account of a visit to Buenos Aires sometime after 1750. With Argentina's smaller Indian population, less Church influence, and heavier commercial activity in mind, the rest of what Concolorcorvo describes could just as well have happened in Quito or Lima or Mexico City. At the time it was written, Buenos Aires was part of the viceroyalty of Peru—hence the reference.

A Rogue Visits Buenos Aires

By Concolorcorvo

The city is situated west of the voluminous La Plata River, and it seems to me that it may be considered the fourth largest in the great realm of Peru, according first place to Lima, second to Cuzco, third to Santiago de Chile, and fourth to this city. The first two surpass the other two in elaborateness of churches and buildings. The one in question here has advanced greatly in size and in number of buildings since the year 1749, when I was there. . . .

The expanse of the city is 22 common blocks, both from north to south and east to west. The men and women dress like European Spaniards, as is the case, in varying degrees of refinement, between Montevideo and Jujuy [two other cities in the area]. In my opinion the ladies of this city are the most refined of all the Spanish American women, comparable to those from Seville, inasmuch as, although they do not possess as much spark of wit, they do pronounce Castilian more purely. I have seen a soirée, attended by 80 women, robed and coiffed in the latest fashion, accomplished in French and Spanish dances; and, although not comparable in cost to that of Lima and the rest of Peru, their dress pleases with its cut and adornment. All the common people and the majority of the principal ladies do not patronize tailors since they cut, sew, and embellish their gowns and toilettes with perfection because they are clever and exquisite seamstresses; without any prejudice toward the other ladies of ability I have heard extolled in Buenos Aires,

I observed for many days the great art, prudence, and talent of the beautiful and creative Spanish lady Doña Gracia Ana, in copying the finest needlework and embroidery brought to her from Spain and France.

Those ladies of middle class, and even the poor ones, whom I do not choose to call second and third class lest they become angered, not only make and adorn their own clothes, but those of their husbands, children, and brothers as well—particularly if they are from Tornay, they say—with extra profits realized from washing and starching done by some of their slaves. The men are circumspect and of considerable creative talent.

Inasmuch as there are no secular schools, some send their children to Córdoba and others to Santiago de Chile, not desiring an ecclesiastical career for them in their own country, since it provides a very small income, sufficient only for a frugal life. . . .

This city is well located and laid out in a modern fashion, divided into equal blocks and having streets of equal and regular width, but they become impassable on foot in the rainy season because the heavy carts that transport supplies and other materials make holes in which even horses become mired, and thus passage for those on foot is impeded, particularly in crossing from one block to another, obliging people to retreat and, many times, to miss Mass when they find it necessary to cross the street.

The residents who had not built homes in early times and who had plots or bought them later built houses with an elevation of more than 1 *vara* [roughly a yard] and surrounded them with a balustrade 1½ *varas* high, along which people pass with considerable ease, but the old houses are seriously damaged by the traffic of carts and horses heeling toward them, which often makes exit from them impossible; and if the rains are copious the houses are inundated, leaving most of the rooms uninhabitable, a situation almost without remedy.

The city square is not complete, and only the sidewalk of the town hall has arcades. On it are the jail and offices of the notaries; the high constable lives above. This town council has a special practice in that when they go to the fortress to get the Governor for the tournaments the honors of lieutenant general are accorded him within the fortress where the Governor's guard is. The entire fortress is surrounded by a very deep moat, and one enters it by means of a drawbridge. The building is large and solid, and in its main patio are the royal money chests. Its walls are of considerable elevation on the side by the river so as to be level with the top of the cliff, which overlooks the river. The present cathedral is a very small chapel. A large and substantial temple is being constructed, and even if they succeed in completing it, I do not believe the present generation will see it with fitting adornments because the bishopric is poor and prebends of the canons do not exceed 1,000 pesos, nor do those of most of the parish priests. The rest of the churches and monasteries are of very common and ordinary aspect. There is a great wealth of merchants, and even on the most remote streets one sees clothing shops. I believe there must be four times as many as there are in Lima, but all of them together are not as great as four of the largest in that city because the big merchants have stores from which they supply all of Tucumán and more.

I know only one large-scale farmer, Don Francisco de Alzáibar, who has an infinite number of cattle divided among several farms on the other side of the river, but even with all this it has been a long time since 4,000 pesos could be found in his house at one time. I have not heard of any family estates, nor do the residents think of anything other than their business, being content with a good home and a country plot which serves only for recreation. Meat is in such abundance that it is taken in quarters to the square by the cart load, and if by accident a whole quarter slips off, as I have seen happen, the driver does not dismount to recover it, even if he is aware of it, and if by chance a beggar passes, he does not take it home because it is not worth the trouble of carrying it. At the hour of the Angelus, meat is often given away gratis in the slaughter houses because each day many animals, more than are needed by the town, are killed, merely for the hide.

All the dogs, which are in great number without distinction as to master, are so fat that they can scarcely move, and the rats go out at night for fresh air, in efficient detachments, because in even the poorest home they have an overabundance of meat, and they feed on eggs and chickens which come in great quantities from the neighboring regions. . . .

I do not believe the number of carriages in the city exceeds 16. In former times, when there were fewer, residents brought mules from the country and tied them to a stake at their homes, leaving them without food until they were emaciated and could not work, whereupon they ordered that others be brought in. . . . At the present time they have applied themselves to raising green barley, which they bring into the city with loads of hay for the riding horses which live very poorly, with the exception of those belonging to a few people who gather straw and barley from the nearby fields. . . .

The colonies were established, and Spain dispersed its laws and government throughout Latin America. But, as we have seen in the Introduction to this part, there was no guarantee that the laws would be carried out. Dissension and intrigue made the colonies difficult to control. Extended struggles for power resulted in frequent assassinations, and a continual flow of new viceroys and Spanish officials attempted to bring order and obedience. This selection discusses the arrival of Blasco Núñez Vela, a new viceroy, into Lima in 1544. Núñez Vela was supposed to enforce the new laws, royal decrees forbidding the mistreatment of the Indians and their general enslavement at the hands of the Spaniards. The new laws met with stiff resistance in the colonies, as Núñez Vela soon discovered. The colonists voiced their opposition, and when talk failed, they rose in revolt. The new laws were never adequately enforced, and the treatment of Indians continued as before. Gómara, a historian of the colonial period, describes the conflict.

The New Laws in Peru

By Gómara

Blasco Núñez [a viceroy] entered Trujillo amid great gloom on the part of the Spaniards; he publicly proclaimed the New Laws, regulating the Indian tributes, freeing the Indians, and forbidding their use as carriers against their will and without pay. He took away as many vassals as these laws permitted, and vested them in the crown. The people and the town council petitioned for repeal of these ordinances, except for those which regulated Indian tribute and prohibited the use of Indians as carriers; of these provisions they approved. He did not grant their appeal, but instead set very heavy penalties for those judges who should fail to execute the laws, saying that he brought an express order of the emperor for their enforcement, without hearing or granting any appeal. He told them, however, that they had reason to complain of the ordinances; that they should take their case to the emperor; and that he would write to the king that he had been badly informed to order those laws.

When the citizens perceived the severity behind his soft words, they began to curse. Some said that they would leave their wives. Actually, some were ready to leave them for any reason, good or bad, since many had married their lady-loves or camp-followers only on account of an order that stripped them of their estates if they did not do so. Others said that it would be much better not to have a wife and children to maintain, if they were to lose the slaves who supported them by their labors in mines, fields, and other pursuits; others demanded payment for the slaves that were being taken from them. . . . Still others said that they were ill-requited for their labors and services, if in their declining years they were to have no one to serve them; these showed their teeth, decayed from eating toasted corn in the conquest of Peru; others displayed many wounds, bruises, and great lizard bites; the conquerors complained that after wasting their estates and shedding their blood in gaining Peru for the emperor, he was depriving them of the few vassals that he had given them. The soldiers said that they would not go to conquer other lands, since they were denied the hope of holding vassals, but instead would rob right and left all they could; the royal lieutenants and officials complained bitterly of the loss of their allotments of Indians, though they had not maltreated them, and held them not by virtue of their officers but in return for their labors and services.

The priests and friars also declared that they could not support themselves nor serve their churches if they were deprived of their Indian towns; the one who spoke most shamelessly against the viceroy and even against the king was Fray Pedro Múñoz, of the Mercedarian Order, saying how badly the king rewarded those who had served him so well, and that the New Laws smelled of calculation rather than of saintliness, for the king was taking away the slaves that he had sold without returning the money received from them, and that he was taking away Indian towns from monasteries, churches, hospitals, and the conquistadores who had gained them; and, what was worse, they were laying a double tribute and tax on the Indians whom they took away in this fashion and vested in the crown, and that the Indians themselves were weeping over this. There was bad blood between this friar and the viceroy because the latter had stabbed the friar one evening in Málaga, when the viceroy was *corregidor* there. . . .

Besides the political and economic machinery that we have discussed, the only other Spanish institution of real importance to the colony was the Church. (The military was not very well organized at the time.) During the first days of the colony, the Church was made up of proselytizing friars, who lived in isolated villages with the Indians they were attempting to convert. Whatever unity existed in the early Church was shaken by the internal debates and struggles over the treatment of Indians. A small group of Dominican friars led by Father Montesino (the subject of this selection) and Bartolomé de las Casas (the author) began to speak and work against the *encomiendas* (forced Indian labor) and the way the Indians were handled by the Spanish. The whole ecclesiastical debate hinged around the question of whether the Indians already had souls, or whether (since they had never been exposed to Christianity) they were somewhere on a lower social order, and could be treated accordingly. Montesino and Las Casas believed the Indians merited the same human compassion as Spaniards or anybody else. The selection from a Montesino sermon, given on the island of Hispaniola as an answer to those who demanded that he retract an earlier sermon of similar content, needs no further explanation.

Although it has no direct relation to Montesino or Las Casas (and in fact preceded both of them), I include the selection by Bernal Díaz del Castillo, Cortés' aide, because it summarizes the counterarguments that were popular throughout the colony. In Díaz's view, the Indians themselves were barbaric, believed in human sacrifice, and committed such gruesome excesses on each other that any Spanish mistreatment paled in comparison.

By the time the towns were populated, the Church people, like the military conquerors, lost their militant fervor and became part of a stolid and conservative institution. Picón-Salas, in his selection, describes how the missionaries turned into city priests, how rituals and wealth replaced the messianic fervor, how the Church created its elegant and imposing baroque structures that can still be seen in major Latin American cities today. The Church became a rock in Latin America, and from then on was essentially immobile—until recent times.

About the time the Church was solidifying its position and power in Latin America (it took over a fifth of the land in most countries), the Inquisition was in full swing back in Spain. Heretics and other nonbelievers were punished or put to death during the massive Counter Reformation, the Catholic backlash to Martin Luther and the Protestant rebellion in Europe. The Inquisition, run by the Holy Office, was also brought to the colonies, and its practices and effects are described here. The general point to remember about the Church during this period was its defensive, reactionary character; no longer openly confronting the task of converting Indians, the priests retreated behind a wall of doctrine, ritual, and organization.

There was one exception to this hardening—the missionary spirit carried on by the Jesuits, especially in Paraguay. Germán Arciniegas, a modern Latin American historian, shows how the Jesuits established utopian colonies, first fighting off warlike Indians and then the Portuguese adventurers and slave-hunters—the people he calls Paulistas (from São Paulo) and Mamelukes (mixed Indian and Negro ancestry). The Jesuit experiments survived until the middle of the eighteenth century, when the order was expelled from Latin America. The rest of the Church hierarchy feared and disliked these militant zealots. The influence of the Jesuits, though, is still obvious in Paraguay, whose Guaraní Indians have an intense cultural pride that the missionaries helped create.

The Strange Sermon of Father Montesino
By Bartolomé de las Casas

Sunday having arrived, and the time for preaching, Father Antonio Montesino rose in the pulpit, and took for the text of his sermon, which was written down and signed by the other friars, "I am the voice of one crying in the wilderness." Having made his introduction and said something about the Advent season, he began to speak of the sterile desert of the consciences of the Spaniards on this isle, and of the blindness in which they lived, going about in great danger of damnation and utterly heedless of the grave sins in which they lived and died.

Then he returned to his theme, saying: "In order to make your sins known to you I have mounted this pulpit, I who am the voice of Christ crying in the wilderness of this island; and therefore it behooves you to listen to me, not with indifference but with all your heart and senses; for this voice will be the strangest, the harshest and hardest, the most terrifying that you ever heard or expected to hear."

He went on in this vein for a good while, using cutting words that made his hearers' flesh creep and made them feel that they were already experiencing the divine judgment.... He went on to state the contents of his message.

"This voice," said he, "declares that you are in mortal sin, and live and die therein by reason of the cruelty and tyranny that you practice on these innocent people. Tell me, by what right or justice do you hold these Indians in such cruel and horrible slavery? By what right do you wage such detestable wars on these people who lived mildly and peacefully in their own lands, where you have consumed infinite numbers of them with unheard-of murders and desolations? Why do you so greatly oppress and fatigue them, not giving them enough to eat or caring for them when they fall ill from excessive labors, so that they die or rather are slain by you, so that you may extract and acquire gold every day? And what care do you take that they receive religious instruction and come to know their God and creator, or that they be baptized, hear mass, or observe holidays and Sundays?

"Are they not men? Do they not have rational souls? Are you not bound to love them as you love yourselves? How can you lie in such profound and lethargic slumber? Be sure that in your present state you can no more be saved than the Moors or Turks who do not have and do not want the faith of Jesus Christ."

Thus he delivered the message he had promised, leaving his hearers astounded. Many were stunned, others appeared more callous than before, and a few were somewhat moved; but not one, from what I could later learn, was converted.

When he had concluded his sermon he descended

from the pulpit, his head held high, for he was not a man to show fear, of which indeed he was totally free; nor did he care about the displeasure of his listeners, and instead did and said what seemed best according to God. With his companion he went to their straw-thatched house, where, very likely, their entire dinner was cabbage soup, unflavored with olive oil. . . . After he had left, the church was so full of murmurs that . . . they could hardly complete the celebration of the mass.

An Answer to the Sermon
By Bernal Díaz del Castillo

. . . Let us anticipate a little and say that these were the great cruelties about which the bishop of Chiapas, Fray Bartolomé de las Casas, wrote, and was never tired of talking. He insisted that we punished the Cholulans [a Mexican tribe] for no reason at all, or just to amuse ourselves and because we had a fancy to. He writes so persuasively that he would convince anyone who had not witnessed the event, or had no knowledge of it, that these and the other cruelties of which he writes took place as he says, whereas the reverse is true. Let the Dominicans beware of this book of his, because they will find it contradicts the facts. I should like to say also that some good Franciscans, who were the first friars His Majesty sent to New Spain after the capture of Mexico, went to Cholula to inquire into the details of this punishment and the reason for it, and examined the actual *papas* [priests] and elders of the city. After questioning them thoroughly they found the facts to conform exactly with the account I have written, and not with the bishop's. If we had not inflicted that punishment, our lives would have been in great danger from the companies of Mexican warriors and Cholulans, and their barricades and breastworks. And if we had been so unfortunate as to be killed, this New Spain of ours would not have been conquered so rapidly, nor would another armada have dared to set out, or if it had done so it would have met with greater difficulties, because the Mexicans would have defended the ports. And they would still have remained in a state of idolatry.

The Church and the Inquisition
By Mariano Picón-Salas

As the sixteenth century merged into the seventeenth, the Church likewise grew more sedentary and fond of luxury. It was more interested in dominating the Creole society of Spanish Americans than in harvesting Indian souls. To gain this control, Franciscans were at odds with Dominicans, Dominicans with Jesuits in the colonial universities, monks with secular clergymen in the bishoprics, and the Church in general with the state. These conflicts mainly took the form of petty feuds over matters of jurisdiction and ceremonial etiquette. Immense wealth became unproductive as it flowed into the coffers of the religious orders and of the dioceses from the tithes and first fruits, from contributions of the crown and of feudal overlords, from dowries of nuns and friars on entering convents and monasteries, from legacies and bequests, and from parish fees that were much higher than in Spain. All this income and property were held in mortmain and hence inalienable. According to the conservative estimate of Lucas Alamán, by the end of the colonial period at least half of all property, urban and rural, in the viceroyalty of Mexico alone was thus controlled.

The church-fortress, or evangelistic training center, of the early missionaries evolved into the elaborately ornate baroque structures of Spanish Creole architecture, and most of the intrigues in colonial cities emanated from the locutories of sumptuous convents. Every viceroy and bishop was threatened by monkish uprisings as, for example, when Bishop Palafox was

forced to resign in Mexico after long-drawn-out litiga-
tion with all civil and ecclesiastical authorities and including appeals to the pope and the king; or again
when an ignorant and fanatic mob was incited against
the viceroy Carillo de Mendoza and began to set fire
to the viceregal palace, shouting "Lutheran" and
"heretic." The medieval quarrels between Church and
state crossed to America to become even more puerile
there. Since it was inexpedient to attack royal patron-
age, that is, the control of the Church granted by the
popes to the Spanish kings, conflict arose over simple
matters of hierarchy and jurisdiction. Whenever the
inquisitors visited the viceroy, for example, an exact
record had to be made of his manner in receiving
them—whether he was standing or seated, and what
were the ceremonial acts or courtesies that one party
extended to the other. Any formula of politeness considered inadequate to the occasion was immediately
subject to the most distorted interpretation.... A
mere lack of formality might stir up a controversy that
could reach even the ears of the king who acted as a
mediator and arbitrator in matters of petty gossip
through his royal decrees. He had to decide on the
seating order at the observance of Holy Thursday,
which authority was entitled to the key to the taber-
nacle, and other trivial matters of protocol. In the
administrative language of the time Spain seemed like
a mandarin government that gave all its attention to
the properly chosen rite, to the excessively cere-
monious formula, and to subtle interpretation of the
intrigues of any official, which became a public problem; and a parasitic superstructure of colonial functionaries, clergymen, and lords of entailed estates
rested upon a vast pedestal of servile classes.

The Inquisition and the Spirit
of the Counter Reformation

The Inquisition, like no other institution, exempli-
fies the defensive character of seventeenth-century
colonial culture, its narrowness and spiritual steril-
ity.... The Holy Office [administrators of the Inquisi-

tion] was not an integral part of life in the Indies until near the end of the sixteenth century when it was formally established in Lima (1570) and Mexico City (1571). From then on this tribunal acted as a superorganism whose intrusive and vaguely delimited powers alarmed both the civil and ecclesiastical authorities. Many a viceroy feared the inquisitors and tried to pursue a prudent and ingratiating policy in their presence. The undefined scope of the legal functions of the Holy Office, the fact that its decisions were not subject to appeal, and the unquestioning obedience and coöperation that it demanded as the "secular arm" of the Church, all constituted an invitation to abuse. Such abuse included both the fanatical type of justice entrusted to the Church and the perquisites and privileges that the Inquisition enjoyed in administering seized properties and the monetary gains which it sometimes derived from illicit trafficking. As early as 1605 the king wrote to the Mexican inquisitors stating that he had heard that several of them, especially the treasurer, had suddenly become very rich and "owned large estates and sheep and cattle ranches. . . ."

The Inquisition would busy itself with trivial matters such as that of a Negro slave girl who "talked from her chest." This possibly ventriloquist trick led many to think that it was an antic of the Devil. The investigation covered reams of paper with a jargonized prose after which the slave's owners were sentenced to sell her and to dispose of her within a stipulated number of days far beyond the limits of Mexico City. A familiar figure in the Inquisition records was the Devil who had grown more devilish in the American environment owing to what he had learned in his dealings with Indians and Negroes. Unlike Dr. Faustus, the humble half-caste or offspring of an Indian and a Negro did not need the Devil to propound a metaphysical problem or to ask for the boon of eternal youth. Rather, his need of Satanic intervention was for more tangible and concrete things. There was the instance of Francisco Rodríguez, a *zambo* or Indian-Negro mixture, "forty-three years old, occupation coachman and herdsman," who accused himself, in proceedings dated April 6, 1646, "of having had a pact with the Devil, paid him homage, and deeded himself as a slave for nine years at the expiration of which his Satanic majesty would carry him off to Hell." According to the inquisitors' report, the benefit to be derived from this supernatural deal (as witness whereof the Devil had offered Rodríguez a likeness of himself printed on a piece of parchment) was the gift of

> being able to fight off a thousand men, have any woman he liked, however high her rank and class, fight bulls or ride horses with no personal danger, journey back and forth to this city and elsewhere in a single night, however far away he might be, and many other fearful and dreadful things much too outrageous and offensive for proper Catholic ears. . . .

In another respect the Inquisition followed a restrictive policy in the colonies, affecting their intellectual culture. The defensive system of the Spanish Counter Reformation had taken elaborate precautions against the spread in the Indies of even the slightest echoes of the great schism agitating Europe. Ever since 1543 the crown had forbidden the exportation to America of "books of fiction and on secular matters or of fanciful character such as the Amadis romances of chivalry." The highest aspiration of the Counter Reformation ideal was to transform the colonies into an immense meeting house for prayers and devotions. The whole of paragraph xiv of the Laws of the Indies deals with the expurgation of books, and another law requires that "no book dealing with the Indies be allowed, permitted, or printed without special license of the Council of the Indies." When a ship arrived in port, royal officers made a careful inspection to ascertain whether it carried any works of a forbidden nature, as set forth in the Inquisition's list of prohibited writings. . . .

But in the seventeenth century—the period of repression *par excellence*—wordiness, affectation, and the retreat from reality prevailed far more than any direct testimony of persons or things, or any literature of action properly speaking. Permeating our attitude toward life and our ways was that strange, historical complex called the baroque. . . .

The Jesuit Experiment

By Germán Arciniegas

The greatest Jesuit experiment was made in Paraguay. In 1607 the General of the Company resolved to make the missions of Paraguay completely independent of those in Peru. Earlier they had covered a vast region containing parts of present-day Paraguay, Brazil, Bolivia, and Argentina. The original idea was to group the Indian population around the communities of new converts in the care of cells under Jesuit rule. They proselytized in ever widening areas, initiated the catechumens into the arts and crafts, and developed a comprehensive plan of colonization. During the eighteenth century, the communities of converts expanded to the number of thirty. One hundred and five thousand native colonists lived in this communal republic, which the Jesuits kept jealously isolated from the surrounding Spanish and Portuguese colonies. The colony was an actual state, governed by not more than four hundred members of the Company. The Jesuits were attempting by this means to provide the Indians with a shelter against the power of the white laymen who were exploiting them on the *encomiendas,* and as long as the Crown sponsored them, they were able to evade any interference from the Spanish authorities.

Each community was like a small municipality containing houses for the Indians all built according to the same plan, common workshops for handicraft, schools, and a staff of *corregidores* and native officials who were themselves supervised and directed by the priests of the Company. The system must have been inspired, at least in part, by the Incan plan for its indigenous communities rather than by any European scheme. Most of the converted community was under the *Tupa-Mbae*, meaning God's share, whereby all the Indians had to work a certain number of days each week, as a kind of tithe, to defray the general expenses of the community. Tools, seed, and animals were owned in common. Handicraft from the workshops of the community was handled in the same way. The printing press was introduced in the communal missions of Paraguay earlier than in Argentina, and the books in the Guaraní language that came off the press were printed from wooden fonts carved by the Indians themselves. Guaraní was the spoken language, but the hymns and prayers were in Latin. As the Indians returned home in the afternoon from their work in the jungle on rafts steered along the great rivers, they sang in Latin to the accompaniment of a harp. The harp became the instrument of popular music, and remains so in Paraguay today. The ruins of the churches and workshops still bear witness to the scope of this experiment, during the time of which Utopia came true for a century and a half.

The missions in Paraguay made such an impression in Europe that writers as astute as Montesquieu never shied away from their belief that Plato's Republic had been built on that spot in America. Articles in Montesquieu's *Encyclopédie*, published before the expulsion of the Jesuits from France, described the missions in the most laudatory terms.

Yet the missions had not made an easy start. First they had to fight the Indians. Fathers González de Santa Cruz and Rodríguez y del Castillo died the death of martyrs in 1628 and were beatified during the papacy of Pius XI. Later they had to stand off the Paulistas and the Mamelukes, who were spreading out around São Paulo in Brazil and had destroyed several communities of converts. For all that, the fathers managed to keep their republic under firm discipline until

1767, the year of their expulsion. To be sure, they protected the community so paternally that none of their villages was capable of governing itself, and when they left, the jungle grew up behind their footsteps. But the idea that the missions should be set apart and sheltered against the surrounding whites sank into the Paraguayan mind. . . .

In 1767, the year of the expulsion of the Jesuits from the Spanish dominions, the number of the Company's members in all Spanish America barely totalled 2,200; yet they had 700,000 Indians in their care. They owned schools, hospitals, dockyards, and workshops where they trained the Indians to spin, tan, and make pottery. They had accumulated immense wealth. No other order had received as many legacies as they received during the last century of their stay in America, or held so much land. When the Company fell into disgrace with the monarchs and lost the favor of the papacy, the other orders, already jealous, joined in the effort to have the order suspended throughout the Catholic world, which meant also that they themselves would automatically fill the vacuum left in America by the expulsion. . . .

PART V.

THE BREAK WITH SPAIN

Introduction

Latin America was created by contradiction. Since the 1790's, the idea of revolution had been in the air; various rebellions had been attempted and put down by the Spanish authorities. But the first serious threat to the power of Spain came in 1810, after Napoleon Bonaparte had invaded Spain and installed his elder brother, Joseph, on the throne. The French invasion triggered a large-scale military revolt in Latin America, but it was hard to decide whether the Creoles in the colony were making trouble to defend Spain against the French invaders or to assert their independence from Spain, or what.

Whatever the real impetus for revolution, the match hit the powder keg all over Latin America. There were many famous generals, intellectual authors of independence, and military geniuses, but the two men who stand above all the others are Simón Bolívar from Venezuela and José de San Martín from Argentina. Both men were radically different in personality—Bolívar the undisciplined and brilliant conversationalist, the sexual charmer, and ferocious combatant; San Martín the taciturn and somewhat morose fighter. Both had spent time in Europe; both were aware of the bankruptcy of Spanish authority at the time and of the ideas of revolution that were circulating from France and the United States.

Whatever the impetus for the revolution of 1810, when it began, things got out of hand. Each section of Latin America seemed to have its own problems and timetable for revolt; a liberation army could be routed in Venezuela while one was still being formed in Colombia. The revolution is hard to follow, but in general it was a battle between the Creoles (Spaniards born in the New World) and the *peninsulares*, European Spaniards who were sent to govern the colonies. There was great resentment between these two groups; the former was gaining

118

economic power but had not been allowed any political control or social prestige. The Creoles rebelled and formed various types of governments in the colonies to challenge the authority of the Spanish administration. Most of these governments floundered in debts and political infighting.

The revolution of 1810 received a setback in 1814, when Fernando VII, the legitimate Spanish ruler, was restored to the throne. No longer were the colonies rebelling against the French, and the restored Spanish monarchy promised some reforms. Except in Argentina, all of the independent governments created during 1810–1814 were dismantled; the republican armies were beaten back by the Spanish. The monarchy seemed solidly restored.

But in 1817, San Martín, who was residing in Argentina, began a famous march across the Andes with his army, a march that has been compared to Hannibal's crossing of the Alps in terms of tedium, cold, and danger. Taking the Spanish by surprise, San Martín moved in with his tired men and captured Santiago, the capital of Chile. This victory gave the revolution new life, and while San Martín marched north to Peru, Bolívar was chipping away at the Spanish armies in Venezuela. For the next few years, these two generals squeezed the Spanish in a pincer play—Bolívar heading downward, San Martín upward—until the two of them met in Ecuador in 1822. San Martín retreated from involvement in the revolution after that historic meeting; nobody has ascertained what words crossed between the two men, but it is surmised that there was a quarrel over objectives and neither would be subordinate to the other. San Martín, who favored a monarchical system in the new republics rather than democratic government, apparently realized he couldn't work with Bolívar.

The revolution continued in isolated spots until 1824, when Antonio José de Sucre, who was the recipient of the letter by Bolívar reprinted in this part, defeated the remaining Spanish army in Peru. Independence for Latin America had begun.

The entire revolution was full of crossed signals, amateur armies, hurried mountain sorties, and makeshift warfare that for the first time acquired the name "guerrilla." The confusion, especially within the new governments that were supporting the independence effort, was awing even to the participants. Bolívar's letter to Antonio José de Sucre, another of the great generals, is a typical example of a week in the war, when nobody knew who his allies were, where supplies were coming from, or for whom he was fighting. The American Revolution, for all its flexible tactics, seemed almost computerized by comparison.

When the whirlwind subsided, though, it was like dust settling on granite. The revolution of 1810 had ostensibly been fought in the name of principle and the masses, but it turned out to be a power play between the American-born upper-class Creoles and the Spanish-born upper-class *peninsulares*. The Creoles won and made it to the top of the pyramid by lopping off Spain. But, as Victor Alba shows, the rest of the pyramid didn't shift at all—and the Indians, Negroes, and various other lower-caste groups, whose name had been the inspiration for victory, found themselves in the same place as before. A popular Latin American saying—the revolution ended two hundred years of oppression and began two hundred years of the same thing—sums up the situation. Out of the chaos, the social hierarchy survived intact, perhaps even strengthened, just as it would survive future less glamorous revolutions.

After the revolution, the armies and caudillos and the political leaders who had taken part in the fighting came back to an incredible morass, a tangled political rout. This was the beginning of the age of the caudillo, the strongman who wrested power from the vacuum, who often roamed the countryside, ruling through terror and to his own personal benefit. Caudillo, the man on horseback, became a synonym for government in Latin America; the image of the self-serving, militaristic, grabby tyrant later evolved into the modern idea of the dictator.

The puzzled account of an unknown journalist in Ecuador, writing just after the revolution, explains the exasperation of the inheritors of the new Latin America as they returned to their capitals looking for the government. What they found was an unbelievable succession of double-crossings, intrigue, and musical chairs that frustrated even Bolívar. He had tried to unify the northern part of South America into a federation like the United States, but his dream of Gran Colombia, as he called it, failed as Ecuador fell from Colombia in a feud. Bolívar's vision was mocked in many ways, and the liberator ended up saying that his revolution had merely "plowed the sea."

Latin America was born. Across the continent Brazil seemed to slide or dance into independence, with no pain. It was almost flawless, natural, like everything else in Brazil. There was no bloodshed, no army, no planting of flags over dead soldiers. Dom Pedro, the son of the Portuguese king, in charge of Brazil at the time, merely declared independence by uttering the words.

This selection recounts the Latin American movement for independence from Spain. Ureña takes us from the first sporadic uprisings (which failed) at the turn of the nineteenth century, through the growing opposition to colonial authority, and finally to the full fledged warfare between the Spanish armies and sympathizers and the liberation armies led by Simón Bolívar to the north and José de San Martín to the south. The situation was similar to the American Revolution against the British in the sense that there were Latin American "Tories" and the regular Spanish army on one side, and a whole menagerie of dissidents from various social classes on the other. But the Latin American war lasted longer (from 1810 to 1824) and was generally more chaotic than the American Revolution. A series of clashes covered the entire continent; governments were created and disbanded; there was no clear sense of who was running the movement for independence. As the excerpt shows, North American and European thinkers had a great influence on the Latin American desire for independence; it was in this period that relations between the United States and the rest of the hemisphere were at their most cordial.

The Roots of Revolution
By Pedro Henríquez Ureña

The idea that the American colonies would become independent of Spain and Portugal was very old. It was only natural that the Indians, particularly those who belonged to the two great subjugated empires, Mexico and Peru, should think of recovering dominion over their native lands. Indian uprisings, both large and small, began early and broke out repeatedly, reaching a climax in the famous revolt led by Túpac Amaru, a descendant of the Incas, in 1780. The Europeans, and later their descendants, also launched rebellions. The first were those led by Gonzalo Pizarro, brother of the conqueror of Peru, in 1542–44, and by Martín Cortés, son of the conqueror of Mexico, in 1566, in which the rebels went so far as to talk of secession, though there is no evidence that this idea was accepted by the leaders. In any event, none of these uprisings, whether of Indians, of Spaniards, or of *criollos* (Europeans born in the New World), succeeded in seriously jeopardizing the unity of the Spanish empire.

From time to time, someone would put forth the idea that independence was destined to come in the future, but this prophecy was not made in a spirit of rebellion. In 1783, the Count of Aranda, minister to Charles III of Spain, advised the King to create three monarchies, ruled over by Spanish princes of the blood royal: one in North America and two in South America. . . .

Three events led finally to the movement for secession among the colonies: the United States Declaration of Independence (1776); the French Revolution (1789); and Napoleon's invasion of Spain and Portugal (1807).

Since the middle of the seventeenth century . . . the colonists had been reading the works of French and English thinkers whose writings contained such doctrines as the social contract (which, starting with Grotius and Althusius, had arrived, by way of Spinoza and Locke, among many others, at Rousseau's influential statement), the sovereignty of the people, and the separation of powers in the government of nations. With the revolutionary turn of events in France and North America, these doctrines acquired a dangerous vitality—dangerous for traditional authority. The Spanish Americans not only ignored the injunctions against reading works containing these doctrines, but persisted in reading the documents of both great revolutions and the writings of the thinkers who had participated in them or had supported them, such as Thomas Jefferson. The Declaration of the Rights of Man promulgated by the Constituent Assembly in Paris, translated into Spanish by Antonio Nariño (1765–1823), and printed clandestinely in Bogotá in 1794, circulated throughout a large part of Spanish America.

When Napoleon invaded the Iberian Peninsula, the Portuguese monarchs transferred their court and more than 10,000 followers (counting their retinue and public officials) to Brazil. They left Lisbon at the end of 1807 and arrived in Rio de Janeiro early in 1808. In March of 1808, the King of Spain abdicated.

The Spanish colonies were now confronted with an unprecedented situation. They had no legitimate government; their king had abdicated, and they refused to recognize the rights of the usurper. At the outset, the tendency was to ignore the authority of Napoleon and to proclaim loyalty to the deposed Spanish monarch through the *ayuntamiento,* or municipal council, the only body whose authority might be said to derive from the people, if only in part. This was especially so when it took the form of the *cabildo abierto,* or town meeting, with the participation of citizens, who, however, exercised no official function. What resulted was a combination of the doctrine of popular sovereignty, very much in favor at the time among enlightened persons, and the old Spanish tradition of the autonomous *cabildo* or *ayuntamiento.*

This movement failed in Mexico (September, 1808). It triumphed temporarily (only to be defeated later) in La Paz (July, 1809), Quito (August, 1809), Caracas (April, 1810), Bogotá (July, 1810), and Santiago de Chile (July and September, 1810). Only in Buenos Aires (May, 1810) did it achieve a lasting success; thenceforth, local power stayed in Argentine hands.

Meanwhile, in Spain, in the region that Napoleon's

forces had not managed to dominate, a parliament was convoked (it was modeled on another traditional Spanish concept—the Cortés), and the "overseas provinces" sent their representatives. This parliament, or congress, held its most important meetings in Cádiz, where peninsular Spaniards and Spanish Americans worked together to discuss and draft the first constitution of Spain, promulgated in March, 1812. It was, in the main, liberal. They decreed, furthermore, liberty of the press (November, 1810) and abolished the tribunal of the Inquisition (February, 1813). Among the Spanish Americans, the one who labored most zealously to shape the constitution was the Ecuadorian José Mejía (1777–1813), who was considered the leading orator of the congress.

But Spanish America was restless and could not be satisfied by the Cortes of Cádiz. The desire for independence was felt everywhere, and soon it erupted in violence in many places. In North America, the insurrection began in Mexico in September, 1810; independence was achieved in 1821. As a consequence, Central America was declared free without a struggle; it comprised Guatemala (seat of the captaincy-general from which the rest of the region had been governed), El Salvador, Honduras, Nicaragua, and Costa Rica.

In South America, the movement had two points of departure: Venezuela and Argentina. As early as 1782, the liberation of Spanish America had been envisioned by the Venezuelan Francisco de Miranda (1750–1816), "the Precursor," a man with an extraordinary career. In the name of Spain, he took part in the United States War of Independence in 1781–82, and in 1792, as a general of revolutionary France, he captured the city of Antwerp. (His name is inscribed on the Arc de Triomphe in Paris.) Moreover, he traveled widely in Europe, going as far as Russia, Sweden, and Turkey. He launched the Venezuelan campaign for independence in 1806, and failed; he raised another expedition in 1810, failed again, and died in prison. Either directly or through the Lautaro Lodge (a secret society founded in Buenos Aires to press for independence), he influenced many of the Spanish American liberators, among them Bolívar, San Martín, and O'Higgins. Simón Bolívar (1783–1830), a military genius, finally liberated Venezuela and then New Granada and Ecuador. In the meantime, José de San Martín (1778–1850), another military genius, in 1812 assumed command of the campaign that had begun in Argentina in 1810, and carried the war to Chile (1817), where he was joined by the forces of Bernardo O'Higgins (1776–1842), and then to Peru (1820). The final battles of the South American wars were entrusted to Bolívar, who won the battle of Junín (August 6, 1824), and to his lieutenant Antonio José de Sucre (1795–1830), who triumphed at Ayacucho against a force led by fourteen Spanish generals (December 9, 1824). Aroused by Bolívar's campaigns, the Spanish Antilles, too, tried to achieve independence. Santo Domingo succeeded without a struggle, but Cuba and Puerto Rico remained subject to Spain until 1898.

In Brazil, the Portuguese king, João VI, after residing at Rio de Janeiro with his court for thirteen years, returned to Lisbon (April, 1821), leaving his son Pedro as regent of the colony. Pedro was summoned shortly afterward to the Congress of Portugal. However, on the advice of his Brazilian friends, especially José Bonifacio de Andrada e Silva (1765–1838), he chose to remain. He made the historic declaration of his intent—"*eu fico*" ("I stay")—on January 9, 1822. On September 7, 1822, he proclaimed the independence of Brazil—Grito de Ipiranga (the Cry of Ipiranga)—and on December 1 he had himself crowned emperor. The weak Portuguese attempts at reconquest were easily repulsed. The Empire was organized as a constitutional monarchy, and Pedro I (1798–1834) governed until 1831, when he was deposed. He was succeeded by his son, Pedro II (1825–91), who ruled until 1889, in which year Brazil became a republic.

The following letter was written by Simón Bolívar, the great Venezuelan general, to Antonio José Sucre, another general, near the end of the wars for independence in January, 1824. Bolívar had taken Colombia, and was on his way to Peru, where, as the letter shows, he was in for some problems. The specific names, dates, and places included in this excerpt are not important—I include it to give the reader some idea of the chaos of the war and the local governments that were supporting it, the difficulty in finding soldiers and supplies, and the mental state of Bolívar at the time.

Letter to a General

By Simón Bolívar

To GENERAL ANTONIO JOSÉ DE SUCRE

January 16, 1824

My dear General:

...I came here ill, but I feel better now, though I am still weak. I shall be here two weeks to convalesce and to seek funds from the government in Lima. I shall not go to Lima to lose time and patience. At the end of the month, I shall leave for Trujillo to direct the troops that are arriving from Colombia and to give them any needed assistance. Then I shall proceed to the sierra, after I have collected, along the coast, all the horses and mules that the army needs. In that region there is no shortage of horses or of pasture....

I have threatened the government that I will leave Perú if, within the month, they have not supplied me with money to maintain the army. I have expressed dissatisfaction with the government and disgust concerning the general state of affairs. I have written Congress in strong terms, demanding sacrifices for the army. All this will produce something, but not much. I have asked Colombia to equip the troops that are coming by way of the Isthmus. I have ordered everything to be brought to Trujillo, convoyed by two or three ships of war so that the privateers, who are doing great damage, will not capture our supplies. As all this will result in many delays, you may be sure that our troops will not arrive for at least four months; that is, the sum total of what we are expecting from the first two divisions that I requested so long ago: to be exact, the 3,600 men of whom over 1,000 have left for Guayaquil and Perú, while the remainder should now be either at the Isthmus or on their way here; and the other 3,000 that I requested when I learned of Santa Cruz' defeat, over three months ago. The Vice President has promised me everything except money. Colonel Ibarra went to fetch another 6,000 men, and I reason that, by the time you receive this letter, he should be in Bogotá. . . .

Pineda and Ante tempted fate in an uprising: Pineda was sent to me as a prisoner, and Ante was left in Quito. They say that the whole matter is of no consequence. I am returning Pineda and giving orders for the conspirators to be punished, so that one example may discourage possible future victims. Guayaquil, Cuenca, and Loja are doing well. . . .

Mosquera has left for Bogotá, commissioned by me to notify the government and people that I am resolved to return to that city and to forget the war in the south unless they send me the 12,000 men I have requested. What is more, I have sent Congress my resignation, expressing my disgust with the ingratitude of the people. This step should not fail to produce some results, just as it did in Lima. Otherwise, I shall simply resign from the service outright. I am determined not to have Colombia lost at my expense, much less to have to liberate her a second time. That is a task that cannot be done twice. I am ready to fight the Spaniards to end the war in America, but no more. I am tired and old, and I now have nothing more to expect from fortune. On the contrary, I am like a rich miser, in constant fear that I will be robbed of my savings: all is fear and anxiety with me. It seems to me as if, at any moment, I am about to lose my reputation, which is all the reward and wealth that I have amassed at such great cost. You no doubt will feel the same way; nevertheless, I must remind you that you are still very young, and you have much to live for. If only I were in your place and had no need to tremble for my own fate; at least I should have desires, at least I should have hopes to cheer me. . . .

I do not know what else to tell you, save that I am extremely impatient to receive better and more definite news of the early arrival of our troops. I am certain that with another 6,000 Colombians, which will leave us with a reserve of an additional 6,000 in the south, the war in Perú will be ended.

I understand that the President of Perú, in agreement with the envoy from Buenos Aires, will approach the Spaniards [in Upper Perú] to have them declare their stand on the armistice—an affair as broad as it is long. Of course the Spaniards will derive considerable advantage as they will receive war supplies and will have ample opportunity to trade and communicate with Spain [by way of Buenos Aires]. We, on the other hand, will despair, eat our hearts out, and mark time until peace comes. For my part, I shall do nothing to aid these negotiations. In this way I shall assume no responsibility; hence, the Spaniards will know that we are not afraid.

Good-bye, my dear General. I am your devoted
Bolívar

Bolívar and some of the other liberators had dreams of a united Latin America, but they disappeared soon after the fighting ended. A nation called Gran Colombia—a conglomeration of Venezuela, Colombia, and Ecuador— was established for a short time, but it fell apart in bickering and factionalism. This account of the chaotic political conditions after the war was published anonymously in an Ecuadorian newspaper in 1829. The names and dates and places cited in the article are not particularly important; the overall impression is that the Latin Americans, in charge of their own affairs for the first time, did not exactly establish peace, tranquillity, and order. These early years of independence were depressing for the theoreticians of the revolution, who somehow were never able to fashion a cohesive political body like the United States. In fact, the anarchy that began after the break from Spain became a model for centuries of impossible government.

The Dust Never Settled

Anonymous

... On May 25, 1810, the city of Buenos Aires began its political existence. As its example was not followed by the other provinces, it was necessary to use force in order to compel them to espouse the revolutionary cause. While so engaged, the troops of Buenos Aires set a precedent for their subsequent harsh and ignorant behavior by killing the Viceroy Liniers, who had earlier freed that country from the British troops. At the same time they began to persecute the pastors of the Church, in the person of a bishop who was guilty of nothing more than obedience to his vows. . . .

The Río de la Plata [Buenos Aires and vicinity] has had but one man who proved capable of serving his country nobly and well. Saavedra quickly proved himself capable of presiding over the destinies of that Republic, but his death soon deprived the country of its one remaining hope. Since that time there has been no order or pattern in Argentine affairs. The federal government took possession of the land, and the land became its victim. Every province recovered its individual sovereignty, which God has given to every man, but that every man tacitly relinquishes to society, which thereupon assumes responsibility for the individual's safety. Nothing is so perilous as inconsistency between a political system and natural law. Each province governed itself, and every military expedition sent against them went down in humiliating defeat. The towns armed and fought each other like enemies. As a result of federation, the nation fell heir to blood, death, and crime of every description, due to the unleashing of the passions of a people who, although they had broken their chains, were devoid of the concepts of right and duty, and could only avoid enslavement by becoming tyrannical themselves.

Elections were characterized by riots and intrigue. Many times armed soldiers marched to the polls in formation, something unknown even in ancient Rome or in the island of Haiti. Force, faction, and bribery determine everything. And to what purpose?—momentary control amidst times of trouble, battle, and sacrifice. Virtually every government official has been replaced by a blood-stained victor, and those who are removed are made to suffer the misfortune of banishment, proscription, or violent death. Rare are the elections that are free of terrible crimes, and fewer still are the government leaders who have held their posts for the term provided by law or have been succeeded by legally elected leaders. . . .

However, let us be fair to the Río de la Plata. What we have just described is not peculiar to that country: its history is that of all Spanish America. We shall again see these same principles, these same processes, these same consequences in every republic, one country differing from another only incidentally, and modified only by circumstances and regional variations.

Throughout America we shall see but a single trend in public affairs. The cycles are similar, varying at most according to time and conditions, but otherwise paralleling the stages and the events in the other newborn states.

Nowhere are there legal elections; nowhere do those elected come to office according to the law. . . . If a Dorrego has been assassinated, assassinations are also being committed in Mexico, Bolivia, and Colombia— September 25 is too recent a date to be forgotten. If Pueyrredón plunders the public treasury [of Buenos Aires], there are those in Colombia who do the same. If [the Argentine province of] Córdoba and Paraguay are ruled by bloody hypocrites, Perú has its General La Mar in a donkey-skin, with the claws of a tiger and an insatiable lust for American blood. If anarchic movements occur in every Argentine province, Chile and Guatemala set such horrible examples that we can scarcely hope for peace. In the Argentine provinces, Sarratea, Rodríguez, and Alvear have compelled their country to house, in the capital, bandits who call themselves liberators. In Chile, the Carreras and their henchmen have committed similar acts. Freire, the director, destroyed his own government, the control of which he has obtained only by subjecting the Congress to extreme violence; moreover, as a result of his inability to govern, anarchy soon held sway. Urriola legislated for the legislature, after first defeating the government troops and the Director himself, who had led them with distinction. And is there any crime of which Guatemala is innocent? The lawful authorities have been removed; the provinces have rebelled against the capital; brother wars upon brother—a horror which the Spaniards had prevented—and this war is to the death. Town fights town; city stands against city, each with its own government, and every street is a self-constituted nation. In Central America all is bloodshed and terror!

Though it is true that a government in Buenos Aires lasts scarcely a week, it is equally certain that Bolivia has now followed this monstrous example. No sooner had the illustrious Sucre left that unfortunate country than the traitor Blanco seized, through intrigue, the government which legally belonged to General Santa Cruz. Yet Blanco did not hold it five days before he was captured and killed by a dissatisfied faction, to be followed by a legitimate head, Velazco, who was in turn succeeded by Santa Cruz. Thus, hapless Bolivia has had four different leaders in less than two weeks! Only the Kingdom of Hell could offer so appalling a picture discrediting humanity!

We are amazed at the almost infinite number of subdivisions in the territory of the Argentine, whose condition resembles that of the baronies of old, so that this federation under freedom is like the feudal estates under monarchy. The barons imposed levies, built castles, and ruled as they pleased; they thus defied their sovereign, and on occasion they even fought him. Buenos Aires, Chile, and Guatemala imitate and surpass the practices and doctrines of those barons; thus, extremes clash, and, for the same reasons, personal ambition.

But recent events in Mexico dwarf everything that we have so ruefully mentioned respecting the Río de la Plata and the rest of America. Buenos Aires must, therefore, bow before opulent Mexico, now a rabble-ridden city. Horror and crime stalk that fair land. A new breed of sans-culottes, or rather sans-chemises, occupies the seats of government and controls everything. . . .

. . . From one end to the other, the New World is an abyss of abominations, and, were anything lacking to complete this terrible chaos, Perú could more than supply it. A partisan of the tyrannical Spaniards during the war for independence, Perú, with her liberty not yet fully won, in the very first days of her existence, was the scene of a fraticidal struggle. The country had been cleared of Spaniards from Trujillo to Ica by valorous General San Martín, at the head of the Chileans and Argentines. In the eyes of the people of Lima there was no more of Perú to liberate; thereupon, some promptly undertook to rid the country of San Martín, whose services were most urgently needed. This act of ingratitude interrupted all political progress in Perú. . . .

There is no good faith in America, nor among the nations of America. Treaties are scraps of paper; constitutions, printed matter; elections, battles; freedom, anarchy; and life, a torment. Such, Fellow-Americans, is our deplorable situation. Unless we change it, death is to be preferred. Anything is better than endless conflict, the indignity of which appears to increase with the violence and the duration of the movement. Let us not delude ourselves—this evil, which increases revolts and mutinies in the armed forces, will eventually compel us to reject the very first constructive principles of political life. We lost all individual rights when, in an effort to obtain them in perfect form, we sacrificed our blood and all that we cherished most, prior to the war—for, if we look back at that time, who will deny that our rights were then more respected? Never were we as badly off as we are at present. At that time we enjoyed positive and tangible benefits, whereas today we have dreams bordering upon illusion, hope feeding upon the future, and disillusionment forever tortured with the bitterness of reality....

Spanish-speaking America struggled for its independence, but it was granted to Brazil without a shot ever having been fired. The Portuguese king, João VI, was forced to move his court to Rio de Janeiro during the French occupation of his country, which corresponded to the occupation of Spain. The king returned the royal court to Portugal in 1821, but his son, Dom Pedro, stayed behind as governor of the Brazilian colony. After some urging from his advisers, Dom Pedro simply declared Brazil an independent nation. Germán Arciniegas explains how it happened.

Brazil's Glide into Independence
By Germán Arciniegas

The story of how Brazil gained independence is a world wonder. The country passed from colony to independent nation with a gentleness and serenity that might have been expected of Canada, where the cold freezes even the formidable channel of the St. Lawrence River, but not of a green tropical paradise in which the sun and the music might have been expected to stimulate more hot-blooded solutions. The transition was made with great ease during the period of Dom Pedro's rule as regent in the name of the House of Braganza. Some of the gentlemen in the government went to the prince and explained that the nation would like to become independent. All of formerly Spanish America already was independent;

the United States was independent; and therefore it was absurd that Brazil should continue dependent upon Lisbon. In short, they said to Dom Pedro: "Would you like to be our emperor?" Dom Pedro accepted, saying: "Independence or Death." And without more ado the country became independent. The change-over gave the people a reason for celebrating, the army a holiday, and everyone an excuse to parade. Nothing was heard from the armed forces, except band music.

Sixty-seven years went by; then the Brazilian empire made an equally smooth transition to a republic. Dom Pedro II was the last of the great enlightened monarchs. A founder of academies and libraries, philosopher, scholar, friend of the most illustrious men of Europe. But still an emperor. The republicans went to call on him. "Your Majesty," they said, "what Brazil wants is a republic like the republics all over America." His Majesty could find no objection. "So be it," he said. The gentlemen who had come calling escorted Dom Pedro to the port, accompanied him to his stateroom, a luxurious one, and bade him godspeed as they waved their handkerchiefs on the shore. Dom Pedro spent the rest of his life quietly in Europe, highly respected by the Brazilians. The republic was proclaimed in a box in a newspaper. Another holiday for the people. The soldiers, like the great philosophers they were, celebrated their own little revolution in the military college by reading the works of Auguste Comte and by placing on their nation's flag the two magical words "Order and Progress."

What kind of society emerged from the revolution? Who benefited from the defeat of the Spaniards, and who did not? Victor Alba, in this selection, traces the formation of the ruling class that would take the place of Spain. The word "Creole" refers to American-born Spaniards whose allegiance was with Latin America during the revolution. A "caudillo" is a strongman military leader, usually with a personal army.

Creoles and Caudillos

By Victor Alba

The Roman and Spanish empires probably were the only two that truly acted as civilizing forces. That is, they were the only colonial empires that, when they were forced to withdraw, left their colonies in a situation almost identical with that prevailing in the motherland. When the hour of independence struck for Spanish America, the colonies were not very different from Spain; their social structure and administrative apparatus were identical with those in the Peninsula.... The main difference between Spain and Spanish America lay in the composition of the two populations: The colonial populations contained a high percentage of Indians, Negroes, mestizos, and mulattoes. But in neither the colonies nor the motherland did the common people themselves play any political role.

A popular saying aptly described the situation: "The conquest was the work of the Indians; independence was the work of the Spaniards." The conquistadors relied on the help of some Indian groups to subdue other hostile Indians whom they were determined to dominate. Later, in 1810, a great many Indians fought in the armies of the King of Spain because the monarch was their protector whereas, generally speaking, the Creoles (American-born Spaniards) fighting for independence were their exploiters. The Creoles started, led, and capitalized on the war for independence. In the beginning, the purpose of the struggle was not so much to separate from Spain as to refuse obedience to the King, whom Napoleon had placed on the Spanish throne, a man too liberal for the Creoles' taste. Independence was, at first, a reactionary social movement....

At the time of the outbreak of the wars for Latin American independence, the people in the principal cities in each province came together and proclaimed open town meetings to decide what to do about the anomalous situation that had arisen in Spain. Most of the assemblies set up juntas to take charge of the government. The juntas appointed leaders with executive power, and draft constitutions were drawn up and approved in public meetings. The juntas performed more or less the same functions as the Continental Congress in the North American colonies, or as the National Assembly and the Convention in France.

Before long, however, the root of municipal popular government began to wither. The poor Creoles (whom we would now call middle-class Creoles) who headed mutinies and tried to win support from the Indians and mulattoes were displaced. The Creoles from the great families became the leaders in the wars for independence. An attempt to unite all the people—the Creoles, Indians, Negroes, mestizos, and mulattoes—might have laid the foundations of a nation, and, indeed, some pioneers did speak about a nation. For them, independence had a social as well as a political meaning. But, to the wealthy Creoles, the movement was solely political, and its objectives were economic. Their idea was not to reform society but to hand it over to other political administrators. . . .

Augustín de Iturbide (1783–1824), Simón Bolívar (1783–1830), and José de San Martín (1778–1850), all wanted to preserve the old order insofar as that was possible. . . . Bolívar went so far as to say that "the Army and the Church were the most efficacious, if not the only supports for an authority that could save us and a stable government." And yet, Bolívar was the most democratic of the liberators; he tried to be close to the people. José María Morelos (1765–1815), of Mexico, was perhaps the only leader who could give a popular ring to his words. His humble origin, and that of some of those who rebelled with him and later joined the armies of Iturbide, in the long run, were largely responsible for endowing the Mexican political experience with a character completely unlike that of the other Latin American countries and for giving it a greater *national* quality. . . .

It would be a mistake, though, to think that the Liberators were inflexible oligarchs. That was left to their descendants. The Liberators tried to satisfy the common people, to attract to their cause, if not the masses, at least the majority of the whites and even mestizos. (It is worth remembering that, in many places, class lines then followed—as they still do—color lines and divisions, and that racism, although it is disguised and not legal, has never been wholly absent from Latin American society. Racism there is hypocritical and paternalistic but no less discriminatory than in countries where it is overt. Even today, racism influences Latin American life, though everyone denies that it exists.) While the Creoles tried to satisfy other social groups, they never intended to give them the slightest chance to gain political power. . . .

There can be no doubt that the people saw the war for independence as their chance to obtain land and to destroy the caste system. This lent their participation a social purpose that the Creoles deliberately glossed over or stifled. Miguel Hidalgo (1753–1811), of Mexico, promulgated a law that ordained the distribution of land to the mutinous peasants. Bolívar, despite his social conformism, realized that, if he were to recruit armies and stabilize the new countries, the masses had to be placated, and he had been the first to raise the question of land reform in Venezuela. But, in 1830, military bonds were issued instead of parcels of land, a move that served to line the pockets of speculators and some of the caudillos. Hidalgo and Bolívar were, in fact, exceptions. Hidalgo was executed and Bolívar was exiled from Venezuela by the Creole oligarchy. In the end, the war strengthened and consolidated latifundism [the system of large estates] instead of destroying it. . . .

The flood of optimism felt by the masses during the war dried up. Except for the political change, everything remained as before. Existing privileges were augmented by new ones. A flaw in the new order of things—the oligarchic system—kept the countries from following the road taken by the peoples of Europe and the United States; the old colonies had won political freedom, but they retained the landholding system of Spain, and its injustices were aggravated by the absence of the safeguards and protection that the Spanish monarch traditionally tried to give his people. While industry in Europe and the United States in the wake of the French Revolution and the Napoleonic Wars was becoming mechanized under the rule of capitalism, Latin America still clung to an obsolete, uneconomic social system. The maintenance of this system demanded the oligarchy's total control of political life and the exclusion of the people. The first generation of government officials after independence met both requirements and managed to conceal their basic objectives, including the manipulation of their countries' constitutions—a favorite sport of Latin American politicians—beneath a constant flow of rhetoric in praise of democracy.

In this society, in which there still were no political parties, or in which parties took the form of rival Masonic lodges—for example, the Scottish rite and the York rite in Mexico, the conservatives issuing from the one and liberals from the other—the people were without a voice. From those elements of the masses who had distinguished themselves and won promotion in the war came the caudillos, who expressed the social aspirations of the people. That is, for want of a better way, the people tried to make their aspirations felt through these popular military figures. But the caudillos were by definition bad politicians; if they had been good, they would never have reached caudillo status. The oligarchies tamed them easily, now with sweet talk, now with social embarrassment, now simply by bribery. Yet, if the caudillos were not much good as representatives of the people, they played a very important historical role by becoming the pioneers of militarism. That is, they made it an accepted,

or at least an acceptable, fact that the armed forces
would have a voice in politics. After the officers who
had taken part in the war for independence had
died, the only desires of the second generation of
militarists were for power and booty. Naturally, they
let themselves be led by whomever could fulfill their
wishes, and that meant the Creole oligarchs. Consequently, the common people remained disfranchised,
and the oligarchs acquired a supplementary police
force to protect their social system. . . .

As in Spain—which to this day has not come up
with a structure that will permit the various nations
on the Peninsula to live together successfully—the
men of the independence era in Latin America, although they made efforts to rise above local interests
(quickly aborted), did not succeed in creating anything more than a group of scattered states. San
Martín planned a state that would comprise all the
lands South of Panama; Iturbide established a short-
lived empire that embraced all the Spanish lands
north of Panama; Bolívar managed temporarily to
unite most of the territories that had made up the
viceroyalties of Peru and New Granada. The goal of
an abortive Pan American Congress in Panama in
1826 was to form a federation that would comprise the
entire old Spanish Empire in America. But each group
of Creoles preferred a state, an army, and a flag of its
own. The Creoles still thought like colonials. . . .

The desire for separation won out over the idea of
union. Bolivia and Peru separated; Greater Colombia
broke into its three component parts. Both Colombia
and Venezuela wanted to carry division still further.
For a time, Colombia was little more than a feeble
alliance of independent states; Venezuela worked out
a compromise—federalism. Central America soon
broke its bonds with Mexico, and Mexico seemed for
a time to be on the verge of greater fragmentation as
Texas briefly enjoyed the life of an independent republic before the United States annexed it. The only
practicable way of coping with localism was the federal system. But, in Central America, even that failed,

for the single republic was replaced by the five tiny nations that still decorate the varicolored map of the isthmus.

Thus, independence destroyed those features of the Spanish heritage that might have led to the creation of nationalities: the spirit of the *cabildo*, which gave the people an opportunity to take part in political life, and the idea of integration, which might have united small territories into a major state or federation of states. Militarism came into being because the people ceased to participate in the life of the state. Localism came into being because no real federations or confederations existed.

The men who won independence belonged to the Creole aristocracy and the oligarchies, and, though certainly not revolutionaries, they were endowed by the magnitude of the task they had undertaken with a certain breadth of vision. The oligarchies supported them as a necessary evil. Later, they apotheosized them into overblown figures of a gilded myth that served to distract attention from what was going on. No wonder, then, that, by the time their work was done, the caudillos of independence felt disillusioned. San Martín, Bolívar, José Gervasio Artigas (1774–1850), Bernardino Rivadavia (1780–1845), and many others died ostracized or in exile. Sucre was assassinated. Bolívar, embittered, wrote shortly before his death, "In South America there is neither trust nor faith neither among men nor among the various states. Every treaty is here but a scrap of paper and what are here called constitutions are but a collection of such scraps." If, in moments of optimism that come with the flush of victory, he predicted a brilliant future, in others, he showed a pessimistic side: "Inevitably, America will fall into the hands of the unleashed rabble, only to pass gradually into those of petty tyrants of every color and race."

When he saw what was happening all around him, Bolívar came to the heartbreaking conclusion, seldom mentioned in Latin America, that "we who have struggled for the independence of America have plowed the sea." He was right. The Latin American countries did not achieve independence. They proclaimed themselves independent, but they remained dependent on the landholding Creole oligarchs who monopolized economic power and permanently dominated those who exercised political power. A Chilean positivist, José Victorino Lastarria (1817–88), later made a pronouncement that still provides the key to Latin American nationalism: "Independence was the work not of the people but of armies, armies that might more rightly have been called the armies of the caudillos. . . ."

The struggle for Latin American independence was won by men who were not and never could be nationalists. The task of making nations out of the countries and their people was left to succeeding generations.

PART VI.

THE LATIN AMERICAN CHARACTER

Introduction

After cutting himself away from Spain, the Latin American was left alone to figure out who he was. He was not any one thing, of course; there seemed to be a pool of traits from which he could draw. There were urges, restraints, and emotions that made him different from other cultures, from, say, the North Americans. It is some of these qualities, which the Latin American sees as dividing himself from the rest of the world, that this part attempts to describe.

Latin American writers have been pondering their cultural identity ever since the revolution of 1810, and their wonderment has been more agonized than that of North American writers attempting to do the same thing. To generalize a bit, there seems to be more confusion, more puzzlement, in the efforts of Latin Americans to say who they are. They are the products, first of all, of two incompatible forces, neither of which can be totally acceptable. As Salvador de Madariaga shows in the beginning selection, the people who emerged from the revolution—the mestizos, who were born both of Spain and of the Indians—were pulled apart by their guilt over Spanish conduct and their fear of Indian blood. They could neither fully embrace nor reject the Spanish or the Indian, which left them in a cultural limbo.

From these extremes of ancestry, the Latin American seemed to string himself out between many other polar opposites—between revolution and inertia, between, as Victor Alba shows here, the truth of the word and the truth of the deed, between the Virgin Mother and the prostitute. It is this vacillation, this trembling betweenness, that falls to the bottom of the Latin American soul, pushing him violently between extremes.

144

Latin Americans have never agreed on the traits that make up their culture, that separate them from others. Some of them are matters not of content, but of style. Both Latin America and the United States could, in their special ways, be thought of as violent cultures; but the nature of the violence makes them strangers. Latin America is almost miraculously devoid of territorial wars, of the calculated, grinding kind that have plagued Europe. A Latin American nation would, I think, be incapable of pursuing a Vietnam war, not because they wouldn't have the strength, but because they would be so uncomfortable with cold, mathematical violence. Latin violence has always been the volcanic, bursting kind, the quick knife flick, not the violence of the Pentagon Papers or the drawing board. Georgie Anne Geyer's account of the 1968 Peruvian soccer game in which more than three hundred people were killed shows the explosive side of the Latin American character and how it can be touched off.

The concept of Latin violence is wrapped in the macho, the cock-strutting, fist-pounding, hot god of love and destruction. The classic macho, like Superman, is a stereotype, even the subject of comic books.. But there is enough loud virility in Latin America to impress the visitor that macho exists. It can be anything from a husband's demand that his wife be pregnant every year so that he won't be accused of being homosexual, to the urge to fight a bull single-handed, or to turn over tables in a bar, or verbally to annihilate a friend. There is a lot of macho in the North American culture, but the Spanish-speaking kind is more poetic, more stylish, more involved with honor. The macho demands everything; through his antics he reduces the world to nothingness, to original chaos, to ashes, and then struts triumphantly away—as Octavio Paz puts it.

The macho type also has his counterpart in Latin American politics. The free-wheeling caudillo, forerunner of the strongman dictator, was usually a macho par excellence. Domingo Sarmiento here describes part of the career of one such macho, Facundo, who terrorized and ruled much of the Argentine countryside during part of the nineteenth century. Facundo is an extreme case, but you get the idea.

But the Latin American has other releases from the boredom and constraints of his life, and one of them is the fiesta. North Americans, thinking of fiestas as mere parties, are always mystified at the number of them, and at their importance to Latin Americans. There must be a genius sitting in every country's archive, I used to think, who figures out a reason for a national holiday every other day. But there is a profound reason for these interminable fiestas, which seem always to begin in pious rigidity (boys on one side of the room, girls on the other) and end in screeching abandon. Octavio Paz, the Mexican philosopher, tells in one of the selections how the fiesta satisfies the *latino's* urge to purge himself, to annihilate, to break things apart. The fiesta, Paz says, is a revolution in the truest sense of the word, and anyone who has been in the streets at the height of one of them knows what he means.

The explosive, perhaps suicidal, urge underlying the violence, the *macho,* and the fiesta is enough to lead the Latin American to distrust himself, to seek an authority figure, someone who is totally in control, a father, or perhaps a dictator. The penchant for strongmen, the other reason for the outbreak of caudillos, has little to do with the availability of tanks or the lack of understanding of the constitution. If Latin America is restless with democracy, it is only because democracy does not correspond to the makeup of its character. Fernando Guillén Martínez, in another of the selections, tries to reach the sources of paternalism in the upbringing and beliefs of the Latin American, to discover on a personal level why he tends to distrust himself in politics. Paternalism also has something to do with the Spanish aristocratic notion, the source of a widespread unwillingness to get one's hands dirty. Moritz Thomsen's excerpt shows how this attitude is adopted even by some of the poorest people. The dislike of manual labor, however, once a cliché to describe Latin America, seems to be diminishing among the new Latins. Ché Guevara, the hero of millions of students, was not afraid to live in a tent, clean his own gun, and cook his own food.

There are also some exuberant qualities about Latin Americans, such as their generosity, their romanticism, their loyalty, their belief in people instead of schedules or events. Where else would a bank open its doors for you at eight P.M., or a bus pick up a passenger even though he was far from an authorized stop? Where else would a host, if you compliment something in his or her house too persistently, insist on giving you the object? There is a wonderful transcendent quality about Latin American people, a mystical, fantasylike world that demands, and often receives, the most incredible gestures of courtesy or heroism. The North American soldier will die only for a cause, while the Latin American soldier will die for pride, for a chimera, for a lark if his honor is at stake. There is mysticism and honor everywhere. The stuff of mysticism is dissected here in an account of the life of a Brazilian priest, but it also appears in every facet of Latin American life. The conflict of honor in the short story "The Pin" can be found in the wars of jealousy of every household.

All of this business about the Latin American character, however, must be taken only half-seriously; as that continent moves toward an urban, industrial existence, the special traits are submerged in nostalgia—just as the agrarian ethic slowly dissipated in the cities of the United States. The youth of Latin America, the middle classes and upper classes, are beginning to sound, dress, talk, and think like their counterparts in Europe and the United States. The culture that remains most unchanged is the culture of poverty, a distillation, perhaps, of a Latin American identity that is breaking up from above. Moritz Thomsen, a Peace Corps volunteer who lived for three years in the poor Ecuadorian coastal town of Río Verde, and then wrote a book about it, describes what life is like there.

As we have seen, the Latin American is principally a product of the Indian and Spanish cultures. Most Spanish-speaking people from the continent, whether they happen to be Mexican or Peruvian, are a mixture of the two races—mestizos. The mestizo blends not only the physical characteristics of the white Spaniard and the Indian, but also the thoughts, feelings, and beliefs of the two groups. Madariaga charts the soul of the mestizo, and the tension between the two influences that comprise it.

The Mestizo Dichotomy
By Salvador de Madariaga

Nothing is more complex than the soul of a mestizo. Compared with it, the subtlest soul of a pure blood— white, black or Indian—is as transparent as water. The typical feature of the mestizo soul is its swift-changing hue, calling to mind those iridescent tinctures or shot silks which change from green to blue and react to the slightest movement in the incidence of light. This feature has often been put to the debit of the mestizo as shiftiness and unreliability. "Pray, be seated, *gentlemen*"—a South American President is said to have requested the Minister of a neighbouring republic known for its predominantly mestizo population. "But, I am alone, Mr. President." "Oh"— smiled the President—"you people of your country, you are always each at least two." Now, the President meant it in a neighbourly, i.e., in a poisonous way. But he was right, though not in intention. The mestizo is always at least two: a White and an Indian.

This means a world of possible swift changes, because there is in him a world of possible attitudes. The mestizo carries with him the vigour of the conqueror, the leisurely pride of the settler, the creative charity of the early friar, the vicious, lascivious epicureanism of the later friar, the greed of the *corregidor*, the barbarous contempt of the brutal priest for the passive and long-suffering Indian; the tacit assertion of the right to rule which the abler stock of men assumes towards its subjects, all the virtues and vices of the Spaniard. But he does not carry them in their natural and spontaneous state. All these features in him live constantly under the inner opposition from his other self, the Indian, object and often victim of them. The Indian in him is just as rich and complex as the White. He is subservient and faithful to that White who has conquered him; ready to flatter him and to shape himself and truth and the world to please the White; and he is proud of his own native blood and history, which in Mexico and Peru had given rise to two great well-ordered empires; he is aloof, contemptuous of the White intruders who came to occupy the land in which he, the Indian, was rooted; distant, strong in his superoriental capacity for suffering, and in his patience to weave a destiny out of threads too long and thin for a Spaniard to see; at times he is wildly resentful; grateful at times; now confiding and credulous, like a child, now as immovable in his perennial wisdom as the oldest of men. The tension within the soul of the mestizo between the two strains of men living together under his skin in the closest intimacy could not be more acute. But it was a rich tension, vibrating with the mutual attractions and repulsions of powerful opposites. And it might have resolved itself into something wonderful if left to mature in a healthy moral climate. Unfortunately, the moral climate was unhealthy. The two men, the White and the Indian, come to live together from those two continents of the spirit so distant from each other, had to breathe a social air which challenged them both, humiliated them both, by setting them socially aside, always as half-castes, often also as bastards. Under this pressure and this challenge, the complex tensions within the mestizos soon turned aggressive. They answered challenge with counterchallenge, and kept a kind of permanent warfare against the environment, as a matter of habit, whatever the environment might be. Indian to the White, the mestizo was white to the Indian. But in both these attitudes, he benefited from the advantages and suffered from the handicaps of his other blood. Indeed, the mestizo was an Indian who, at war with the White, was in alliance with a White; and a White who, at war with the Indian, was in alliance with an Indian—alliances which nothing could break, since the two allies co-existed within the same skin. . . .

Such were the contradictions in which the soul of the mestizo was apt to live. Towards the Indian, they must out-white the White. "They declare themselves vassals of the king of Spain"—write Ulloa and Jorge

Juan—"and though mestizos, they take pride in being Spaniards and in descending from Indians, in such a curious way that, though they have an equal share of both, they are most bitter enemies of the Indians, who are their own blood." This enmity towards the Indian was not born merely of a desire to assert his white blood and status over the downtrodden and conquered people; but also of an equally ardent desire to avenge on the beaten people the humiliation of the defeat which the Indian within the mestizo felt more bitterly than the pure Indian by all the Spanish blood in him. Similarly, when he took up a challenging attitude against the Spaniard, as, despite Ulloa and Jorge Juan's optimistic report, the mestizo often did, both individually and collectively, what animated him was not merely his desire to assert his Indian blood and to restore to it its pre-conquest proud and independent stature—a desire stiffened and stimulated by his own Spanish impulses—but also the urge to avenge on the Spaniard the humiliation of the Spaniard within him, a misfit of a conqueror, and a mean exploiter and tormentor of Indians.

The two sides of his soul acted thus upon each other like the two plates of an electric condenser, raising each other's pitch, and therefore the tension between the two. The somewhat shallow and wilful enmity of the white Creole against the European Spaniard was enriched and deepened in the mestizo by all the unfathomable injuries and memories of the repressed and oppressed Indian, while the passive aloofness of the pure Indian borrowed a passion and a purpose from the Spanish blood which flowed together with his own in the veins of the half-caste.

It is easy to see to what a rich gamut of states of mind, feelings and emotions this set of inner tensions could lead, according to the individual condition of mind and character, the upbringing and social rank, the ups and downs of fortune, and the thousand petty incidents of life, when the subtle and complex soul of the mestizo came into friction or collision with a subtle and complex society as variegated as that of the Indies. The chief feature of this psychological situa-

tion was its extreme mobility and instability: no relation to the turbulence and gaiety of the Negro, to the
energy of the mulatto, still less to the impassivity of
the ever silent pure Indian. The mobility and instability of the mestizo are all inward. They are due to
a constant ebb and flow between the opposite currents
in his life blood, and to the ever unexpected way in
which they will react to outer challenges. Now fiercely
pro-Indian, now contemptuous of the native, at one
time as proud a Spaniard as a pure Castillian, at
another a violent opponent of the Spanish tyranny,
the mestizo will be the tortured and twisted stem in
which the sap from the new earth rises through the
Indian to meet the sunrays from the Spanish foliage
in the grafted tree of that complex life; the centre of
all the ideas, feelings, emotions, movements for or
against everything, the only spirit wide enough, tor-
mented enough, fully to incarnate the history of the
Spanish New World.

Suspended between the opposing forces of his creation,
the Latin American has a profoundly different view of the
world than the North American. His cultural conflicts are
not resolved, Alba says, and his thoughts and actions also
become part of a dichotomy, an ambivalence that leads
outsiders to believe that the Latin American is hypocritical
or dishonest. Looking at it from the Latin American side,
Alba says this is untrue, and explains why.

Honesty, the Word, and the Deed
By Victor Alba

Perhaps the most common and profound characteristic derives from the fact that, as was pointed out
earlier, the Latin American lives on two different
planes at once, one of action and the other of word
or thought. He acts in one way and thinks in another.
This is not hypocrisy but an involuntary attitude, a
product both of the need for self-defense that the
Indian felt in the presence of the conquistador and

of the psychological ambivalence to be found in all people of mixed blood. Even when the Latin American has a single racial origin—white, Indian, Negro— the fact that he lives in a society in which his single origin is an exception makes him adopt mental attitudes proper to those of mixed ancestry.

There is a widespread impression that people in Latin America are less honest than those in the United States. But we must not forget that what a Latin American says does not have to correspond exactly to what he does. The Latin American, for instance, holds women in high esteem, honors his mother, and treats the female sex with ceremony. At the same time, and without being conscious of any incongruity, the Latin American, as head of a family, as husband, as son, behaves in a way that seems to belie his attitude of esteem and that, to Americans or Europeans, appears irresponsible and even offensive. For the Latin American man, and his Latin American wife, the divergence of word and action is natural; the wife would feel cheated if she were not accorded the outward signs of respect and amazed if this respect were translated into action. The institution of the *casa chica*—the second, nonlegalized family kept by many Latin American husbands—is an example of this dual attitude.

In politics, this ambivalence is shown by the ease with which Latin Americans accept the idea that once a law has been promulgated to solve a problem, the problem ceases to exist—no matter how obvious the persistence of the problem, either because the law is not enforced or because the "solution" has not solved anything. Latin Americans constantly speak, in utter good faith, of constitutionality, in a continent where every year two or three constitutions are violated, altered, or simply annulled. And they boast, for example, that Latin American social legislation is among the most advanced in the world, untroubled by the fact that poverty, exploitation, and even servitude continue because such legislation is poorly enforced, or not enforced at all. For the Latin American, accustomed to the Spanish legalistic spirit, the law itself, rather than its application, is the solution. Thus the recurrence of problems sincerely considered as solved, and the repeated passing of laws dealing with the same question.

... The average Latin American has never had the power to decide his own destiny. Deprived of the opportunity to act, he has taken refuge in word and thought. If he cannot act, he can compensate for this by talking, and in Latin America this has given the word greater importance than it has elsewhere.

The same origin helps to account for other Latin American traits: the tendency to spend rather than to save for the future, and the fondness for gambling and betting. In Cuba, before Castro, there was a lottery every day; in Mexico, there is one three times a week. The Latin American tends to let chance decide his destiny, as if he were so convinced that outside forces determine his life that he wants to emphasize this by playing his own games of chance. ...

Many Latin Americans would not agree with Georgie Anne Geyer's characterization of them as "losers," but her description of a fatal soccer game says a lot about the nature of violence in that part of the world. It is hard to imagine three hundred North Americans killing themselves over a football game, but on the other hand, it is hard to imagine Latin America pursuing a Vietnam war. So there is at least a different quality of violence on both sides of the Rio Grande. It is worth noting where the Peruvians place the blame for all these deaths— intense nationalism plays a big part in inter-American affairs, in the difficulty of getting countries to work together.

Violence at a Soccer Game
By Georgie Anne Geyer

"All the battles we celebrate are losses, but they are grand losses."—A Latin American.

"I am a Peruvian, and I could not allow them to

annul the goal of my people."—Victor Matías "Bomba" Campos, who started the 1964 soccer riot in Peru in which 319 persons lost their lives.

If it were only outsiders who had always perceived Latin Americans as a people who never win, the judgment would not be so corrosive. But, it is they who perceive themselves as chronic failures. Their historic inferiority complex is a pervasive reality that poisons every aspect of Latin American life. As individuals, as nations, as a unified entity, they have never experienced the luxury of winning. And so generosity of spirit is budding but weak, and confidence shatters at the first slight threat.

One of the predominant strains in the conglomerate psyche of Latin Americans throughout history is that they are a people who cannot bear to lose. Yet they are at the same time a people which has always lost. There are very few Latin Americans who, nationally or personally, have known lives of victory or lives which they have controlled. And so they emerge a people with such deep historic feelings of inferiority that they cannot react with grace to the slightest displeasure from without or exact from themselves the minimal discipline to advance technically in the bigger world. Neither can they accept responsibility for what they are, a fact that leads to the gnawing dependency of blaming everything they are on forces outside themselves.

One of the most pathetic examples of all of this occurred in Lima on May 24, 1964, an ordinary Sunday in an ordinary Lima winter. The capital of Peru is a somber city in the winter, when a low fog creeps over the city and nearly chokes it. The foothills of the Andes are obliterated. Tangible life is reduced to the level of the curbstones and tree trunks, for often you cannot see the tops of buildings or the tops of trees. It becomes hard to breathe and harder still to keep your wits about you. It is not surprising that *limeños* grow cranky, nervous and depressed. Life is hard enough anyway, sitting in the middle of a great desert, being brushed by the cold Humboldt Current that originates in Antarctica, and coping with a life that was better four hundred years ago than it is today. You do not need the added burden of the Peruvian fog from April to October.

That Sunday, Peru was playing Argentina in a soccer match in the Lima stadium, a huge cement ring which is one of many stolid public buildings scattered around the city that were built by the dictator Manuel Odría as proof of how dictators "get things done." It was an important game. Not only were the two countries old enemies—Argentina looks up upon itself as white and European and looks down upon Peru as brown and *indio*—but the winner would represent Latin America at the Olympic Games in Tokyo. All the nameless, faceless *limeños* were there who do not belong to the Club Union, an aristocratic haven where the affairs of the country have historically been settled. They had come in from the *barriadas* and the *callejones* and the other poor sections that infect the old city like a growing poison, and they wanted to win.

Soccer is more than just a sport in Latin America, it is a religious fever. It is the place where the poor go for a cathartic exoneration for their lives, and in many instances a passion for soccer supplants patriotic fervor. Jokes about soccer and national character abound. In a favorite Brazilian joke, a Spaniard, just off the boat in Rio, comes across a crowd running down the street and yelling, "*Botafogo . . . botafogo . . .*" In addition to being the name of a favorite Rio soccer team, this also means "Set fire." The Spaniard, with his politically oriented background, happily joins the crowd, shouting, "*Al palacio del gobierno*"—"To the palace of the government."

But to get back to the story, during this Sunday soccer game at the last moment the Uruguayan umpire suddenly ruled against Peru on a goal that would have made Peru the winner. A howl of rage rose from the stands, but nonetheless it seemed to bystanders that the angry crowd would accept the decision. Several newspapermen left and went back to their offices to file the story: Peru had lost something—again.

Just when the crowd seemed to be quieting down, however, a hulking Peruvian Negro named Victor Matías Campos, known in unsavory circles as "Bomba," could no longer bear the humiliation. Later he told the police, who had made his acquaintance before, "I am a Peruvian, and I couldn't permit them to annul the goal of my people." Eluding the guards, he ran onto the field with a broken bottle to attack the Uruguayan umpire, thus setting off a melee in the stands.

Something snapped. The young Peruvians, whose nerves are always as tight as taut violin strings, poured out onto the field and all the strings suddenly broke. Forming a flying wedge around the umpire and the Argentine team, the police managed to get them safely to their dressing rooms. The bewildered umpire was hidden in a downtown hotel and flown to Argentina in the middle of the night.

As police battled the rioters, the fight grew more and more vicious. A common hatred of the authority of the police erupted. The rioters flung one policeman to his death from the top of the stadium. Another was strangled with his tie. When police were forced to use tear gas, they inadvertently lobbed several bombs into the stands. The masses of soccer fans had been watching the melee with attentive interest, as Latin Americans always observe acts of the most wanton violence with an absorbed, almost scientific curiosity. But now they stampeded to the gates. It was already half an hour after the official closing of the game and the doors should have been opened. But it was typical, too, that the gatekeepers had not opened the gates. They had been watching the riots.

Later that night, in the hospitals across the city, as the infuriated cries of the day faded into the dull dirge of the night, you could see the corpses with the cross marks from the gates impressed on their bellies. In the outdoor patios and the dingy hallways, the bodies lay in long lines. As they stampeded from the stands, hundreds of persons had been caught at the closed gates. And as body pressed against body, the life was squeezed out of them. Later, when the gates were opened, the corpses tumbled onto the pavement: three hundred and nineteen of them. Before the bodies could be transported to the hospitals, the local toughs of Lima put a final touch on the Kafkaesque scene by robbing them of watches and money.

Early in the evening the fog turned into a fine, steady rain, unusual for Lima. There seemed to be air nowhere. Lines formed outside the hospitals—long patient lines. People spoke in low voices; inside, there was an eerie quiet. Methodically, people were allowed in in sixes and sevens. They crept from body to body— many were children—seeking to identify. Occasionally a woman would find a son or a husband. One middle-aged Peruvian woman, with a black mantilla over her head, suddenly came upon her sixteen-year-old son. "I knew it, I knew it," she screamed, "I knew he was here." She fell to her knees, clasping her hands. The man supporting her said to the empty room around him, in stupefied explanation, "It was her only son."

Lima is a city that had to be careful as to how all this was handled. Mass funerals were held the next day. President Fernando Belaúnde immediately proclaimed a state of siege, for he feared that leftist elements would attempt to exploit the ill-defined, amorphous violence.

And then the questioning began. Latin Americans are not, in general, notably self-analytical, but a certain amount of investigation had to be done. A reason had to be found and given for the carnage. And the explanations for the greatest sports tragedy in history poured out in a welling up of righteousness and indignation.

With no exception—either among individuals, in newspapers or in government communiqués—there was only one explanation ever offered: the umpire—a foreigner—had ruled against Peru. No one claimed that the umpire had ruled incorrectly. It was never mentioned that, right or wrong, the umpire rules and his will must be accepted, that such is the essence of good sportsmanship. What was central to everything at the time was simply the fact that he had ruled against Peru.

Neither were such sentiments reserved exclusively to the poorer classes. When a high-level investigating commission of judges, public officials and lawyers was formed to investigate the reasons for the tragedy, the commission's explanation was that the Uruguayan umpire was the "intellectual author" of the stadium massacre. . . .

The caudillo is a recurring phenomenon in Latin American politics. People seem to await the coming of the strongman, the leader on the white horse, who will take matters into his own hands and sweep problems away. One of the classic examples of a caudillo in action is Facundo Quiroga, an Argentine bandit-leader who ruled vast expanses of that country during the middle of the nineteenth century. There are also benevolent caudillos in Latin American history, but the term is often used in criticism of a selfish dictator—as it certainly applies to Quiroga. This selection was written by Domingo Sarmiento, a foremost Argentine scholar and statesman during the nineteenth century. Sarmiento obviously had little love for Quiroga.

A whole group of caudillos, each with his own personal army, roamed the lands after the wars for independence, filling the vacuum of power and feeding from the political chaos of the period. But caudillo is not only a political term; there is something of the swashbuckling, violent, egotistical dictator that is part of the general Latin American personality. Quiroga is an advanced case of *macho* (a word used to describe the neighborhood caudillo), and traces of Quiroga can be found at all levels of Latin American society.

Machos and Caudillos

By Domingo Sarmiento

Facundo is a type of primitive barbarism. He recognized no form of subjection. His rage was that of a wild beast. The locks of his crisp black hair, which fell in meshes over his brow and eyes, resembled the snakes of Medusa's head. Anger made his voice hoarse, and turned his glances into dragons. In a fit of passion he kicked out the brains of a man with whom he had quarreled at play. He tore off both the ears of a woman he had lived with, and had promised to marry, upon her asking him for thirty dollars for the celebration of the wedding; and laid open his son John's head with an axe, because he could not make him hold his tongue. He violently beat a beautiful young lady at Tucuman, whom he had failed either to seduce or to subdue, and exhibited in all his actions a low and brutal yet not a stupid nature, or one wholly without lofty aims. Incapable of commanding noble admiration, he delighted in exciting fear; and this pleasure was exclusive and dominant with him to the arranging all his actions so as to produce terror in those around him, whether it was society in general, the victim on his way to execution, or his own wife and children. Wanting ability to manage the machinery of civil government, he substituted terror for patriotism and self-sacrifice. Destitute of learning, he surrounded himself with mysteries, and pretended to a foreknowledge of events which gave him prestige and reputation among the commonalty, supporting his claims by an air of impenetrability, by natural sagacity, an uncommon power of observation, and the advantage he derived from vulgar credulity....

It was the immemorial custom in La Rioja [an Argentine province] that the *estrays*, or the animals that were not marked at a certain age, should become the lawful property of the treasury, which sent its agents to collect these gleanings, and derived no contemptible revenue from them, but the annoyance to the proprietors was intolerable. Facundo demanded the adjudication to himself of these animals, to meet the expenses he had incurred for the invasion of the city; expenses which were reducible to the summons of irregular forces, who assembled, mounted on horses of their own, and lived constantly on what came in their way. Already the proprietor of herds which brought him six thousand bullocks a year, he sent his agents to supply the city markets, and woe to any competitor who should appear! This business of supplying meat for the markets was one which he carried on wherever he ruled, in San Juan, Mendoza, or Tucuman; and he was always careful to secure the monopoly of it by proclamation or simple notification. It is with shame and disgust that I mention these disgraceful transactions, but the truth must be told. . . .

I do not intentionally dwell upon these things. How many I omit! How many misdeeds I pass over in silence which are fully proved and known to all! But I am writing the history of government by barbarians, and I am forced to state its methods. . . . Facundo, on the contrary, not only rejects all recognized civilization, but destroys and disorganizes. Facundo, who does not govern, because any government implies labor for others' good, gives himself up to the instincts of an immoderate and unscrupulous avarice. Selfishness is the foundation of almost all the great characters of history; selfishness is the chief spring of all great deeds. Quiroga had this political gift in an eminent degree and made everything around him contribute to his advantage; wealth, power, authority, all centered in him; whatever he could not acquire,—polish, learning, true respectability,—he hated and persecuted in all those who possessed them.

His hostility to the respectable classes and to the refinement of the cities was every day more perceptible, and the governor of La Rioja, whom he had himself appointed, finally was forced, by daily annoyances, to resign his place. One day, Quiroga, feeling inclined to pleasantry, was amusing himself with a young man as a cat sports with a frightened mouse; he liked to play at killing; the terror of the victim was so ludicrous, that the executioner was highly diverted, and laughed immoderately, contrary to his habit. He must have sympathy in his mirth, and he at once ordered the *general* to be beat throughout the city of Rioja, which called out the citizens under arms. Facundo, who had given the summons for diversion's sake, drew up the inhabitants in the principal square at eleven o'clock at night, dismissed the populace and retained only the well-to-do householders and the young men who still had some appearance of culture. All night he kept them marching and counter-marching, halting, forming line, marching by front or by flank. It was like a drill-sergeant teaching recruits, and the sergeant's stick travelled over the heads of the stupid, and the chests of those who were out of line. "What would you have? this is the way to teach!" Morning came, and the pallor, weariness, and exhaustion of the recruits showed what a night they had passed. Their instructor finally sent them to rest, and extended his generosity to the purchase and distribution of pastry, each recipient made in haste to eat his share, for that was part of the sport.

Lessons of such a kind are not lost upon cities, and the skillful politician who has raised similar proceedings to a system in Buenos Ayres, has refined upon them and made them wonderfully effective. For example: during the periods between 1835 and 1840 almost the whole population of Buenos Ayres has passed through the prisons. Sometimes a hundred and fifty citizens would be imprisoned for two or three months, to be then replaced by two hundred who would be kept, perhaps half the year. Wherefore? What had they done? What had they said? Idiots! Do you not see that this is good discipline for the city? Do you not remember the saying of Rosas [another famous Argentine dictator] to Quiroga, that no republic could be established because the people were not prepared for it! This is his way of teaching the city how to obey; he will finish his work, and in 1844, he will be able to show the world a people with but one thought, one opinion, one voice, and that a boundless enthusiasm for the person and will of Rosas! Then, indeed, they will be ready for a republic! ...

Fiestas are much more important to Latin Americans than they are to North Americans, and they seem to recur without end. We might condemn the Latin American love for fiestas as frivolous, but Mexican philosopher Octavio Paz sees beyond the fiesta itself to the serious social purpose it serves—as a momentary revolution when the culture is destroyed, when the hidden Mexican can escape from his encrusted shell. Paz sees in the fiesta the entire personality of Mexico, and his observations are indispensable clues to how the Mexican thinks and acts. He emphasizes the special character of his own country, but I think that what he says can be applied to the rest of the continent as well.

The Day of the Dead

By Octavio Paz

The solitary Mexican loves fiestas and public gatherings. Any occasion for getting together will serve, any pretext to stop the flow of time and commemorate men and events with festivals and ceremonies. We are a ritual people, and this characteristic enriches both our imaginations and our sensibilities, which are equally sharp and alert. The art of the fiesta has been debased almost everywhere else, but not in Mexico. There are few places in the world where it is possible to take part in a spectacle like our great religious fiestas with their violent primary colors, their bizarre costumes and dances, their fireworks and ceremonies, and their inexhaustible welter of surprises: the fruit, candy, toys, and other objects sold on these days in the plazas and open-air markets.

Our calendar is crowded with fiestas. There are certain days when the whole country, from the most remote villages to the largest cities, prays, shouts, feasts, gets drunk and kills, in honor of the Virgin of Guadalupe or Benito Juárez. Each year on the fifteenth of September, at eleven o'clock at night, we celebrate the fiesta of the Grito [the call to arms against Spain 1810] in all the plazas of the Republic, and the excited crowds actually shout for a whole hour . . . the better, perhaps, to remain silent for the rest of the year. During the days before and after the twelfth of December, [fiesta of the Virgin of Guadalupe] time comes to a full stop, and instead of pushing us toward a deceptive tomorrow that is always beyond our reach, offers us a complete and perfect today of dancing and revelry, of communion with the most ancient and secret Mexico. Time is no longer succession, and becomes what it originally was and is: the present, in which past and future are reconciled.

But the fiestas which the Church and State provide for the country as a whole are not enough. The life of every city and village is ruled by a patron saint whose blessing is celebrated with devout regularity. Neighborhoods and trades also have their annual fiestas, their ceremonies and fairs. And each one of us— atheist, Catholic, or merely indifferent—has his own saint's day, which he observes every year. It is impossible to calculate how many fiestas we have and how much time and money we spend on them. I remember asking the mayor of a village near Mitla, several years ago, "What is the income of the village government?" "About 3,000 pesos a year. We are very poor. But the Governor and the Federal Government always help us to meet our expenses." "And how are the 3,000 pesos spent?" "Mostly on fiestas, señor. We are a small village, but we have two patron saints."

This reply is not surprising. Our poverty can be measured by the frequency and luxuriousness of our holidays. Wealthy countries have very few: there is neither the time nor the desire for them, and they are not necessary. The people have other things to do, and when they amuse themselves they do so in small groups. The modern masses are agglomerations of solitary individuals. On great occasions in Paris or New York, when the populace gathers in the squares or stadiums, the absence of people, in the sense of *a* people, is remarkable: there are couples and small groups, but they never form a living community in which the individual is at once dissolved and redeemed. But how could a poor Mexican live without the two or three annual fiestas that make up for his poverty and misery? Fiestas are our only luxury. They replace, and are perhaps better than, the theater and vacations, Anglo-Saxon weekends and cocktail parties, the bourgeois reception, the Mediterranean café.

In all of these ceremonies—national or local, trade or family—the Mexican opens out. They all give him a chance to reveal himself and to converse with God, country, friends or relations. During these days the silent Mexican whistles, shouts, sings, shoots off fireworks, discharges his pistol into the air. He discharges his soul. And his shout, like the rockets we love so much, ascends to the heavens, explodes into green, red, blue, and white lights, and falls dizzily to earth with a trail of golden sparks. This is the night when friends who have not exchanged more than the prescribed courtesies for months get drunk together, trade confidences, weep over the same troubles, discover that they are brothers, and sometimes, to prove it, kill each other. The night is full of songs and loud cries. The lover wakes up his sweetheart with an orchestra. There are jokes and conversations from balcony to balcony, sidewalk to sidewalk. Nobody talks quietly. Hats fly in the air. Laughter and curses ring like silver pesos. Guitars are brought out. Now and then, it is true, the happiness ends badly, in quarrels, insults, pistol shots, stabbings. But these too are part of the fiesta, for the Mexican does not seek amusement: he seeks to escape from himself, to leap over the wall of solitude that confines him during the rest of the year. All are possessed by violence and frenzy. Their souls explode like the colors and voices and emotions. Do they forget themselves and show their true faces? Nobody knows. The important thing is to go out, open a way, get drunk on noise, people, colors. Mexico is celebrating a fiesta. And this fiesta, shot through with lightning and delirium, is the brilliant reverse to our silence and apathy, our reticence and gloom.

. . . In certain fiestas the very notion of order disappears. Chaos comes back and license rules. Anything is permitted: the customary hierarchies vanish, along with all social, sex, caste, and trade distinctions. Men disguise themselves as women, gentlemen as slaves, the poor as the rich. The army, the clergy, and the law are ridiculed. Obligatory sacrilege, ritual profanation is committed. Love becomes promiscuity. Sometimes the fiesta becomes a Black Mass. Regulations, habits and customs are violated. Respectable people put away the dignified expressions and conservative clothes that isolate them, dress up in gaudy colors, hide behind a mask, and escape from themselves.

Therefore the fiesta is not only an excess, a ritual squandering of the goods painfully accumulated during the rest of the year; it is also a revolt, a sudden immersion in the formless, in pure being. By means of the fiesta society frees itself from the norms it has established. It ridicules its gods, its principles, and its laws: it denies its own self.

The fiesta is a revolution in the most literal sense of the word. In the confusion that it generates, society is dissolved, is drowned, insofar as it is an organism ruled according to certain laws and principles. But it drowns in itself, in its own original chaos or liberty. Everything is united: good and evil, day and night, the sacred and the profane. Everything merges, loses shape and individuality and returns to the primordial mass. The fiesta is a cosmic experiment, an experiment in disorder, reuniting contradictory elements and principles in order to bring about a renascence of life. Ritual death promotes a rebirth; vomiting increases the appetite; the orgy, sterile in itself, renews the fertility of the mother or of the earth. The fiesta is a return to a remote and undifferentiated state, prenatal or presocial. It is a return that is also a beginning, in accordance with the dialectic that is inherent in social processes.

The group emerges purified and strengthened from this plunge into chaos. It has immersed itself in its own origins, in the womb from which it came. To express it in another way, the fiesta denies society as an organic system of differentiated forms and principles, but affirms it as a source of creative energy. It is a true "re-creation," the opposite of the "recreation" characterizing modern vacations, which do not entail any rites or ceremonies whatever and are as individualistic and sterile as the world that invented them.

Society communes with itself during the fiesta. Its members return to original chaos and freedom. Social structures break down and new relationships, unexpected rules, capricious hierarchies are created. In the general disorder everybody forgets himself and enters into otherwise forbidden situations and places. The bounds between audience and actors, officials and servants, are erased. Everybody takes part in the fiesta, everybody is caught up in its whirlwind. Whatever its mood, its character, its meaning, the fiesta is participation, and this trait distinguishes it from all other ceremonies and social phenomena. Lay or religious, orgy or saturnalia, the fiesta is a social act based on the full participation of all its celebrants.

Thanks to the fiesta the Mexican opens out, participates, communes with his fellows and with the values that give meaning to his religious or political existence. And it is significant that a country as sorrowful as ours should have so many and such joyous fiestas. Their frequency, their brilliance and excitement, the enthusiasm with which we take part, all suggest that without them we would explode. They free us, if only momentarily, from the thwarted impulses, the inflammable desires that we carry within us. But the Mexican fiesta is not merely a return to an original state of formless and normless liberty: the Mexican is not seeking to return, but to escape from himself, to exceed himself. Our fiestas are explosions. Life and death, joy and sorrow, music and mere noise are united, not to re-create or recognize themselves, but to swallow each other up. There is nothing so joyous as a Mexican fiesta, but there is also nothing so sorrowful. Fiesta night is also a night of mourning.

If we hide within ourselves in our daily lives, we discharge ourselves in the whirlwind of the fiesta. It is more than an opening out: we rend ourselves open. Everything—music, love, friendship—ends in tumult and violence. The frenzy of our festivals shows the extent to which our solitude closes us off from communication with the world. We are familiar with delirium, with songs and shouts, with the monologue ... but not with the dialogue. Our fiestas, like our confidences, our loves, our attempts to reorder our society, are violent breaks with the old or the established. Each time we try to express ourselves we have to break with ourselves. And the fiesta is only one example, perhaps the most typical, of this violent break. It is not difficult to name others, equally revealing: our games, which are always a going to extremes, often mortal; our profligate spending, the reverse of our timid investments and business enterprises; our confessions. The somber Mexican, closed up in himself, suddenly explodes, tears open his breast and reveals himself, though not without a certain complacency, and not without a stopping place in the shameful or terrible mazes of his intimacy. We are not frank, but our sincerity can reach extremes that horrify a European. The explosive, dramatic, sometimes even suicidal manner in which we strip ourselves, surrender ourselves, is evidence that something inhibits and suffocates us. Something impedes us from being. And since we cannot or dare not confront our own selves, we resort to the fiesta. It fires us into the void; it is a drunken rapture that burns itself out, a pistol shot in the air, a skyrocket. . . .

One of the frequent descriptions of Latin Americans is that they are paternalistic—that they are always looking for a father figure, a strongman, to manage their affairs. While North America was founded on self-reliance and individualism, Latin America supposedly was built on grandeur and dependence. Because of this, some say, we have democracy while they have dictatorships. I have doubts about this viewpoint, but it is widely held. In this selection, Fernando Guillén Martínez traces what he believes to be the source of paternalism, both in governments and in families.

Paternalism and Tiger Worship
By Fernando Guillén Martínez

In the vernacular catechisms utilized by the Spanish missionaries in order to conquer the souls of the natives in the Amazon regions and to facilitate the oral confession of the natives to the new catechists, one can read questions like these: Have you worshipped tigers? Have you been angry with God or thought badly about the saints? Have you been angry with your relatives, judges, governors, or have you whispered about them? Have you disobeyed your parents, judges or elders?

There is no doubt that the most important part of moral life for the Spanish catechists was obedience. The convert was required to obey the old authorities of his tribe, to obey the new master-conqueror, to obey the priest and the group of relatives. Individual rebellion was compared with such serious transgressions as idolatry. And up to now, that characteristic has persisted in a constant manner in Spanish American life, generating a social paternalism of submissive appearance and of characteristic and irresponsible perspective. There is visible today the tendency of the population of all Latin America to obey blindly all kinds of political, religious, or economic authorities without rational discrimination among them and to require of these same powers unrealistic capability of domination and decision. It might be said that social inertia creates the necessity for a master to submit to, to hate, to praise, or to cheat.

The responsibility, individual or collective, of the people has seriously deteriorated among the Latin Americans. One can refer to a feeling of the "magic of power" as the constituent element of most human relations.

If an ordinary Latin American (a "progressive" industrialist, a city worker, or a sharecropper) is asked what he can do toward self-progress, he certainly will answer that the "government" has not wanted to solve his problems, or he will say that he intends to ask the "government" to correct some of the personal misfortunes he has suffered. The Marxists, of course, will respond that the only thing that they can do is make a "revolution" in order to change the government.

There is, no doubt, a paternalistic psychological structure (of national hate and love toward power) at the bottom of all Latin American activity. In order to analyze it, it is necessary to take into consideration that "the government" does not signify political authority solely; it implies in an unconscious manner any source from which there arises the power of decision. Therefore, the armed forces, economic wealth, or the repressive energy of the Church are also "government," and the people react to all those forms of co-active violence in the same basic way.

The conquest of power (and its counterpart, the winning of protection through power) seems to be actually the only psychological goal in Latin America. Other social benefits, such as wealth or individual liberty, have a secondary and subordinate place in personal preferences. It can be affirmed that wealth and liberty are appreciated only so long as they hold the promise of dominion over others and they are scorned when they seem to obstruct the anxiety for protection and paternalism which forms the maximum "right" of existence.

A Colombian educator and writer, formerly Rector of the National University, Mario Laserna Pinzón, observed with great acumen that Colombian life was founded under the sign of magic and he proceeded to define it: "What characterizes magic is to attribute definite effects to definite acts without knowing the intermediate acts from cause to effect. Moreover, the chain, or causal mechanism, works not only in an unknown way but on the premise that it has nothing to do, rationally, with the anticipated effect." That is to say, magic searches through imaginary and irrational means dominance over others and instantaneous satisfaction of the necessities of the individual and of the group through *sentimental* adhesion to that power which is presumed absolute.

Toward the "government" one therefore reacts compulsively. People associate themselves indiscriminately with the source of power or combat it to the death to obtain—through cajolery or compulsion—benefits to which they believe themselves to have an unconditional right. . . .

To believe in tigers (as magic incarnations of vital potential) or to see in the judge or mayor or the group of relatives a feared but easy substitute for collective or individual responsibility, was the foundation of the reaction of the indigenous Amazonians. All present-day Latin American society seems to have been symbolically contaminated.

A series of strange phenomena result from these facts. The political "governments" are not representative of their electorates even if they have been elected by the majority of the votes of the people, the Church does not interpret, nor is it the true vehicle of feeling in the population; business and industry are instruments of social oppressions over the masses who do not understand their systems or the fundamentals of their activity. . . . Richard S. Aldrich asserted in *Life* magazine, in referring to the mistake of the Alliance for Progress: "in general, it has attempted to create the human infrastructures through the mediation of national governments. This could only be effective if there existed any real intercommunication among governments and peoples, if the governments were effectively based on the will of the governed, if constitutional systems were firm. But the truth is that these conditions, for the most part, do not exist in Latin America."

The above quoted statement written by a foreign observer of Latin America, is useful in explaining the profound sentiment of the associated elements in Latin American life. In spite of the fact that power may seem to derive from the consent of the population, it was not conceived by the social will. People organize power with the exclusive object of demanding from it satisfaction for what they implore or else of attacking it ferociously if their request fails. But the people do not feel responsible for the powers constituted by themselves, nor do they understand that they are yielding to those powers the totality of their autonomy and their own capacity for salvation. "Power" for its part responds in a correlative form: to deny society any capacity for intervention and encircle it with a mythical prestige disproportionate to any real capacity for action. The result is chaos, a mixture of arbitrary authoritarianism and emotional anarchy.

Although at times this seesaw masquerades in the dress of "capitalism" or tf "popular suffrage," it is not, for all that, identical with the phenomenon expressed by the military coup or by associations or landowners or by ecclesiastical excommunication.

Neither are the people responsible for the direction of economic and social life, nor do those who are try to interpret the common will. The association is one of magic obedience which gives rise to an equally magical subversion. In other words, the Latin American people do not participate in power, nor do they seem to have a conscious desire to become responsible for eventual equal participation.

The majority of Latin American governments represent the direct interests of a small group of people who have succeeded in manipulating the armed forces or in creating political parties directed from above (without conscious participation on the part of the masses) and they control likewise the most important businesses and the powerful newspapers and magazines. Such governments organize—regularly or irregularly—elections in which the average voter lacks all chance of becoming acquainted with public problems, which he could not understand anyway due to lack of proper education. In addition, the media of publicity and information which have a truly national breadth are always in the hands of governmental groups. The possibilities for a conscientious and informed opposition are negligible. . . .

The dominant Latin American group justifies itself with the argument that people need direction and protection. The dominated people, in their turn, demand of that "government" magic powers and excessive generosity in exchange for their irrational adhesion. The explanation must be found in historic evolution, which formed a subconscious idea that paths leading to arbitrary privilege are open to all. . . .

In this climate of irresponsibility and of magic subjugation, personal autonomy and awareness of individual power become impossible. A deaf anger and a blind and impassioned subjection are the psychological elements of common existence. . . .

A Latin American industrialist or politician is much more interested in continuing to maintain absolute authority over the electorate, or over his employees, than to satisfy his own ambition for economic profit. The empty pure forms of democracy serve to maintain the myth of popular sovereignty, and verbal generosity in "helping" the humble classes (without sharing authority) creates in the foreign eye the complete illusion of a false desire for reforms. This paternalistic attitude is a permanent brake on economic development and on the appearance of civic and individual responsibility. Paradoxically, the resulting misery is interpreted as a cause and not as a result of paternalism. One thinks that the people are irrational because they are poor. Nobody imagines that they are poor because they are irrational. Therefore, the Marxist infection gains support because its doctrines about the absolute authority of the state coincide surprisingly with the traditional Latin American psychology. All social life is interpreted from the exclusive point of view of the economic. In the struggle initiated in the world between socialist totalitarianism and the desire for human liberty, it has been forgotten that the development of liberty is not exclusively a financial effort.

On facing the social and economic underdevelopment of half of the American continent, the importance of which in world strategy is not overlooked by anyone today, Europe and the United States have interpreted the fight as a simple dilemma between riches and poverty, between comfort and hunger. . . .

It follows that by financing and supporting exclusively governments and the groups currently dominant, the Europeans and North Americans have not done anything except fortify in the eyes of the Latin American people the image of a single powerful and arbitrary authority. And they have helped the "oligarchies" and the masses of the whole hemisphere to interpret "power" as an invincible force from which all can make demands without the necessity of supporting it or sharing in its responsibilities. . . .

The mistaken strategy of the "West" (that is to say,

of the democratic forms of bourgeois civilization) in the Western Hemisphere is symptomatic of the growing antagonism that separates the "poor" countries from the "rich" countries and the farming regions from urban manufacturing centers. The capacity for initiative of the masses of farmers and workers is paralyzed by the compulsive force of government, which has generated an *anarchistic socialism* which does not dare to confess its name and which is financed by international effort. . . .

It is scarcely necessary to say that the Latin American world has found in its absurd political division one of the most persistent obstacles to economic development. Lacking large domestic markets for consumption, the industries of Latin America are asphyxiated by a body of controls which contradict the norms of common sense and place in an antagonistic position populations that obviously must have a common aim and some complementary interests.

There is no racial, linguistic, or economic explanation for this phenomenon of Latin American division. One must accept the fact that only the necessity of artificially maintaining government bureaucracy, power, and "leadership" was what divided into twenty authoritarian centralisms what should be a democratic federation of small communities. The necessity of inventing "power" and taking possession of power is the only meaning of that phenomenon which contradicts the elemental interest in Latin America.

Those twenty kinds of authoritarianism have been converted into an acute problem for the rest of the world, particularly for the so-called "Western" world. They have presented their urgent petitions for the consideration of the "powerful countries," demanding satisfaction without any effort on their own part, and convincing their own people that in the end anarchy or poverty or weakness are caused by the "imperialist powers." All the paternalistic power groups, through the mouthpiece of government, use the Marxist vocabulary,—this phenomenon being more acute and perceptible among the large, landed proprietors. . . .

Then is it worthwhile to finance and encourage

further Latin American paternalism by supporting only "governments"? . . .

Latin Americans have always been famous for their aversion to manual labor—to getting their hands dirty. This has been especially true for the aristocracy and for those with pretensions of aristocracy. The prideful disdain for manual labor, always given as an explanation for Latin American "underdevelopment," is diminishing all over the continent, but it is still apparent in many places. Moritz Thomsen, an ex-Peace Corps volunteer in Ecuador, shows how the notions of aristocracy reach even to the poorest people, and perhaps help to keep them poor.

Dirtying Your Hands

By Moritz Thomsen

I began to understand the reasons for Alexandro's poverty; it was a product of his own idea of himself, of how he saw himself in relation to the town. His father was the political lieutenant of the zone, a sort of combined judge, sheriff, prosecuting attorney, and jailer. Alexandro hated his father, but at the same time he felt himself to be one of the aristocratic families, and for this reason there were certain types of work that he could not consider. He would not work with a machete, for instance. "I am not a machete man," he said with dignity when I asked him why he didn't work with some of the younger guys as a day laborer. And when I asked him why he didn't earn a little money ferrying people across the river, he gave me a scornful look, as though I were impugning his manhood. . . .

North Americans are known as pragmatists, skeptics of the spirit; but Latin America is permeated with mysticism, with a belief in ideas that cannot be measured or contained in words, with martyrs and apparitions and transcendence. There have been all kinds of mystics in Latin

America, political mystics who die for impossible causes, religious mystics who create a spiritual fantasia; everybody in Latin America has something of the irrational spirit of Don Quixote. Antonio Conselheiro was a fairly obscure mystic who lived in eighteenth-century Brazil. His followers, who populated mostly the harsh backlands of northern Brazil, were harassed by the army, fought against the government, and were finally wiped out. The details of life in the town (Canudos) where the selection takes us, and of this specific religious sect, are not important; but pay attention to how the people abandon their daily routines, their ordinary life, to heed the call of a traveling wildman.

The Mystic

By R. B. Cunningham Graham

His trenches opened, and the ever-increasing population that had flowed into Canudos [Brazilian town] housed, or at least sheltered in their huts, Antonio Conselheiro's first care was to draw up a scheme of life for them. He was, of course, supreme, after the fashion of all prophets and democratic leaders when they have attained to power. When a man is convinced, as was Antonio Conselheiro—for without doubt he was quite honest in his faith in himself—that he is God's vicegerent upon earth, nothing more natural than he should make himself obeyed. . . .

Feeling himself secure, at least for a considerable time, he set about to mould the lives of the inhabitants according to his will. Conduct he left to individual taste, setting but little store upon it, as it would seem, for faith was his chief stronghold, in a world so soon to disappear. Ninety per cent of all their worldly goods the faithful paid into the treasury, esteeming themselves happy with the little that remained to them, for mere material needs. "Blessed are those who suffer" was the theme that he embroidered on in all his sermons to his followers. He enjoined strict fasting, giving the example in his own person, and prolonging abstinence till he was nothing but a skeleton. Most of the day had to be passed in singing hymns and litanies. Sermons were frequent and all the population had to attend them under pain of penance and of punishment. . . .

Antonio Conselheiro dwelt often in his sermons to his well-armed saints upon the theme of "Blessed are the sufferers," exhorting all his hearers to avoid comfort, good food and clothes as they would shun the plague. Better a mortal sin, he said, than an excess of comfort, holding, as did the monks of the Thebais, that dirt and ignorance, idleness and maceration of the flesh, were things more acceptable to Him who at the same time had given reason to mankind by which to shape their lives.

So prophets from the beginning have assumed to know God's mind better than He Himself; for vanity and pride disguised in rags and misery have been their guiding stars. Still, it was evident Antonio Conselheiro preached in good faith and all sincerity. Had he not done so, he would have had no followers, for let the ecstatic, mystic, revolutionary, or any other class of men doubt of the leader's faith, they follow him no more.

Antonio Conselheiro practised all he preached, fasting to the point of actual starvation, sometimes remaining hours upon his knees in ecstasy before the rough-hewn figures of the saints, at others busying himself with public matters—for he was priest and king. . . .

One day a follower wasted with fasting came to visit him, and was invited to sit down to share his frugal meal. When he departed he proclaimed, though he had eaten hardly anything, he felt as if he had risen from a banquet, strong and refreshed with meat. The wondrous news ran through the town and all rejoiced, both at the miracle and because it was a sign the Lord had given to their Councillor. Whether Antonio Conselheiro wished to bring the people's bodies low by fasting and thus exalt their minds, no one can say; but it is certain that the whole population of Canudos lived, as it were, upon a pilgrimage of body and of mind. A people in this state is moved more easily to acts of heroism and of self-abnegation than those who pass an ordinary life, marrying and giving in marriage, buying and selling and setting down accounts by double entry. The greater part of the prophet's followers were simple folk, who no doubt really thought the destruction of the world was close at hand, and practised fasting and the rites of their religion in absolute good faith. Others arrived, of a far different complexion; these he accepted without a question, holding, perhaps, that their adhesion to his cause wiped out their crimes; or, understanding that if the aim is sure, it matters little if the hand that fires the gun be steeped in villainy. So, homicides and cattle-stealers, the broken men of the Sertão, flocked to Canudos, and were received into the fold. . . .

"Honor" is a word used frequently in Latin America, especially in connection with sex and love. Latin Americans (mostly the men) have constructed an elaborate and rigid code of ethics; if they are deceived by their wives or by their friends, then they are expected to seek revenge. This is a generalization, of course, but Latin Americans are more ready than North Americans to feel that their pride has been wounded or their character dishonored by the actions of another person. This selection from a short story, "The Pin," shows how well accepted the motives for revenge can be.

The Pin: An Affair of Honor
By Ventura García Calderón

The horse collapsed, dying, soaked with sweat and blood, as the rider leaped to the ground at the foot of the massive stairway of the Ticabamba ranch. Above the heavy cedar balcony appeared the stern head of the owner Don Timoteo Mondaraz. In a bantering bass voice the imposing old man called out to the visitor, who was trembling:

"What ails you, Borradito? Why, your knees are

knocking together. Speak up, man, we don't eat people alive here—"

Borradito, so nicknamed through the valley because of his pock-marked face, clutched his straw hat desperately in his hands and tried to explain so many things at the same time—the sudden tragedy, his gallop of twenty leagues that night, with orders to get to his destination as quickly as he could, even if it killed the horse—that for a moment he could not get a word out. Suddenly, without breathing, he poured forth in a jumble:

"Master, I am here to tell you that Mr. Conrado told me to tell you that just last night Miss Grimanesa took sick and died."

It must have been by a special dispensation of Providence that Don Timoteo did not whip out his revolver, as he always did when excited, but he clutched the servant's arm as though to tear further details out by the roots.

"Last night—dead—Grimanesa?"

He must have sensed something in Borradito's vague explanation, for without saying any more, leaving orders that his daughter Ana María was not to be awakened, he went himself to saddle his best riding horse. In a few moments he was on his way to the ranch of his son-in-law Conrado Basadre, who the year before had married Grimanesa, that lovely, pale Amazon, the best catch in the whole valley. The wedding was like a festival, with fireworks, Indian women dancing in their purple dresses, Indians still lamenting the death of the Incas, which took place centuries before, but which still lives on in the dirges of the downtrodden race, like the lamentations for Zion in the sublime stubbornness of the Bible. Then along the best paths through the planted fields there had come the procession carrying ancient images of saints. And the happy marriage of his lovely girl to handsome, dashing Conrado Basadre had ended like this—

Burying his buck spurs in the horse's flanks, Don Timoteo recalled that festival with horror. He was trying to make it to Sincavilca, the estate of the Basadres, in four hours.

Late that afternoon there came the sound of another swift gallop clattering over the stones of the mountain road. To be on the safe side the old man fired a shot into the air, calling out:

"Who goes?"

The rider coming toward him reined in his horse, and in a voice that could not conceal his emotion, called out in turn:

"Don't you know me, sir? The overseer of Sincavilca. I'm going for the priest."

The rancher was so upset that he did not ask why he was hurrying so fast to get a priest when Grimanesa was dead, or why the chaplain was not at the ranch. He waved good-bye with his hand, and urged on his mount, which set off at a gallop, its flanks running blood.

Over the huge gate that closed the courtyard of the ranch the silence hung like a pall. Even the dogs were silent in the presence of death. The great doors, with their silver nailheads of colonial days, were draped with black crepe in the form of a cross. Don Timoteo crossed the vast, deserted rooms without removing his spurs till he reached the bedroom of the dead woman, where Conrado Basadre sat sobbing. In a voice choked with tears the old man asked him to leave him there for a moment alone. And after closing the door with his own hands he gave himself over to his grief for hours, insulting the saints, calling Grimanesa by her name, kissing her limp hand which fell back upon the sheet, covered with Cape jessamine and wallflowers. Grave and solemn for the first time in her life, Grimanesa lay like a saint, her hair hidden under the coif of the Carmelite nuns, and her lovely body imprisoned in the habit, as was the religious custom of the valley. On her breast they had laid a tremendous silver crucifix that one of her grandfathers had used to brain Indians in an uprising long ago.

As Don Timoteo bent over to kiss the sacred emblem the corpse's habit parted, and he observed something that horrified him, for he drew back from the body with a strange revulsion. Looking quickly about him, he hid something under his poncho, and without

taking leave of anybody, mounted and returned to
Ticabamba that same night. . . .

[A few months later, Don Timoteo receives a visit
from the dead girl's husband.]

They went into the old-fashioned drawing-room,
where the portrait of the dead daughter still hung.
The old man sat in silence while Conrado with great
embarrassment explained in a hesitant, abashed voice
that he would like to marry Ana María. A long pause
followed. Don Timoteo sat with his eyes closed, as
though he had fallen asleep. Then swiftly, lithely, as
though the years had passed over his robust rancher's
body without leaving an impress, he got up and
opened an iron box, whose old and complicated lock
had to be gently coaxed open. Still silent, he took out
of it a gold pin. It was one of those stick-pins the
Indian women use to hold their shawls together, the
head shaped like a coca leaf, but longer, sharper, and
stained dark with blood.

When Conrado saw it he fell to his knees, whimper-
ing like a convicted criminal.

"Grimanesa, my poor Grimanesa!"

But with a brusque gesture the old man indicated
that it was not the moment for tears. Making a super-
human effort to control his growing distress, he mut-
tered in a voice so blurred that his words could hardly
be made out:

"Yes, I took it from her breast as she lay dead— You
had driven this pin into her heart— Isn't that true?—
Had she been unfaithful?"

"Yes, Father."

"Did she repent as she died?"

"Yes, Father."

"Does anybody know it?"

"No, Father."

"Was it with the overseer?"

"Yes, Father."

"Why didn't you kill him too?"

"He ran away like a coward."

"Do you swear to kill him if he comes back?"

"Yes, Father."

The old man cleared his throat solemnly, clasped

Conrado by the hand, and said in a voice almost too low to hear:

"If this one deceives you, do the same with her. Here!"

And he solemnly handed over to him the gold pin, as in olden times a sword was handed to a newly made knight. Then pushing him roughly away, and putting his hand over his aching heart, he made a sign to his son-in-law to leave the room, for it was not good for anyone to see stern, implacable Don Timoteo Mondaraz weeping.

For millions of Latin Americans, character is formed not only by history or ancestry but also by the extreme poverty in which they live. Moritz Thomsen, writing about his experiences as a Peace Corps volunteer in Ecuador, describes the effects of poverty on the people who are sentenced to exist in it.

Living Poor

By Moritz Thomsen

Living poor is like being sentenced to exist in a stormy sea in a battered canoe, requiring all your strength simply to keep afloat; there is never any question of reaching a destination. True poverty is a state of perpetual crisis, and one wave just a little bigger or coming from an unexpected direction can and usually does wreck things. Some benevolent ignorance denies a poor man the ability to see the squalid sequence of his life, except very rarely; he views it rather as a disconnected string of unfortunate sadnesses. Never having paddled on a calm sea, he is unable to imagine one. I think if he could connect the chronic hunger, the sickness, the death of his children, the almost unrelieved physical and emotional tension into the pattern that his life inevitably takes he would kill himself.

In South America the poor man is an ignorant man, unaware of the forces that shape his destiny. The shattering truth—that he is kept poor and ignorant as the principal and unspoken component of national policy—escapes him. He cries for land reform, a system of farm loans that will carry him along between crops, unaware that the national economy in almost every country sustained by a one-crop export commodity depends for its success on an unlimited supply of cheap labor. Ecuador needs poor men to compete in the world banana market; Brazil needs poverty to sell its coffee; Chile, its tin; Colombia, its cacao and coffee, and so on. The way United States pressures shape the policies of the South American governments can make a Peace Corps Volunteer who is involved and saddened by the poverty in his village tremble to his very roots.

Death, of course, is the great release. I lay in my house one night trying to sleep, while up the hill a fiesta went on until dawn—drums in an endless and monotonous rhythm connecting a series of increasingly complicated songs, some chanted by women, some by men, some by mixed voices. It gradually became beautiful and moving, but I was puzzled because the celebration was just a week before the great *Semana Santa*, Holy Easter, a fiesta that everyone saves up for and that leaves everyone broke and exhausted.

"Why were they *bombiendo* all night on the hill?" I asked someone.

"They were celebrating the death of Crispín's firstborn," I was told. "He was born dead, an *angelito*." There wasn't a bit of sadness in the town; it was a real celebration. Crispín's son had struck it lucky; he was one of God's angels without all of that intervening crap.

The incapacity of the poor to see the pattern of their lives is occasionally breached. I took a color photograph of Wai and his family standing in front of their house, and when the people of the town saw it, it had the curious power to make them weep. It was just a picture of a man, like any other in the town, with his eight children formally lined up in ascending order, his pregnant wife, and his mother. But there was something awful in Wai's rags, in the tilt of his head, in the foolish pride that showed in his mother's face for the voracious horde of naked kids. The picture summed up his whole life, a symbolic rendering of his past and future. The people would look at it and gasp. "Oh, my God, poor Wai." Perhaps for just a moment they saw themselves. Wai, of course, was the poorest, but not by much. You could measure degrees of poverty in Río Verde with one pot or one woven mat or a dollar's worth of fishhooks.

One week, which seemed to contain a few extra big waves, I tried to keep track of some of the things that happened in my town, the unexpected riptides, the sudden squalls that threatened the people.

There was nineteen-year-old Lucho. I had met him on the street in Esmeraldas one night where he had borrowed twenty-five cents from me to buy, he said, groceries to take back to Río Verde—a head of cabbage and some beets. What he brought back instead was a case of gonorrhea from a two-bit whore. He sat on the dock for three days, sinking into a deep depression, lacking the twenty sucres that he needed for penicillin and afraid to tell his father what was wrong. I broke his confidence and told Alexandro, who instead of being angry was rather proud, a reaction I had half-anticipated, knowing something about his lusty old man. He immediately sold one of the ten chickens that he had been raising for his wife's approaching confinement, the only time when, to rebuild a woman's strength for the next assault, chicken is eaten in great quantities. He bought penicillin; a happy ending for Lucho. (Poverty makes a thief of a man who doesn't have monumental character. I found out months later that part of Lucho's depression had been simple fury. Just before his sickness Lucho had stolen the schoolteacher's ring. But in Esmeraldas no one would buy the ring, it was so obviously stolen. There he sat with eight hundred sucres of nonnegotiable assets in his pocket, his manhood polluted, too poor to cure himself.)

I met Alvaro staggering down the beach late one afternoon that week, his jaw swollen and his lips flecked with blood. He had been suddenly overwhelmed by the most violent toothache; too poor to go to an Esmeraldas dentist, he had walked up to Roca-fuerte, the next town to the north, where one of the storekeepers did emergency work with a pair of pliers. He told me about it; it was almost a joke by then. "Oh, that *pendejo*. He looked in my mouth and everything was swollen and he didn't know which tooth to pull. 'Oh, Christ man,' I said, 'pull them both, then; pull them both.'"

One of Orestes' two children came down with typhoid fever. He loaded up half the chickens that he had been pampering until they laid and sent them into Esmeraldas with his wife and child. In one day he lost the work of months.

That week, the week of the spring flood tides, the waves swept high up on the beach and carried away half of Pablo's coconut plantation. For three days as I walked back and forth along the beach I saw Pablo, a deaf old man who walked with a cane, wandering dazedly around in the remains of his *cocal*, the ground littered with piles of balsa chunks, debris from the flooded river, and fallen palm trees. Pablo had other assets, a *salón* by the dock, but this plantation had in his youth been the foundation of his relative affluence, bringing him in perhaps a hundred dollars a year, and it came as a great blow to lose it in one night.

A little farther up the beach the waves broke through the sand barrier and cut away the foundations of Wai's house, fulfilling his mother's prophecy. The sea washed away the steps and the balsa fence that confined his two ducks, three chickens, and a Peace Corps turkey whose feet had been badly gnawed away by rats. The day after the first high tide I found the whole family tearing the sides off the house and getting ready to move it farther back from the beach on the other side of the salt grass.

"You'll need some help with the big timbers," I said. The four corner posts of the house were of *guayacán,* the hardest, heaviest wood known to man.

"Yes, and with the roof sections," Wai said. "I've got to use the same roof. But I haven't got the money to buy new palm thatch, nor money for the *aguardiente* for a *minga*." (It was dishonorable to organize a *minga* without serving cane alcohol and food to the participants.) I waited a week and nothing happened. I couldn't bear to see Wai and his family sleeping on the beach without a roof, so I bought a bottle of *aguardiente*. Wai killed one of his ducks and invited his friends to help him dismantle his house, and one morning we all gathered at Wai's.

As the *aguardiente* began to take effect, the pace of the work gradually accelerated and the style disintegrated. The roof sections, which Wai desperately wanted to save, turned to powder as they crashed to the ground, released too suddenly on ropes held by drunken hands. The roof was made of ascending strips of bamboo to which had been laced palm leaves, but the bamboo was dry and rotten and the leaves were as brittle as eggshells.

By noon the house-wrecking had turned into a hilarious farce, marred but somehow made funnier by the fact that a four-by-four mahogany roof beam had crashed down and broken Santo's nose. We were all caught up in the joy of destruction, walking warily through the pools of Santo's blood. At one o'clock we gathered together for duck soup in the shattered remains of Wai's house, of which nothing remained standing but the four main corner posts, deeply sunk into the sand. Around us was absolute chaos.

"*Jodido pero feliz,*" Wai said, surrounded by friends and family and tipping up the last of the Cayapa. Screwed but happy.

PART VII.

BLACKS, BRAZIL, AND THE CARIBBEAN

Introduction

While the Spaniards were taking over the Pacific coast of Latin America, the Portuguese were busy colonizing Brazil, and various other European nations scrambled to establish bases in the Caribbean. One of the few similarities between these non-Spanish colonies was their use of black slaves, imported from Africa, to work the sugar plantations. The Brazilian sugar culture, as the first excerpt shows, demanded a different personality and social structure than, say, the *encomienda* system in the Andes. And what is said to apply here to Brazil could also apply to the Caribbean areas, where similar plantations stretched across the islands.

Brazil, the largest country on the continent, promises to be a world superpower, the first industrial giant in Latin America. With its Afro-Portuguese tradition, Brazil seems like a flapping edge on a starched shirt: its language and its people bend, the whole culture is more sensual and more flexible than that of Spanish America. Although it abolished the slave trade relatively late, Brazil is known today for racial tolerance; its people are a resolution of white and black—there is no outright segregation. There is a certain amount of class prejudice in Brazil, but it is more social than racial, following the Brazilian saying "A white man who is poor is black; a black man who is rich is white." The two selections written by Poppino are general descriptions of Brazil—its people, politics, and economy. The excerpt on macumba is just one example of how the African tradition affects the music, religion, philosophy, and the entire way of life in Brazil.

The Caribbean islands are so diverse that it is difficult to lump them together. French Haiti and the British Bahamas are as alien to each other as the United States is to Peru. The selection attempts to describe the various island cultures and how they developed in their separate ways. Central America was largely a Spanish product, but I include it here because the area also opened itself to black culture and to aspects of tropical life similar to those found in Brazil or in the rest of the Caribbean.

Unlike the rest of Latin America, Brazil and much of the Caribbean imported thousands of black slaves from Africa, for use on the tropical plantations. Frederick Pike describes how and why the slaves were brought to Brazil. The hunger for cheap labor was just as strong in the Caribbean as it was in Brazil, and blacks arrived there in similar fashion.

The Sugar Culture
By Thomas E. Skidmore

... From the time the land was discovered by the Portuguese in 1500, the Europeans in Brazil faced a labor problem. The Indians of the region, who were much less advanced than the Indians whom the Spanish encountered in the Andes and Middle America, at first furnished the manpower for a primitive barter economy in brazilwood (valuable for its qualities as a dye). By the middle of the sixteenth century, however, barter had already ceased to entice the Indians sufficiently, and the scattered Portuguese settlers began enslaving them in order to ensure the wood supply. The need for slaves became even more pressing when the Portuguese discovered the great profits to be gained in the Brazilian Northeast from growing sugar, the crop that was to form the backbone of the export economy until the end of the seventeenth century.

But the Brazilian Indians soon proved to be unsatisfactory for plantation labor. First, their background as a hunting and fishing people had given them no experience in the routine of regular field labor. Second, they quickly fell victim to the numerous European diseases against which they had no immunity. Third, the Church partially blocked the use of Indians as slaves. In Brazil, as in Spanish America, the Church sought with varying degrees of intensity to prevent the enslavement of the Indian. This intervention, motivated largely by theological concern over the Indian's status as a potential convert to Christianity (which was the regal and papal rationale for Iberian conquests in the New World), certainly did not keep the Indian totally free. Indeed, many of the Catholic orders themselves owned slaves in sixteenth-century Brabil. But the Church's sporadic attempts to protect the Indian—culminating in the abolition of all Indian slavery in the 1750's—did help force Portuguese planters to look elsewhere for their labor supply.

The logical place to look for better plantation laborers was black Africa. Even before the Spanish and the Portuguese came to America, they had successfully exploited African slaves on the plantations—primarily sugar plantations—of their Atlantic island possessions. Furthermore, the Portuguese African possessions offered an inviting supply of captives. The Portuguese began systematically importing enslaved Africans into Brazil about 1570 in a stream that was eventually to total three and half million before the slave trade was suppressed in 1850.

Working the sugar plantations or *fazendas* was the first major task of Brazilian slaves. By the seventeenth century, the humid northeastern coast of Brazil had become the world's leading sugar producer, generating a per capita income for the area that has never been equaled since. This prosperity was based squarely on the Negro slave, who was aptly known as "the hands and feet of the planter." The handsome profits from Brazil's productive Northeast attracted foreign invaders—first the French and then the Dutch. The latter occupied the coast of Pernambuco from 1630 until their expulsion in 1654. Quickly appreciating the basis of Brazilian wealth, the Dutch for a time seriously considered a plan to conquer Angola, Brazil's "black mother," a dream that was never realized. The South, on the other hand—from the province of São Paulo southward—had a largely non-export economy that did not require plantation labor, and this area continued to use primarily Indian rather than Negro slavery. . . .

In general, the rigidity and harshness of Brazilian slavery tended to decrease in regions suffering economic decline, especially the Northeast and the old mining areas of Minas Gerais. Although these areas were in economic retreat by 1800, other regions soon experienced the next great agricultural boom of Brazilian history. In the 1830's and 1840's slave labor was in great demand for the coffee plantations of the province of Rio de Janeiro, southeastern Minas Gerais, and São Paulo. Just as sugar had ruled in the seventeenth century and gold and diamonds in the eighteenth, coffee became king in the nineteenth. By 1850 Brazil had become the world's largest producer of the new drink that rapidly captured the fancy of the prosperous inhabitants in the industrializing North Atlantic world. Negro slave labor seemed as indispensable to the huge coffee plantations as it had once been to the sugar plantations and the mines. But the coffee boom differed from earlier ones in a basic respect: Now the end of the African slave trade was imminent, and abolitionist opinion had grown strong. For economic and social reasons, therefore, the coffee planters had to think in terms of alternative sources of labor. . . .

———————

Brazil's black population, its Portuguese background, its gargantuan size, and its unreserved aspirations come together to make up a different culture from the rest of Latin America. Poppino sounds like he is writing about the nineteenth-century United States when he describes Brazil—with its natural wealth, its exploding cities, the optimism of its people. Brazil has become one of the most repressive military dictatorships in Latin America during the last few years. There are those who believe that a tight military state is the only way to achieve rapid economic growth in Latin America, and Brazil is the test of that belief.

The Continent of Brazil

By Rollie Poppino

"Brazil is a continent." This statement is not literally true, but it is frequently used by Brazilians to describe their country, to set it apart from the rest of Latin America, and to indicate the magnitude of its problems, accomplishments, and promise. The expression is employed to evoke a vision of the vastness, complexity, and unity that distinguish Brazil from Spanish America and from the recently independent countries of tropical Africa and Asia. Brazil lends itself to such exaggeration on the part of admirers and critics alike. In sheer size, in the wealth of its natural resources, and in the make-up of its burgeoning population, Brazil can seldom be considered in the terms applied to its neighbors in Latin America or to underdeveloped nations in other parts of the world. Its negative aspects, also, are usually described in superlatives.

Brazil occupies approximately half of the continent of South America and accounts for one-third of the region known as Latin America. It covers 3,286,478 square miles, dwarfing the largest Spanish American republics. Brazil has three times as much territory as Argentina and more than four times as much as Mexico; and it is larger than the continental United States by about 185,000 square miles. Only China, the Soviet Union, and Canada surpass Brazil in contiguous land area.

Brazil's endowment of natural resources matches its "continental" dimensions. Sharing two immense river systems, the Amazon and La Plata, Brazil has one of the world's greatest potential sources of hydroelectric power. Its subsoil deposits, still not fully explored, include nearly a quarter of the proven iron ore reserves in the world and abundant quantities of most other minerals prized in an age of steel and atomic energy. The supply of essential fuels, however, is inadequate. Coal is of poor quality, while petroleum production is far below present needs. Traditionally, Brazil's principal source of wealth has been its land. The rich clay soil of the northeastern coastal strip and the red loam of the southern plateau have made Brazil a leading producer of tropical and sub-tropical plantation crops since the sixteenth century. And after more than 400 years, three-fourths of the land has yet to be turned to plow or pasture. Much of the unused area is comprised of steep, eroded slopes and of dense tropical forests, but enormous stretches of arable land in the central-western region are still awaiting settlement.

One of Brazil's most distinctive features is its population, which is an uneven blending of three major strains of the human race. While by no means all Brazilians are of mixed blood, the fusion of European, African, and Amerindian (originally from Asia) has proceeded farther in Brazil than in any other area. Perhaps even more striking than the degree of miscegenation is the success of the Brazilian experiment in racial democracy. It is unrivaled in the Western Hemisphere.

The Brazilian census ignores race but distinguishes four colors in the population: white, brown, black, and yellow. The white segment, made up of persons of predominantly European ancestry and others accepted as such, comprise about 60 per cent of the total population. The browns are mostly mixed-bloods, and constitute well over one-fourth of all Brazilians. Approximately 10 per cent are identified as blacks, the descendants of Negro slaves who once represented the largest ethnic element of Brazilian society. The yellow category is comprised almost entirely of Japanese immigrants and their descendants; it accounts for less than 1 per cent of the total. Gilberto Freyre, a leading authority on miscegenation in Brazil, believes that Brazil, in some areas at least, is developing a new ethnic type similar to that in Polynesia. At the same time, he and most other authorities agree that the Brazilian population is gradually becoming whiter, or more "Aryan," as it becomes more mixed. In the absence of new infusions of African blood in more than a century, the Negro population is slowly being absorbed into the mulatto segment, while the white element is growing in absolute numbers through continued, though minor, immigration from Europe and by the passing of fairer mulattos into the white category.

Despite the high degree of racial tolerance of which the Brazilians are proud, there is discrimination and lack of full equality between ethnic groups in Brazil. By and large, the whiter an individual's skin, or the more European his physical characteristics, the greater his opportunities and the higher his standing on the social scale. But "whiteness" is determined as much by a person's activities, dress, manner, and education as by his color. A man who conforms to the popular stereotype of "white" is apt to be considered white, regardless of his skin tone. Mixed-bloods and even persons of unmixed African descent who combine native talent and ambition with education are not barred from high position in society, government, business, or the church, but the percentage of the colored population which achieves such positions is still extremely small.

After more than four centuries, the overwhelming majority of the people in Brazil continue to live within a relatively short distance of the sea. In 1970, more than 20 per cent of all Brazilians resided in the band of states from Maranhão in the north to Rio Grande do Sul in the south. Only one of these states—Minas Gerais—has no seacoast; and in nearly all of the coastal states the largest cities and heaviest concentrations of rural population are well within one hundred miles of the Atlantic. The situation in Brazil today is somewhat comparable to that of the United States at the time of independence. Although isolated islands of settlement have existed far inland since late colonial days, the interior is still thinly populated. In the four southern states in recent decades there has been a fairly steady movement of the line of permanent settlement inland, as prime agricultural land closer to the coast has been pre-empted or exhausted. In the Northeast, however, where the immediate hinterland has poor soils and an unattractive climate, most of those with sufficient resources and ambition to migrate usually seek the promise of a better life in or near the urban industrial centers of the South and East. The others remain on the land where their families have lived for generations or crowd into the mushrooming port cities on the hump of Brazil. Only since the transfer of the national capital to the central plateau of Goiás in 1960 has there been a deliberate, political effort to induce large numbers of people to move from the seaboard to the central-western frontier. But despite official encouragement of the "March to the West," migration from rural areas to the cities throughout Brazil continues to be much greater than from the coast to the interior.

With more than 100 million people, Brazil is emerging as one of the giants of the world community. One out of every three Latin Americans is Brazilian. There are two Brazilians for every Mexican, some four for every Argentine, and about a dozen for every Cuban. Brazil ranks eighth in population among the nations of the globe, and none of the top seven—China, India, the Soviet Union, the United States, Indonesia, Pakistan, and Japan—equals Brazil's annual growth rate of nearly three per cent. It is likely that another century or more must pass before the number of Brazilians can compare with the masses of humanity found in China and India, and for at least another two generations the population of Brazil will remain smaller than that of the Soviet Union or the United States. But at present growth rates Brazil should require only one generation to overcome the numerical gap separating it from Japan, Pakistan, and Indonesia. Brazil already has a larger population than any Western European power. This fact receives a great deal more attention in Brazil than does the nation's status in comparison with the developing countries of Asia. Brazilian spokesmen take pride in pointing out that Brazil is first among Latin nations; that it has long since surpassed tiny Portugal as leader of the Portuguese-speaking community; that it has far more people than Italy; and that it has more Roman Catholics than France and Spain combined. It seems destined, moreover, to outstrip all Latin Europe in numbers before the end of the century. By that time, even by conservative estimates, the population of Brazil should approach 200 million.

Few Brazilians are alarmed by the population explosion, for Brazil is still one of the sparsely settled regions of the globe. Its average of close to thirty persons per square mile is comparable to that of Kansas. Throughout its history, Brazil has been plagued with a shortage of manpower, while its enormous empty areas were apparently capable of absorbing almost unlimited numbers. The high rate of growth in recent years has not basically altered this situation. Under the circumstances, there is virtually no pressure for a reduction in the birth rate or for restrictions on the flow of immigration into Brazil. Rather, a continuous rapid expansion of society is regarded as inevitable and highly desirable. It is widely held that the future contribution of the increased population toward national development more than compensates for the very real immediate problems of accommodating the rising numbers of new citizens. The present generation in Brazil tends to equate a large population with national greatness.

The great majority of Brazilians are convinced that their country is destined to become a world power and that this destiny will be achieved within a short time. The foregoing glimpse of Brazil's resources suggests the basis for such optimism. Clearly, the raw ingredients necessary for great power status are to be found in more generous quantities in Brazil than in any other country of Latin America. But mere possession of the ingredients of power does not guarantee that Brazil must inevitably soon emerge as a leader of the international community. Generalizations about Brazil's actual and potential assets in almost every category must be rigidly qualified. National totals and per capita averages mask enormous discrepancies in the disposition of physical and human resources within this vast nation. Over the short term at least, the difficulties in overcoming these discrepancies appear nearly as monumental as the resources themselves.

The very size of the country and the population boom that encourage Brazilian aspirations compound the difficulties inherent in the effort to transform Brazil into one of the powerful nations of the world.

Brazil has long been known as a land of extreme contrasts and contradictions. Pessimists have called it a land of unlimited impossibilities. Certainly a great deal in Brazilian experience appears to justify their contention that each progressive step in one sector tends to increase the weight of inertia in another. The South on the whole is modern and the North remains traditional. Much of the potential wealth of the nation is in the interior, while the great bulk of the population is crowded into the coastal states. Rail and water transport are woefully deficient even for present needs. Crop surpluses and critical food shortages may occur simultaneously in neighboring states. Trucks have been used to carry iron ore worth less than the gasoline burned in transporting it. But the enormous distances involved raise the cost of an adequate national transportation system to prohibitive levels. Brazil has the most extensive industrial complex and the largest urban labor force in Latin America. It also has a rural populace larger than the total population of most other Latin American republics, and it remains the area's leading producer of a long list of plantation products. Coffee alone continues to be by far the largest single source of foreign exchange earnings. For decades rural Brazilians have been pouring into the cities in a rising flood. At the same time the number of those extracting a bare subsistence from the soil increases every year. Between 1960 and 1970, for example, the urban sector expanded by about 20 million persons, from 45 to 56 per cent of the total population. During these same years the rural population increased numerically by 2.6 million.

Education in Brazil reflects an almost identical paradox. Because of the phenomenal rate of population growth, a gradual decline in the percentage of illiterates is accompanied by a staggering increase in the absolute number of persons who can neither read nor write. Industry and modern agriculture require a literate populace. Yet, a larger number of Brazilians than ever before—about half of the adult population—is completely illiterate, and nearly a third of the children between seven and fourteen years of age have no school to attend. The bulk of those who are formally literate, moreover, has received less than three years of elementary training. The existence of this untrained mass poses a continuing problem for the nation's leaders and accounts for much of the current gap between reality and aspiration in Brazil.

The distribution of the population by age group is characteristic of the pattern found in most underdeveloped countries in the postwar period. Brazilian society is composed largely of young persons, for the high rate of population growth is due almost entirely to improvements in health and sanitation which have drastically reduced the incidence of infant mortality in the more densely settled areas of the country. The average life expectancy is still below fifty years of age. In 1950 less than 10 per cent of all Brazilians were over age fifty. At the same time, nearly 42 per cent of them were under age fifteen, while slightly over half the total was under twenty years of age. The preponderance of youth is now even greater than in 1950. This situation places a tremendous burden on the relatively small, economically productive, adult population, which must support the large proportion of children. It also taxes beyond present capacity the ability of government to provide educational facilities for minors, and strains the economy to the breaking point. Brazil is expected to provide as many new jobs each year as does the United States, with two and a half times as many people. One of the consequences is widespread underemployment, while there continues to be a shortage of technically proficient labor for industry.

Closely related to this situation are two other problems which challenge Brazil's leadership and the public at large; the so-called "revolution of rising expectations" that has swept through the middle and lower classes, and the legacy of inflation—a by-product of the postwar urgency for rapid economic development. With the spread of mass communications media in Brazil after World War II, the common people discovered that their traditional way of life could be changed, while alert politicians vied with each other in promising the masses greater social welfare, improved economic status, and enhanced personal dignity. At the same time, the forced-draft industrialization in which Brazilians take pride was largely financed until 1964 by inflation of the currency. During the preceding decade there had been at least a tenfold increase in the cost of living and a comparable rise in the cost of government services. Thus, while the clamor for a better life was becoming more strident, it was increasingly difficult for the individual to satisfy his personal desire for a higher living standard and for the government to satisfy mounting popular aspirations for "social justice." This dichotomy was at the heart of the political revolution of 1964, and has remained a prime concern of the administrations in power in Brazil since that time. . . .

While international economists have predicted happiness for Brazil and its rising gross national product, millions of its people do not share in the prosperity. The growth of the cities that Poppino described has also brought droves of poor people from rural areas into Rio or São Paulo in search of a job. The *favelas*, as the slum areas are called, ring the cities like rotting packing straw around a shiny gift. *Favelas* are called by different names in other countries—*callampas* (mushrooms) in Chile, or *barrios suburbanos* (ironically, suburbs) in Ecuador—but slums encircle almost all the major Latin American cities. Rural peasants flock to the cities, looking for a way to make some extra money or to break out of poverty. Those entering *favelas* can't always find a place to live even among the shacks; some of them camp out in abandoned buildings. The conditions of the *favelas* have become a hot political issue all over Latin America, with people asking for more armies to put down potential slum rebellions on one side, and those asking for more social justice for the *favela* dwellers on the other. So far, little has been done to change conditions in the *favelas*. Carolina María de Jesús wrote about her life in the *favelas* during the 1960's, and her book became a bestseller in Brazil. Part of her diary is excerpted here.

The *Favela*: City of Straw
By Carolina María de Jesús

May 23. I got up feeling sad this morning because it was raining. The shack is in terrible disorder. And I don't have soap to wash the dishes. I say "dishes" from force of habit. But they are really tin cans. If I had soap I would wash the clothes. I'm really not negligent. If I walk around dirty it's because I'm trapped in the life of a *favelado*. I've come to the conclusion that for those who aren't going to Heaven, it doesn't help to look up. It's the same with us who don't like the *favela*, but are obliged to live in one. . . . It doesn't help to look up. . . .

I made a meal. The grease frying in the pan was beautiful. What a dazzling display! The children smile watching the food cooking in the pans. Still more when it is rice and beans—it's a holiday for them.

In the old days macaroni was the most expensive dish. Now it's rice and beans that have replaced the macaroni. They've crossed over to the side of the nobility. Even you, rice and beans, have deserted us! You who were the friends of the marginal ones, the *favelados*, the needy. Just look. They are not within reach of the unhappy ones of the Garbage Dump. Who has not flown off is senhor cornmeal. But the children don't like cornmeal.

When I put the food on the table João smiled. He ate and didn't mention the black color of the beans. Because black is our life. Everything is black around us.

In the streets and shops I see the posters with the names of candidates for deputy. Some names are already known. They are the repeaters who have already failed once at the ballot boxes. But the people are not interested in elections. Our elections are just a Trojan Horse that appears once every four years.

The sky is beautiful, worthy of contemplation because the drifting clouds are forming dazzling landscapes. Soft breezes pass by carrying the perfume of flowers. And the sun is always punctual at rising and setting. The birds travel in space, showing off in their happiness. The night brings up the sparkling stars to adorn the blue sky. There are so many beautiful things in the world that are impossible to describe. Only one thing saddens us: the prices when we go shopping. They overshadow all the beauty that exists.

Theresa, Meryi's sister, drank poison. And for no reason. They say she found a note from a woman in her lover's pocket. It ate away her mouth, her throat, and her stomach. She lost a lot of blood. The doctors say that even if she does get well she will be helpless. She has two sons, one four years old and the other nine months.

July 8. I wasn't feeling well and went to bed early. I awoke because of the clamor in the street. I couldn't understand what they were saying because everyone was talking at the same time and there were many voices. All sorts of voices. I wanted to get up and ask them if they would mind letting people sleep. But I know I'd be wasting my time. All of them were drunk. Leila was giving her show. And their shouts didn't let the neighbors sleep. At 4 o'clock I began to write. When I wake up it's difficult to go back to sleep. I started thinking of this troubled life and of the words Brother Luiz gave us in his humble sermons. I thought: if Brother Luiz was married, had children, and earned the minimum wage, I would like to see if he would be so humble. He said that God blesses only those who suffer with resignation. If the Brother saw his children eating rotten food already attacked by vultures and rats, he would stop talking about resignation and rebel, because rebellion comes from bitterness.

I sent João to buy ten cruzeiros of cheese. He met Adalberto and told him to come and talk to me. That I had found some boards and was going to make a little room where I could write and keep my books. I went out in search of paper. There is little paper in the streets because that other poor soul is also picking it up. He sells paper, buys *pinga*, and drinks. Afterward he sits down and weeps silently. I was so sleepy that I couldn't even walk. Dona Anita gave me some candy but my paper only brought me 23 cruzeiros. When I got back to the *favela* João was reading a comic book. I warmed up the food and fed them. That noise at night that I heard: the women were gossiping that the men drank 14 liters of *pinga*. And Leila insulted a young man, and he beat her. They threw her on the ground and kicked her in the face. An act of the jungle. But when Leila drinks she annoys people. She even bothered Chiclet, a good Negro who lives here in the *favela*. He didn't want to touch her but she degraded him so much that he hit her with such force he broke off two teeth. That's why everybody now calls him "The Dentist." Leila's face swelled up so bad she had to take penicillin. Today is the day of the wailers. There is a *nortista* who lives here that when she drinks, burns up your patience. Her son took a lover. A woman who could be his grandmother. The future wife came to live with his mother. When the old lady drinks she gets nasty and argues. She never gave them any peace. So, he ran away with the woman. Now the old lady is wailing. She wants her son back.

It's 5 o'clock. José Carlos arrived. I'm going to change his clothes and take him to Gouveia's Store and buy him a pair of shoes. At Gouveia's he picked out his shoes. 159 cruzeiros. Senhor Gouveia let me have them for 150. José is happy. He watches people as they go by to see if they are noticing his new shoes.

When I got back to the *favela* I met Senhor Francisco. He loaned me his wagon and I went to look for boards. I put Vera inside the wagon. And José Carlos and Ninho came too. Going, it was easy. The wagon sped over the concrete as if it were automatic. I found all kinds of wood. I piled it in front and in back. I figured I'd have to carry it in two loads. What I have to do, I do. Without even thinking of the work involved. At the corner of Araguaia and Canindé there is a lot of mud and I ran into trouble because I was barefoot and my feet slipped in the mud. There was no way I could solidly plant them. I fell. A man appeared and pulled the wagon for me. He told me to steady the pile of wood. I thanked him and went on. Going over the streetcar tracks the boards fell off the wagon. José Carlos appeared, saw my troubles, and said:

"Why don't you rest? Now you have a man to help you."

I gave thanks to God when I finally got back to the *favela*. There was a woman waiting for me. She told me that João had hurt her daughter. She said that my son had tried to rape her two-year-old daughter and that she was going to tell everything to the Judge. If he did this, then the person who should lock him up is I. I wept.

I put José Carlos to bed and went out with João. I went to the court to see if there was a possibility they might lock him up. I had to take him out of the streets because now anything that goes wrong they'll say he did it. At the court a nice gentleman who was on duty told me to come back on the tenth because the ninth was a holiday. I left the court and took a streetcar because it was cheaper. At the end of the line João stood in the doorway of a bakery shop and sat down to rest a little. When I returned to the *favela* it was midnight. I was upset.

The music, architecture, and literature of Brazil all reflect an indelible African influence—a loose, lyrical happening unlike the stiff forms of Spanish culture. This selection describes, in a firsthand way, the effect of African influence on Brazilian folk religion, and the magnetism of the folk culture as it affects even the urban middle class.

Macumba: A Folk Religion

By Susan Berns Wolf

Macumba horrifies the Catholic priest. Its rituals incorporate African traditions, the ancient jungle Indian religions, as well as the trappings if not the teachings of Catholicism. Those who practice it use several indigenous psychotropic plants which induce trancelike states, visions, chants, and dancing that continues for hours. The macumba altars are covered with various bowls of liquid and many statues, ranging from tiny Buddhas to Virgin Marys and Catholic saints known for the hideous martyrdom of their deaths. Many strange, rootlike objects are strewn about.

Several years ago I accompanied an American acquaintance of mine, Danielle Padwa, and a Brazilian man to one of these macumba services. He was a citified *carioca* (from Rio de Janeiro) who was returning to the small town where he grew up, and he was almost embarrassed to take me to what he referred to as an uneducated gathering.

We entered a small, plain adobe chapel. The benches were wooden, the walls were cracked, and the room flickered with candles. As we passed through the door, an old woman blessed us by putting her hand in our hands and making a sign (not of the cross) in front of our faces. We were then led to the altar, which held all the small figures so oddly juxtaposed—a Virgin, a cheap doll from a penny arcade, a cupid, a Buddha, Saint Sebastian with arrows piercing his side, and a Saint Lucy whose eyes were placed on a platter that she held in her hands. My Brazilian friend was offered a sip from a wooden bowl containing a murky substance. I was offered a drink as well, but only pretended to take it. We were then led to our seats. The others, about forty people of all ages, men and women, all appeared to be Indian or at least a great deal Indian. They wore white, shapeless, thinly made robes, and their hair was disheveled.

Their eyes were staring and not seeing, at least not seeing the room itself. Someone started beating a drum, and everyone began to chant; the chanting got more frantic, and the congregation started to move, my friend along with it. He no longer looked so civilized; his posture was unfamiliar to me. Each person went into a frenzy of wild epileptic jerks, somewhat similar to what people at the revival churches do. My Brazilian friend was no longer an ally in this strange place, but someone who had come home. I knew I could never accept the city people as city people again. Those who came from the country still kept within them a strange secret place which responded to the ancient communality of their ancestors.

The Caribbean is too diverse for all its aspects to be treated adequately in this reader. This selection is intended to summarize the major differences that occur between the various islands and possessions that comprise the Caribbean, and also the few similarities that give this group of countries a unified character.

The Caribbean Community
By Robert Crassweller

From many points of view, this strange aggregate of lands and peoples appears to be characterized by large differences and contrasts and by a remarkable diversity. This is true even in the most elementary physical sense. The observer sees, instead of the small region generally evoked by the word "Caribbean"—a region containing neighborly islands and nearby mainland territories narrowly demarcated by water, as if the area consisted only of the Leeward and Windward Islands—vast spaces punctuated and bounded by widely separate island and land areas. Guatemala is more than 2,250 miles from Guyana, about the same distance that separates Washington and Los Angeles, or London and Damascus. Even within the smaller circle of the Commonwealth Caribbean, Jamaica in the center lies almost 800 miles from British Honduras in the west and more than 1,000 miles from Trinidad and Tobago in the east. The latitude of Georgetown, Guyana, is more than 1,350 miles south of that of Great Abaco in the Bahamas. . . .

Of all the formations that history gave to Caribbean life, two may be considered of supreme importance. The first is the colonial experience. . . . In this there has been a basic dichotomy, a polarization into what may be termed the northwest European and Iberian heritages. The latter was decisive in the Spanish Caribbean and the former in all other areas. The tremendous persuasion of heritage, and of the differences and divisions it generates, is seen in every social and human aspect of Caribbean life. Religion, race relations, social organization and hierarchy, the varying social skills applied to the problems of daily life, attitudes toward economic enterprise and political practice, receptivity to change, the nature of the ideal— in short, everything that relates to patterns of value— all find their spirit and formulation in colonial heritage.

The second important historical inheritance in the Caribbean, intimately related to the first, has been slavery. Again, in assessing impact, one is led to a cleavage or, rather, to two cleavages. The Caribbean as defined here may be divided in so far as slavery is concerned into the area that experienced the plantation economy as a way of life and the area that did not. The line between them runs northward and westward along the shore of Central America. To the east of that line, encompassing the Guianas and all the Caribbean island nations and colonies, is what Charles Wagley has described as "plantation America: a culture sphere." Here came those anonymous thousands and hundreds of thousands of Africans so diverse in their tribal and regional origins that slaves on one Caribbean island often could not communicate with their counterparts on another island within sight of the first—the Africans who created, unwillingly and unknowingly, the structure and sociology of the Carib-bean. To the west of the line, in Central America, lies an entirely different culture area, in which slavery was a minor influence in comparison to that of a large indigenous Indian population.

And, when slavery ended in the nineteenth century, its functions were to some extent taken over by yet another source of Caribbean variation—the system of indentured labor that brought to Guyana and Trini-dad, over a span of four decades, almost 400,000 hardworking and prolific East Indian immigrants.

Other evidences of dissimilarity are conspicuous. Racial diversity is one of these. Much of the Caribbean is still distinctively African. But in Guyana the East Indian strain is now one-half of the population, while in Trinidad and Tobago it is more than one-third. Guatemala is one-half pure-blooded Indian. Surinam has extensive Hindu and Moslem populations whose origins were in Java and the other East Indian islands. Mulatto and mestizo mixtures, subtle in their degrees and variations, are found everywhere. Small groups of pure white derivation appear more numerous than they really are. Levantine strains are widely distrib-uted, and so are the small Chinese minorities. . . .

Another consequence of the multiplicity of in-digenous and imported peoples and the intricacy of their historical experience is that diversity of tongues that even today is an important barrier to Caribbean unity. Wide areas have always spoken English or Spanish. French is the language of Martinique and Guadeloupe and of Haiti as well, although in that per-plexing country (and also to some extent in other areas where the French colonized) the popular lan-guage is the combination of French vocabulary and West African grammatical patterns and verb conjuga-tions that is known as Creole. In Guatemala more than fifteen variants of the Maya-Quiche dialects are spoken by perhaps 30 per cent of the population. In the more racially mixed Caribbean countries, enclaves may be found here and there, not only of well-known languages like Portuguese and Chinese but also of such exoticisms as Hindi, Urdu, Tamil, and Telegu.

Local patois, archaic and eclectic and impenetrable as tropical undergrowth, exist in many countries, including those of the Commonwealth Caribbean, and occasionally find their way from the public market and the cockpit into national literature.

Every form of economic diversity is equally apparent in the Caribbean. Agriculture predominates in the region as a whole, but it may be the traditional sugar agriculture of Cuba and Barbados and the eastern Dominican Republic and many a smaller island, or the mountainside coffee agriculture of the Central American highlands, or the small-plot mixed agriculture of the Cibao region in the Dominican Republic, or the banana agriculture of Panama, Costa Rica, the Windward Islands, and northern Honduras. In the midst of all this, Jamaica, Surinam, and Guyana, are, respectively, the first, third, and fourth producers of bauxite in the Western world; Trinidad and Tobago bases its economy on oil; Puerto Rico is industrialized to a degree that reduces agriculture to a secondary position; the Bahamas live on tourism and banking; Curaçao depends on refining imported petroleum; and Panama flourishes as an intrepôt trading and servicing center. And many a small island, devoid even of size, exists on little but hope and emigration.

These dissimilar economies yield correspondingly dissimilar results. Per capita gross national product, a not very precise tool of economic analysis that is tolerated for want of something better, is an astonishing $1,340 in Puerto Rico, the great economic success of the Caribbean. But three hundred miles to the west, in scrawny Haiti, it is only $70 and even that is guesswork.

Political and social characteristics reflect the underlying diversity as visibly as does economics. Costa Rica enjoys a functioning democracy based on a population that is 84 per cent literate; Haiti is hardly 10 per cent literate and recently endured a dictatorship as firm as any of the tyrannies in its long history of misfortunes. In the Dominican Republic there is one doctor for every 1,620 people, but at the other end of the same island, in Haiti, the doctor would serve no less than 14,980 people. Barbados, serene and steady in mood, almost totally literate, inherits political traditions that can be traced back in unbroken sequence to the House of Assembly that first sat in 1639, only twenty years after the initial meeting of the Burgesses in Williamsburg. But Guatemala, torn and violent, distressed. by factions and endless upheaval, only 38 per cent literate, finds its own unbroken historical sequence in the successive attempts at political unification of Central America in which it has participated with its neighbors since 1838: twenty-five separate formal efforts to find appropriate institutions of unions in 133 years, all of them fruitless. . . .

What then remains? What similarities, what common relevance can be shaped out of all this diversity? Why should one define the Caribbean as it has been defined here, and then write about it?

There are several justifications, several unities that harmonize the disparate elements, and these may be discerned on two levels. The first, and more obvious, is the level of appearance and emotional impact, for at first glance the sea-scattered profusion of the Caribbean does have a kind of common identity. Perhaps romantic imagination is the integrating element. The old language of adventure lives on in the place names—the Windward Passage, Port Royal, Balboa's Peak in Darien, mythical El Dorado, and, most of all, the Spanish Main and the visions it summons out of childhood. Nor is romantic imagination limited to the things of the past. New substance for it emerges from the politics of this decade, out of turbulence among the volcanos of Central America, Cuban intrigue, the aftermath of one colorful tyranny in the Dominican Republic and the recent demise of another in Haiti. Even the products and the flora of the lands—cocoanut palms by the sea, sugar cane moving under warm winds, the scarlet berries and white flowers of coffee trees approaching harvest, banana plantations astonishing in their sensuality—transcend the market place and find higher reality in a mythology of the tropics.

There is more to these assumptions of identity than mere imagination. There is indeed in the Caribbean the climate and mood and style of tropicality. There *is* the wide oceanic milieu of bright water and beach. There *is* the trade wind that blows over all things with unwavering constancy. There *are* the stabbing, crushing rains, walls of water that move across hill and valley with the firmness of a judgment, striking broad leaves and hot earth with a hissing crackle heard long in advance, like the oncoming of a cosmic scythe. There *is* a pace and tone of life, a curious blending of languor and passion, of excitement and unconcern, that announces the tropics. These felt sensations, crowding all about in the island Caribbean and in the lowland littoral, become attenuated in the Central American highlands, but even there the contrast with, say, Buenos Aires or Lima is so evident that no one would mistake the Caribbean reality.

The second level of unity exists beyond and beneath the panorama of imagination and sensation. There is unity of geography; all of the countries that are central to this study either border the Caribbean sea or are islands within it or, in the case of Guyana, Surinam, El Salvador and the Bahamas, are close by and maintain connections with the Caribbean nations proper. There are similarities of scale and of development that set these Caribbean countries apart from the larger and more technologically advanced nations to the north and the south of them. There is of course a conspicuous difference in size between Barbados, the smallest of the states considered here (with 166 square miles, it is only one-fifth of the area of Jacksonville, Florida, the second smallest independent country in the world, and the second least populous) and the largest, Guyana, approximately the size of Minnesota. But all of them are quite distinguishable from Venezuela, Colombia, and Mexico, the smallest of which is more than four times the size of Guyana. There is likewise a considerable difference between the primitive development of Haiti and the sophisticated level that Puerto Rico has achieved. But in comparison to the same three mainland countries, the Caribbean nations as a group are seen instantly for what they are: an assortment of small countries that have not yet attained full participation either in the technological age or in sociopolitical modernity. . . .

A third strand of similarity is the relatively short distance that the Caribbean countries have advanced along the road to self-understanding and the discovery of entity. The independent nations among them are striving for the reality, as opposed to the juridical seal, of sovereignty. All are searching for the uniqueness and public personality and purpose that demarcate one people from another. . . .

Finally, the Caribbean nations are united in a particular and distinctive relationship to the United States as a paramount regional power, a relationship in which history and geopolitics and economic interdependence and political concern and psychological interplay are all combined in a subtle continuum. For the Caribbean countries, the relationship with the United States has always been an important concern, and present developments on the world scene as well as those that are foreseeable indicate that this concern will almost certainly become stronger and more intimate. For the United States the Caribbean relationship has also been traditionally regarded as significant in itself, an element in the national welfare. And by reason of the world role of the United States, the relationship may additionally be regarded as a component, by no means inconsiderable, of the global balance of power which it rightly deems necessary for the constructive discharge of its world role.

It has not been customary to conceive the Caribbean littoral and islands as a single unity, bound to the United States in a relationship of reciprocal significance, and relevant also to the North American power in terms of the international scene. Tendencies in the Caribbean and in the larger world, however, now indicate that the time for such a viewpoint has arrived. In no other way can urgent needs of the present, and even more the needs of the future, be well served.

———

The politics of Central America are thought to be more volatile than those of their southern neighbors; the area is noted for power squabbles, wars, and heavy nightstick dictatorships. Central America has been controlled for many years by U.S. money, through such corporations as the United Fruit Company, and family-style dictatorships like the Somozas in Nicaragua, where rule seems to pass from father to son.

The dream for Central America has always been unification into a single nation, but none of the plans in that direction has progressed very far. A Central American common market, thought to be the beginning of an overall Latin American common market, was established in the 1960's and is still in operation.

This selection summarizes the important political history of these countries. Pay special attention to the section on Panama. The canal is still an issue of sensitive importance to Latin Americans. The sixty-nine-year-old treaty by which the United States pays Panama for the use of the canal has come under severe criticism in Panama. Panamanians feel that their country should get more than the two million dollars a year they receive under the current plan, and they have always been incensed at the presence of the Canal Zone, a veritable U.S.-run colony in the middle of their country. Negotiations have been proceeding for several years to modify the treaty.

Central America: An Active Volcano
By Dwight B. Heath

The Central American republics celebrated the 150th anniversary of their independence in September, 1972. If the rhetoric of unity and progress was still as much in the air as ever, the spirit and the prospect of realizing either unity or progress in significant degree seemed as remote as a century ago.

In a world of massive power-blocs and super-blocs, small countries too often tend to be ignored unless a natural disaster or a deliberate play for attention briefly attracts journalists. In Central America, where seven countries have a population of less than 18

million and an overall area only slightly larger than
California, the problem of scale is especially acute.
Too many North Americans find it difficult to take
so-called "banana republics" seriously, and tend to
discuss recurrent coups, military dictatorships, guerrilla insurrections, and other forms of violence there
as having a specious "comic opera" quality. Similarly,
few look beyond those symptoms to the more fundamental and pervasive problems, such as widespread
poverty, disease, illiteracy, unemployment and underemployment, that characterize the entire area.

This is a volatile region in many senses—active volcanoes still occasionally change the face of the land;
many national borders remain in dispute; ethnically
diverse populations are often antagonistic; and political and economic rivalries are often deadly.

Although Central America lies entirely within the
tropical latitudes, differences in altitude are so great
that each country has a wide range of flora, fauna and
climate, as well as varying modes of life. Its inter-
continental position makes it important to many kinds
of scientists, although contemporary developments
there often tend to be ignored among current events
on the world scene. Botanists and zoologists enjoy
studying a remarkable variation in life-forms within a
limited area. Archeologists are busily tracing styles,
techniques and cultural motifs from both centers of
pre-Columbian American high civilization, Meso-
america in the north, and the Andes to the south.
Linguists and ethnographers are only beginning to
analyze in detail the rich variety of cultural and symbolic systems that persist in the vast areas that are still
remote from cities and roads.

Even the Spanish conquistadors paid little attention
to Central America, which did not offer either great
mineral wealth or large concentrations of Indians who
could be dominated to provide cheap labor. Because
of the economic poverty of most of the area and its
people—at least in comparison with more densely
populated areas to the north and to the south—they
were more neglected than exploited. The entire area
(except Panama) was governed by the *Audiencia* of

Guatemala, and many of the controversies over present-day national boundaries date back to the imprecise delimitation of *provincias* during the colonial period.

Independence from Spain was neither sought nor actively earned by Central Americans, but it came with the general collapse of imperial control throughout mainland Spanish America. During the ensuing century and a half, the independent republics have made occasional attempts at confederation and other forms of union, but with little success. All of the area that had comprised the captaincy general of Guatemala under Spanish rule was incorporated in the short-lived Mexican Empire of 1822. When it fell apart, the southern states stayed together as the United Provinces of Central America from 1823 to 1825; even after that experiment in confederation failed, the idea of federation persisted until 1839. The five separate republics established at that time have persisted, despite sporadic attempts throughout the last century by strong political leaders to reunite them under the banner of liberalism or conservatism.

In recent decades, political uncertainty and economic confusion have been characteristic of each country much of the time, but not until 1955 was federation again proposed as a long-range goal. At that time, the Organization of Central American States (ODECA) was established as a symbolic focus of unity; based in San Salvador, it has accomplished little in the way of cultural or economic integration, much less political union. A Central American Common Market (CACM), founded in 1962, appears to be on the verge of dissolution even before it achieves its preliminary goal of constituting a customs union.

In this article, I am using the term "Central America" in the geographical sense, which is more inclusive than customary political usage. Whereas the five nations of Costa Rica, El Salvador, Guatemala, Honduras and Nicaragua are often collectively referred to as "the Central American republics," it seems appropriate in this context to include some reference to the current history of British Honduras and Panama, countries to the north and south respectively, which are rarely treated in discussions of North or South America.

Central America, in this sense, has a population of nearly 18 million and one of the highest rates of population growth in the world. Even so, the population is still irregularly distributed throughout the area. The hot humid Caribbean lowlands are everywhere sparsely settled; the central highlands are most densely populated, and the Pacific lowlands vary demographically, but tend in each country to be intermediate between the other regions. The composition of the population also varies. The majority in British Honduras are descendants of black slaves (sometimes called "Bush Negroes" or "Black Caribs"). Nearly one-half of Guatemala's population are Indians who retain their native languages, costume, social organization and many other aspects of culture. The people of Costa Rica, whether appropriately or not, generally pride themselves on their "pure white" ancestry. In isolated areas, scattered Indian, black, and mixed populations reflect a variety of culture histories, but most of them have little contact with the administrative or commercial systems even within their own countries. Throughout the rest of Central America, the majority of the people are mestizos (called *ladinos* in Guatemala), whose physical features and cultures reflect their combined Spanish and Indian ancestry.

The economies of these nations are dominated by agriculture, which occupies more than half of the labor force, and comprises nearly 80 per cent of the exports. The combined patterns of *latifundismo* and monoculture are accompanied by typical problems of underdevelopment. Specifically, large landholdings monopolized by a few mean that the majority are tenant farmers or small-scale peasant cultivators, whose per capita annual income rarely reaches $300. National dependence on one or two crops means not only that a drought or blight can disrupt the entire economy, but that minor fluctuations in the world commodity market (over which no Central Americans have any significant control) can significantly affect the budget of the nation and all its people. Few North Americans consider what a drop of just one cent per pound in the price of coffee means to a country like Guatemala or El Salvador, where over 60 per cent of the foreign currency income derives from that crop. In Costa Rica and Honduras, similar problems derive from a nearly 50 per cent reliance on bananas and a 30 per cent dependence on coffee.

Coupled with large-scale agricultural production for export is the pattern of underproduction of basic food-stuffs. Costa Rica, for example, imports both rice and beans, staples in the popular diet, while exporting thousands of tons of coffee and bananas.

A brief summary of the major political and eco-nomic events of the last three years will illustrate both the causes and the effects of some of the salient social problems that are shared by the people of Central America.

British Honduras

British Honduras, although geographically part of the Central American isthmus, shares little with the other countries there. Although some Guatemalans still belligerently lay claim to it as the stolen province of Belize, its people and their culture reflect a very different orientation that has prevailed since the terri-tory was proclaimed a British colony in 1862. Peopled largely by the descendants of African slaves and Maya and Carib-speaking Indians, the official language is English and insofar as the country looks outward at all, it is more closely linked with the Caribbean islands than with its Spanish-speaking neighbors. The major-ity of the population live in the few towns along the coast; the rest of the country is heavily forested, and there are virtually no roads. The major exports, timber and chicle, go to distant industrialized countries, and imports are few. There was never any question of British Honduras joining the Central American Com-mon Market but, rather, since 1968 British Honduras has been a member of the Caribbean Free Trade Area.

British Honduras was briefly spotlighted early in 1972, when armed forces from the United Kingdom staged "training maneuvers" off the coast, which were widely interpreted as a show of strength to dissuade two very different constituencies, both of which have been vocal in recent years in their opposition to continued British control. A number of Guatemalans, including the incumbent administration, have been calling for the "return" of that area, while the most vocal spokesmen among the British Hondurans themselves have recently been calling for the independence that was promised to them some time ago. There was no international incident, and the rest of the world paid little attention.

Guatemala

Guatemala has continued to be rent by domestic unrest, with extremists on both the right and the left routinely turning to kidnapping, murder, and other tactics of urban terrorism. In the three-way presidential election of 1970, Carlos Arana Osorio won a plurality of the votes, but his 43 per cent did not constitute a majority. Few were surprised when he was elected by Congress, but some were surprised at the moderation he showed for several months after his inauguration in August. The leftist Rebel Armed Forces (FAR) soon claimed credit (or blame) for events that focused the attention of the world briefly on Guatemala: the kidnapping of a United States government employee, and the kidnapping and murder of the ambassador of West Germany. A state of siege was imposed, meaning limited martial law, with the suspension of certain constitutional guarantees. West Germany broke diplomatic relations with Guatemala, but foreign aid from the United States and various loans from international agencies were not cancelled.

Throughout 1971, the state of siege was continued, ostensibly in response to continued internal disorder. Censorship of the press increased, as did tensions between the church and the state, when several foreign clerics were deported whose crime of "political intervention" consisted of promulgating an appeal for a "cease-fire in the undeclared civil war." A short-lived strike by university students and faculty in protest against the state of siege was broken when the administration threatened to revoke the jealously guarded autonomy of the university. Economic and technical aid from the United States and from the World Bank continued, and some economic gains were achieved. West Germany negotiated the resumption of diplomatic relations, and former leftist President Jacobo Arbenz Guzmán died, having lived in exile since his overthrow in 1954.

The state of siege continued in 1972, but did not stem the episodic violence of Castroite and/or Maoist urban guerrillas, which was often matched by retributive violence on the part of rightist vigilantes who call themselves the Organized Nationalist Armed Movement (MANO).

El Salvador

El Salvador is the smallest and most densely populated country in Central America, and the only one without a Caribbean coastline. Nevertheless, it has also become the most highly industrialized member of CACM [Central American Common Market].

During recent years, however, El Salvador has continued to suffer from the undeclared war that has not yet been resolved with neighboring Honduras. Ambitious and industrious Salvadorans had long emigrated across the vaguely defined border into sparsely populated Honduras, where their economic success was resented by poorer local people. The open warfare that erupted in June, 1969, was unfortunately dismissed by uninformed outsiders as an absurd "soccer war," because hostilities erupted immediately following Honduras' defeat by El Salvador in a crucial soccer match. Details of the fighting are still not altogether clear, but deaths undoubtedly numbered in the thousands, and property destruction was considerable in an area where any waste is a luxury. A cease-fire was arranged by the Organization of American States in July, but the tiny unarmed OAS peace-keeping team was unable to prevent sporadic fighting across the 3-kilometer demilitarized zone that was proclaimed. The Pan American Highway was closed at the border—not to all traffic, but to traffic originating in either of the contesting countries. Similarly, mail and telephone service between the unfriendly neighbors was suspended for more than a year, while negotiations dragged on intermittently.

President Fidel Sánchez Hernández proclaimed a limited land reform as part of the continuing policy of "controlled revolution" that has been espoused by a succession of military leaders. Even this modest reform was strongly opposed by the businessmen and landlords who dominate much of the national economy, and by extreme rightists within the ruling military clique.

The elections of March, 1972, appeared important inasmuch as all 52 seats of the Legislative Assembly were at stake. A proposed coalition among the opposition parties did not work out, so Arturo Armando Molina of the incumbent National Conciliation party (PCN) won a plurality in the four-way race, and was elected by the Congress. A coup staged by General José Alberto Medrano (the defeated Independent Democratic United Front candidate) was aborted in March; José Napoleón Duarte (another defeated presidential candidate, of the Christian Democrats) was also implicated, but won widespread sympathy because of the heavy-handed actions of the army and police who seized him in the home of the Venezuelan ambassador.

Honduras

Honduras is at least as much a victim of the continuing hostilities as is El Salvador. Other events of 1971 were the precipitous promulgation of agrarian reform (although the law seems to have been effectively blocked in terms of application in the countryside), and an agreement by the United States to return the Swan Islands (in the Caribbean) to Honduran sovereignty after years of leasing.

Although dissatisfaction had been voiced on many

sides before, Honduras, the least industrialized country in CACM, was the first to withdraw formally from the so-called common market, in January, 1972, and she took no part in the conferences that were held that June in the hopes of revising and reviving it.

The elections of 1972 were imminent before President Oswaldo López Arellano decided not to succeed himself: Ramón Ernesto Cruz of the Nationalist party won over Jorge Bueso Arias of the Liberal party. The March election was marred by an exceptional demonstration of lack of confidence on the part of the several minority parties; their boycott was so effective that barely half the electorate voted, despite universal and compulsory suffrage. Cruz's six-year incumbency, begun June 6, was agreed to only when he accepted Bueso's "national unity plan," whereby the seats in the legislature were divided equally between the major parties. The bipartisan "unity plan" was ignored, and Cruz was not a powerful administrator. On December 4, armed forces spokesmen justified their bloodless coup as necessary to rescue the nation from "its chaotic situation." Installed as President for the remaining five years of the term was Commander of the Armed Forces Oswaldo López, who had been an unelected President before, having led successful coups in 1956 and 1963.

Border skirmishes with El Salvador continued, even while talks were resumed, in San José, Costa Rica. United States recognition of Honduran authority over the Swan Islands was confirmed by treaty in 1972, an event that had enormous symbolic value. The country mourned her ambassador to the United Nations, former President Ramón Villeda Morales, and suffered another critical deficit in balance of payments throughout the year, despite several loans from international agencies.

Nicaragua

Throughout much of 1971 and 1972, elaborate machinations laid the groundwork for the continuity of the Somoza machine, with a nod in the direction of democratic forms. [The Somoza family had run the country for decades.] President Anastasio Somoza Debayle was forbidden, by the constitution, to succeed himself. He and leaders of his Nationalist Liberal party agreed with the Conservatives to have Congress call a constitutional convention and then dissolve itself, leaving Somoza free to rule by decree until the convention actually met. At that time, he was to resign in favor of a junta (comprising two Liberals and one Conservative), thereby becoming eligible for candidacy in the 1974 election. A cynical observer might snicker at this as a transparent ruse, since members of the Somoza family have won elections by overwhelming majorities for almost 40 years—sometimes by more votes than there are voters! A slightly less cynical observer might express some gratification, since even such a gesture toward local and world opinion would have been considered a superfluous nicety only a few years ago. Four minor parties opposed the agreement, but, like the short-lived student protests, they got little attention at home or abroad, and did not interfere with the smooth operation of the plan.

At a time when most member nations were threatening to withdraw, Nicaragua spoke strongly in favor of reforming the Central American Common Market in order to benefit the deficit countries. With respect to inter-American relations, 1972 saw the withdrawal of a vestige of United States "big-stick diplomacy" in Nicaragua, just as in Honduras. The Bryan-Chamarro Treaty was formally terminated, a gesture of immense symbolic importance. Even though there had never been any move to invoke the treaty dating from 1916, pride in national sovereignty was affected by United States relinquishment of the treaty's grant of rights for building an inter-oceanic canal, establishing a naval base, and so forth. The specter of a different kind of imperialism briefly chilled some Nicaraguans when United States billionaire Howard Hughes visited Managua briefly; nothing has yet come of the rumors that he might buy the national airline.

Costa Rica

Costa Rica is a country proud of her pacific and orderly political history. In a sense, that is a recent phenomenon, dating only from the revolution of 1948 which brought upstart José Figueres Ferrar of the National Liberationist party to power. That same "Pepe" Figueres, heading the same party, was elected to the presidency in February, 1970, over Mario Echandi Jiménez, of the National Unification party, and three other candidates of minor parties. Schooled in the United States and fluent in English, Figueres has long been treated in this country as an "elder statesman" on behalf of free enterprise and democratic forms in Latin America. That misunderstanding engendered another, so that, in his own country, he was believed to have strong connections in Washington. At a time of shrinking United States aid and investment abroad, however, he was unable to deliver the kind of support required to back up money that had been flooding from the printing presses in recent years, and so he turned to the Communist countries in order to broaden the market for his country's major exports, bananas and coffee.

In 1972, Costa Rica reestablished diplomatic relations with the Soviet Union, the first Central American nation to do so. It is not yet clear how much substance there may have been behind the sensationalized exposé of a plot against President Figueres that was supposedly planned by the United States Central Intelligence Agency, but he shrugged it off as rumor and remains in office.

There even seems to be a growing rapprochement between the Liberationists and the Republicans on the political front. Economic problems continue to worsen, and the mounting balance of payments deficit led President Figueres to impose a surcharge on all imports—in direct violation of the rules of the Central American Common Market. Although Costa Ricans have never been enthusiastic about the common market, when CACM was threatened with collapse, goods imported from member nations were exempted from the surcharge.

A number of loans were made available by national and international agencies, especially for potable water systems and for agricultural and vocational training. Former President Rafael Calderón Guardia died in 1971, and President Figueres declared that the long period of hostility with Nicaragua (a "cold" war has survived since the brief "hot" war of 1955) should be considered ended. Those who thought the old fighter might have grown soft over the years were treated to an unusual spectacle when President Figueres, tommy-gun in hand, directed a group of policemen who thwarted an international airplane hijacking by shooting up the plane when it landed for refueling near the capital. The dubious distinction of having the world's highest rate of population growth seems to have passed from Costa Rica in 1972, which offers promising long-range implications for the long-awaited renewal of economic growth.

Panama

Panama, like British Honduras, is part of Central America in a geographical sense, but does not share a common history with the five other isthmian republics, nor is she economically linked with them in any significant degree. During the colonial period, she was administratively linked with New Granada, unlike the northern provinces which were governed from Guatemala, and only in 1903 did she become independent of Colombia.

The Panama Canal links the country's few cities with markets halfway around the world, at transportation rates cheaper than those overland to her Central American neighbors; the Inter-American Highway remains unpaved in Panama and the southern half of Costa Rica. Agriculture occupies most of the labor force, but major sources of revenue are services and commerce in connection with the canal.

During the past few years, a variety of machinations have provided a superficial appearance of democratic forms, while Panamanian political reality is markedly dictatorial. Since he came to power in a bloodless coup in 1968, General Omar Torrijos Herrera has held a tight rein, through strict control of the press, vigorous opposition to the church (including the exiling of some clerics who voiced their opposition), virtually continuous use of the "state of siege" provisions that suspend constitutional rights "in time of national emergency," cancellation of the 1970 elections, consistent opposition to the formation of cooperatives and other grass-roots organizations, and so forth.

In August, 1972, a new constitution made the presidency a largely ceremonial post, vesting power in the newly created Chief of Government. In effect, this confirmed the status quo, making President Demetrio Lakas legally a figurehead for Chief of Government Torrijos. The United States granted a huge loan for completion of the Pan American Highway, across the swampy Isthmus of Darien. Negotiations between the two countries were reopened concerning the present Canal Zone and the projected new sea-level canal. Few North Americans seem to appreciate the emotional and symbolic significance of the Canal Zone that cuts all the way across that small republic, as a 10-mile-wide quasi-colonial enclave. In an unusual move, to focus world attention on her 69-year-old grievances, Panama has invited the United Nations Security Council to meet there in March, 1973, when Aquilino E. Boyd, Panama's chief delegate, will take his turn as president of the Council. If that does happen, United States diplomats may also have to face renewed Cuban claims to Guantánamo, and Puerto Rican claims for independence—challenges that are often voiced, but that may have special impact in a Latin American setting.

PART VIII.

THE SECOND CONQUEST

Introduction

While caudillos were still settling their grudges, and the great agrarian fiefdoms entrenched themselves across the land, a second conquest of Latin America began almost without notice in the late 1800s. United Fruit Company was eyeing the Caribbean, the British were playing Monopoly with Argentina, and countless ore plunderers, fruit pickers, grub stakers, cattle magnates, and railroad barons started looking at Latin America as a potential investment. These were not hopeful Spaniards with a cross and an empty pocket; these were the foreign capitalists with machines and money and economic theories, who brought Latin Ameria into the world of heavy industry, single-export economies, international debts, urban proletariats, and balance-of-payments deficits.

Latin America was no longer a simple duet between Spaniards and Indians, with a few blacks on the side— as the first excerpt, by James Scobie, shows. Buenos Aires, as one example, was filled with Italians, some Germans, and Englishmen; waves of immigrants brought European literature, art, music, and a whole new urban class to this exploding city. The money also began to come in, as Latin America moved from being a depleted gold producer for the Spanish crown to a premier mineral producer for the corporations of the United States and industrial Europe. The second selection, by Jerome Levinson and Juan de Onis, shows how each major country was tied to the capitalists, usually producing only one major product. With the money came some technicians, and the beginnings of a Latin American middle class, a class that was supposed to jolt the society out of its feudal mold—with a few rich at the top and many poor at the bottom.

The Andean countries and the Caribbean nations were not as drastically affected by the second conquest, but none of them completely escaped the effects of the changes. Just as the town, the *encomienda*, the colonial bureaucracy, and the Church were the legacy of Spanish authority, so the large city, the blue-collar worker, the middle-class technocrat, and the foreign investor were the new symbols of industrial authority.

Latin American countries found their capital cities inundated with foreign money; their roads, bridges, and railroads built by outsiders; their economies created and then altered to fit the needs of the factories abroad. Argentina became a cattle farm, Chile a copper mine, Central America a banana plantation, and Venezuela an oil well—all at the convenience of U.S. or British corporations. Latin America was still the dead man's gold tooth.

The social structure that had survived the revolution of 1810 also made it through the industrial revolution. Some landowners became industrialists, some middle-class people could fashion a respectable living for themselves, and the upper classes retained opulent control. But while the first revolution had threatened Spain's power but not its values, the arrival of industry in some ways traumatized the Spanish spirit. In Mexico the government turned against the piety of its people with a fierce anticlericalism that burned churches and punished priests for practicing the outlawed Catholicism. The passage from Graham Greene's novel *The Power and the Glory* shows the strength of the government's repression and the Mexican people's reaction to it. While the Church retained its stronghold in most other countries, and the people continued to pray and to believe even in Mexico, the emergence of anticlericalism is just one example of the questioning and wrenching of the Latin American personality inherited from Spain.

If there was a new philosophy to challenge the religious mysticism of the Spanish, it was liberalism—not of the kind that we understand today, but rather a belief in a technical, secular utopia. In places like Mexico and Argentina, the ideas of Comte, of social salvation through material progress, grew in power as that of the saints shrank. Like almost everything else in Latin America, liberalism was elevated to the plane of belief, and in Mexico investment was described with the awe of a Catholic conversion, and the economists and technocrats were treated as priests. Liberalism was at its strongest in Mexico, where an explosive fervor surrounded the regime of Porfirio Díaz and his *científicos* (scientists). Díaz took over Mexico during the period following the popular regime of the Indian patriot Benito Juárez. He ruled the country for almost thirty years.

Díaz's dictatorship became a blueprint for many Latin American strongmen who later imitated him, but the popular enthusiasm for Díaz in Mexico was rarely equaled in other countries. As the excerpt by Lesley Byrd Simpson shows, he brought in money, investment, and industries, and the people put up with his police-state tactics. His regime was relatively uncontested because people didn't trust themselves to do any better. Besides, Díaz was turning Mexico into the only industrial power south of the Rio Grande, and his formula was repeated throughout the twentieth century.

Díaz's regime, ironically, ended in revolution—one of the two real revolutions, some say, ever to occur in Latin America (the other being the Castro revolution in Cuba). We will discuss the reasons for this revolution in the next part, but it has always been a puzzlement. How could what many people consider to be the only real social upheaval (except for Cuba) in the history of Latin America occur at the end of perhaps the most progressive dictatorship in Mexico's history? Perhaps there is a lesson here for the believers in the Alliance for Progress, who saw quick industrialization and prosperity—precisely the things that seemed to fuel the Mexican revolution—as a defense against the communist revolutionary threat.

The Díaz regime is one model for Latin American political life at the turn of the century, but there were also various attempts at democracy. Most of the countries had by this time developed political parties: usually the Church-oriented, landed aristocracy made up the conservatives; and the urban, industrial middle-class groups joined the liberals. In Ecuador, the battle between these two groups ended in various assassinations, and throughout Latin America, intermittent military intervention was already the rule. Even where democracy had a chance, the form of the politics was mocked by what actually happened. There were so many splinter groups, and so much switching of allegiances, that the notion of the political party was lost in chaos. Democracy seemed about as comfortable in most of Latin America as monarchy would have been in New England; and the Latin Americans themselves were comfortable with neither.

The overall political picture of Latin America in 1900 is worth remembering, especially for those who now believe that the continent is a vast powder keg, with Cuba as the match—or even for those who believe that slow political progress is taking place. At least on the level of politics alone, Latin America in 1900 was a remarkable rehearsal for Latin America of the 1960's—with Díaz playing the role of the Cuban dictator Batista, the Mexican revolutionary Emiliano Zapata of Castro; with the radicals, in Argentina sounding like today's Marxists in Chile; with the promise of industry pitted against the realities of an impoverished society; with the U.S. military invading the Caribbean; with a seemingly endless alternating current of dictatorships and democracies. Of course, the countries that have re-created these political events have changed, and many of the details are different. But the history of Latin American politics is a great cure for impatience—an idea often lost to observers who seem to vacillate endlessly between undiluted hope and undiluted despair, and who are fooled by both. Latin American politics seems most faithful to the Aztec philosophy—that history is an endless rolling hoop rather than a straight line to perfection.

Especially in Buenos Aires, the commercial capital of the day, the first non-Spanish immigrants began to trickle in about 1800. The news of the advantages and successes they found in Latin America must have influenced the wave of immigration that followed them during the industrial surge in the latter part of the century.

The New European Immigrant
By James Scobie

A sizable number of Europeans . . . reached Buenos Aires during the first half of the nineteenth century, most of them motivated by a thirst for adventure and fortune. Except for the several hundred families who arrived under colonization contracts in the 1820's, almost all possessed resources of their own. Many were younger sons of middle-class or wealthy families. Others were shopkeepers and tradesmen anxious for a new start or herdsmen and farmers who had heard of the opportunities in sheep raising. The great majority of the new arrivals were young men. Wives or sweethearts were occasionally sent for after the man had made good, but until the 1850's few families immigrated. Hardly any immigrants came with the intention of staying: to make a fortune and to return to their homeland was the common dream. Consequently emigration often exceeded immigration, and the ebb and flow of Europeans responded closely to depression or expansion, civil wars or peace, drought or plenty. Manual labor frequently provided the key to success. In the coastal region where the natives, wealthy or poor, considered the use of a shovel, plow, hammer, or trowel beneath their dignity, such work brought handsome wages. One traveler in the 1840's noted that Irishmen digging ditches on *estancias* in southern Buenos Aires received ten to twelve shillings per day—enough to buy a flock of fifteen hundred sheep with three weeks' labor. Wages for servants and construction workers, prices for dairy products and vegetables, profits from making shoes or repairing carriages followed a similar scale.

The Irish sheepherder, the English merchant, the French shopkeeper, the Italian river captain profited enormously. Thousands of their countrymen swelled the *porteño* population, added talents and labor to increase livestock production, and provided the services and products needed in the major urban center. Hundreds remained, married into creole families, and added their blood and culture to a nation in formation. Although their influence did not revolutionize Argentina, they provided Buenos Aires with a strength far beyond their numbers. The Irish and Basques, who laid the foundations for sheep raising, introduced more intensive use of the land, brought families and settlement to rural areas, and added an important export to *porteño* trade. At the northern and western edges of the city of Buenos Aires the first extensive use of the pampas' crop potential flourished under the care of foreigners—garden produce of fruits and vegetables and harvests of corn and wheat. The Genoese captains and their immigrant crews who built their own ships and carried most of the trade between river ports facilitated Buenos Aires' role as commercial emporium for the Río de la Plata. As for technical skills, Argentina in the nineteenth century still depended on foreigners as much as in 1607 when several Flemish millers were forcibly detained in Buenos Aires since only they could operate the town's one flour mill. Improvements in the packing of salted meat, processing of leather, and extraction of tallow came from French and English experts. And foreigners owned and operated almost all machinery and engines, which were usually located in the city of Buenos Aires.

Investments and commerce were also concentrated at the port of Buenos Aires. Argentina had exchanged the tutelage of Spain's administration for that of England's trade. Capital and credit provided the sinews for commercial expansion, and these came largely from London, the investment center of the nineteenth-century world. British commerce and shipping now succeeded where redcoats had failed. The invasions had revealed potential markets and raw materials, and special licenses to English merchants in 1809–10 stimulated trade. Although the British Foreign Office could not, because of England's alliance with Spain, grant official recognition to a rebellious Spanish colony, commercial houses at Liverpool and London were not hindered by such scruples. Even before San Martín was well launched across the Andes, the British community at Buenos Aires was the city's largest and most influential foreign group. . . .

Regardless of wrangles over political control or of autonomy versus strong central government, Argentina had to meet the European world in Buenos Aires. . . .

Along with immigrants, the nineteenth century also brought capital to Latin America; when railroads were built in Argentina, mines opened up in Chile, and ports expanded to handle the traffic in raw materials. This selection describes the coming of the capitalists, and their general impact on economic life.

The Invasion of the Dollar
By Jerome Levinson and Juan de Onis

The past century of Latin American history reveals a pattern. Development in a given area has typically begun with major foreign investments, bringing natural resources into production for sale to the industrialized markets of the West. In the nineteenth century the investors were primarily British financiers and entrepreneurs; since World War I, U.S. investors have gradually supplanted the British.

Chile's modern phase began with the mining of nitrates by the British, followed by U.S. investments in copper. Argentina became a major source of beef for Britain and grains for Europe through railroads and ports built by the British to open up the pampa. Cuba became the world's sugar bowl through U.S. investments. Foreign demand for coffee made Brazil and Colombia the world's largest coffee exporters, with production in local hands but marketing controlled by foreign traders. Venezuela came out of poverty and political anarchy through a bonanza in oil, developed by U.S. and British investments. Bolivia was drawn into the world economy by tin, with the ore transported on a British-built railroad to Pacific ports, where it was loaded aboard British ships to be carried to a smelter near London. The United Fruit Company made banana republics of Ecuador and the Central American countries. Panama's major natural resource—a roadway between the Atlantic and Pacific oceans—was developed by the U.S. Panama Canal Company. In more diversified fashion, but still through foreign investments, Mexico and Peru made their way into foreign markets with nonferrous metals, cotton, oil, and fishery products. This process brought Latin America, in a largely passive and dependent role, into the framework of Western industrial capitalism. It had a massive impact on countries that had been relatively isolated from modernizing change after the Spanish and Portuguese colonial enterprises lost their early creative impetus.

Although this form of development is open to the charge of exploitation, it changed economic conditions dramatically. The trade boom raised the export earnings of some countries from tens of millions to hundreds of millions of dollars in just a few years. European immigration moved into some areas even more rapidly than it had into the United States. An extraordinarily large share of the exchange earned by the new exports remained abroad in the hands of the foreign developers, but the capacity of the Latin American countries to import and borrow abroad rose sharply. Their greatly increased consumption, based on foreign products, opened up new avenues of internal commerce. Although this consumption was still confined to a privileged minority, economic expansion significantly enlarged the higher income sectors. Promoted by the new investments, the ports, railroads, sugar mills, mines, and banana plantations served as bases for the first Latin American attempts to form labor unions, gradually giving rise to a wage elite of organized workers. But as Latin America moved into the first stages of economic development a rift opened between the modern sectors and a backward but populous rural society.

The coming of capitalism shattered some of the old feudal ideas of hereditary power and landed gentry. The descendants of the conquerors, and the Spanish institutions like the Church, continued to be powerful, but something in their beliefs was threatened for the first time. In Mexico, for example, ideas of material progress and science began to influence the people. The Catholic Church was outlawed in Mexico, and there was a fierce anticlerical backlash there. This selection from Graham Greene's novel *The Power and the Glory* concerns the efforts of one priest, also a drunkard, to work underground, even though his religious activities were illegal. Greene's novel deals with the whole anti-Catholic era in the second half of the nineteenth century in Mexico, and he obviously believes that the people sympathized with the priests more than with the government. The incident fictionalized by Greene took place in the 1840's; by the time Porfirio Díaz came to power in the 1870's, Catholics were again allowed to practice their religion. But the implantation of the modern state dealt a serious blow to Spanish influence. Anticlericalism was not as strong in the rest of Latin America as it was in Mexico, but industrialization threatened the old traditions in other ways.

The Whisky Priest

By Graham Greene

. . . The lieutenant barked out: "Attention. All of you. Listen to me." The outer ring of police closed in, pushing the villagers together into a small group in front of the lieutenant: only the children were left free. The priest saw his own child standing close to the lieutenant's horse: she could just reach above his boot: she put up her hand and touched the leather. The lieutenant said: "I am looking for two men—one is a gringo, a Yankee, a murderer. I can see very well he is not here. There is a reward of five hundred pesos for his capture. Keep your eyes open." He paused and ran his eye over them: the priest felt his gaze come to rest; he looked down like the others at the ground.

"The other," the lieutenant said, "is a priest." He raised his voice: "You know what this means—traitor to the republic. Anyone who shelters him is a traitor too." Their immobility seemed to anger him. He said: "You're fools if you still believe what the priests tell you. All they want is your money. What has God ever done for you? Have you got enough to eat? Have your children got enough to eat? Instead of food they talk to you about heaven. Oh, everything will be fine after you are dead, they say. I tell you—everything will be fine when *they* are dead, and you must help." The child had her hand on his boot. He looked down at her with dark affection. He said with conviction: "This child is worth more than the Pope in Rome." The police leant on their guns: one of them yawned—the turkey-cock went hissing back towards the huts. The lieutenant said: "If you've seen this priest, speak up. There's a reward of seven hundred pesos. . . ."

Nobody spoke.

The lieutenant yanked his horse's head round towards them; he said: "We know he's in this district. Perhaps you don't know what happened to a man in Concepcion." One of the women began to weep. He said: "Come up—one after the other—and let me have your names. No, not the women, the men."

They filed sullenly up and he questioned them: "What's your name? What do you do? Married? Which is your wife? Have you heard of this priest?" Only one man now stood between the priest and the horse's head. He recited an act of contrition silently with only half a mind—". . . my sins, because they have crucified my loving Saviour . . . but above all because they have offended . . ." He was alone in front of the lieutenant—"I hereby resolve never more to offend Thee . . ." It was a formal act, because a man had to be prepared: it was like making your will—and might be as valueless.

"Your name?"

The name of the man in Concepcion came back to him. He said: "Montez."

"Have you ever seen the priest?"

"No."

"What do you do?"

"I have a little land."

"Are you married?"

"Yes."

"Which is your wife?"

Maria suddenly broke out: "It's me. Why do you want to ask so many questions. Do you think *he* looks like a priest?"

The lieutenant was examining something on the pommel of his saddle: it seemed to be an old photograph. "Let me see your hands," he said.

The priest held them up: they were as hard as a labourer's. Suddenly the lieutenant leant down from the saddle and sniffed at his breath. There was complete silence among the villagers—a dangerous silence, because it seemed to convey to the lieutenant a fear. . . . He stared back at the hollow stubbled face, looked back at the photograph. "All right," he said, "next," and then as the priest stepped aside: "Wait." He put his hand down to Brigida's head and gently tugged at her black stiff hair. He said: "Look up. You know everyone in this village, don't you?"

"Yes," she said.

"Who's that man, then? What's his name?"

"I don't know," the child said. The lieutenant caught his breath. "You don't know his name?" he said. "Is he a stranger?"

Maria cried: "Why, the child doesn't know her own name! Ask her who her father is."

"Who's your father?"

The child stared up at the lieutenant and then turned her knowing eyes upon the priest. . . . "Sorry and beg pardon for all my sins," he was repeating to himself with his fingers crossed for luck. The child said: "That's him. There."

"All right," the lieutenant said. "Next." The interrogations went on—name? work? married?—while the sun came up above the forest. The priest stood with his hands clasped in front of him: again death had been postponed: he felt an enormous temptation to throw himself in front of the lieutenant and declare himself—"I am the one you want." Would they shoot him out of hand? A delusive promise of peace tempted him. Far up in the sky a buzzard watched: they must appear from that height as two groups of carnivorous animals who might at any time break into conflict, and it waited there, a tiny black spot, for carrion. Death was not the end of pain—to believe in peace was a kind of heresy.

The last man gave his evidence.

The lieutenant said: "Is no one willing to help?"

They stood silent beside the decayed bandstand. He said: "You heard what happened at Concepcion. I took a hostage there . . . and when I found that this priest had been in the neighbourhood I put the man against the nearest tree. I found out because there's always someone who changes his mind—perhaps because somebody at Concepcion loved the man's wife and wanted him out of the way. It's not my business to look into reasons. I only know we found wine later in Concepcion. . . ."

If any one regime symbolized the Golden Age of Industry—with foreign money, strong national governments, and new ideas of materialism and progress—it was the reign of Porfirio Díaz in Mexico. Díaz came to power in 1870 and held virtual dictatorial sway over the country until 1910. He was a ruthless despot in many ways, but he also industrialized Mexico earlier and faster than any other Latin American government. Díaz's tactics and beliefs had great influence throughout the early twentieth century, as other countries scrambled to imitate the success of Mexico.

Díaz's government was followed by the revolution of 1910, a bloody ten-year affair that tore apart the nation's ruling class. People have speculated why the first real revolution in Latin America (as opposed to palace revolts and coups) since the wars for independence emerged from Porfirio Díaz; there are no clear answers. This selection—from Lesley Byrd Simpson's *The Rise and Fall of Don Porfirio*—characterizes the spirit of the time, the history of the Díaz regime, and the original rumblings that turned into revolution, a social revolution that preceded the Russians' by seven years.

Porfirio Díaz and Mexican Liberalism
By Lesley Byrd Simpson

The legend of Don Porfirio is full of magic. In all Mexico there is only one Don Porfirio. His name evokes the nostalgic longings of the disinherited who, since the Revolution of 1910, have been looking back on the Age of Don Porfirio much as Lot's wife looked

back on Sodom and Gomorrah. The good old days of
Don Porfirio have become a kind of cult, not limited
by any means to the ex-nobility, for the present de-
votees of the God of Industrialization recognize in
Don Porfirio the prophet who showed them the way
to the Promised Land. . . . For everyone of late feels
kindly toward Don Porfirio, although his most ardent
admirers, naturally, continue to be those who hope
that some day another Strong Hand will take over and
run the country more to their heart's desire. It is one
of the many charming inconsistencies of Mexico that
Porfirio Díaz, the military caudillo and bitter enemy
of Juárez [Benito Juárez, Indian leader who ruled
Mexico after liberating the country from foreign rule
under Maximilian], should have succeeded the Law-
giver of Oaxaca and ruled Mexico for a third of a
century as an irresponsible despot, under the cloak of
the liberal Constitution that Juárez and his devoted
company had fought so long to establish. . . .

Juárez and his Law had been rejected in favor of
rule by force, and the astonished conservatives suddenly found themselves presented with a dictator,
gratis. For the next thirty-four years they were to
enjoy the most efficient despotism ever seen in the
western hemisphere. Don Porfirio's slogan was "Bread
and the Club": bread for the army, bread for the
bureaucrats, bread for the foreigners, and even bread
for the Church—and the club for the common people
of Mexico and those who differed with him. . . .

Porfirio Díaz had the virtues of a great barbarian,
and he needed them. The lesser caudillos who had
elevated him had to be kept quiet, and they had to be
kept harmless. Unlike Juárez, Don Porfirio was not so
naïve as to expect his military chieftains to put their
country's welfare before their personal fortunes. Their
new master had the cunning of a Caesar Borgia. He
gave his generals little jobs and restored them to their
rightful place at the public trough; he kept them apart
and played them off against each other; he split the
army into small units and scattered them about the
country; but he did not trust it. For his immediate use
in terrorizing dissenters he organized a private army

of thugs, whom he called his *bravi* and who could be counted on to wreck newspapers and remove suspected opponents in their own way. The police, of course, could never track down the criminals.

The nation was suffering from its endemic plague of banditry. Don Porfirio's solution was to set up a national gendarmerie called the Rurales, recruited from the gunmen of the cities and from among the bandits themselves. They were given showy uniforms, good salaries, and the power to shoot on sight, and no questions asked. Into their capable hands was placed the task of making Mexico safe for Don Porfirio and his friends. Troublesome Indian caciques, striking workmen, indiscreet speakers and writers, and honest bandits disappeared into the noisome dungeons of the fearful old Belén Penitentiary, or were shot "while attempting to escape," an effective device known as the *Ley Fuga*. In the course of a few years Mexico became the best policed country in the world. It was ruled by martial law, without courts, and the Rurales loved to shoot.

As the years rolled by and Mexico lay quiet in her straitjacket, foreign capital was encouraged to come in; manufactures and agriculture flourished; railroads pushed their way south from the border; American miners reopened the ancient *reales de minas* of the Spaniards, and smelters began to belch their yellow fumes into the desert air. Silver, gold, copper, lead, and zinc flowed north to feed the rapidly expanding commerce and industry of the United States; and coffee, sugar, bananas, and henequen found a ready market abroad. In 1893, Don Porfirio's brilliant Minister of Finance, José Ives Limantour, funded the public debt at a reasonable rate of interest and balanced the national budget. Mexico was solvent! This feat was so close to being a miracle that Don Porfirio was hailed everywhere as the "Coming Man." Grumblers were quiet for once, or, if they had anything to say, they said it to themselves. For many years Mexico saw not a single pronunciamiento, and the *Pax Porfiriana* was a blessing that his country could appreciate meaningfully.

Like Santa Anna, Don Porfirio had to have appropriate monuments to his immortality. The capital was cleaned up and modernized; beggars and *léperos* were kept out of town; electric lights blinked, over the protests, to be sure, of the gas monopoly; streetcars clanged; and a rash of marble palaces broke out, the most hideous example of which is the bastard Palace of Fine Arts.

For the Creole aristocracy the dictatorship of Don Porfirio meant the return of the Silver Age. The hacienda reverted to the pure type of the feudal estate, with the terrible Rurales to call on in the event of trouble. Elegant carriages drawn by high-stepping throughbreds again paraded up and down the Paseo on Sundays. The ladies discarded the graceful Spanish mantilla for the *dernier cri* from Paris. Their sons were sent to France for an education and came back pattering the lingo of the *boulevardier* and scoffing at the barbarism of their own country. The best people went in for building houses in the villainous style of the Second Empire. I was shown through one of them by its proud owner, now reduced to taking in boarders. It was a museum piece of velvet draperies, pier glasses, marble tables, gilt, dazzling chandeliers, spindly chairs, artificial flowers, and stuffed birds. "Isn't it beautiful!" she exclaimed. "They don't build houses like this any more. *There is nothing Mexican in it!*" This good lady belonged to the class of which Charles Flandrau makes such kindly fun in his delightful *Viva Mexico!* Their ready hospitality, their reckless good living and charming manners were one of the pleasantest features of Creole life. Happy days were here again, and Don Porfirio would live forever.

The clergy awoke from their long nightmare and discovered that religion and the liberal dictatorship of Don Porfirio were not necessarily incompatible. The offensive laws of Juárez' day were discreetly ignored; religious schools and thinly disguised nunneries appeared; and should there be trouble the pious Doña Carmen Díaz could be counted on to patch things up with Don Porfirio, who was an indulgent husband. The ranks of the clergy were swelled by

Spanish, French, and Italian priests, until by the end of the régime they numbered some five thousand, against the pitiful five hundred of the dark days of Juárez. Only the native clergy grumbled.

If the dictatorship of Don Porfirio meant the return of the Silver Age for the Creoles and the clergy, for the foreigner it was the Golden Age. Mexico became "the mother of foreigners and the stepmother of Mexicans." The foreigner soon learned that he could buy justice and favors from the swollen and underpaid bureaucracy, which grew to include a large percentage of the literate population of the country. *Empleomanía*, the government-job mania, infected the whole middle class of Mexico. But the foreigner was king, for the new paradise was made possible by his money and industry, and the sweat of Mexican workmen. His factories and mines were rarely disturbed by strikes or similar unpleasantnesses, and, when they were, the Rurales, the army, and the judiciary saw to it that the malcontents gave no more trouble. Strikers were slaughtered by the score and by the hundred at the Cananea mines and the textile mills of Río Blanco. "You can't make an omelet without breaking eggs." Díaz made Mexico a colony of foreign capitalism, principally American, although Mexican capitalists did not suffer. His amazing success was to a considerable extent a by-product of our post-Civil War prosperity; Mexican economy reflected our booms and panics, and began to show signs of weakness about 1907.

Don Porfirio had the intelligence to surround himself with able men, his *científicos*, a brilliant group of lawyers and economists, headed by Limantour, worshipers at the new and glittering shrine of Science and Progress. They honestly believed that a dictatorship was the only possible government for their backward country, and they did their utmost to force modernity upon it. They resembled the Bourbon administrators of the eighteenth century, those efficient administrators of benevolent despotism, and they made themselves into a tight oligarchy, ruling Mexico for her own good. . . .

Beyond question the material and even the cultural advancement of Mexico during the dictatorship of Don Porfirio was very great: so many miles of railroads, so many millions of dollars invested in this and that, so many years of peace and order, eighty millions of pesos in the treasury. It may even be true that Díaz was a superior kind of benevolent despot. It may also be true that some sort of military dictatorship was inevitable after the frightful chaos of the mid-century, and that if Don Porfirio had not taken over, Mexico would have been torn to pieces by the rival caudillos whom he so effectively checkmated. Otherwise, the price of the *Pax Porfiriana* was too high. It threw Mexico back into the hands of an irresponsible autocracy, without the Laws of the Indies or the salutary fear of a royal visitor to curb it. There was no law but the will of Don Porfirio. The legislature became a mockery, kept to lend the color of legality to his acts. He cynically referred to his lawmakers as *mi caballada*, "my herd of tame horses." Elections were such a farce that hardly anyone took the trouble to vote. All of the offices of the Republic were filled with Don Porfirio's men. Between 1883 and 1894, by a series of colonizing laws passed by his caballada, Díaz gave away, to foreign speculators and personal friends, 134,500,000 acres of the public domain, that is, *about one-fifth of the entire area of the Republic*. Not satisfied with this colossal rape, the land sharks prevailed upon Díaz to throw open for seizure and settlement the remaining lands of the Indian communities—which he could legally do under the *Ley Lerdo*. When the Indians objected, as did the Maya and the Yaqui, the army and the Rurales put down the "rebellions," and thousands of prisoners were sold into slave gangs to cultivate henequen in Yucatan and tobacco in the Valle Nacional of Oaxaca. By the end of the Díaz régime not ten per cent of the Indian communities had any land whatever. In short, the Díaz régime was the denial of elementary justice to a large part of the population. The price was blood.

One of the curious things about the dictatorship of Don Porfirio was that its beneficiaries evidently thought, and certainly hoped, that it would never end. But toward the last his feline brain began to thicken and his trigger finger lost its cunning. A handful of revolutionary thinkers, like Felipe Carrillo Puerto and the Flores Magón brothers, Enrique and Ricardo, preached socialist and anarchist doctrines, wrote pamphlets and edited newspapers, and faced death, imprisonment, torture, and exile, but their work went on. In 1908 a mild little man named Francisco Madero published a book entitled *La Sucesión Presidencial en 1910,* in which he brought up the forbidden subject of Don Porfirio's successor. What! Could Don Porfirio die? A year later Andrés Molina Enríquez wrote a shocking book, *Los Grandes Problemas Nacionales,* which somehow got by the censor, although it was later suppressed. Molina's book was a terrifying exposure of the whole hypocritical, stifling miasma of despotism, Porfirian despotism. Books, to be sure, would not have caused anyone's downfall, because most of the reading public was safely tied to government jobs, but they might profitably have been read by the elect and by the foreigners, whose heads were thrust deep in the sand.

The year 1910 was the year of the Great Centennial, celebrating the hundredth anniversary of . . . the birth of Independence. It was also meant to advertise to the world the triumph of progress and *porfirismo.* The irony of the double program was almost too heavy to be ignored, but it *was* ignored. Like a plant whose roots have been cut off, the Golden Age of Don Porfirio threw out its last spray of blossoms with the Centennial, and died. The century died as it had begun, in bloodshed. . . .

The fall of Don Porfirio was as inevitable as it was unplanned. Up to 1908 all suggestions that the Golden Age might end were rigorously suppressed, and their authors expiated their temerity in exile, prison, or death. In 1908, however, the aging dictator granted an interview to an American newspaper man, James Creelman, which was published in *Pearson's Magazine* under the heading "Thrilling Story of President Díaz, the Greatest Man on the Continent." The greatest man on the continent had told Creelman that the Mexican people were now ready for democracy and that he intended to retire in 1910. The story was probably meant for circulation north of the border, or perhaps it was a trial balloon. If the latter, it was soon bouncing wildly about among the politicians and intellectuals of Mexico. The news was too good to be true, for the truth was that the younger generation was bored with its doddering dictator and his senile government. Not a few men were concerned with the fate of the country when Don Porfirio should retire, for no provision had been made for the succession, and several offered themselves as potential saviors of the fatherland.

The one who first capitalized on the situation was Francisco Madero, whose book has been mentioned. Madero was not a revolutionist. Indeed, a more unlikely leader of a revolution can hardly be imagined. He came from a large and rapacious family of landowners of Coahuila. He was a kindly man with no particular training for anything. Following the mores of his class, he had spent part of his youth in Paris, and had managed to complete a semester's residence at the University of California. His diminutive size (five feet two), squeaky voice, and lack of biceps he compensated for by going in for messianic oddities: teetotalism, vegetarianism, and spiritualism. In one of his séances his Ouija board told him that he was to be president of Mexico, and the Creelman article told him that the time was at hand. His first step was to publish his book, which had nothing remarkable about it, being a few mild suggestions, to the effect that it might be a good idea to restore the Constitution of 1857 and give the people a chance to elect a *vice-president*. That vice-president could easily be Panchito Madero, and Don Porfirio might die. Stranger things had happened.

Don Porfirio was good-natured about the competition of his puny antagonist and allowed him to travel about the country haranguing audiences; but to his astonishment Madero was everywhere received by enthusiastic crowds. Madero invented a slogan that caught on: "Effective Suffrage—No Reelection!" It did not mean much, perhaps, but it was at least a protest against the interminable dictatorship of Don Porfirio. Madero's success was so sensational that Don Porfirio became alarmed and had him jailed in San Luis Potosí. Various other candidates were discouraged in one way or another, and Don Porfirio and his stooge, Ramón Corral, were duly elected president and vice-president on September 30, 1910.

Meanwhile, on Independence Day, September 16, the Great Centennial was inaugurated, with 20,000,000 pesos spent on fireworks, decorations, military parades, banquets, speeches, poems, and carloads of champagne, while Francisco Madero, in his cell at San Luis Potosí was writing the "plan" which was to ignite the glorious bonfire of revolution.

After the election Madero escaped across the border to San Antonio and there "pronounced" in heroic style. Nobody seemed to pay much attention to him and, after a laughable fiasco, he gave up his revolution as a bad job and set out for Europe. But down Chihuahua way a rough storekeeper named Pascual Orozco and a gorilla-like bandit whom he had befriended decided to stage a revolution on their own. The bandit was one Doroteo Arango, better known to history as Francisco Villa. At the news of their uprising Madero abandoned his European trip, hastened back to Chihuahua, and persuaded Orozco and Villa to let him lead their revolution under his "Plan of San Luis Potosí." So, in February, 1911, Madero had a party at last and, what was more important, an army. . . .

All the world could now see how rotten the federal army was, and *tumultos* broke out with increasing frequency and violence. The situation of Don Porfirio was patently hopeless, and Limantour accepted defeat and agreed to Don Porfirio's resignation, without even consulting him. Under the terms of the agreement a provisional government would be set up, under Francisco de la Barra, until Madero should be elected president—an event that was taken for granted.

On May 23, 1911, the news of the capitulation broke in Mexico City. The next morning huge crowds paraded down the streets to the Zócalo. *Resign! Resign!* Mobs milled before the National Palace. *Resign! Resign!* Don Porfirio's answer: "Fire!" Two hundred dead. All that evening Don Porfirio, suffering from a raging toothache and the importunities of his family and friends, refused to accept the dreadful fact that his time had come. And then, toward midnight, he retired to his chamber and, in halting and clumsy phrases, penned a long and self-righteous resignation which ended with the prophetic words: "I hope . . . that when the passions which accompany every revolution have been calmed, a more conscientious and substantiated study will cause a more correct judgment to arise in the national conscience which will permit me to die bearing in my heart a just recognition of the esteem which all my life I have consecrated . . . to my fellow citizens."

Congress received the terrifying document in death-like silence. The *caballada* was free at last!

PART IX.

LATIN AMERICA IN THE
TWENTIETH CENTURY

Introduction

As Latin America entered the twentieth century, the continent had already known dictatorships, democracies, caudillos, military juntas, and revolutions. Another round in the fight between the tank and the ballot box was beginning.

The only true social upheaval and economic reform during the early part of the century was in Mexico. The landed aristocrats and the "scientists" of Porfirio Díaz were shattered in a bloody revolution led by Francisco Madero, Venustiano Carranza, Pancho Villa, and Emiliano Zapata. After the actual battle phase of the revolution (the first excerpt in this part) its momentum carried Mexico through fifty years of economic and social transformations: the state solidified into a single political party, land reform was carried out, and major industries nationalized. Andrew Frank's article (in Part X) takes us through the revolution from the Villa days to the 1960's. Frank's observations are still valid, although since his article was written Mexico's government has embarked on perhaps the most brutal repression of dissent since the reign of Díaz.

Just as Cuba and Chile stand today as two products of a general revolutionary ferment, the 1920's in Latin America were a time for dreams of overthrow, of change. The most influential thinker of the time was Víctor Raúl Haya de la Torre, a Peruvian who founded APRA (American Popular Revolutionary Alliance). Aprismo was an attempt to create a purely Latin American style of development, and the theory and practice of Aprismo in Peru are discussed in the two selections on Haya de la Torre. While Aprismo never had a real chance of success in Peru at the time, it formed the basis for reform in other countries. The APRA formula of nationalization of industry increased government power and responsibility; heavier

248

taxation and more extensive land redistribution have been applied even in recent years, as the excerpt on Betancourt's Venezuelan experiment in the 1960's illustrates.

APRA, like the Alliance for Progress, depended on the idea that a society could be overturned through the ballot box, and rich groups would accept the changes foisted on them by political persuasion. But the promise of the idea was swamped by a series of dictatorships that seemed to appear simultaneously all over Latin America in the 1930's. The case of Rafael Trujillo, as presented here, is not completely typical—because none of the dictators did it exactly the same way—but it shows how one man could come from nowhere to immobilize a country in his private web.

Trujillo was one of five famous dictators to take over during the same general period. The selection by Tad Szulc discusses the fortunes and tactics of the other four—Vargas in Brazil, Rojas Pinilla in Colombia, Perón in Argentina, and Odría in Peru. The durability of a Latin American dictatorship is proven by the example of Perón, who recently returned to Argentina after seventeen years of exile and immediately became the principal political force in the country.

The people who lived under these dictatorships and viewed the democracies around them often had little to envy. Life went on, the Latin American political arrangements seemed almost divorced from people's daily problems, and the bewilderment of democratic anarchy can be exasperating. Chile, for one, believed in the democratic process and tried to make it work; so did Costa Rica. But in most other places, there was skepticism at best. The Latin American love for form comes into play here; in Ecuador, almost every political upheaval of the century has been followed by a new constitution. The new constitution is always written as if it might erase the people, their beliefs, the causes of political failures in the past. But it is a ritual purgative; the words are switched around, but the same people and the same problems remain. The strange career of Latin American democracy is contained in the famous case of José María Velasco Ibarra, the Ecuadorian president who has come to power five times since 1933 and has been able to finish only one complete term in office. The crazy Velasco Ibarra pendulum—one year the savior, the next year banished to

Argentina by the military, only to be asked to return again to save the country—is particularly chaotic, but similar stories could be told about the other countries. Velasco Ibarra's political history also uncovers the Latin American's lack of adherence to specific ideologies (one year Velasco Ibarra is a communist, the next year a conservative, the next a liberal), which makes the politics tricky to understand.

When Velasco Ibarra is thrown out of office, it is usually by a used U.S.-made tank, rolling up to the government palace in Quito—a scene that has become a cliché in the U.S. view of Latin America. And yet, as the Edwin Lieuwen excerpt explains, the military is not that easy to categorize: it cannot always be associated with dark sunglasses, fat generals, repression, corruption, and favoritism to the upper classes. Lieuwen points out that the military is one of the few places where a poor man can make his way into professional life, and the rise of such people into military power in Peru may be what makes that country's current junta so sympathetic to social reform.

Most Latin American countries, far from being either dictator-prone or democracy-prone, have walked a jagged line between all the styles of government described here. Peru, Venezuela, Brazil, Argentina, and Chile have all recently attempted APRA-style reforms under democratic leadership. In three of these countries—Brazil, Argentina, and Peru—the attempts have ended in military takeover. The tenuousness of electoral politics in the face of a strong military, a chaotic party system, and an impatient country is shown in the excerpt describing Frondizi's election in Argentina. Like Betancourt in Venezuela, and Haya in Peru, Frondizi attempted discreetly to shake down the privileged classes, nationalize industries, and distribute land. The military put an end to his efforts— the same thing that happened to the 1952 Bolivian reform and the Brazilian regimes of Quadros and Kubitschek in the 1960's.

Whatever the specific reasons, the original hope that democratic reform and economic change could be brought about simultaneously has not been fulfilled. Most Latin American countries are now more concerned with the pocketbook than the ballot box, and they seem to prefer running their governments through military regime—whether socialist like Peru's or capitalist like

Brazil's. The only real test of whether rapid economic redistribution can happen in a democracy was Chile, but the test failed when Allende was deposed. Chile had been looked on as a new departure, but in a way it was the sole survivor of APRA, Betancourt, Haya, Frondizi, Quadros, and the rest of the great democratic reformers.

Since the Mexican revolution of 1910 is considered to be one of the few true social upheavals ever to occur in Latin America, it is worth finding out how it started. A little background is necessary to understand this selection: after Díaz abdicated, the country was run for a brief period by Francisco Madero, the liberal reformer who hastened Díaz's downfall. The *científicos* (old Díaz supporters) didn't like Madero, and rebellions were breaking out across the country. A military coup took place, Madero was deposed and murdered, and a Mexican general named Huerta (a Díaz supporter) was put in power. Instead of stepping down after a short time and permitting elections, as he had promised to do (something that occurs often with Latin American interim presidents), Huerta attempted to solidify his power. The selection takes it from there.

Villa, Zapata, and the Revolution
By John Womack, Jr.

... A bitter civil war spread through the country. Local communities dissolved into refugee masses. The economy decayed and retracted from world patterns. By the spring of 1914, Huerta's force had run down. To help rout him, the United States Navy occupied Veracruz. From every direction, revolutionary armies pressed into the strategic center of the country. In July 1914, Huerta left for Europe. The old regime was in crisis, but its principal worthies could not rally. In August, they surrendered to the main revolutionary force. They lost all offices and many contracts, and the Army mustered out. Thus the class that had dominated Mexico for a generation disintegrated into ruins. The plutocrats fled into exile.

The whole country now hung in suspense. To reorganize it, neither Great Britain nor the United States would intervene directly, because war had just begun in Europe. Responsibility for a new order therefore weighed on the Mexicans themselves, specifically on three revolutionary factions. These were alike in their popular origins, their fresh national pride, their democratic assumptions, and their ideological crudity. But in their visions of their task they were quite distinct. The strongest faction, which had taken authority in the capital, was essentially entrepreneurial. Its chiefs were tough young Northerners who had resented the Porfiriato for its monopolies and who wanted to make Mexico a land of opportunity for all, where any man of gumption and talent could succeed. They had the best connections with workingmen's unions. Ironically, their First Chief was an old Porfirian politico, Venustiano Carranza, whom they did not like but for tactical reasons respected. Another faction, almost as strong and also Northern, had for its hero Francisco Villa, once a bandit, then a rebel chief under Carranza's orders, but now independent. The Villistas had no definite interests. The Mexico they dreamed of was simply a place where buddies could prosper and carouse. And into their headquarters crept remnants of the old regime angling for restoration. The third faction was Southern, forged in the agrarian rebellion that had raged continually in the South since 1911. Its chief was Emiliano Zapata, a determined countryman. Though the Zapatistas were a small and amateurish force, they probably represented the inarticulate hopes of the majority of the nation. The Mexico they foresaw was basically a traditional commonwealth of market towns and villages.

At issue in 1914 was whether these three factions could work together to refound their country. And in a solemn Revolutionary Convention they tried—and failed. The Villistas then wormed the Zapatistas into an alliance to destroy the Carrancistas. The Carrancista chiefs reconcentrated their forces and counterattacked. Organized workingmen enlisted in their ranks. For two years an immense, bloody civil war blasted Mexico. Swarms of refugees registered its terrible cost. Twice the United States intervened, indirectly in 1915 to recognize Carranza's claim to govern and directly in 1916 to send troops over the border on a wild-goose chase after Villa. But the struggle continued. Though at times it seemed that the rival revolutionaries would tear the country apart, that Mexico was less a nation now than ever before, Mexicans were learning in their common pain and courage a new lesson—their identity as a people.

The Carrancista entrepreneurs emerged victorious. The organized workingmen tagged along. By late 1916, though Villa and Zapata still had raiders in the field, Carranza was able to start building a regular regime. In an exclusively Carrancista convention, his lieutenants ratified their victory and proclaimed their own radical plans in a new Constitution on February 5, 1917. They promptly rigged elections to put themselves in authority. Congress opened. Carranza became president, incorporated his legions as a National Army, and appointed a Cabinet. Governments soon formed in most states. After seven years of profound instability and change, the Republic was back in business again.

It often wobbled, however. The economy was a shambles, the populace miserable yet militant. Usually the jolts came from natural mistakes in fabricating the new political system. But the real rub was Carranza, who hardly fit in the regime he presided over. He held his post almost by leave of the Army, and he would not sponsor reforms to gain popular support. In fact, he only superintended while his lieutenants negotiated among themselves over who would succeed him.

Just before elections in 1920 they finally acted. When Carranza balked at their claims, they dumped him (and accidentally allowed his murder), subsumed into their party the rebel remnants still in the field, and carried their toughest and canniest colleague, Álvaro Obregón, into the presidency. Evidently the true masters were now in control, and Mexico was on its true course—bereft through the last decade of hundreds of thousands of lives and poorer by billions of pesos, but somehow heading home. That fall, for the first time, officials commemorated the anniversary of Madero's revolt ten years before. As it began, so the Revolution ended—a thoroughly native operation.

It took Mexicans the next twenty years to make sense of this awful experience. They did so not deliberately, not even in terms of their radical new Constitution, though it survived, but rather in working out troubles as they went along. They could do so because they had already destroyed the class that might have obstructed them. And in their search they still proceeded on their own: Despite the confusion of the world in the 1920's and 1930's, despite appeals and threats from the United States, and despite the tempting models of Soviet Russia, Fascist Italy, and Nazi Germany, the Mexicans went their independent way. And for all their ideological rhetoric, which they often believed, they remained pragmatic in practice. . . .

During the 1920's, efforts were made to define a completely Latin American political movement—one that did not copy either European socialism or American democratic capitalism. Víctor Raúl Haya de la Torre, a Peruvian leader, created such a movement in the Alianza Popular Revolucionaria Americana (American Popular Revolutionary Alliance), or APRA. The philosophy is called Aprismo, the participants are Apristas. The selection deals with the founding of APRA and treats the effects of Haya's philosophy on other Latin American leaders. Venezuela, Argentina, Brazil, Mexico, and Peru have all attempted APRA-style reforms at one time or another since the 1930's, and Haya's thinking is a good basis for understanding the Latin American democratic left today.

In the Hirschman selection, *ejido* refers to the communal land system of the Indians in Mexico. *Latifundio* is the predominance of large *haciendas,* and generally describes the feudal land system traditional in Latin America.

Aprismo Explained
By Albert O. Hirschman

Up to the first decade of the 20th century this [Latin American economic] literature with its passionate self-criticism and its advocacy of laissez faire and a social and economic system similar to that of the advanced industrial nations was perhaps dominant. In the next phase we encounter a greater tendency to find fault with the outside world rather than with oneself. Correlatively, a search begins for specifically Latin American solutions to the area's economic problems. United States interventionism in Panama, the Caribbean and Mexico, the loss of face of Europe as a result of the First World War, and the Russian and Mexican revolutions all contributed to this change. Yet cohesive theories of social and economic reform were slow to emerge. The Mexican Revolution was remarkable in that it wholly belied the Napoleonic maxim that a revolution is an idea that has found bayonets— here it was rather the revolution which found its ideas as it proceeded with varying speed and over a large number of years along its pragmatic road.

Paradoxically, the most ambitious attempt at revolutionary theorizing about Latin American society arose in a country that up to this day at least has gone through a minimum of social change [Hirschman wrote this before the recent upheavals in Peru—described later in the book]: I am speaking about Peru and the writings of Haya de la Torre....

Haya de la Torre formulated his thinking in the early twenties, in an intellectual climate dominated by the October Revolution. He soon felt the need to differentiate himself from orthodox communism and set out to discover the peculiar character of Latin America's problems. Thus, he considered Lenin's definition of imperialism as the last stage of capitalism and noted that for the nonindustrial countries, imperialism was rather *their first* experience with capitalism. For this reason, Haya de la Torre maintained that a revolution in Latin America could not be undertaken by the weak and submerged proletariat, but must also rely on the intellectuals and the middle classes, which, according to him, were endowed with far more fighting spirit in Latin America than in Europe.

Under these conditions, the struggle must be conducted under an anti-imperialist rather than an anti-capitalist banner. Action against imperialism was the first point of Haya's five-point program, the others being: political unity of Latin America, nationalization of land and industries, internationalization of the Panama Canal, and solidarity with the oppressed people and classes everywhere. But like some of these latter points (e.g., nationalization) Haya's anti-imperialism was subject to interesting qualifications. For Haya explicitly recognized Latin America's need for foreign capital, but, so he argued, if only Latin American countries stopped competing for foreign capital, and united in an anti-imperialist coalition, they could obtain it under far more favorable conditions since capitalist countries have a compelling need to export capital. . . .

Stripped of rhetoric, this simply means that the state should exercise control over the direction of investment—a condition which is today frequently demanded by the foreign (e.g., World Bank) capital itself, rather than imposed upon it.

Haya's search for an "Indoamerican Way" rests upon closer inspection essentially on the desire for economic development without some of the disruptions and injustices that have marked the process elsewhere:

> Why not build into our own reality "as it really is" the bases of a new economic and political organization which will accomplish the educational and constructive task of industrialism but will be free of its cruel aspects of human exploitation and national vassalage?

Attribution of backwardness to imperialist exploitation, direction of economic development by the state, avoidance of the excesses that have marked the early stages of capitalist development in the West, and the community of interests of all of Latin America—these are basic ingredients of Haya's thought which as we shall see have left a deep mark on Latin American economic thinking.

A final element is the search for elements in the Indian or primitive past of Latin America that are not only worth preserving but that can be used in building a better social and economic order. Haya speaks eloquently about the dualism of the Peruvian economy and about the need to preserve and to build a new agrarian society on the collectivist tradition of the Indian economy. In the work of another influential Peruvian, the Socialist José Carlos Mariátegui (1895–1930), the preservation of the communal *ayllu* (corresponding to the Aztec-Mexican *calpulli-ejido*) and the call for its victory over the *latifundio* are principal themes. Actually, U.S. anthropologists who have done field work in Peru have expressed serious doubts about the vigor of the communes and about the extent to which they still hold land in common, engage in reciprocal labor, etc. Nevertheless, the continuing belief among intellectuals that it may be possible to build on the Indian past is in itself of interest. It is part of the attempt to find an "own" way to economic progress and social justice.

Whether or not the currents thus far reviewed qualify as economic theories, knowledge of this background is important to an understanding of contemporary thinking. For, essentially, the debate is still defined by two principal questions: One, where lies the responsibility for our lag? In ourselves or in the outside world which exploits us? Two, how can we make progress? By imitating others (the West or Russia) or by fashioning our own way?

There were other styles of dictatorship than Trujillo's. Tad Szulc, a reporter for *The New York Times*, describes four of them. The quintet of Vargas in Brazil, Odría in

Peru, Rojas Pinilla in Colombia, Perón in Argentina, and Trujillo cover the gamut of strongarm techniques, and the advantages and disadvantages of despotic rule. There is a tendency to return to old dictators, in the manner of paternalism that Guillén Martínez describes in an earlier part of this book. Argentina, for instance, went into ecstasy over the return of Perón after seventeen years of exile in 1972. Perón instantly became the most powerful political force in that country, even after nearly two decades of absence.

Four Other Dictators

By Tad Szulc

Getúlio Vargas

This man was Getúlio Dornelles Vargas. In order of time, Vargas, an outwardly cheerful, deceptively mild-looking man endowed with much erudition, great personal magnetism, immense toughness, and amazing political shrewdness, was the first of the remarkable modern South American dictators. In 1937, after seven years in office, he formally launched his Estado Novo (New State) regime as the Brazilian version of European fascism and corporativism, rich in studied demagoguery, political opportunism, and social appeal. He set himself up as the first contemporary "populist" president on the continent.

In point of personal and historical interest, Vargas towered over his more bombastic and superficial dictatorial colleagues of later days. While functioning as a dictator, he showed something akin to political brilliance. As a constitutional president, freely elected five years after his ouster from dictatorial power, he was a dismal failure, a tragic figure who finally chose suicide as the denouement of his long life. And from his deathbed he made the parting gesture of demagogic drama in the form of a political last will in which he proclaimed that he was giving his life to defend the working people from rapacious international interests.

Because he led Brazil, perhaps in erroneous fashion but always with conviction, through her greatest social revolution since the nineteenth century's abolishment of slavery and the change from empire to republic; because he was closely associated with the destinies of the largest and potentially the wealthiest of all the Latin-American nations for well over a quarter of a century; and because he was a man who commanded as much love as hate among his fellow citizens, Getúlio Vargas has left a deeper permanent mark on his country than any other modern dictator in his part of the world.

He is best remembered for revolutionizing political thinking in Brazil, fostering economic development, introducing social legislation, and instilling social consciousness into the masses that were being transformed from chattel-like farm hands and unskilled city workers into a fairly articulate rural and industrial proletariat. His policies and attitudes were paternalistic, his social legislation was so far ahead of the day that it often did more harm than good to the country as a whole, and in his dictatorial heyday he ruled with a constitution faithfully copied after European fascist charters. . . .

Proceeding along a tortuous political line, adapting himself with enormous flexibility to the requirements of the moment, Vargas presided over the process of transforming Brazil from an economically feudal and almost completely agricultural nation into the dynamically expanding, partly industrialized country of today. Of course, this change was bound to come sooner or later, but Vargas, appearing on the scene at the historic moment, quickened it and directed the different forces at play into channels of his choosing. By centralizing all national controls in his hands and in the capital of Rio de Janiero, he went far toward unifying Brazil politically and curbing the exaggeratedly autonomous powers of the twenty states forming the federal union. . . .

Another fact setting Vargas apart from the other dictators was that he did not enrich himself in office—though most of his friends and relatives did in scandalous fashion and thereby set the stage for the final tragedy of his suicide. His personal life was quiet and unostentatious; he was a devoted husband and a good father. When Vargas died in 1954, he left behind a cash debt of about $40,000. His assets at his death were limited to the family ranch in the south of Brazil and an apartment in Rio de Janiero. In sharp contrast, such dictators as Perón, Rojas Pinilla, Pérez Jiménez, and Batista amassed fortunes of millions of dollars during their tenures in power.

Juan Perón

A dictatorship infinitely more outrageous and one almost completely barren of any of the positive aspects of the Vargas era in Brazil was the gift to Argentina of Juan Domingo Perón, army colonel turned politician. Perón rose to the presidency in 1946 through free elections, although some months earlier a mob-supported coup d'état had placed him in a commanding position to capture the votes of millions of workers who had fallen prey to his labor rabble-rousing. Like Vargas, but aping Mussolini's balcony-shouting techniques he had learned during his years in Italy, and which the Brazilian dictator never had to use, Perón presented himself and his wife Eva as the friends—the only friends—of the Argentine workingman. While he also controlled the army, Perón derived most of his power from the labor unions, whose leaders he made and unmade. Despite all abuses, the rank and file gave him their loyalty and support for a long time, perhaps mistaking the disruptive force he had handed them for the dignity and importance they had sought. And, damaging and distorting deeply Argentina's economy, he saw to it they were well off—no matter what was happening to the rest of the country. The loyalty of the Peronista workers did not end with Perón's overthrow in September, 1955. Greatly influencing from exile the political activities in Argentina, he issued instructions to vote for Arturo Frondizi in the February, 1958, elections that were obeyed by two million voters.

But Frondizi turned his back on the Peronistas almost immediately after taking office, and the ex-dictator's followers became the worst thorn in his side, as they violently opposed his austere and courageous program of economic rehabilitation for Argentina.

Perón's strength stemmed chiefly from his appearance on the national scene at the psychological moment when he could take advantage of a social explosion resulting from the disintegration of Argentina's cycle of rural semifeudalism. He passed on to the workers and their families the inebriating sensation that they, too, were running the country through something along the lines of a dictatorship of the proletariat, although Perón himself was never known to have used this expression. This approach, heavy on the social aspects of national life, explains why Perón and Vargas were the only ones among the five dictators to have retained a very substantial following for years after their exit from power.

But the decade of Perón's rule left Argentina, a once wealthy country, on the brink of economic ruin. Whereas Vargas had made a fairly serious attempt to find a new basis for the solution of Brazil's emerging social and economic problems, Perón's ideological contributions were his Justicialismo and Peronismo—two vague doctrines based almost exclusively on demagoguery, chauvinism, and mob rule in the streets by workers whipped into hysteria by his fascist methods. Vargas had never stooped that low in his dictatorial days, and, strangely, it took the return of democracy in Brazil to send him scurrying demagogically after the crowds. . . .

Manuel Odría

If one would set out to make a case for an enlightened, benevolent dictatorship that has done a nation some good despite a denial of liberty, the eight years of the unspectacular regime of General of Division Manuel A. Odría in Peru could be singled out as the best modern example in Latin America. It cannot be put in the same class with the Vargas government because, while the Brazilian president led a social revolution along with his political experimentation, General Odría concentrated merely on sound administration, and, if anything, sociological transformation in the deep sense was arrested in Peru during his period. But important progress was made in improving the lot of the people through the development of the country's wealth, along with its social welfare and educational programs.

Odría assumed the presidential office in 1948 as the result of a military revolt designed to end the chaos into which Peru had been plunged by the attempts of a rabble-rousing political party, the APRA, to impose quick radical solutions for the country's deep-seated social problems. The age-old Andean problem of the destitute but stirring Indians—the problem that also is at the root of the revolutionary upheavals of neighboring Bolivia—was one of them. A disorderly and confused social revolution had been in progress in Peru when Odría stepped in at the head of his troops. The process of social ferment was then bottled up for eight years while the military regime successfully worked to restore peace and stability to Peru.

This done, General Odría took a step that became his main achievement and distinction: fulfilling an earlier promise, he allowed the holding of free elections in 1956. When the time came for the inauguration of Manuel Prado y Ugarteche, an old-line civilian politician and former president who emerged as his freely elected successor, Odría bowed out into the wings. Political democracy returned to Peru, and General Odría deserves his share of the credit for it. It was this unusual, and probably unprecedented, voluntary end of a military dictatorship that helped to make Odría and his period so worthy of note. It is an objective fact that he had been an efficient and successful administrator who, in eight years, led Peru from abysmal economic and political confusion to relative stability and a prosperous economy. . . .

As was to be the case later with Rojas Pinilla in Colombia and Pérez Jiménez in Venezuela, Odría's advent in Peru was greeted with much hope by the conservative classes, who saw in the military revolution a promise of the restoration of political peace and the consequent return of a favorable business and economic climate. This they found in the Odría regime, but they found also repression or denial of most of the freedoms. Thus, these influential but short-sighted people who were willing to go along with Bolívar's "able despotism" formula must share the blame for the initial strengthening of the dictatorship. But in time they learned their lesson and they showed it by helping to establish a public-opinion climate that must have played a key role in leading Odría to keep his word about restoring democracy to Peru.

With all that can be said in his favor, Odría was still a dictator, and in matters of freedom there evidently can be no rationalizations or compromise. He won an earlier election by imprisoning his opponent; he allowed no independent political parties to function in any real sense of the word; he tolerated no freedom of the press, except during the period immediately preceding the 1956 elections; he exiled many of his enemies and imprisoned others. Yet his rule was not characterized by the shocking police excesses of Perón's Argentina, Pérez Jiménez' Venezuela, or even Vargas' Brazil. . . .

Gustavo Rojas Pinilla

In sharp contrast to the easygoing but efficient Odría in Peru, neighboring Colombia was run between 1953 and 1957 by an inept and vain military dictator, General Gustavo Rojas Pinilla. As commander in chief of the armed forces, Rojas Pinilla directed a coup d'état that threw out of office Dr. Laureano Gómez, a cantankerous right-wing dictator during whose presidential period the lingering civil war between the Conservatives and Liberals had reached bloody and alarming proportions. When democratic rule returned to Colombia late in 1958, the death toll for the decade of civil war stood near two hundred thousand. The country's population was under twelve million.

Rojas' coup was hailed throughout Colombia as an act of salvation. The general promised a government that would end the internecine strife and bring about the national unity needed to restore Colombia's traditional democracy and allow her to get back on a normal path of progress.

But the bright hopes did not last long. Rojas Pinilla, surrounded by a palace clique of rapacious relatives and friends, soon became a full-fledged dictator, imprisoning his critics, silencing the free press, and erecting a system of self-glorification, special privileges, and corruption. He participated in the latter with complete abandon and immense personal profit, and during his tenure in the presidency he became one of Colombia's biggest cattle owners.

Rojas flooded the country with his portrait in gala army and navy uniforms, with Caesarlike busts, and even with wrist watches bearing his picture on the face. With all this, Rojas Pinilla's performance in terms of being a successful dictator added up to total failure when compared to the records of his colleagues. Despite its opposition to him, the majority of Colombia's public opinion was willing to let him serve out his term ending in 1958, but Rojas, through a series of unnecessary and ill-advised measures, precipitated the 1957 revolt and his own fall. A member of Pérez Jiménez' dictatorial regime in Venezuela, a lethally efficient group, remarked once to this writer that "Rojas is downgrading and cheapening through his stupidities the whole institution of dictatorship." Yet the irony of it was that the Venezuelan dictator repeated some of the very same errors of Rojas and thereby brought doom upon himself.

Unlike Pérez Jiménez, General Rojas left very few important works as a monument to himself—a crucial dictatorial failing even if allowances are made for the fact that Colombia's resources and revenues were not comparable to Venezuela's. Finding a reasonably prosperous land despite years of civil war, Rojas turned it back to its people riddled with internal and external debts—and with precious little to show for them. He did not wreck Colombia's economy as efficiently as Perón did Argentina's—perhaps because he was not very efficient at anything and because he had only

four years, against Perón's decade, in which to inflict
the damage. To help eradicate all manifestations of
independent political life in the nation—always a
threat to a dictator—Rojas Pinilla came up with the
slogan of "Motherland Above the Parties." Then he
proceeded to build around himself a political faction
called the Third Force that, in crude and pathetic
imitation of Perón's Justicialismo, sought to draw support from organized labor and to do a considerable bit
of glorification of the Supreme Chief. In further imita
tion of the Peróns, General Rojas' daughter Maria
Eugenia took over Colombia's social assistance organization, but, having neither the looks, intelligence,
nor personality of Evita, she did not extract from
these activities important political dividends for her
father.

Like Perón before him and Pérez Jiménez afterward, Rojas Pinilla collided with the powerful Roman
Catholic Church, which had just launched its new
liberal policy in Latin America and would not toler-
ate his awkward excursions into the realm of "populist" pseudo social experiments. In May, 1957, Rojas
Pinilla, the man who was fully and tragically convinced until the last moment that he was truly be-
loved by his people, tumbled from power when all of
Colombia rose in protest against his arrogant attempt
to have his rubber-stamp National Constituent Assembly re-elect him a year ahead of time for another
term in office. The democratic government that succeeded the post-Rojas Military Junta allowed him to
return to Colombia late in 1958, and the deposed dictator, still dreaming of power, wasted no time in preparing a conspiracy. But so tiny was the support he
commanded in the nation that the government had no
difficulty breaking up the plot, even before it was
actually staged, and arresting Rojas. . . .

Thus, caught in a maelstrom he did not fully understand, Rojas was little more than a throwback to the
old-fashioned Latin-American military man on horseback. But he, too, performed his historical function:
the anti-Rojas revolution united the two warring parties
as nothing else could have done. It stopped organized

Liberal-Conservative warfare and it has finally put Colombia back on the democratic track after an up-heaval-punctured lapse of eleven years. . . .

The ideals of APRA were lost in an era of dictators that took over various Latin American countries around the 1930's. While each of the strong-arm leaders described in the Szulc selection (Vargas in Brazil, Odría in Peru, Rojas Pinilla in Colombia, and Perón in Argentina) differ dramatically in personality and the methods they used to gain despotic power, taken together they give a good overview of the way dictators operate in Latin America. There is a tendency to return to old dictators, in the man-ner of paternalism that Guillén Martínez describes in an earlier selection. Argentina, for instance, went into ecstacy over the return of Perón after seventeen years of exile in 1972. Although he didn't run for office himself, Perón instantly became the most powerful political force in that country, despite nearly two decades of absence.

The selection by Goff and Locker shows the potential importance of United States support to a Latin American dictator, in this case, Rafael Trujillo of the Dominican Republic. Trujillo fashioned perhaps the most outrageous *personal* empire ever seen in the continent—and the U.S. government was an indispensable part of his strength. Long years of Trujillo led to conditions that created a bloody civil war in 1965, as we shall see later in this book.

Portrait of a Dictator: Trujillo
By Fred Goff and Michael Locker

When the National Police was transformed back into the army in 1928, Trujillo assumed the role of chief. Maneuvering carefully behind the scenes he engineered a fake uprising followed by the seizure of cities and the confiscation of weapons on the pretext of preserving order and preventing bloodshed. One of Trujillo's greatest concerns in this plot was to insure that the government he established would be recognized by the United States. Close contact with the American legation and his influential old Marine Commander, Colonel Cutts, guaranteed Trujillo U.S. support and ultimate success.

Once in power Trujillo proceeded to erect a pervasive and repressive totalitarian regime. The army was his private instrument of coercion and terror; the oversize officer corps benefited materially and enjoyed privileged status. At home and abroad he developed a huge espionage apparatus providing the kind of intelligence needed to predict events and manipulate people. By recruiting their sons Trujillo cleverly forced most of the oligarchy into collaboration; blackmail, threats, and economic pressure compelled virtually every man of ability to serve him. Torture and assassination awaited those who resisted. Political opposition was erased or manipulated by co option, imprisonment, exile, or murder. The Generalissimo personally selected all the national and local appointments, and his own party, manned by an endless string of relatives and cronies, administered a sizable social-welfare program. Every official, high or low, was subjected to constant rotation, public humiliation, or sudden elevation on short notice by orders from "El Jefe."

Beyond this traditional caudillo system, Trujillo constructed a fantastic personal economic empire. . . . Funds collected from the public and from elicit operations were invested in every conceivable agricultural and industrial enterprise; monopolies usually followed. Import-export taxes and license fees facilitated the harassment and eventual takeover of corporations dealing in foreign trade, the lifeblood of the economy. Moreover, U.S. commodity shortages at the end of World War II raised prices on agricultural exports and propelled the island's elite into relative prosperity. After centralizing banking operations, Trujillo could sell any of his unprofitable businesses to the state for a large profit and make timely reacquisitions. It has been estimated that between 65 and 85 percent of the entire economy eventually ended up in his hands. The monetary fortune accumulated from this empire was not trivial, and the variety of devices it afforded for exercising power was crucial to maintaining the regime.

In the late forties and during the fifties, Trujillo made his move for the most coveted prize in the Dominican economy—the cane sugar industry. A sharp rise in postwar sugar prices attracted Trujillo's attention, but with the exception of relatively small properties held by the Vicini family the entire industry was owned by foreign capital—mainly United States. Fully aware of the financial and political complications involved in entering this economic sector, he proceeded cautiously. After acquiring a small independent mill in 1948, he pushed forward with the construction of an enormous milling installation, Rio Haina, that was put into production in 1953. In order to supply enough cane, he acquired large tracts of land from Dominicans, Canadians, Puerto Ricans, and finally Americans with small holdings. The largest single sugar complex on the island, La Romana, a subsidiary of the American-owned South Puerto Rico Sugar Co., was then handed the technical task of building a railroad for the efficient transportation of cane and managing the entire operation on a profit-sharing basis.

These accomplishments pushed Trujillo into the largest economic deal of his reign—acquisition of the prized U.S. West Indies Sugar Company. A product of the Marine occupation and the efforts of antiguerrilla expert Edwin Kilbourne (president and director of the company), West Indies was the largest geographically dispersed sugar complex on the island: four high-volume mills, along with 30,000 head of cattle, considerable pasture land, coconut plantations on Samana Bay, some coffee *fincas,* and a great deal of underdeveloped land. Unlike La Romana with its powerful South Puerto Rico Corp. connections to Kuhn, Loeb & Co. and Rockefeller interests, West Indies could not elicit enough political influence to bring about U.S. intervention. After some pressure was applied and the word of Trujillo's desire to buy got out, the stockholders negotiated a favorable figure

($35,830,000) in three cash installments. As for South Puerto Rico, Trujillo realized its technical skills were not replaceable and its powerful connections could be mutually advantageous in raising the island's U.S. sugar quota.

The sugar acquisitions demonstrated that Trujillo still retained his keen understanding of power relationships within the United States as well as the limitations they imposed on his actions. Geographic proximity and the economic strength of the United States forced any Dominican government to depend on close and cordial relations with powerful U.S. citizens. To this end, Trujillo devoted boundless energy and resources in the form of business deals, sex, flattery, campaign contributions, bribes, blackmail, even murder. Joseph E. Davies, the archetype of Trujillo's influential American, was a multimillionaire corporate lawyer (with a major interest in General Foods) turned New Deal diplomat. In 1931, Davies visited the Republic for President Roosevelt and brought back a highly favorable assessment of the new regime, which led, in turn, to a lifesaving moratorium on debt payments and opened up new lines of credit. A long friendship ensued, Davies visited often to serve as financial counsel on business ventures and fiscal policy. Along with Davies, industrialist Herbert May, construction tycoon Felix Benítez Rexach, diplomat-businessman William Pawley, and the molasses dealers A. I. and J. M. Kaplan served as Trujillo's economic liaison with the U.S. financial and business community.

Trujillo never found an equivalent to Davies in the political sphere of the U.S. Establishment, though he managed to significantly influence governmental decisions and public opinion through a chain of well-paid politicians, lawyers, journalists, and lobbyists. Nobody knows how many millions of dollars were passed directly or indirectly to Senators, Representatives, Executive Department employees and other powerful Americans in public life who might protect and promote Trujillo. Such dignitaries, critics as well as supporters, were often invited to his private fiefdom, wined and dined, provided with women and then secretly photographed. . . .

In conjunction with these unsavory tactics, Trujillo produced a continual barrage of propaganda geared to project a favorable image of the Dominican Republic and its benevolent leader. Elections were staged, figureheads occupied the president's office, the capital was "beautified" and anti-Communism took on the trappings of a holy crusade. In order to inflate the country's importance, extravagant foreign embassies were maintained, glamorous trips undertaken, and a world's fair hosted in the capital. In a most clever move to obtain the influential good will of American and European Jewish leaders, an offer was made in 1940 to admit 100,000 Jewish refugees on very liberal terms. Most of these programs and many others were of course meaningless, but in public relations terms they would have to be judged a success. A countless number of public officials and newsmen praised the nation's "progress built on stability" and cooperated with its operations out of innocence, stupidity, or greed. . . .

. . . Castro's revolution was obviously a mixed blessing [for Trujillo]. On June 14, 1959, Dominican exiles launched an invasion from Cuba which, though unsuccessful, shook Trujillo's regime to its roots. Torture, arrests, and assassinations of prominent Dominicans followed, and for the first time in thirty years, opposition on a large scale developed. By January, 1960, in an unprecedented event, the Roman Catholic Church finally denounced the Trujillo regime. During this same period huge arms expenditures began to sap the economy's strength. In a fit of desperation, Trujillo lashed out in an assassination attempt on an archenemy, Venezuela's social democratic President Rómulo Betancourt. The Organization of American States (OAS) was called into session, Trujillo was denounced, and economic sanctions were imposed.

U.S. support for OAS condemnation and sanctions demonstrated how far Trujillo's U.S. power base had diminished. U.S. investments failed to increase after the early fifties because of the dictator's drive for total monopoly over the economy and massive corruption. . . .

. . . Increased U.S. reliance on Dominican sugar imports strengthened the push to stabilize the situation by removing Trujillo. Diplomat-businessman William Pawley, along with his close friend Senator George Smathers (D.-Fla.), visited El Jefe to plead for his abdication in order to facilitate a smooth transition toward democracy. Trujillo refused to comply, military assistance and arm shipments were terminated, and Ambassador Joseph S. Farland contacted the growing internal underground before the United States vacated his diplomatic post in May, 1960. . . .

The Communist Party was legalized and only Russian disinterest prevented the establishment of close political relations with the socialist countries. The disestablishment of the Catholic Church and the expropriation of all U.S.-owned property were urged in public. But in contrast to these anti-U.S. moves, Trujillo desperately tried to protect the country's much-valued sugar quota from OAS-inspired sanctions. His lobbyists and diplomatic representatives went to work in and outside the government on the close-knit sugar community. Lawrence Myers, head of the Agriculture Department's sugar office, Thomas Murphy, deputy to Myers, and William Case, an official in the sugar office, were secretly contacted. The lobbyists convinced Representative Harold Cooley (D.-N.C.), powerful Chairman of the House Agriculture Committee, to block legislative moves by the Eisenhower Administration to suspend the quota. When Congress adjourned without final action, executive power prevailed through an order imposing a special tax on Dominican sugar, thereby abolishing windfall quota profits.

Kennedy's rise to power gave Trujillo's lobbyists a new chance to alter U.S. policy. State Department consultant and sugar company executive Adolf A. Berle, Jr., and Under Secretary of State Chester Bowles were reached in an effort to have the special sugar tax lifted. Moreover, a special lobbyist (Igor Cassini) convinced Joseph Kennedy that a revolutionary situation was developing and that it would be helpful to send a special envoy to Ciudad Trujillo to assess matters. The State Department's top troubleshooter, Robert Murphy, paid an informal visit and again sought a liberalization of the regime. It was clear to the Kennedy Administration that support among Latin Americans for anti-Castro activities (including the Bay of Pigs) rested in part on anti-Trujillo moves. Without a power base in the executive branch of the United States Government the Dominican dictator was helpless to determine his own fate.

The failure of the Murphy mission set in motion the final stages of a CIA-supported plot to assassinate Trujillo. Chiefly organized by some of his own military officers, the assassination was successfully carried out on May 31, 1961. As an obstacle to, rather than an instrument for, domination, the Great Benefactor had to be removed.

The 1960's brought another era of reform and excitement, similar to the 1920's period before the dictatorial rash. The country that attempted the most serious transformations under the framework of elective politics was Venezuela during the regime of Rómulo Betancourt. Betancourt was a great friend of John Kennedy's and believed in the principles of the Alliance for Progress (discussed in the final part of this book). Venezuela was viewed as a proving ground for slow, nonviolent political change that was supposed to provide an alternative to Castro's Cuba. The selection is quite pro-Betancourt, but even so, one can easily see the problems that plagued Betancourt, the reasons that neither Venezuela nor any other Latin American country has made radical alterations under moderate, compromise politics.

Can Democracy Work?
Betancourt in Venezuela

By Robert Alexander

The most obvious observation that one can make about the Venezuelan Democratic Revolution concerns the magnitude of the programs that were launched in order to transform Venezuela, to convert the country into a modern nation with a balanced economy, a relatively equitable distribution of wealth, and a democratic political system. It set out to abolish the conditions of life and the patterns of thought that made it possible for a long series of military dictators to rule the country. It sought to transform the semi-dependent economy in which the majority of the people lived under the primitive conditions of several centuries ago.

Through its agrarian reform program, the Betancourt government began a massive redistribution of the national wealth. Through its projects for economic diversification and industrialization, the regime sought to develop new wealth and establish a balanced economy. Through its education, housing, and health efforts, and its program for providing basic social services to the rural people and the residents of towns and cities, the Betancourt government attempted to develop the country's human resources, and to raise the standards of living of its people.

The regime's oil policies as well as the industrialization program were designed to develop a greater degree of national independence in the economic field. Finally, through its handling of the armed forces and its general political policies, the Betancourt administration tried to establish the basis for a stable democratic form of government in Venezuela.

In carrying out its various programs, the government of the Venezuelan Democratic Revolution had certain advantages. These put it in a relatively favorable situation when compared with some of the other Latin American countries that are faced with more or less the same problems as Venezuela.

First of all, the country has been receiving and will probably continue to receive, for many years, a sizable income from the oil industry. This petroleum income meant that in spite of the temporary economic and financial crisis that marked the first years of the Betancourt administration, the regime could count on relatively large resources for financing its various reform and development efforts.

In the second place, the regime had the advantage of being led by two political parties which were well disciplined, well led, and which knew what they wanted and how they wanted to achieve their ends. The leaders of the Venezuelan Democratic Revolution were seasoned by long political experience, but were not so old as to have lost willingness to experiment and a feeling of enthusiasm for the fundamental changes that they were trying to bring about in Venezuelan life.

Finally, the Betancourt regime was fortunate to come to power at a time when the policies of the United States in its relations with Latin America were undergoing a decided alteration for the better. As a result, the Venezuelan democratic government had the benefit of receiving considerable moral, political, and financial support from the United States, particularly after the inauguration of President John F. Kennedy.

These advantages were partly offset by a number of serious handicaps which made the path of the regime a rough one and in some ways limited the effectiveness with which the administration was able to carry out its objectives.

The first such handicap was the economic-financial crisis that marked the first half of the Betancourt administration. Arising largely from circumstances created by the Pérez Jiménez and provisional regimes, this crisis limited considerably the financial resources available to the government, and forced it to spend large sums on projects that probably it would not otherwise have favored. . . .

The second major handicap that the government of the Venezuelan Democratic Revolution faced was the recalcitrance of its political opposition. The Right-wing opponents of the regime refused to give up their belief that the Betancourt government was "Communist" and that it should be overthrown by the time-honored but presently discredited means of the military conspiracy and coup d'état. The Left-wing opposition, for its part, made little secret of the fact that it repudiated political democracy and would overthrow the Betancourt government by insurrection in the streets or guerrilla warfare in the mountains if the opportunity to do so presented itself. This type of opposition made it exceedingly difficult for the Betancourt regime to be as simon-pure in preserving full civil liberties as its leaders would have liked. Even the democratic opposition frequently tended to go to extremes and to skirt on the edge of subversion in pressing its dissidence with the administration. . . .

A third difficulty of the Betancourt regime was the necessity to continue to spend too large amounts on the armed forces. Although under Betancourt the military item became for the first time only the third largest part of the budget, it continued to be necessary to spend impressive sums on the military. This remained the case not only because the regime did not want to run the risk of creating widespread discontent among the soldiers, sailors, and airmen, but also because of the genuine military dangers to the regime arising from action by disgruntled and displaced elements of the old Pérez Jiménez dictatorship, and from possible armed attacks on the government by the Movimiento de Izquierda Revolucionaria and the Communist party, with the backing of the Cuban regime of Fidel Castro. . . .

The agrarian reform got well under way during Betancourt's term of office. Although the leaders of the revolutionary democratic government had no illusions about completing the process of land distribution in a few years, let alone training fully the new landowners to use their land efficiently, they made a start on both under Betancourt. In the central part of the republic, the land redistribution program basically altered the pattern of ownership. A somewhat less dramatic impact was felt in the area around Lake Maracaibo and in the mountain states. The small holding was on the way to becoming typical in Venezuelan agriculture by the end of the Betancourt regime.

The Betancourt regime's program of industrialization also made very marked progress. Through a policy of protection for important branches of manufacturing, coordinated with the lending policies of the Corporación Venezolana de Fomento, the textile industry became capable of producing all but a small percentage of the country's needs, and the food-processing and metallurgical industries made important progress to the same end. By the end of the Betancourt administration, the country was also self-sufficient in automobile assemblies, pharmaceuticals, basic steel, and fertilizers.

Besides stimulating the growth of privately owned industries in many fields, the democratic government went ahead with the development of state enterprises in the field of heavy industry. It proceeded with the building of the steel and petrochemical plants, and undertook the establishment of an aluminum factory, in conjunction with the Reynolds Aluminum Company as a minority stockholder. It also pushed energetically the construction of a nation-wide government-owned electricity network to serve as a basis for further widespread industrial development.

During the Betancourt administration the basis was laid for a new nationalist policy for dealing with the country's principal source of foreign exchange, petroleum. The policy of giving no further concessions was firmly established. The organization late in 1960 of the Corporación Venezolana del Petróleo laid the foundations for a Venezuelan government-owned sector of the nation's oil industry, and opened the possibility for the gradual and orderly taking over of the industry by the government without disrupting it as a source of foreign exchange.

The most spectacular progress made by the Betancourt government was in the field of education. School attendance rose dramatically, and the government undertook to change the orientation of the nation's educational system to conform more closely to the needs of a rapidly developing economy and society. . . .

Finally, it may be argued that the fact that it was necessary to suspend some constitutional guarantees over a considerable period of time was a partial defeat for a government such as that of Rómulo Betancourt.

This regime was pledged to carry out a social revolution in a democratic manner. Therefore, any restriction on democracy would indicate that the government was falling short of its aspirations and its intentions. It must be underscored, however, that the suspension of guarantees was forced by serious attempts of the Left-wing opposition to overthrow the regime, or to provoke Right-wing military elements to do so. It should also be emphasized that the suspension of guarantees had little effect on the functioning of the three powers of government, and that the opposition had a wide range of legal activity open to it in spite of the suspension of guarantees. Nonetheless, it is to be lamented that such action had to be taken.

On balance, the Betancourt government was successful in planning for and carrying out the kinds of economic development and social reform programs that were promised by President Betancourt and Acción Democrática before and during the 1958 election campaign. For those who look for perfection, there is much to criticize in what the Betancourt regime did or left undone; however, when one considers the vastness of the problems involved in the Venezuelan Democratic Revolution, the achievements of the Betancourt regime far outweighed its errors of omission and commission.

One of the reasons that democracy seems unsuited to Latin America is that it becomes part of the cycle of salvation and redemption, the Indian notion that the world is constantly destroyed and re-created. Latin Americans have a different use for democracy than as a straight line toward progress on a stable succession of elected leaders. A leader may be exiled today, only to return with unanimous acclaim tomorrow; he may call himself a conservative today and radical tomorrow; his friends may embrace him today and plot his removal tomorrow. The most famous case of chronic election is that of José María Velasco Ibarra, the skeletal Ecuadorian who has been made president of his country five times from 1933 to 1968, only to be ignominiously shoved out of office four of those times. Why do they keep shunting him back and forth from exile to the presidency like a Ping-Pong ball?

How Democracy Fails:
Velasco Ibarra in Ecuador

By John Rothchild

A search for purity runs through Latin American politics. A rousing speech about the perils of poverty is often more appreciated than a detailed plan to do something about it: the Latin American has no natural affinity for compromises and gritty details, or for pushing toward a common denominator. The political forces seem to vibrate outward toward extremes, toward moments of exuberance and moments of despair and great empty spaces in between.

The Latin American politician himself is often strung out between sainthood and excommunication, between being heralded as the savior of his country and being unceremoniously banished from office. This cycle of total acceptance and total rejection is what makes democracy such a tenuous and artificial arrangement. For democracy thrives on trading and settling, on finding solutions completely satisfactory to nobody and partially satisfactory to all. This bartering and center-seeking does not fit the Latin American leaning toward esctasy, mysticism, and cosmic purification. Politics is not a tool in Latin America so much as it is a revival. Democracy had to be tailored to fit the Latin American character—the rigid postures, ideological impasses, and the destructions and redemptions of the Aztec gods.

Consider the strange career of José María Velasco Ibarra, the Ecuadorian leader who has been given the power to run his country five times, ranging from 1933 to 1968. By now, Velasco's longevity has made the white-haired, skeletal, ascetic figure into a famous political case—he has probably held the presidential office more times and longer than any leader of the modern world. But the most amazing thing about Velasco is that he is thrown out of the palace with the same consistency and the same enthusiasm as he is invited in. His campaign slogan, "give me a balcony and I will become president," is supported by a ferocious ability to excite the country, to unite it behind him, to make euphoria out of a political habit. But then the slogan has a reverse side, and there is always a balcony to throw Velasco off. Out of the five times he has come to power, Velasco has managed to complete a term of office only once, from 1952 to 1956. In each of the four other cases, he has been deposed by the military and forced into exile. The military itself is usually responding to the desires of a rival political faction, but by the time the tanks are rolled into the palace to escort Velasco out, the popular acclaim on which he is always elected has miraculously vanished. People say, "Well, Velasco has failed again. The old man has a good heart, but his ministers steal the country blind." Then this popular opposition evaporates as quickly as it was created, and in two or three years Velasco is invited back to another tumultuous welcome, and another attempt at finishing a four-year term.

The history of Velasco is a testimonial to the fickleness of Latin American politics, and while he represents the extreme case, most of the other countries have plenty of their own Velasco stories. In 1933 the young, liberal intellectual, supported by almost everybody in the country's congress, was named president by virtually unanimous popular acclaim. A few months later, none of the changes that he had promised were either apparent or forthcoming, and some of the legislators began to get restless and to criticize Velasco in public. He put them in jail, to reaffirm his control, to demonstrate his popularity, and to show the country that he was still the father figure who could punish with the upper hand. But in this act of jailing his opposition, Velasco created more opposition (the disillusionment was getting rampant), and he found himself facing a dissident congress. This phenomenon of a congress, pulling out its support from under a president is unknown in the United States—where party loyalties ensure a certain amount of stability—but in Latin America loyalty can be a very conditional thing. Velasco responded to the opposition not by trying to calm tempers, to move toward the center, to compromise, but by resorting to more extreme measures to quiet the criticism and return to a pure state of unqualified support. He dissolved the congress by presidential decree and convoked a new one, filling it with his own loyalists. His cleansing of congress is a favorite tactic of Latin American politicians, who seem to dislike the idea of living with ambiguity or accepting the validity of opposition. When there are severe problems with the government in Ecuador, the constitution is usually rewritten, and the country has gone through nineteen of them since independence. The constitution never changes much—a few words are added or deleted—but the purpose of replacing it, like dissolving the congress, is to create the illusion of starting all over again. But the same people and the same schisms remain.

After Velasco abolished the congress, his control was smothered in factionalism. Political life became unmanageable, because Velasco had been discredited and there was no machinery of government to make order out of his downfall. No machinery, that is, except the army, which is often called on to restore not only martial order but also political order. Velasco was sent into exile for the first time, and democracy received a setback.

In 1944 Velasco was returned to power for the second time (he ran unsuccessfully in 1940, and still claims he lost because of vote fraud). During the campaign of 1944 he sneaked in across the Colombian border because he was not yet officially welcome in Ecuador. He wrested power from a crumbling government in a coup popularly called the revolution of May 24, and his presidency was ratified after the fact by a congressional coalition that included socialists, communists, and conservatives. (Strange alliances are another trademark of Velasco politics.) Gradually, the leftists in this coalition abandoned Velasco, and he responded by putting some of them in jail. Just as it had happened during his first presidency, the rebellion grew, and this time legislators demonstrated their disrespect by burning pictures of Velasco on the floor of congress. Velasco dissolved the ungrateful body and presided over the formation of a new congress, composed mainly of conservatives who still supported him. The constitution was rewritten—this time it would be more to the conservatives' liking. The name of God was returned to the preamble, after it had been omitted in earlier constitutions to please the then-powerful liberals.

This Velasco-packed congress was supposed to get together and vote on a new president for the country; presumably the winner would be either Velasco himself or one of his supporters. After all, hadn't Velasco hand picked the congress? But leaving nothing to chance, Velasco didn't even trust his own manipulations at this point. He ordered the army to roll its tanks out to the legislature, to force the congress to vote for him. His fears were not entirely groundless, because a conservative candidate, who had secretly been assured of victory, was left holding his tuxedo specially tailored for the swearing-in. Velasco was named president again.

These pressure tactics served Velasco until 1947, when a group of military leaders again overthrew him for the purpose of restoring order between the warring political factions. Velasco was sent into exile for the second time.

But in 1952, just four years later, the country that had banished him to Argentina returned Velasco to the presidency by one of the largest pluralities in Ecuadorian history. The congress, with an unusually short memory for the way Velasco had treated it in the past, declared him unanimously elected. By this time, Velasco had gotten the reputation of being an innocent man, perhaps even a saint, who was so naïve that his trusted ministers would steal the treasury blind while he wasn't noticing anything. Velasco's downfalls were popularly attributed to the orgy of graft that accompanied his presidency, and the voters were probably not wrong in their opinions. (An orgy of graft has accompanied almost every Ecuadorian presidency.) But in the 1952 attempt, Velasco was able to survive the critics and actually finish a four-year term. He had unusually strong political allies during this period, especially Camilo Ponce Enríquez, one of the most powerful conservatives in the country, who served in Velasco's government. To reciprocate, Velasco supported Ponce for the 1956 presidential campaign, and Ponce won. (The version of the constitution then in force said that no president could succeed himself.)

Velasco ran for president again in 1960, this time against a man who was widely recognized in the United States as Latin America's only hope for democracy. North Americans could understand Velasco's opponent, Galo Plaza Lasso.

A product of a rich, conservative, landowning family, Galo Plaza was educated in the United States, spoke perfect English, and even played football at the University of Southern California. He was popular with U.S. audiences, partly because they could understand him, but also because Plaza preached a reassuring philosophy. He talked about how Latin Americans had not been prepared for democracy, how they were like children finally coming into voting age, and how the United States had to be patient during this critical maturing process. Plaza had served as president of Ecuador from 1948 to 1952, and he was instrumental in bringing foreign capital into the country. He was also boastful of the fact that his government was run efficiently, that he looked at his watch and arrived on time, and that the country had progressed under his Nelson Rockefeller-style leadership. The 1960 election, then, was an important choice between a low-key, rational, English-speaking technocrat and a haranguing, inspiring prophet whose greatest achievement was merely staying in office. Ecuador's voters chose Velasco, the latter figure, over Plaza by a whopping margin. Galo Plaza, understood so well in the

United States, was rejected by the electorate of his own country, proof of how different the political notions are on each side of the Rio Grande. (Later he became secretary-general of the Organization of American States, a post he still holds today.)

Velasco was now sixty-seven years old, the dean of Ecuadorian politics, and people thought that with all his training, and with such a large margin of support, he would surely finish out the term. They were, of course, wrong. After he had held office for a year, a group of military officers and plotting politicians (including Carlos Julio Arosemena, Velasco's vice-president at the time) pulled off a successful coup, and Velasco again found himself in exile, with time to reflect on how he had failed again.

Velasco's undignified exit was followed by the usual breakdown. Carlos Julio Arosemena, who had betrayed Velasco, became the president for a time. But he was abruptly removed by the military in 1961, after he reportedly urinated in the punchbowl at an official government function. Arosemena was replaced by a military junta that was in turn followed by a new congress, a new constitution (the eighteenth), and two provisional presidents.

Velasco, now well into his seventies, returned to his country in 1968 to be elected president for an incredible fifth term.

The 1968 election shows how short the Latin American political memory, how unimportant the political parties and their labels. Ecuador, like most of the other countries, has been traditionally divided between a liberal party and a conservative party, with splinter groups appearing and disappearing around the side. The liberals are known for their industrial, urban, coastal supporters, the conservatives for representing the Church and the old landed aristocracy. But as the Velasco example shows, political parties are often of no consequence in the real life of Latin American governments. During his career, Velasco has ruled in the name of all of Ecuador's factions, including the Marxists, switching his alliances easily and abruptly during the moments of trauma. Party structures may remain intact, but the politicians can quickly embrace them or shrug them off when such moves are convenient. There is little adherence to strict party doctrine or philosophy. For instance, once a groundswell for Velasco is detected, everybody rushes to his side; the liberals support him in return for key ministries in the government, the communists for recognition as a political party, the conservatives for financial favors. Inconsistencies and ideologies are forgotten as the candidate's power increases; strange bandwagons are formed. Even personal loyalties and the matters of honor discussed in other parts of this book do not always survive the requirements of politics. Carlos Julio Arosemena, the man who stabbed Velasco in the back during the coup of 1960, was one of the old man's first welcomers when Velasco returned to the country in 1968. Both Arosemena and Velasco rode together down the lined streets of Guayaquil, the country's largest city and major port, embracing each other and smiling.

The Velasco story seems endless—reelected in 1968, deposed again in 1970, the country beginning a whole new round of military rulers and provisional governments—but it says a lot about Latin American politics. Since party lines are not to be trusted, the politician can never be sure what alliances or coalitions are forming behind his back. Since unanimity is the goal of politics, the leader can hardly accept a little rebellion, or mollify the opposition; in Ecuador he tends to want to crush the opposition to affirm his power. This usually only strengthens the opposition and hastens a downfall. Since the army has a traditional role as a political power, a leader never knows when he might face exile, when a small coalition will be created to overthrow him.

The Ecuadorian people, for their part, do not trust politicians—even less than the average North American voter; they do not believe that government action will do them any good. In one of the poorest countries in Latin America, where the government is notoriously corrupt and the bureaucracy unmanageable, they have reason to disbelieve. Perhaps for that reason, or for the more profound reasons that the Guillén Martínez article on paternalism describes, the Latin American voter seeks a savior, through whom he can forget the problems of the day. And for the same reason that a savior like Velasco is created, he is also destroyed; when changes do not occur, the savior becomes a scapegoat and must be purged from the system. In all of these fractured comings and goings, this cycle of purification and rejection, democratic politics take on a meaning that is foreign to the North American observer. Leaders change unpredictably, but the system that invents them does not; the occupants of the presidential palace are removed, but the office itself is not remodeled.

Throughout modern Latin American history, the military has played a significant role in making and breaking presidents. The military has gotten a bad name in all this —a reputation for buying too many surplus jets, for wearing dark glasses, for preferring exotic tortures, and for intervening too easily in politics. In this selection, Edwin Lieuwen concludes that the Latin American military has no tactical purpose and is strictly a political institution. As a political party, the military provides organ ization and stability, and is called on during times of chaos to unify a nation or to cleanse it by forcing a presumed villain into exile. This is far different, say, from the military's role in the United States. Later we will see that the new generals of the 1960's have further altered the military's function—even to becoming a radical force in some countries.

The Military as Politician

By Edwin Lieuwen

To understand the nature of military intervention in Latin America today, it will help to dispose first of a prevalent myth. This is the notion that the armed forces are primarily a military institution. That this notion is erroneous becomes clear when their actual functions are scrutinized. There are two—and only two—legitimate military functions for an armed-forces organization to perform, namely, to defend the nation against external aggression and to defend the government by preserving internal order. However, in Latin America not only is there no real threat of extracontinental aggression, but the armed forces are totally unprepared to defend against it should it come.· . . .

As to protecting incumbents against internal disorders, more often than not, when civilian opposition to a constitutional government arises, the military, rather than come to the defense of such a government, will generally supplant that government with one more conducive to the maintenance of law and order. Furthermore, in the eyes of the military, the government exists to defend the armed forces, rather than vice versa. When this inversion of the military function occurs, as it does in most of Latin America today, then that function becomes purely political.

What of the military paraphernalia—the aircraft carriers, the destroyers, the jet fighters, the bombers, and the tanks? What are they for? Obviously, they are not for defense against Russia, or even Cuba. This hardware is sometimes purchased to keep pace with one's neighbors. For example, there is the struggle for supremacy among the Peruvian, Ecuadorian, and Venezuelan Air Forces and among the Argentine, Brazilian, and Chilean Navies, but national pride and jealousy, rather than preparations for future wars, explain the purchase of such equipment. For all the nations of Latin America are allied militarily under the 1947 Inter-American Treaty of Reciprocal Assistance (the Rio Pact), and the peace machinery of the Organization of American States has, in effect, outlawed war within the hemisphere.

In fact, the military hardware is exclusively for internal use and is utilized by the armed forces mainly for political rather than military functions. These arms, particularly the tanks and planes, were used to topple seven popularly elected governments between March 29, 1962, and April 2, 1964 (an average of one every 105 days), and in the aftermath of the coups, to cow the deposed regimes' student, labor, and peasant supporters.

Brandishment of these arms has been generally sufficient to enable the military to seize power from the civilian authorities, but the only arena in which the arms are actually employed in battle is against rival services within the country, such as the Air Force versus the Army in Ecuador in 1961 and in Guatemala in 1962, the Air Force and Army versus the Navy in Venezuela in 1962, and the Air Force versus the Navy in Argentina in 1963. In addition, these arms may be employed in intraservice fighting, particularly within the armies, such as in the case of the engineers versus the infantry in Ecuador in 1961 and the cavalry versus the infantry in Argentina in 1962. The acquisition and use of arms for conducting internecine service warfare within a country can hardly be considered a legitimate military function, for the various services, or branches thereof, invariably fight over political issues—constitutionalism in Brazil and Ecuador in 1961, and also in Guatemala and Venezuela in 1962, and elections in Argentina in 1963. All these matters were resolved in favor of the military faction having the greater number of units of effective firepower. That the issues themselves are resolved with bullets rather than ballots does not obscure their essentially political nature. . . .

In terms of political institutions, there is no civilian political force or combination of forces able to compete with the armed forces. Once that institution makes up its mind on a given issue, nothing can prevent it from having its way. This is largely because the military has arms, a monopoly on the means of violence, and thus the incontrovertible argument of force on its side. But it is also because the military possesses an organizational structure far superior to that of any civilian political party. Its centralized command, its hierarchical structure, and its disciplined membership make it capable of acting with complete unity. However, the recent armed-forces schisms have served to weaken somewhat the military's heretofore customary advantages in weapons and organization.

The armed forces hold that they have a legitimate political mission above that of the government. Their first allegiance is to the nation and to the constitution, as they interpret it, rather than to the ephemeral civilian politician who happens to occupy the presidential chair at a given moment. Thus, the military's custodianship of the national interest, a heritage from the wars for independence, makes its political involvement inevitable.

Normally, the armed forces will support the duly elected civilian government, but the moment the situation departs from what they view as normal, they begin to re-examine their position. If public order threatens to break down as a result of growing opposition to the policies of the incumbent government, then the military feels a constitutional duty to intervene, usually only temporarily, to provide the nation with a more viable administration. The armed forces always disclaim any desire to exercise political power themselves; they wish only to guarantee that the civilians who exercise it are doing it properly in the true national interest and are not perverting their functions. Perversion of the governing function includes, in the eyes of the military, any actions inimical to the interests of the armed forces, such as any humiliation, material weakening, and moral undermining of the armed-forces establishment. . . .

This selection is about politics in Argentina, but it illustrates the thin tightrope that an elected leader must walk, how he must appease the conflicting interests, how he must constantly fear a military coup. Frondizi was also a democratic reformer; the groups that caused his downfall have done the same to other Latin American progressive leaders who rely on the democratic process.

The Political Tightrope
By Jerome Levinson and Juan de Onis

Nine months after Quadros [President Janio] resigned in Brazil, the Argentine armed forces overthrew President Arturo Frondizi, who had taken office in 1958 after a landslide electoral victory. Frondizi had been the candidate of the moderate left wing of the Unión Cívica Radical (UCR) party. Like Quadros in Brazil (elected as an independent), Frondizi had extended his electoral base beyond his own party, primarily by wooing the outlawed Peronists (followers of the former populist dictator, Juan Perón) with campaign pledges of social legislation, nationalism, and state control of heavy industry. The week before the election, reports circulated that Frondizi had made a deal with Perón to legalize the Peronist Justicialista party. But once elected, he acted upon his own view of the immediate economic and political realities and did the opposite of what he had pledged.

He opened up the oil industry to foreign investment and initiated an ... economic stabilization program; the peso was devalued, multiple exchange rates were scrapped, tight credit restrictions were imposed, consumer subsidies were eliminated, wage increases not linked to production increases were discouraged, and a determined effort was made to balance the budget. Labor felt betrayed, particularly when Frondizi called in the military to break major strikes. Financial austerity hit consumers, and businessmen chafed at credit restrictions.

In his efforts to steer his way among the various interest groups of Argentine society, Frondizi offended all of them. In order to garner Roman Catholic support he placed private religious educational institutions on an equal footing with state schools, and thus incurred the wrath of anticlerical liberals and socialists. In order to conciliate the Peronists, he returned control of labor unions to elected Peronist leaders, and thus angered the right-wing military. In order to curry favor on the left, he espoused a policy, like Quadros' in Brazil, of nonintervention in the hemisphere and neutrality toward Cuba, and thus infuriated Argentine conservatives. Like a circus performer on a shaky highwire, Frondizi moved from one breathtaking crisis to another, until, in March 1962, he lost his political footing and fell.

In the general elections of March 1962, Frondizi allowed the Peronists to compete openly under the colors of their own political party, the Frente Justicialista. The Frente won 35 percent of the vote, more than Frondizi's own party (28 percent), and gained forty-five of the eighty-six contested seats in the Chamber of Deputies and nine of the fourteen governorships. The military forced Frondizi to prevent Andrés Framini, a Peronist labor leader who had been elected as governor of Buenos Aires province, from taking office. A wave of Peronist-led strikes ensued and Frondizi had to call on the military to control them.

The military was increasingly divided between those pushing for an outright coup and those who, concerned that the whole world was watching, wanted just to keep Frondizi under control. Frondizi tried to check the rising conspiracy of anti-Peronist politicians, particularly in the right wing of the UCR, and military chiefs, particularly in the Navy, by collaborating with the wing of the military opposed to a coup, but in the showdown the constitutionalist military lost out. The U.S. military attachés in Buenos Aires strongly advised the Argentine military against a coup, but to no avail. On March 29, 1962, Frondizi was arrested at the presidential residence by military officers and imprisoned on Martín García Island. The Supreme Court invested as president José María Guido, president of the Senate and constitutional successor to the presidency. The military justified its action, in what was to become a standard line throughout the hemisphere, as "necessary to maintain democratic procedures."

Latin America is increasingly turning to military governments to bring about social change and economic
progress. The two most notable of these governments
exist in Brazil and Peru—the Brazilian model representing
political repression and favoritism to foreign capital and
private industry, the Peruvian example tending toward
socialism, expropriation of private industry, and redistribution of land. What are the successes and failures of each
of these models? We will look at right-wing Brazil in
this part; an evaluation of Peru's left-wing governmnt
appears in the next section of the book.

Brazil at the Crossroads

By Robert M. Levine

In April 1973, Brazil's "revolutionary" military government will enter its ninth year. Already it has
achieved a longevity exceeded in modern times only
by Getúlio Vargas, in and out of power as chief of
state during a total of 20 years between 1930 and
1954. Whether the present regime collectively will surpass Vargas' record remains to be seen. Official plans,
at any rate, call for presidential elections in 1974, although the President himself holds discretionary powers to modify or cancel the election schedule. Present
indications suggest that Brazil's military leaders, hostile to the prospective return to open political debate,
will opt for a closed process of selection, leaving the
choice of the next President to the armed forces high
command, subject to technical ratification by the duti-
ful federal Congress.

Recent statements by Senator Felinto Müller, the
majority leader of the official pro-government party,
the Aliança Renovadora Nacional (ARENA), hint that
national elections will not be held in 1974. Müller,
who was Vargas' chief of police during the fascistic
Estado Novo (1937–1945), suggested early in 1972
that a gradual return to civilian government would be
permitted; but later in the year he reversed his stand,
stating publicly that the "principal virtue" of his party
would continue to be "obedience," and that attempts

to discuss the presidential succession would be inappropriate.

Government officials have not been insensitive to the question of the restoration of democracy. A 1971 Rand Corporation study which speculated that the Brazilian military might remain in power until the year 2000 widely irritated Brazilian authorities, who have taken pains, especially outside of Brazil, to affirm the transitory nature of their authoritarian regime. . . .

Despite President Costa e Silva's earlier pledge to "humanize the revolution" after assuming office, anger over vocal dissidence from a minority group of congressmen—one of whom, Márcio Moreira Álves, allegedly insulted the honor of the armed forces (and publicly accused the government of the use of physical torture against political prisoners)—prompted the government to decree, on December 13, 1968, Institutional Act Number Five, a repressive law which closed federal, state and municipal legislatures, suspended the constitutional right of *habeas corpus*, and set the stage for mass detentions of persons suspected of subversion under the act and the Revised National Security Law of March, 1969.

Rising incidents of political kidnapping, hijackings, and terrorist acts . . . exacerbated tensions, as authorities pressed their campaign of political repression. Nearly 100 federal legislators were purged, as were three justices of the Brazilian Supreme Court and numerous civil servants and university professors. In the aftermath of the abduction of United States Ambassador C. Burke Elbrick (who was released in exchange for 15 imprisoned students and militants), the government issued Institutional Act Number Fourteen, which imposed the death penalty for "psychological warfare and revolutionary or subversive activities against the state."

After the incapacitation of President Costa e Silva by a cerebral hemorrhage in August, 1969, the military's unwillingness to permit a civilian to accede to the presidency even temporarily led to the suspension of the constitution and the seizure of control by the chiefs of the three armed services. In consultation with the supreme military command, they chose General Garrastazú Médici, the former head of the Brazilian Security Agency (SNI), as Chief of State. In his first public statement, Médici declared his intention to restore democracy by the completion of his term of office. In May, 1970, however, he changed his mind, stating that the military government would remain in power "as long as it might take to implant the political, administrative, juridical, social, and economic structures capable of raising all Brazilians to the minimum level of well-being."

Stricter Military Control

The turn to stricter political control after December, 1968, reflected the military's continuing disillusionment with seemingly inept and corrupt civilian politicians, and its firm belief that economic growth, made possible by foreign confidence in Brazil's stability, must be given precedence over social justice. By late 1971, urban terrorist activities subsided, the result of the fragmentation of the guerrilla movement.... In turn, authorities relaxed the campaign of repression which had raised cries of protest abroad, but refused to relax the strict censorship of the press and media....

To its supporters, and particularly to the international business community, these issues stand as necessary annoyances which permit Brazil to achieve economic development and strive toward her stated goal of becoming a world power. Under the post-1968 "third phase," the regime has initiated a wide variety of programs, including massive highway construction designed to link Brazil to each of her South American neighbors by 1973, the industrialization of the underdeveloped northeast, expanded facilities for higher education, especially in technical subjects, and economic growth under a new "Brazilian model," based upon neutralizing inflation, promoting exports, encouraging private investment, increasing national savings and maintaining foreign confidence.

The record has been impressive, although doubts can be raised regarding the significance and the social costs of the gains to date. Economic progress, while dramatic, has not affected the country evenly, either in terms of regional growth (the urban centers of the south have fared best) or in income distribution. In short, the rich are getting richer and the poor are getting poorer. While the overall growth rate in 1971 was announced at 11.3 per cent and the per capita GNP rose an estimated 6 per cent, real wages for the majority of the population fell by 38 per cent between 1964 and 1969, although for the tiny percentage of university graduates they have risen by approximately 50 per cent in a comparable period. . . .

. . . For most wage earners—particularly outside the highly developed Rio de Janiero–São Paulo–Minas Gerais triangle, the gap between the rising cost of living and real wages has not been bridged by "national" economic progress.

Opening the Interior

In a talk at Columbia University in October, 1972, ex-President Juscelino Kubitschek—still stripped of his political rights at home—praised the current regime's economic policies, suggesting that the "revolutionary" government's efforts to attract foreign investment and to open the Brazilian hinterland represented the culmination of programs initiated under his own presidency from 1956 to 1961. In any case, the military has harvested extensive mileage from its dramatic program of highway construction, the symbolic (and effective) key to its goal to achieve meaningful national integration and *de facto* Brazilian presence in remote frontier regions. . . .

Highway construction has provided jobs, including temporary work for thousands of destitute drought refugees during 1970–1971 who were briefly organized into work gangs as a form of welfare employment. Indigenous tribes residing in the path of the new highways will be relocated on federal reservations, not only to preserve their way of life (their numbers have been savagely depleted by the penetration of civilization and alleged acts of systematic extermination which created an international furor in the late 1960's) but to allow for the transfer of as many as one million initial settlers. These families will be placed in new "agrovillages," supervised by military authorities, in the regions opened up by the Trans-Amazon road. Ironically, the dramatic industrialization of the northeast under government incentives has failed to provide employment, since most of the investment has been capital-intensive; some critics suggest, perhaps not unfairly, that the decision to construct the Trans-Amazon indicates evidence that authorities have given up on SUDENE, the northeast's development agency, and are seeking a safety valve for the region's surplus population.

Skepticism persists in other areas as well. Ecologists warn that the destruction of the Amazon rainforest may alter the world's climate within a generation and threaten its oxygen supply within a century. The Brazilian delegation to the United Nations conference on the environment in Stockholm in June, 1972, actively opposed proposals for international restrictions on pesticides and other ecological measures on the grounds of national sovereignty, an argument rejected by the congress almost unanimously. Agronomists point out that unless the new settlers of the Amazon adopt rational agricultural methods, they will exhaust the soil after one or two crops have been cultivated. The FAO, in fact, has refused to cooperate with the Brazilians as long as current plans for agricultural development are retained. Some of the best land bordering the highway has already been purchased by speculators, including Bradesco, Brazil's largest private bank. . . .

The Armed Forces

Brazil's military establishment, the backbone of the "revolution," has not remained a static force; rather, major changes have occurred in the relatively short period of time since 1964. Although the military's budget stands relatively low on a per capita basis, the armed forces have received extensive military aid from the United States, and are currently attempting to diversify equipment, with recent major purchases ranging from a $20-million Australian anti-submarine system to French Roland ground-to-air missiles. The Brazilian Air Force, seeking to establish its autonomy from the other two services, is completing a major effort at modernization, topped by an order for 112 "Xavante" fighter-bombers under Italian license and 16 Mirage III aircraft; pilots have also received training in the use of napalm.

A carefully planned modification of the military's career structure carried out under President Médici has already produced results; its impact may be far-reaching. In order to speed promotions of younger officers and avoid top-heavy concentration in the upper ranks, the military command has ordered that officers must retire at 66, or after four years in the same post. As a result, many generals who rose to power after 1964 with Castelo Branco and Costa e Silva are leaving the service, some to accept lucrative jobs in private industry, but in any event, strengthening the hand of President Médici, who by late 1972 had appointed six of the ten generals in the army's high command.

Most of the newly promoted figures appear colorless in comparison to the "hard line" colonels and generals who seemed to dominate the early phases of the "revolution." Their replacements, in contrast, seem to have been chosen for their anonymity, their administrative competence, and their professional dedication to the armed forces. The highest military officials remain almost entirely outside public view. Speculation on whether General Médici will seek "reelection" is forbidden, although observers perceive a low-keyed struggle developing between potential backers of Médici and supporters of General Ernesto Guisel, brother of the Minister of War, Orlando Guisel. Some suggest that Médici personally favors an active role for the military in social change, but that he is waiting to consolidate his own power and the retirement of older officers who might raise opposition. . . .

Cracks in the Facade?

During 1972, a number of problems have come to light, marring the image of optimism and progress which the regime has cultivated. The stock market, driven up during a frenzied 18-month boom, reached a peak index of 5,280 in June, 1970. Thousands of middle class Brazilians, lured by tax incentives and get-rich-quick schemes, joined the bandwagon, only to find the market reversing itself, reaching a low of 1,280 in August, 1972. In the wake of the debacle came the dismissal of the presidents of the São Paulo and Rio de Janeiro stock exchanges (for alleged "short" selling), rumors of mismanagement and misappropriation of public funds, and the near downfall of Treasury Minister Antônio Delfim Neto and Justice Minister Alfredo Buzaid. The seriousness of the matter prompted the government's decision to intensify press censorship, adding unfavorable discussions of economic matters to the list of previously proscripted themes.

In the area of education, substantial gains in university-level enrollment—from 92,000 places in 1961 to nearly 650,000 in 1972—have been made, supervised since 1969 by the no-nonsense Education Minister, Colonel Jarbas Passarinho. On the other hand, restrictions on student activity continue, intensified after mass student protests in the late 1960's; professors considered politically or pedagogically independent have been prematurely "retired," and tuition costs for many university students have been rising. Despite well-intentioned programs to reduce illiteracy among the general population, 35 per cent of all Brazilians cannot read or write. Primary school openings grew from 9.3 million in 1963 to only 13.3 million eight years later, a modest increase, considering Brazil's annual population growth rate of 3 per cent.

Relations between the government and the Catholic Church worsened in mid-1972 over the issue of a hunger strike among 36 political prisoners, three of them Dominican priests, in São Paulo's Tiradentes penitentiary. The church has tended to support the military regime, although hundreds of priests and nuns have opposed it; some were implicated for having assisted urban terrorists, and one archbishop, Dom Helder Câmara, considered a renegade by the church hierarchy, has spoken out sharply against the government outside Brazil. . . .

Industrial gains, accompanied by rising exports of manufactured goods to neighboring Latin American countries, the United States and Europe, buoyed confidence in the regime, but raised questions concerning the capacity of the domestic market to absorb consumer goods and the efforts of industrial modernization to produce selective unemployment, especially among older workers. The steady stream of migration from the impoverished northeast to the prosperous south, a problem which has persisted for decades, has acted to depress the labor market and has created potentially dangerous social tensions as the gap between skilled and unskilled labor lengthens. . . .

There is growing reason to believe that high government officials, military as well as civilian, are becoming dissatisfied with the inability of the economic "miracle" to benefit the majority of the population. In 1972, President Médici himself remarked that while the economy was faring well, the people were faring less well. . . .

What all this suggests is that military leaders are quite unlikely to consider the "revolution" sufficiently successful to permit a return to civilian government in the near future. . . .

In 1960, under five million working Brazilians earned less than 98 cruzeiros, or about $17 per month; in 1970, the number rose to more than seven million. With the military government no longer reluctant to recognize such dilemmas publicly—although its statements have been muted—it is unlikely to relinquish power, especially under formulae which it considers obsolete and self-serving. . . .

PART X.

THE REVOLUTION: DEAD OR ALIVE?

Introduction

The Cuban revolution is almost fifteen years old, and we know very little about it. The United States feared that Castro would stimulate successful guerrilla operations in other countries, a fear that led to a massive build-up of Latin American military strength. We ignored the causes of the Cuban revolution from the beginning—the special nature of Cuba, the coincidences and historical factors that led to Castro's success. The selection by Ramón Ruiz explains these factors; Castro comes off not as a charlatan or an aberration, but as a consequence of the traditional flow of Cuban politics. The results of the revolution have also been obscured, because it is difficult to get information from Cuba and because the United States has been so worried about Castro's influence abroad that it has not stopped to examine what the revolution has accomplished at home.

Barry Reckord is a Jamaican playwright who visited Cuba about four years ago. He saw in the revolution not so much a political example as a social experiment—an attempt to create what Castro calls the New Man. Some of Reckord's observations may be a little dated, but at least he asks the right questions about Cuba. Reckord views Castro, like Mao Tse-tung, as one of the few modern leaders who have tried to reform the lives and beliefs of their people, to wrench apart the way cultures have always done things. According to Reckord, Castro had not resorted to either Stalinist forced labor or greedy capitalist incentives to get the people out into the cane fields. When the New Man cuts the cane, he is not supposed to be lured by carrots or pushed by sticks, but by his own private devotion to Cuba. This experiment in voluntarism, as Reckord describes it, has not been a complete success; a high absentee rate was partially responsible for Cuba's failure to harvest ten million tons of sugar in 1968, the

300

year when spirits were highest and the most energy was put into the cane fields.

The interesting thing about Castro's experiment is that it challenges what have always been considered immutable Latin American traits, some of the traits that we have discussed in this book. Castro has tried to eliminate the resistance to manual labor by middle- and upper-class people; the belief in titles, bureaucracy, and hierarchy; the fatalism; the indifference to anything outside of the immediate family. As Reckord tells it, Castro pretty much abolished the bureaucracies, got the professional classes out of the cities to cut cane alongside the *campesinos*, shattered the traditional family unit, overturned the school system, and seemingly cut away at several layers of the old culture.

This attempt to change a culture seems more important than the mere nationalization of industries or whether the Cuban economy can survive in the world market or how the government is being run. I don't know what the results of the experiment are, or how long the Castro regime—new man or old man—can survive. But Reckord's line of questioning is worth pursuing, not only for the sake of the rest of Latin America, but even for the United States—trapped in its own way by professionalism, immobile bureaucracies, fatalism, and indifference. Cuba may be the most ignored and the most important social laboratory in the world.

Some people in Cuba attempted to export the revolution, either by direct invasion or by inspiration, but the efforts have failed. Castro's lieutenant Ché Guevara left the island in the middle 1960's and tried to take the revolution with him. After finding no luck in Africa, Ché sneaked into Bolivia with a few other veterans from the Sierra Maestra campaigns. Ché chose Bolivia perhaps because the 1952 Indian rebellion in the tin mines had been a revolutionary inspiration to him. In doing so, he made the same mistake as the U.S. leaders who feared that Castro could overtake the entire hemisphere. Ché also believed that the revolution could be exported, that the idea was stronger than custom or nationality, and that a few men with guns and good hiding places would be enough to bring off the revolt.

This belief was mocked by the feuding Bolivian communist parties, many of whom actually opposed his efforts; by the cold, distrustful Indians, who saw Ché as a foreigner; and by the aimlessness of some of his guerrilla band, who sold out as spies to the regular Bolivian military. The few members who remained of Ché's pathetic army were ferreted out and killed in a series of skirmishes in an isolated mountain area during 1968. Ché was captured and later informally executed in a little Indian town near the last battlefield. A section of Ché's diary, reprinted here, shows the frustrations, the heroism—and how far Bolivia was from the Cuban Sierra Maestra.

Ché's death, a revolutionary failure, turned him into the symbol of a revolutionary success. After 1968 the threat of Indian revolts seemed diminished all over Latin America (except perhaps in Central America), and the armies turned themselves into sophisticated antiguerrilla outfits, courtesy of U.S. assistance. The revolutionary impulse was carried on by two rather curious groups—the priesthood, long considered the fattest, most backward, indolent, and conservative institution in Latin America; and the university students, usually from the privileged white upper classes.

What leads a Latin American priest from an elite family to put down the cross, take up the machine gun, and head for the hills to fight? The selection on Camilo Torres, a Colombian priest who became a guerrilla and was killed by the army, shows how he got there—a route taken by a large number of Latin American students and intellectuals during the late 1960's.

All of these revolutionary efforts begun in cities or among the sons of the privileged have, to my knowledge, been crushed—the massacre and arrest of hundreds of Mexican students before the 1968 Olympics, the elimination of the Tupamaros in Uruguay, the torturing of revolutionary cadres in Brazil, the death of Ché and Camilo Torres—and the revolutionary impulse seems dormant for the moment. The efforts of people like Camilo Torres had an aura of martyrdom about them; they did not possess the hard ingredients that forced Batista out of Cuba or Díaz out of Mexico in 1910.

The armed revolutions have not generally succeeded, but some of the goals of the struggle have ironically been adopted by the very groups that were supposed to fight against them. The Latin American militaries, strengthened to meet the Castro threat, have in some places become the vanguard of a new revolutionary society. The Peruvian military regime, as Georgie Anne Geyer describes it here, has instituted some of the changes that Castro brought to Cuba—nationalization of foreign industries, expropriation of *haciendas*—and the U.S. businessmen who supported the strengthening of the armies are amazed and dismayed. The Cubans themselves are saying that they will have to reevaluate their traditional opposition to Latin American militaries, that their greatest enemies may turn out, in the end, to be their greatest ally. (This exuberance must be tempered, of course, by the fact that some of the current military regimes, such as Brazil's and Argentina's, are both politically repressive and favorable to U.S. corporate interests.)

There is a sense, after a decade when leftists believed that arms and bullets were the only way to make revolutions, that perhaps more radical ends can be achieved by much less radical means. Regis Debray, leftist philosopher and friend of Ché, reevaluated his own attitudes after spending time in Chile under the elected Marxist regime of the late Salvador Allende. We will never know whether Allende's campaign to nationalize the copper mines and establish a socialist state might have worked or been permitted to work. But what happened in Chile had a real importance how a country brings itself freely to choose socialism and where that choice takes them. Joseph Kraft traveled around Chile, and his reactions to the Chilean experiment are presented here.

There is a feeling in Latin America, as it enters the 1970's, that anything is possible: the military can be revolutionary; even the Catholic church (as the Veliz selection points out) can work for social upheaval; democratically elected regimes like the one in Chile can bring about socialism; dictatorships can preserve capitalism or communism; elitist students can defend peasants. The political stereotypes don't fit anymore; the expectations are twisted in strange shapes; there are no sure results. But after Cuba, Chile, and to some extent Peru, the question still remains: is Latin America a revolutionary society? The same question was asked after the Mexican revolution of 1910. There is growing poverty but not always growing restlessness, slums but not always rifles, despair but not always the will to fight, machete revolts but not always social upheaval, heroic leaders but not always followers. The desire to overturn has always been a part of Latin America, but Cuba, like Mexico before it, does not help us to measure the potential lifespan of the Nicaraguan dictatorship or the Brazilian military junta. Some say that revolutions come when people have nothing more to lose; some say that empty-bellied guerrillas do not fight as well as full-bellied ones who struggle in the name of toasters and cars and television sets.

Every Latin American country is seeking economic progress, and all the different tactics seem to be enclosed in two alternatives. There is the Brazilian model, the straitjacket military state that favors the foreign corporation, exactly like the Díaz Mexican regime did in 1900. Prosperity will come faster, the Brazilian proponents say, if people will tighten their belts in deference to attracting corporations. Then there is the Peruvian or Chilean or Cuban model: take over the industries, give land back to the people, risk the international economic sanctions, untie yourself from the large corporations. Prosperity will arrive, the proponents of this alternative say, if people will tighten their belts and wait for socialism to work. How revolutionary these alternatives are, whether they will result in more bloody civil wars, or whether they will fulfill their promises, is difficult to say. Whatever the answer, the United States, in the concluding view of Mexican novelist Carlos Fuentes, should stay out of it.

After Fidel Castro turned against the United States, we tried to find the source of his power in communist doctrine: when was the exact moment he accepted communism? We ignored Cuban history, the long resentment of the United States, and the steady development of leftist politics that produced Castro and his beliefs. Many people wanted to think that Castro deceived his own people—a communist posing as a democrat—but this selection traces back the roots of the revolution and explains why Cuba created Castro.

It is worth mentioning that the United States helped Cuba liberate itself from Spain in 1898, when Theodore Roosevelt took San Juan Hill. However, the Cubans have always resented the fact that the U.S. military occupied and ran the country after independence was achieved.

Why Cuba Found Castro
By Ramón Eduardo Ruiz

Cuba presents Americans with the perplexing paradox of a relatively rich country which underwent a major social cataclysm. Until 1958 the island was simply another Caribbean republic, the "sugar plantation" of the world; yet that mono-cultural economy, the target of bitter and persistent criticism, had produced one of the highest standards of living in the Western Hemisphere. Judged by the extremes of the North American "paradise" and the inferno of Haiti, the poorest of the Caribbean republics, Cuba was a purgatory. But, to the surprise of the experts, it was Cuba and not its poverty-burdened neighbors that had a social revolution.

Although no one can say precisely why a radical upheaval engulfed the island in 1959, Cuba's history contains the key to the probable causes. The shape and course of the Revolution were determined primarily by internal circumstances which were the products of a special society. Foreign events helped to transform the Revolution, but the transformation would have been impossible if the particular historical development of Cuban society had not encouraged it. . . .

Although it is true that the ideological shift which occurred when Cuba embraced Marxism-Leninism in 1961 marked an abrupt departure from a neo-capitalistic system and the old reliance on the United States, the Revolution did have roots in national development. There was continuity between the thwarted revolution of 1933 and the upheaval of 1959, and both reflected the mood of the independence struggle of 1895. The new Marxism had roots not only in the Cuban Communist party, the most successful in Spanish America, but in the island's labor movement—which Marxists of varying hues had built in the 1930's and dominated until the late 1940's. . . .

The triumphant Revolution of 1959 represented no sharp break with the past; instead, as Castro has said, it climaxed a long historical struggle, the ultimate success of which had been dreamed of by people who began to fight in the nineteenth century. Nor were the tactics of the Revolution either new or original. From the day in 1953 that Castro and his militants attacked Fort Moncada until the victory of 1959, the revolutionaries copied a pattern of action nearly a hundred years old. The guerrilla warfare adopted in 1956, writes Armando Hart, one of Castro's intimate friends, followed a blueprint that dated back to the nineteenth century, the architects of which were the mulatto warrior Antonio Maceo and the men of 1895 who, inspired and led by José Martí, initiated the final battle for independence. Only national Communism was an innovation, and even that was not entirely alien to Cuban history. . . .

These sentiments were the product of long domination by the United States. For more than a hundred years of colonial life Cubans had been the stepchildren of a declining Spain which was compelled, on more than one occasion, to reject brash American bids for the island. No sooner had Cuba achieved independence from Spain than it was forced by the United States to accept the Platt Amendment, which severely circumscribed the island's freedom of action. The winning of independence, and later the implementation of the ideal, required a militant nationalism which politicians learned to wield effectively for domestic purposes. Castro was not the first politico to exploit fear of imperialism. Nearly every Cuban intellectual had done so, invariably blaming the Wall Street dragon for the island's difficulties. Anti-American tirades were familiar reading. Although they were frequently tongue-in-cheek or simply patriotic propaganda, the youth of Cuba believed them. Castro and his patriots were among the naive who accepted the simplistic diatribes. Ironically, hundreds of these former critics of the United States, who certainly influenced the thinking of their current enemies in Havana, are now in Miami. . . .

Cuban leaders also imitated America politically. Not only was the Constitution of 1901, and to some extent that of 1940, modeled after the American prototype, but the division of Cuba into six provinces reflected the political structure of the United States. Even the famous system of readings in the tobacco factories, which included propaganda favoring independence, developed in imitation of the public readings popular in the United States.

Economically, Cuba profited from its association with the United States, ranking in 1958 as one of the most advanced countries in the Spanish-speaking world. To those Cubans satisfied with the status quo, their country had, in the words of W. W. Rostow, reached the "take-off" stage. According to statistics of the Banco Nacional de Cuba for 1956, per capita income was 336 pesos (the peso was on a par with the dollar)—the second highest in Latin America. The national sugar industry was a highly mechanized system, operating in conjunction with one of the three highly developed railway networks in Latin America and with up-to-date highways and ports. On a per capita basis, Cuba was the most heavily capitalized of the Hispanic-American countries, and second in gold reserves and foreign trade. Only Mexico, Brazil, and Chile outranked Cuba in the value of industrial production. One of every five Cuban laborers was a skilled worker, while over two-thirds of the population could read and write—a figure surpassed only by the "European" countries of South America. Cuba ranked third in the number of physicians, first in the number of television stations and receiving sets; only North Americans attended movies more frequently than Cubans. For these and other advantages, United States citizens, capital, and skill were at least partly responsible. The island, observed Arthur M. Schlesinger, Jr., was the perfect test for the thesis of the Eisenhower administration that "unhampered private investment was Latin America's road to salvation. . . ."

Yet the question of social revolution rests not merely on the issue of economic development, but more precisely on the degree of social justice. Are the majority of the people, and particularly the emerging middle classes, receiving a just share of the fruits of economic development? Has national progress satisfied "rising expectations?" The facts demonstrate that, in the opinion of many Cubans, economic progress had not brought about a sufficient degree of social justice for all Cubans. Schlesinger concedes that there were "shocking disparities in the distribution of wealth, especially between city and countryside and between white and Negro." Furthermore, statistics do not reveal a growing equality in the distribution of income. Only a fraction of the population enjoyed a monthly per capita income of 540 pesos, while the majority of rural families survived on seven pesos. . . .

Denied a full share of the economy, the Cuban middle sector turned to political activity. From 1940 to 1952 politicians of this sector had more or less controlled the political apparatus. The Auténticos, the party of Ramón Grau San Martín and Carlos Prío Socarrás, won the national elections of 1944 and 1948, and individual members of the middle sector held political posts at the local, state, and national levels from the twenties. Despite the tardy collaboration of Batista and his sergeants, the frustrated revolution of 1933 was essentially the contribution of the middle sector.

Unfortunately for Cuba, the middle-sector politician failed to offer able class or national leadership. Instead, more frequently than not, he coveted public office for personal profit, thereby making both the middle sector and the nation suffer. Ultimately, the politicians formed a distinct and separate class, which was castigated for its disregard of the public good, and by 1958 had little prestige among the people of Cuba.

The Cuban experience casts doubts on the validity of the theory popular among some political scientists who envisage the salvation of Latin America in terms of middle-sector rule. For in Cuba, where the middle sector exercised political power, it totally discredited itself and, in the eyes of lower-class Cubans, the system of representative government. The lower classes saw themselves as no better off under the middle-sector politicians than they had been under the former insurgents and sugar barons of the era from independence to 1940. . . .

But the fact that middle-sector unrest existed does not prove that the Revolution was middle class. Castro's rambling speech at the Moncada trial, a potpourri of middle-class panaceas, quasi-Marxist remedies, and paternalistic attitudes, eventually received public approval from the middle sectors, but for varied and conflicting reasons. Each of the middle sectors thought it perceived its own special indictment of Cuban ills in Castro's analysis of Cuba's problems. Later, the various sectors were to disagree vociferously, with Castro and among themselves, over what Castro had promised and about what Cuba needed in the way of reforms. . . .

The Revolution had few leaders outside of those from the nebulous and divided middle sectors, the most notorious example being Castro himself, the son of a planter. Labor remained aloof from the Revolution; only the upheaval of 1933 had drawn the worker into its vortex. In the general strike of that year, the worker had advanced beyond the protest advocated by his leaders; labor radicals had even organized "rural soviets" in the sugar mills. In 1933, however, jobless and hungry men had been driven to extreme measures, but no such motivation existed in 1958. The worker was not living in conditions of intolerable poverty. The urban worker, especially, remained more or less neutral in the conflict between Batista and his enemies. Not once did organized labor heed Castro's call for a general strike. In the earlier struggle against Gerardo Machado, the Communists had fomented work-stoppages, but they opposed Castro until the summer of 1958. Blas Roca, one of the Communist stalwarts, called Castro and his circle "petty bourgeoisie."

Nor did peasants furnish the leadership or provide the program of the Revolution. Castro's Revolution was not a peasant revolution, for Cuban peasants formed only a tiny minority of the rural workers who labored on the tobacco farms or sugar plantations—

which were more like factories than farms. To cite Draper, the few peasants or *guajiros* in the Sierra Maestra "were utterly alien to" Castro and his cohorts. That *guajiros* later supplied the rebels with food, as Ernesto Guevara claimed, is true; but since Castro's small band never numbered more than 300 guerrillas, only a fraction of the rural population participated directly in the armed conflict. Not until the guerrillas had virtually triumphed, late in 1958, did the people of the countryside join the vocal supporters of the Revolution. Castro's agrarian promises ultimately awakened a rural discontent which, although it had remained dormant throughout most of the period of anti-Batista protest, was easily kindled and provided Castro with the backing he later sorely needed.

The Revolution moved with astonishing speed. One reason for this can be found in the absence of insuperable barriers in its path. Cuban society was weak. Split by economic, social, and ethnic divisions, it was a dependent society, the child of American tutelage and of Spanish rule. As noted, no homogenous middle class or national bourgeoisie existed, while the welfare of both the middle sectors and the sugar barons depended on the United States. Neither group had a clearly defined or class interest to defend; both were international in character, more reliant on foreign interests than on local factors. Politically, Cuba had reached the end of an era; parties and politicians were bankrupt, and therefore the structure of society simply crumbled. The guerrilla phase of the Revolution lasted a short two years, and fighting was sporadic and limited in territorial scope. Castro's militants alone did not vanquish Batista; the caudillo fell because he lost the support of the politically aware segments of the population. The government contributed to its own defeat. Without the inherent weakness of Cuban society and Batista's own mistakes, Castro's band could not have triumphed.

Similarly, the absence of ideology in the Fidelista camp characterized the prerevolutionary picture, for Cuba lacked a concise national ideology or set of universal beliefs. Of the political groupings, the Communists alone provided ideological and political unity. They had successfully organized and controlled union labor in the thirties and forties and offered Castro the discipline, organization, and ideology he needed to rally the worker behind him. Confronted with the need for political allies and sharing a similar analysis of Cuban history and ills, Castro turned to them.

Finally, Cuba had a cataclysmic revolution because its political structure had almost always relied heavily on a national chieftain. From the days of Antonio Maceo and José Martí to those of Batista, Cubans had obediently and often enthusiastically followed such a leader. In Martí, the most famous of these, the Cubans had created a national ideal, a hero to enshrine and worship, both for his philosophy and for the revolutionary leadership he offered in the struggle for independence. In Fidel Castro the Cubans found their latest leader, a bold, politically acute, and charismatic young caudillo who claimed that he spoke for the ideals of the immortal Martí.

To the outside world, Cuba was first a philosopher's revolution, and commentators were too absorbed by Castro's Marxism to see anything else. Then it became a statistician's revolution, the success or failure of Castro hinging on whether the country reached its goal of harvesting 10 million tons of sugar. Although Cuba never actually achieved the 10 million (its highest production was 8.5 million in 1968), the country has seen drastic changes in education, the family, and the work life of the people. It is hard to interpret these changes, or to decide whether people are better off or worse off under communism than under Batista's dictatorship. There are conflicting reports. But the most important thing about Castro's revolution is how it changed a solid and established culture, how many of the Latin American "qualities" described in this book—the aversion to manual labor, the belief in the immediate family, and the distrust of politics, of the government, and of progress—have been attacked and overcome.

Barry Reckord, a Jamaican playwright, spent several months traveling in Cuba during 1969, talking to people—

the inspired, the disgruntled, the indifferent. He brought
back conflicting conversations that orbit around the question of how a nation can inspire its people without resorting to the individual profit motive or to the force of
the state. Cuba, he says, is attempting an appeal to conscience and voluntarism, and the results may make Cuba a
lesson not only for South America but for the United
States as well.

What Castro Is Trying to Do

By Barry Reckord

The Absentee Worker

The absentee and his wife were watching a Cuban
television drama, an incredible business of slapped
faces that snapped back defiant, chained hands, and
blazing revolutionary eyes. Her head was in his comfortable lap. They offered to turn down the telly, but
I said I'd come again. The comfort seemed unbreak-
able.

I managed to see him two weeks later. He was still
happily loafing, taking two or three days off a week.
Since there's little to buy, many Cubans can live on
half a month's wages, so absenteeism is a serious problem in Cuba and the subject of many a government
campaign. A report published in *Granma*, the official
newspaper, for example, in October, 1969, made it
clear that on one farm in Camaguey attendance was
as low as 45 per cent, and in most places no higher
than 65 per cent.

Taking care of the workers still means small things
like making refreshments available to them. Large
scale improvements like better housing will have to
wait many years. But the government is avoiding
repression. Cuban production could probably be
doubled if there were no absenteeism; and there is a
desperate shortage of labor, yet Castro avoids even
standard coercive devices like raising prices or lowering wages so that absentees would be forced to work
harder to live. The revolutionary method is appeal to

conscience. This most central problem of socialism, the problem of incentive, is to be solved neither by Stalinist repression nor neo-capitalist devices, but by conscience. I wonder how this worked in practice, what actually happened in the factories.

"I don't get paid for the days I don't work," the absentee said, "so no problem."

"What do they actually say to you at work?"

"They are very joky," he said, sarcastically. "They say 'Well, Comrade, in Havana you think about nothing but food. And where to find a little woman. You think of nothing else. Sex and rice. So agricultural work will be good. The clean open air. The country. You will fall in love with the country. Very exciting.'"

"What do you say?"

"Man, the last thing I want is to leave Havana. You know there's this woman I see. She's a staunch Party member on her block, but left to her I'd never get to work. . . ."

"What's the job?"

"Nothing. Sticking labels on bottles. Women can do that."

"Why don't you study if you don't like sticking labels?"

"I don't like studying. When the revolution came I was 16. Out of school. No steady job, left school at 12. At nine really. Then revolution and they send me to school. I nearly finished junior high school. But I'm no good for studying. I married. Got a job. My wife too. And my mother. Everybody. We work, go to pictures. Eat at restaurants. We live like kings. I lose pay for not going to work but I earn all I need to live. So why work every day?"

The Ex-Manager

"Of course Fidel can talk," said an ex-manager I talked to, out in the country. "He's like a school teacher with a cane. He doesn't have to use it. He has it, and he tells you, 'Oh, it's easy, just coax them; look how quiet they are. It's beautiful. *You* get the same results.'

"Well, I didn't get the same results. In my factory we had a high loss in man days—sometimes half the place absent, sometimes 30 per cent, that is three out of 10. Of course, then the party rolls in with this guy in a car, chauffeur, everything, even cigars to hand round, all the way from Havana, chats them up— these peasants, they gawk and there are no absences for a few days and he says, 'See, just coax them. No brute force. You don't have to transfer them. It's not their fault. It's yours.' You hear that? *My* fault. Just a little firm coaxing. And when he phones a month later to check, two out of the usual three have gone absent again but he says, 'See, it's a great success. Thirty per cent success, with one visit. If I could be there all the time—100 per cent.' The man from Havana leaves me in trouble with my people. They glance at me as if to say, '*He* could get us back, but *you* couldn't.' So I packed the whole thing in. My God, oh my God. They keep on saying good management would cut down absenteeism, good managers like Fidel, yes, but do I have what he has, the cars, the cigars, all that over-head? The army took over my factory.

"How I got the job? Oh, I was the buddy of a buddy—how do people get jobs in Cuba? A friend says to Fidel 'I know a man. . . .' Fidel says, 'I'm tired of men, I want a genius. Preferably an Oriente peas-ant.' Like this bastard who's taken my job. This melon. No background. This black arse-hole known only to himself. And he's in charge. And then he'll get fired like me and want to shoot Fidel. That's Cuba. Land of mystery and women."

The New Manager

I talked to the new soldier/manager, a typically unsophisticated Cuban, about 35, black, a growing reputation in the province, one or two comforting cliches at his fingertips, not much more.

"What is your rank?"

"Does that matter? No, no, that doesn't really mat-ter. . . . The man who drives a tank can drive a tractor. It's got nothing to do with giving or taking orders. The army at present has the most knowledgeable people around. Also some of the most revolutionary. As I said, the dream of every Cuban boy is to be Ché. Not dream, determination. Dreams won't create the new man in America."

"Who is he? Describe him."

"New men with socialist natures."

"You feel you're a new man?"

"Well in the sense that I act on my ideals. That is the way I was brought up. I can fight. I can produce. My education was that of the new man. I am willing to go anywhere in Cuba to increase production and I don't ask how much they'll pay me. . . ."

I said, "The general pattern since the revolution has been falling production and broken promises, yet the masses still avidly listen to Fidel, the young support him, and there have been no defections from among the top leaders of the revolution. Why is that?"

"Because the revolution has been so logical. Get rid of the old order, push, push, push the people's education, guard their health, look around for the right things to grow and manufacture, solve nothing by force and think big. Underdeveloped people think in tens and twenties. Fidel has taught us to think in millions. On this program the grass must grow. If not today, tomorrow. The people themselves are planting it. They are not waiting for manna from any government. Increasingly it's like that in Cuba. Democratic. The work and will of the people. Here we plant manna. . . .

"You see, any agricultural project is an accumulation of scores of mechanized, skilled operations and we are still a highly unskilled people. We are still superstitious people who believe in magic and mystery and can never quite believe that one and one make two, every day, all the time. We wouldn't do the same thing two days running because we'd never believed it would work two days running—whatever power controlled things wasn't scientific. So all sorts of funny things happened. . . ."

Fidel and the Bureaucrats

In a speech congratulating steel workers who had built 800 harrows in 23 days, Castro showed the happier results of this work-style.

The work began January 25, not just on heavy 17,000-pound harrows but also on 10,000-pound harrows. And in record time, just 23 days, the 800 harrows needed were produced. . . .

This is a good example of what can be done when revolutionary methods of leadership are employed, of what can be accomplished when bureaucratic red tape is avoided. . . .

What aroused the enthusiasm of the workers in the various enterprises that participated in this plan? . . . Was it an organizational diagram? It wasn't the paperwork; it was the spirit, the antithesis of paperwork, offices, and even organizational diagrams. . . . It is not hard to make organograms. A line here, three there, squares, and more squares. It develops in someone's mind, as an idea, a sheer abstraction. Someone feels that life must adjust to this diagram. And instead of trying to adjust the forms of organization to life, he tries to adjust life to those abstract forms of organization. And that's how everything gets tangled up.

I don't know whether I am an efficient or a deficient minister, but I do recall something of which I will always be proud. The first thing I did was to completely close down an office called the Office of the Prime Minister, when I found out it answered no need whatsoever. . . . If we had followed the bureaucratic concept, we could have asked for the largest building and drawn up the largest of all organization charts. . . .

Everyone knows, for example, all that education has done throughout the country, and how it was done. And to spark off all this activity, they did not require a building, nor a huge organization chart, nor a 10 or 12-million peso budget. And there you have the importance of concepts. Adhering to the old concept would have cost the republic 80 million pesos in eight years of revolution. . . . The capitalists had a lot of bureaucracy, and we have not eradicated it; we have, on occasion, increased it. There are factories, production units, where a capitalist owner employed three or four office employees, and we have 25 to 40. Why? We have to go to the root of the problem.

The root of the problem is bureaucracy, and the Cuban cure for bureaucracy is to create the worker-intellectual. The worker-student program will no doubt be facilitated by automation which cuts down the hours and harshness of labor so workers won't be too tired to study.

But is Fidel going to have to push the program through almost single-handed? He set up a committee to cut down bureaucracy and soon had to denounce it for becoming bureaucratic. Cuba is full of die-hard bureaucratic elitists who believe in the division of labor. They continue, for example, to treasure chauffeurs.

A fear of bureaucracy partly explains Fidel's ambivalent attitude to the communist party, which he often regards as the great red hope of Cuban democracy, but occasionally cold-shoulders. . . .

It may be that an elected party will at some stage emerge in Cuba, just as the constitution now being worked on by Blas Roca, an old communist, may one day materialize; but the fact is that Castro not only wants to retain power in his own hands, but has a rooted distrust of saddling the Cuban people with a Soviet-style party bureaucracy—representatives entrenched in privileges, offering more and more "guidance" while doing less and less work, setting a bad example to workers, a host of multiplying middlemen between the plan and its performance, so that work is seen once again as a curse, needing special rewards and incentives to make it bearable.

Socialism or Sociolism

In Cuba the word *socio* means buddy and there is a well-known joke that sociolism reigns, not socialism. I asked a member of the Central Committee of the Communist Party where the manager of the factory

I'd visited got his house. He said probably the same place he got his fence. It wasn't important, since the vast majority of houses were being built for workers on the state farms who had nowhere decent to live.

"For us equality is good economics as much as idealism. The minute we develop an elite in Cuba, voluntary labor is dead; and this country runs on voluntary labor. Our greatest effort, the 10 million tons, is based on voluntary labor and the sharing of dirty work. Clearly no man is going to cut cane if the Major is at the beach with his wife and a basketful of fried chicken."

"But what about cutting cane side by side with some major who arrives in a car and goes home to fried chicken?"

"The people don't worry about that much because they know on the whole the leaders have more responsibilities, and are working like hell for general abundance. And, better yet, are achieving it. There is a broad equality which justifies voluntary labor; and voluntary labor is the central tool of this revolution. It was Ché's creation, Ché's weapon. It was tried, as you know, in Russia, but its hour hadn't come and it gave way to individual incentives. But Ché pushed it through in Cuba. Ché believed that even if most people are selfish and suffering from 'human nature,' some have idealism which should be harnessed. For example, you have a factory full of selfish people who won't even come to work, so instead of threatening them with unemployment you call on the few idealists in the factory to do the work, express their idealism in deed, work 10, 12, 18 hours a day till the plan is fulfilled. What the loafers drop, the revolutionaries pick up.

"Any future Latin American revolution," he said, "must use voluntary labor as a central revolutionary principle. In the early years how would we have solved the unemployment problem without voluntary labor? You know what happened; at the revolution's triumph there was vast unemployment. Well, we sent some to school and used the rest building an infrastructure, paid for with the assets we seized from the

Yanks, plus red gold later on. Also we padded the existing workplaces a bit. So what happened? With full employment all the barefoot people wanted easier jobs. The sugarworkers got out of the sun and into air-conditioned offices making coffee for bureaucrats. Nearly every Cuban who could, found himself a sinecure. Without voluntary labor to cut the cane we would have had to whip all those people back into the canefields. Instead the army of conscience swarmed over the fields, cutting cane. They ruined some of it but there was a net gain, because money gradually became a secondary matter in Cuba. It was no longer a silver scale with which men carefully weighed out their labor to the nearest ounce. Wage slavery was abolished, *chico*. You know, voluntary labor nearly killed me. I couldn't face manual work. Say manual labor to a Cuban and he says yes, yes, all right, but really his back isn't shaped that way. Now every Cuban child picks coffee at 10 and cuts or weeds cane at 15 as part of education. . . . Labor is fashionable."

The first stage in the development of voluntary labor in Cuba was to deal with the aversion of bourgeois culture to manual work so it could more easily be shared. The second stage, now under way, is to deepen people's understanding of shared labor as the key to a classless, educated society.

The great symbol of this second stage was the 1970 goal of a 10-million-ton sugar harvest, described by Herbert Matthews of *The New York Times* as "certainly beyond the range of probability." The work was to be done largely by volunteers; they were to cut as much as they could, and among them there was no question of piecework. The incentive was conscience, not money.

The 10-million-ton failure was an emotional blow for Fidel, with incalculable political consequences, since it deepens his debt to the Russians. Nonetheless there was a record harvest (8.4 million tons) which in an earlier speech Castro described as a triumph for the people in the canefields. He attributed their falling short of 10 million tons to the inefficient management of sugar mills, and mentioned the late arrival of vital machinery, some of it from strife-torn Czechoslovakia. He assumed general responsibility for the failure and offered to resign, but most Cubans are so keenly aware of his personal anguish that his standing among them is unshaken. On the other hand there will be disenchantment among the uncommitted, and bitter division in the society. Under these circumstances the door seems to me to be wide open for repressive bureaucratic measure, but what Fidel actually proposed was more say for the workers. Collective leadership would be organized in factories, with workers having as much say as the administrator and the representatives of the Communist Party—the Chinese road, in fact, on Russia money, a tightrope walk that it will be difficult for Fidel to survive. But *if* over the next few years Cuba can maintain a yearly sugar harvest of eight-and-a-half million tons, worth nearly one billion dollars, this should go far to ensure economic stability.

Perhaps the purely economic effects of the harvest have received too much attention both in Cuba and abroad. Equally important is the fact that the harvest was produced, not by hungry and ignorant wage-slaves working 16 hours a day for four months and unemployed the rest of the year, but by volunteers who were more politically and culturally aware. This moral currency has, of course, little value, and Castro's survival will depend on hard cash.

Voluntary Labor

I decided to try voluntary labor. The hotel staff were going out on Sundays to work in coffee, so I got up early, joined the people drinking coffee and eating a biscuit in the throaty five o'clock dark, caught a truck that came two hours late. I grumbled, but they all said, "Progress, it used to be four hours late," and we drove happily through the Cuban morning. Then I started digging holes in the ground, to fill cellophane bags with earth for the coffee plants, and learned the art of packing them evenly in rows.

I soon realized that I preferred writing plays, but people around me seemed quite relaxed, and I persisted until my back ached. That I could bear, but not the boredom. It all seemed like playing in dirt. Dig and fill, dig and fill; I longed for, watched for, the breaks for cold sugar and water, then lunch. A man shouted gaily, "What, no music, no baseball?" Everybody laughed except me. They turned on the damned sound system. I preached to myself the gospel of work—as revolutionary for the bourgeois, I said, as Christianity for the Graeco-Roman aristocracy. My dry, dirty paws couldn't grip the chalky cellophane bags; my teeth were on edge, my nerves cringed. I wanted a bath. I thought of delights in far-away places, but the sun was insistent. I said to my happy neighbor, "People don't write books in order to read them, why should I have to plant coffee to drink it?" I walked 300 yards for a large shovel, and wondered what the hell it must be like cutting cane.

"The new man," said an aging doctor, "is a man who works in agriculture, God bless him, then goes and performs an operation. Of course you might say it won't be a good operation, insufficient practice, too much time in the cane, but all the good surgeons I know used to spend hours on the golf course, so why not the canefields or driving a bus? There is your classless society. Your equality. No laboring class. Now you will still have brilliant doctors and bad doctors, and there's choking inequality, but choking I fear ends in heaven and we are in Cuba. And of course if people study medicine for love and aptitude, not money and kudos, there'll be fewer charlatans. There will still be unequal talents, you know, and envy. I like to be in charge of something, some program, but I'm quite satisfied that by and large, by and large, mark you, I approve of the medical program in Cuba, by and large. Nobody quite does anything your way, but then neither do you do things their way, so just let the thing be done, so long as it's very broadly correct, it doesn't matter by who."

Castro did not have too much success in exporting his revolution to other countries. Ché Guevara, the Argentine doctor who fought in the Cuban revolution and became one of its heroes, secretly entered Bolivia wtih some followers in 1968, with the idea of starting revolution there. He found out that being a revolutionary does not always obscure the fact that you are a foreigner, and that the Latin American powder keg was not as dry as he had expected. Ché's frustrating life in the Bolivian wilds, where only a few loyal supporters from a fragmented Bolivian communist party fought with him, ended in disaster, as he was captured and killed by the Bolivian army. His death seemed to snuff out whatever enthusiasm remained for a continent-wide peasant revolution. These selections from two months of Ché's diary (in 1968) show the frustrations.

Ché in Bolivia

By Ché Guevara

August, 1968

It was, without any doubt, the worst month we have had since the war started. The loss of all the caves containing the documents and medicine was a hard blow, above all psychologically. The loss of two men at the end of the month and the subsequent march on a horsemeat diet demoralized the men and provoked the first case of giving up, Camba, which would constitute a net gain except under these circumstances. The lack of contact with the outside and with Joaquín and the fact that prisoners taken from him have talked, also demoralized the troops a little. My illness caused uncertainty in several others and all this was reflected in our only clash, in which we should have caused several enemy losses but only wounded one. On the other hand, the difficult march through the hills without water brought out some negative aspects of the men.

The most important characteristics:
1. We continue without contacts of any kind and

without reasonable hope of establishing them in the near future.

2. We continue without any incorporation on the part of the *campesinos,* logical to understand if we take into account the little contact we have had with them in recent times.

3. There is a lowering, I hope temporary, of the fighting morale.

4. The army does not increase its effectiveness nor its combativeness.

We are in a downward period in our morale and in our revolutionary legend. The most urgent tasks continue to be the same as those of last month, i.e., to reestablish contacts, to incorporate fighters, to supply ourselves with medicine and equipment.

It should be taken into account that Inti and Coco excel ever more firmly as revolutionary and military cadres. . . .

September, 1968

It should have been a month of recuperation and it was on the point of being so. But the ambush in which Miguel, Coco, and Julio fell spoiled everything, and then we have remained in a dangerous position, besides losing Leon. As to Camba it is a net gain.

We had small clashes in which we killed a horse, killed and wounded a soldier, and Urbano exchanged shots with a patrol, also there was the ominous ambush in La Higuera. We already have left the mules, and I believe that for a long time we shall have no more animals of that type, unless I should relapse into an asthmatic condition.

On the other hand, some of the news about the dead in the other group seems to be true, and that group should be considered liquidated, although it is possible that a little group is roaming, avoiding contact with the army, because the news of the joint death of the seven may be false, or at least exaggerated.

The characteristics are the same as those of last month, except that now the army is showing more effectiveness in its action, and the mass of *campesinos* does not help us at all and they have become informers.

The most important tasks are to escape and look for more propitious zones; later [reestablish] the contacts, despite the fact that the whole apparatus is badly disjointed in La Paz, where they have also given us hard blows. The morale of the rest of the men has been sustained fairly well. My only doubts are about Willy, who may take advantage of some clash to try to escape by himself unless I have a talk with him. . . .

What have been the results of the Mexican revolution in the sixty years that have followed it? Was anything accomplished for the peasants and workers, who were both the justification and the soldiers for the revolution? Andrew Frank's essay is ten years old, but general conditions in Mexico are about the same, and the problems he describes have not been solved. The "PRI" that he refers to is the official political party, the one that has controlled Mexico since the revolution.

Mexico: The Revolution Revisited
By Andrew Gunder Frank

Mexico's revolutionary break with her 19th-century legacy of feudalism and imperialism, carried out at the cost of a million lives, began in 1910. Many of the political, economic, and social fruits of the Mexican Revolution were slow in ripening, and many will be gathered only in the future. From the U.S. point of view, Mexico seemed to be setting the worst kind of example to the rest of Latin America. Accordingly, the U.S. first interfered economically and diplomatically, then sent troops to capture Vera Cruz, and even as late as 1937 labeled the Mexican government "Bolshevik." At the same time, Latin America, still beset by the alliance between feudalism and imperialism, came to view the Mexican Revolution as a guiding star and shining example. By now, much has changed. Today, the U.S. is full of praise for Mexico's

example of "economic progress with political stability"; . . . Latin America, in the meantime, has turned
eyes toward Cuba and asks if the example of Mexico's
50-year revolution is one to follow after all. Let us,
therefore, turn to the lessons that Mexico's experience
holds for Latin America and the world.

The Mexican Revolution resulted in a tremendous
release of popular energy, which, after the fighting
ended, went into the construction of a new society.
The destruction of feudalism radically changed the
social relations of man to man. The peasant's accession
to human dignity, when compared with the conditions
of servitude which still persist in, say, Guatemala and Peru, is perhaps the Revolution's most important accomplishment. That same energy was also
released through improved health (the mortality rate
has fallen by two thirds since 1910) and transformed
into large increases of work, education (illiteracy rate
reduced by one half), and skills, which in turn, particularly since 1940, have been transformed into
Mexico's remarkable economic growth. Only a post-
or non-feudal society could permit and produce such
land reform (millions of small landholdings created),
roads (sevenfold increase since 1940 so that now
nearly half of all goods travel by truck and almost all
passengers by bus), irrigation (an elevenfold increase
since 1940 so that a third of all cropland is now irri-
gated), urbanization (to nearly 50 percent), industrialization (3.6-fold increase from 1940 to 1959),
agricultural output (3.4-fold between 1940 and 1959);
and, despite one of the world's highest rates of population growth, GNP per capita doubled from $150 to
$300 a year. According to Rostow, Mexico has passed
the threshold into self-sustained economic growth. Indeed, the annual rates of growth during the postwar
years of both industrial and agricultural output rank
Mexico among the first half-dozen countries in the
world.

And yet Mexico's revolution has had another face
as well. Her crude death rate of 12.5 remains higher
than that of Bolivia or Peru, her infant mortality rate
of 81 in a 1000 higher than that of Argentina. Her

ratio of doctors to people (1 to 2,200) is lower than Chile's and less than half of Argentina's. The 43 percent illiteracy that remained in 1950 hardly compares with 19 percent in Chile and 13 percent in Argentina. The ratio of working population engaged in manufacturing remains at 12 percent; and Mexico's per capita income of still less than $300 ranks her behind Chile, Argentina, Uruguay, and Cuba, to say nothing of oil-rich Venezuela. After the large-scale redistribution of lands, over a million heads of rural families remained without land of their own; and, with population growth, the number may have risen to nearer 2 million (out of a total of maybe 4 million) since 1950. The average Mexican diet has a caloric deficit of −24.4 according to the UN's Food and Agriculture Organization; and the 3 million indigenous Indians out of today's population of over 30 million remain economically as badly or maybe worse off than the *poorest* of their forefathers of the time before the Conquest, four and a half centuries ago. However large the social change, the economic benefits of the Mexican Revolution have not reached, or have been withheld from, large parts of the population; about 50 percent receive today only 15 percent of the national income; and it has been estimated (although also challenged) that only 1 percent of the population disposes of 66 percent of the *money* income. Further, the inequality of income distribution is increasing, not decreasing.

The wealth and elegance of downtown Mexico City dazzle the visitor, and the heavy industry of Monterrey impresses as another Pittsburgh; but equally do the miles of Mexico City's shanty slums depress, as does the poverty of rural Tlaxcala and Chiapas dumbfound. The question inevitably presents itself: have Mexico's 50 years of revolution really been a success or have they been a failure? . . .

Behind the two Janus faces of the Mexican Revolution there is a single head in a single and by now intricately balanced and developing organism. To learn Mexico's lesson for Latin America and the world, we must try to fathom the development, current operation, and future prospects of Mexico's revolutionary organism.

The history of Mexico seems to fall conveniently into the following periods: (1) the four centuries from the Conquest until 1910; (2) the nearly 15 years of violent revolution, counter-revolution, and reconstruction, symbolized by Madero, Huerta, and Carranza; (3) the 15 years of reform, carried through by Presidents Calles and Cárdenas; (4) the 15 years after 1940 of the beginning of industrialization and the growth of bourgeois power, symbolized by President Alemán; and (5) the current consolidation of the "Mexican System...."

The Mexican Revolution was the product of alliance between the bourgeoisie, represented by Madero, and the peasants, led by Emiliano Zapata and Pancho Villa. They faced a common enemy, the feudal order and its supporting pillars of Church, army, and foreign capital. But their goals inevitably differed—freedom from domestic and foreign bonds and loosening of the economic structure for the bourgeoisie; land for the peasants. Although Zapata continued to press the interests of the peasants until his murder in 1919, the real leadership of the Revolution was never out of the hands of the bourgeoisie, except insofar as it was challenged by Huerta reaction and American intervention. (Even in the 1958 presidential election, only 23 percent of the population voted.) The elimination of feudal social relations was of course in the interest of the emerging bourgeoisie as well as of the peasants. Education became secularized, Church and state more widely separated. But accession to power by the peasantry was never really in the cards.

None of the early presidents were radicals in any sense of the word, nor could they have been and retained their positions. In the middle 1920's, during the administration of President Calles, there began the program of public works, and to a lesser extent irrigation, on the foundation of which much of Mexico's subsequent economic development rests....

Abroad, the Cárdenas administration (1934–1940) may be best known for its expropriation of Mexico's privately owned petroleum, a step which was also provided for by . . . Article 27 of the Constitution of 1917. But still more important domestically, the administration of President Cárdenas expropriated and redistributed more land than all other administrations, before and since, put together. Pursuant to the Constitution and the laws of the Calles administration, these lands were taken from the territories surrounding particular villages and were ceded to them communally as *ejidos,* to be worked in some cases collectively but in most cases individually. An *ejido* bank was established to provide the new owners with agricultural credit. Irrigation and other capital investment in agriculture was not, however, expanded at the same time. In fact, in retrospect it is clear that, although he undoubtedly had his heart in the right place, Cárdenas, as head of a bourgeois government, did not provide Mexican peasant agriculture with nearly enough resources to get it over the hump into self-sustained development. . . .

The exigencies of World War II had given impetus to domestic expansion of industry in Mexico as elsewhere in the underdeveloped world. Further industrialization was promoted by Alemán and his successors. Investment in industry and commerce has also been guided into the same eight favored states, with particular concentrations, of course, in the Federal District and Nuevo Leon, the sites of Mexico City and Monterrey. The older, more populated states were left largely unaffected and far behind. A significant portion of the investment funds, and particularly of the necessary foreign exchange, undoubtedly was contributed by the earnings from agricultural exports as well as from the rapid increase of tourism in Mexico and migrant *bracero* labor to the United States. But simultaneously, American direct investment which had fallen to the depression and post-petroleum-nationalization low of $267 million in 1939 began again a rapid increase and now surpasses the $1 billion mark, or about one tenth of U.S. investment in Latin America. . . .

In Mexican agriculture as well, American capital

plays a significant role. Although Americans no longer own large tracts of land, as they still do in Central America, the American cotton monopoly, Anderson and Clayton, distributes about $200 million of credit for the production of cotton from sowing to shipping. Therewith it effectively determines the buyer and the price for the cotton and prevents Mexico from disposing of a large part of her cotton crop where and when she might wish. And worse, . . . this arrangement contributes to the maintenance of monoculture and a plantation economy using hired labor in large parts of the North. With good reason, "Mexicans are beginning to wonder whether they are returning to the days of Porfirio Díaz. . . ."

The foregoing events of the postwar years have had their inevitable effect on the socio-political and economic structure of the society and on the lives of the people within it. They have meant the growth of a neo-*latifundia* agriculture, no longer organized under the feudal *hacienda* system which uses serfs to produce for home consumption, but organized instead as latter-day plantations, run as capitalist enterprises by city-dwelling owners, hiring agricultural wage laborers, and producing non-subsistence and often single crops for export. . . .

The new private landowners, large and small, and some of the old ones as well, are or are becoming bourgeois in every sense of the word. Even the smaller landowners among them, if they have any capital, have a position and income which affords them a middle-class style of life, and often urban life at that. Their agricultural business often affords them a handsome income, which they dispose of sometimes by real investment in Mexico, sometimes by investment abroad, sometimes by constructing and speculating in urban real estate, or luxury imports. And they have power, economic and political. They and their industrial, commercial, and sometimes professional brethren essentially own and run the state. Beginning particularly during the administration of Alemán, they have, as we have seen in part, been able to use that state to pull themselves up by their bootstraps. But it has not, so far, been their interest to pull the peasantry up behind them....

It remains to ask how the "Mexican System" works today ... and what are its prospects for the future. Mexico is a social and economic pyramid, with a political pyramid inside. At the bottom are the indigenous Indians, remaining where they always were. In the next layer are the landless rural people and the unemployed or only occasionally employed urban ones. The latter, particularly, are a veritable lumpenproletariat, dispossessed by the rural and unabsorbed by the urban economy, living on the margin of society, isolated and alienated from it, from each other, and often from themselves. Next come the *ejidatarios* and such private small holders as are poor enough to work their land by themselves. Although economically more secure, they stand socially sometimes even below the marginal urban people, perhaps because the *chances* for social mobility are greater for the latter. Above them are the workers in the narrower sense of the word, particularly the unionized ones, who in Mexico as in many parts of Latin America, Asia, and Africa today comprise a sort of "aristocracy of the proletariat." The next layer may be termed the middle class or petty bourgeoisie. It comprises a large variety of economic walks of life—small landowner, professional, merchant, clergy, government and white collar worker, small politician—but it affords considerable lateral mobility within it, from one occupation to another. Their badge in Mexico is dark glasses as it is a briefcase in Western Europe, however dark it may be outside or however few papers there may be to carry. And that badge is a counterweight to the sometimes higher income of the workers below them. The bourgeois upper class, the principal manipulators and beneficiaries of the system, includes the large landholders, the effective directors of the financial, commercial, industrial, professional, governmental, and military apparatuses, and by *noblesse oblige* some intellectuals. The viable economic base of the more aristocratic upper class was destroyed by the Revolution. But many of its members and their wealth survived. Their money was invested in finance, commerce, industry, and later again agriculture; and the ex-aristo- crats became the nucleus of the new bourgeoisie. Their ranks were soon supplemented by their erst- while enemies, the individual beneficiaries of the same Revolution, many politicians and generals among them. As their economic position became consolidated, so did their political power—exercised through the PRI, the all-powerful Institutional Revolutionary Party through which they have managed Mexico's political, and thereby indirectly economic, life for the past generation. It is the PRI which allocates the pres- idency and other principal political offices (to its faith- ful), and not the electoral mechanism; and manage- ment and control of the PRI, in turn, by no means extends down to the bottom of the social and eco- nomic pyramid.

But Mexico's pyramid is not static; it is not a caste system, as for example that of Peru substantially re- mains; there is mobility. There are economic, political, and social paths which afford opportunities—or, maybe better, chances—for higher rank to those who play according to the rules of the game. There is the migration from Center and South to the North, in- volving as it does not only geographical movement but also economic improvement coupled with some severance of communal ties and participation in a looser society. There is the very substantial rural- urban migration, especially to Mexico City.... Of course, such migration offers no guarantee of social or economic success, but it increases the statistical chances for the migrant. There is movement into white or off-white collar jobs and various kinds of speculation around the loose ends of a growing econ- omy. And, of course, there is education and "suitable" marriage for those who can manage it. These two are perhaps the most important vehicles for the social and economic migrant himself, and virtually guarantee mobility to his children. Social mobility, however, is individual-by-individual....

The Church was viewed as the most retrograde, un-
changeable institution in Latin America during the late
1930's, and yet it produced some of the most dedicated
revolutionaries during the 1960's. A few priests took up
the gun and left the Church to fight with the revolutionaries in several Latin American countries. The most
celebrated of these priests was the Colombian Camilo
Torres. Pay special attention, in this story of Torres' transformation into a revolutionary, to his social background.
The Latin American leftist vanguard comes mostly from
the privileged upper classes.

A Saint with a Gun

By Jean Larteguy

I had just come back from Colombia. During my
stay I had tried—by means of his friends and enemies,
those who had understood him and those who had
rejected him—to retrace the memory of Camilo
Torres. Along with Ché Guevara, he had in one year
become the other symbol of the Latin-American revolution, the symbol that waved the cross instead of
the red flag. Camilo Torres had taken the road to
martyrdom and had uselessly fallen in an ambush,
betrayed by a peasant who did not even know him,
just as Ché was in Bolivia. The myth was growing. . . .

Camilo Torres Restrepo was born in Bogotá, on
February 3, 1929. His father, Calixto Torres, was the
most famous doctor in the city. It was said of his
mother, Doña Isabel Restrepo, that she bore herself so
proudly that she seemed to be a duchess. She was
quick-witted, free-spirited, and strong in character.
Like Doña Celia de la Serna, Ché Guevara's mother,
she was an aristocrat. She had the same contempt for
conventions, the same carelessness about money, the
same way of doing as she pleased.

Camilo Torres spent his entire childhood in Bogotá
society's top level of twenty-four powerful families.
These families are all Hispanic, proud of the purity of
their blood and convinced that their privileges come

to them by divine right. As a group they possess most of the large landholdings on which some of the best coffee in the world is grown. Colombia produces 20 per cent of the world's production. Camilo Torres, after brilliantly completing his studies at the Cervantes School, began his law studies in 1948. It was the same year in which the *violencia* and repression by the army and the police broke out in Colombia. Fidel Castro, then also a student, witnessed this tragedy. He did not become involved; he had just come from Cuba and was traveling for pleasure. But he had entree into the liberal milieu of Jorge Gaitán, who had just been assassinated.

Camilo Torres did not become involved either, but like the future Cuban leader he never forgot this bloody outbreak. He felt that all strength resides in the people, and that even when they seem resigned, once they rebel they are capable of overthrowing the most well-established regime. . . .

In Camilo Torres' circle, politics is the source of power as well as money. It provides women, land, and a clientele—the courtiers who surround those in power. Every peasant in his far-off *pueblo* is linked to politics for his survival, and his life or death, as well as that of his family, will depend on his choice of party.

Camilo Torres therefore decided to go into politics. At Cervantes, he had already founded a newspaper, *El Puma,* and somewhat later he had unionized the bootblacks. It was at that time that he met and became betrothed to the daughter of Dr. Montalvo, but they did not marry. In Colombia, which, like Mexico, is the land of *machismo,* it is not the woman who chooses; she can only be chosen, so one might assume that it was Camilo who ended the relationship. In any case, the young girl became a nun. Camilo's mother, "The Duchess," was single-minded and jealous in her love for her son. She may have precipitated the break.

Camilo Torres withdrew to a monastery to make a retreat. Then he left law school and entered the chief seminary, where he took the cassock. His friends already said of him, "Camilo can become anything—a saint, a great mystic, a dangerous anarchist—anything but a mediocrity."

In 1954, Father Camilo Torres said his first Mass in the Bogotá cathedral. All the best Colombian society was present. Then he left for Europe. For the next six years he studied sociology at the University of Louvain.

. . . Camilo Torres returned to Colombia in 1960. He was named chaplain of the University of Bogotá, and at the same time he held the sociology chair. He quickly became the leader of the students, a factor that somewhat worried the Marxist groups which had until then controlled all the organizations. But the charm and name of Camilo Torres worked its spell. He came from good—very good—society, just as did all those studying at the university. There were no *campesinos* there. The students were among themselves, among their own social class. Even among the revolutionaries, family precedence continued to play a role. Oh, those Latin-American "clubs" that reconstitute themselves even among revolutionaries! Though the conflict between generations often enters into the political conflict, everything happens within this closed circle. . . .

Initially, Father Camilo Torres asked for reforms; seeing that nobody listened, he went further, repeating what so many others before him had said. On December 23, 1965, at the university's student living quarters he declared, "Only armed revolution can bring about the transformation of the political system."

He also said, "The oligarchy knows that it is finished. Either it agrees to turn control over to the people, who are the custodians of all power, or it refuses and we will have to resort to violence to rid ourselves of it."

But he never stopped saying, "I do not want violence." He was even to repeat it a few days before joining the guerrillas. . . .

The church hierarchy reacted against his "revolutionary tendencies." It removed him first from his post as chaplain and then from his chair in sociology. The students demonstrated in sympathy with him. There were riots and arrests.

It was then that Camilo Torres asked the primate cardinal for permission to revert to a lay state for an indefinite period of time. This in no way meant that he ceased to be a priest, that he could marry, or that he could no longer say Mass. He was not under an interdict. He was on "an unpaid vacation" and could at any time ask to be reintegrated into the Church.

Even after he became a guerrilla, he said, "I am first of all a priest and a Christian. I have merely asked to be relieved of the disciplinary laws of the clergy, but I consider myself bound to behave as a priest."

There can be no doubt that his superiors, when they agreed to his renunciation of the cassock, knew that he would end up with the guerrillas. They did nothing to prevent him. What they feared more than anything else was scandal, and they felt there would be less of it if Camilo quit his cassock. . . .

On November 8, 1965, after a disastrous propaganda tour in the province of Santander, Camilo Torres mysteriously disappeared. Three days later, Camilo joined an ALN (National Liberation Army) guerrilla unit operating in the San Vincente de Chucuri region of the same province.

It is difficult to learn just what made Camilo Torres take the final step. According to some of his friends, Camilo suffered a great deal when he realized that people came to see him not because of his ideas but simply as a curiosity, a priest in mufti, preaching revolution in this very Catholic Colombia.

In addition, his communist supporters had withdrawn those crowds which had formerly come to applaud him with remarkable discipline. They wanted him to ally himself more closely with them, to follow their own tactics and discipline.

Father Camilo Torres knew that he could not obtain a single reform, that he had been "burned," that he was thought a communist, that his United Front attempt had failed due to the lack of solid base and cadres. But he had no desire to become an unconditional hostage of the Communist party, which was simultaneously clandestine and official, and whose subtle tactics and compromises sometimes frightened and sometimes disgusted him. It was then that he announced he would join the guerrillas. . . .

Initially supported by the communist-controlled oil unions but then abandoned by them, the ALN could now count only on outside aid, either from Cuba by means of the coast or from the university by means of the road. But the communists had seized control of the university and were trying to dry up this source of supply.

The two leaders of this guerrilla force, Comandante Victor Medina and Fabio Vázquez, had only a very local following. The Castroite rebellion needed a big name to relaunch it. It was stagnating because it had not yet found its leader, its caudillo. Rejected by his own, cheated by the communists, heartsick, knowing that only death could bring about the triumph of his ideas, Camilo went off. The guerrillas were his last chance, and since the communists did not want him, he would join the others. The Castroites had two representatives at the university. They laid seige to Camilo and never lacked for arguments. They spoke of generosity instead of tactics. Without even informing Monsignor Guzmán, his best friend and a man who leaned toward the communist theses, Camilo joined the Santander guerrillas. The communists had had Camilo Torres stolen from them because they had been much too Machiavellian. The Castroites thought they finally had a banner to rally around. They were not to keep it long. . . .

The army soldiers, knowing there was a priest out there, did everything possible to avoid meeting up with him. To primitive believers, killing a priest is the worst crime in the world. The patrols sent off to make contact with the guerrillas with whom Camilo was thought to be, would trudge a few miles, get their boots dirty, fire a few rounds in the air, and return. And then one day a peasant betrayed the guerrillas.

He had been taken in hand by Civic and Military Action, a fighting plan established in Panama.

These methods of psychological warfare had already been used in Algeria, where they were first developed. They were designed to help the army win over civilian populations by supplying them with everything they lacked and should have had: doctors, dentists, teachers, agricultural advisors, roads, substantial housing, and food supplies when famine threatened.

As a result, this peasant felt that the army was worth more than the guerrillas, that it was finally giving instead of taking; he therefore informed a Civic and Military Action team that a small band of the National Liberation Army was making regular forays into a village to resupply itself. An ambush was set up. A patrol of seven men was sent forward as bait. Behind them, sixty more men were hidden along the sides of the path. Camilo Torres was supposed to be with the two guerrilla leaders in some other region, but at the last moment he remained behind. Another mischance made him follow the small group that went down to the village, which until then had been considered safe. The guerrillas swooped down on the patrol, killed or wounded three men, gave chase, and fell into the trap. Camilo was killed just as he was picking up a soldier's rifle. . . .

Dead, Camilo became considerably more of an embarrassment than he had been alive. The priest in mufti had become a martyr. . . .

To the right of the priest with the gun, the established Church in Latin America has also (perhaps grudgingly) begun to press for social reforms. In every country, there is a growing liberal faction of priests who fight for agrarian reform and peasant rights, but within the political structure. This selection deals with how the new Church developed in Brazil; the same thing has happened in most countries. The outcome of the struggle for control of the Church between the traditionalists and these newer groups has not been decided.

The New Church

By Claudio Veliz

The interest of Brazilian bishops in matters of a socio-political or economic nature is something relatively new.... Since 1945 the emphasis has increasingly been on the need for social and economic reforms, on the need to raise the living standards and to change the working conditions of the rural masses—although traditional religious goals, such as Catholic education and the prevention of divorce legislation, have been far from abandoned. In the summer of 1960, for example, before the impending national elections, a "caravan" of five bishops toured Brazil from North to South to enlighten public opinion about the burning issues of the day. These were (rather over-simplified): the holiness of the family—and the utter rejection of any candidate who even hinted at divorce legislation; the right of Catholic schools to integral financial support from the state; the dangers of excessive nationalism; the need for economic development; and the need for serious agrarian reform.

The Brazilian bishops have been discussing their common problems in regular meetings since the foundation, late in 1952, of the National Conference of Bishops of Brazil (CNBB). In these discussions there has been a growing concern with the social and economic conditions which, in such large parts of Brazil, preclude the full human development from which alone genuine religious options are possible. When one reads the pastoral letters of 1962 and 1963 of the CNBB—whose secretary and moving power was, until the autumn of 1964, Archbishop Dom Helder Câmara, one of the most outspoken progressives of the Brazilian hierarchy—the Church as a whole seemed ready to assume the task of "leading the revolution." In fact, of course, each bishop remained autonomous within his own diocese, and what actually did get done was much less uniform and far less radical. Even in the dioceses of the more progressive bishops whole-hearted support for their ideas among the clergy (and the faithful) is often lacking. In a similar way progressive lay élites have not, on the whole, been able to mobilize a substantial rank and file.

Moreover, it is quite clear that the tone of the declarations was influenced, before April 1964, by the general currents of political radicalization in the country. The majority of bishops, bewildered by the opposing extreme views, refrained from dissenting from opinions formulated by the radical vanguard. Since the establishment of the civil-military government after the overthrow of President Goulart the majority has asserted itself more forcefully, and the pronouncements of the bishops on worldly matters have become muted. The replacement of D. Helder Câmara as secretary of the CNBB late in 1964 was probably in part related to these developments. Nevertheless, the overwhelming climate of change prevailing in the Vatican Council has strengthened the position of the progressive bishops in Brazil. The five-year plan adopted by the CNBB during their stay in Rome late in 1965 is couched in theological rather than political language and is concerned primarily with pastoral matters, but it gives plenty of scope for radical action in the socio-economic field to those bishops who wish to accept its logical implications.

It must be said again, however, that as yet the radical enthusiasts are few in number. Of the 230-odd bishops in the country perhaps 10–20 per cent can be counted among the outspoken progressives. . . .

The "progressives" are significantly stronger among the priests who are not engaged in parish work or education than among those who are. Non-educational, non-parish tasks fulfilled by priests are staffing the different diocesan commissions and bureaus, and acting as advisers to various lay groups. Of these Catholic Action must be specially mentioned. This group was imported in 1935 from Europe, inspired perhaps especially by the French and Italian organizations, and has since grown the whole formal apparatus which has also developed in Europe. It has, however, not been really successful in striking roots in the country, whether in terms of coping with the apostolic problems peculiar to Brazil, or in terms of expanding its adult membership. After an early but superficial and short-lived success in attracting large numbers to its mass meetings and manifestations, Catholic Action fell back to the "level of a general staff," a general staff without an army, endlessly discussing hypothetical methods of action. . . .

The [regular church] hierarchy may have cracked down on the most extreme groups among Catholic youth, but in general these movements were left with a great deal of freedom. . . . This was because, in the first place, most bishops were simply overwhelmed by the political and social happenings, leaving the hierarchy divided and unable to come down forcefully on one side or the other. It had also something to do with the fear, quite widespread among Catholics, of being left behind in the overall trend towards reform. As a result, even some of the less wholeheartedly progressive Catholic leaders were willing to let a section of the Church get thoroughly implicated in the wider radical movement. They regretted, certainly more than the young people themselves, the ideological weakness of those jumping on the bandwagon. These middle-of-the-road churchmen gave warning of the dangers of naïveté, but had few, if any, positive and concretely helpful suggestions. They took up the teachings of the Popes on social and economic matters, expounded them, and talked or wrote about the things Brazil needed. But their theorizing remained abstract and divorced from reality. Minimal attention was paid to the obstacles which prevented the achievement of those worthy goals in Brazil, or to the ways of surmounting them. Great stress was laid on the idea that all Catholics are children of the Church; with this went a genuine abhorrence of violence, even conflict. The emphasis of the moderates on the "solidary," harmonious character of the ideal society . . . drove many of those primarily interested in the real Brazil straight into the arms of those people whose theory purported to explain in detail why society lacked both harmony and solidarity....

Ironically, while the United States built up the Latin American military to quell revolutions, the military itself began to take on revolutionary characteristics—at least in Peru. Georgie Anne Geyer talks about the changes in the Latin American military, how it has turned toward the left.

The New Military

By Georgie Anne Geyer

To some observers the New Military of the '60s was no more than a replay of tired old songs. It was Juan Perón all over again, his appeal to the poor against the rich, his cry to the younger officers to pry out the entrenched older ones.

But closer studies made clear that they were, indeed, something new. Perón was a caudillo par excellence, and now there were no caudillos, no charismatic leaders. The new men in charge—Arturo Costa e Silva, Juan Velasco Alvarado, Omar Torrijos, Juan Carlos Onganía—were themselves such gray men, so uninteresting personally and so unattractive politically, that they might better be called anti-caudillos.

They eschewed public popularity. Rather, they institutionalized the junta to a point at which the new phenomena might be called "juntas on horseback." They abhorred public displays of wealth such as, for instance, Pérez Jiménez's in Venezuela, building his pleasure brothel for his Cuban prostitutes on the side of the mountain. These new men were economic sobriety and dull morality itself.

In each country there were of course differences. The sober Argentina regime which took over in 1966 concerned itself exclusively with economics; it abolished politics, and soon set the economic house in order only to be continually plagued by displays of political dissatisfaction. The brutal Brazilian regime which came to power in 1964 was equally overcome with economic problems, but at least talked of reforming the political life of the country.

Peru stood as the most social reformist of the regimes. And although it, too, was imposing everything from above, the colonels there were intensely interested in giving political power and purchasing power to the forgotten marginal people. Panama would rank with Peru in having more interest in redistributing wealth and political power.

And yet, there were certain common roots in all— a rurally influenced propensity toward economic statism, a class tension with the oligarchs, a violent and inclusive patriotism, and a deep distrust of politicians. These had always grown in Latin American soil. Even Bolívar had spoken contemptuously of politicians, calling them "those legislators, more ignorant than evil, more presumptuous than ambitious, who are leading us to anarchy. . . ."

Many Latins came to hate and despise their militaries, who seemed to exist not to fight wars but to oppress their own peoples in the name of the wealthy. Money flowed into the military machines, which had the power to demand what they wanted, whether in salaries or in fancy airplanes. By the late 1950s the military services were costing the nations nearly $1.5 billion annually, or approximately one of every six of their national tax dollars—compared to one in fifteen spent for education.

Between 1954 and 1959, John J. Johnson, the political scientist, points out, Brazil spent more on its armed forces than on all public works and development programs combined.

As the armies formed they naturally took on the contours and styles of their countries. Uruguay's military was always nonpolitical. Brazil's was considered the most democratic. Venezuela's was the most corrupt and meddlesome, until 1958 when the Rómulo Betancourt revolution turned the military into a nonpolitical body. Colombia's was the most professional. In the Caribbean the armed forces tended to be

National Guards formed and trained by the United States—a leftover of American occupation. In almost every country there was one aspect of the Latin military's role that was totally different from that of the North American military. Their constitutions defined them as "guardians of the constitution" or some such similar thing, and gave them the right to step into political life when the security of the country was threatened.

In early times and in certain countries the officer class came in large part from the upper classes. But generally the armies drew from the lower classes and to join the army was the one way for a poor young man to make good. More important, that poor young man most often came also from rural origins and from small landholding families who had no experience with capitalism and distrusted it. This laid the basis for the anti-capitalist tinge to their statist mentality.

For the Latin militaries had a strong tendency toward statism or economic nationalism. The Argentine military long had controlled the steel industry, the airplane industry and a host of smaller but crucial industries; Argentine, as well as Brazilian, military men sat in influential spots on development and planning boards. When the Peruvian military took over in 1968 they clearly were statists—they embarked on a binge of nationalization comparable only with the Cuba of Fidel Castro, the man whose "way" they said they were trying to avoid. To many this represented "socialism without Marxism."

In effect, too, they came out of the marginal population. And here is another example—a crucially important one today—of the New Latins, who formerly took no part in the inner life of their societies, suddenly coming to run them and to impose their own imprint and values upon them. . . .

But . . . different kinds of changes were coming— particularly after the coming to power of Fidel Castro. Father Vekemans early had warned that a "technocratic military" would be a greater threat to real democratic participation than the Marxists, but no one listened. Then, one after the other, democratic governments of differing worths fell to military coups—Brazil in 1964, Argentina in 1966, Peru and Panama in 1968. . . .

The continent began to see, as Dr. Johnson, who is the specialist on the Latin military, said, "the substitution of technically trained managers of violence for the heroic leaders of the past." He warned, too, that things had changed, that no one should expect a repetition of the past. . . .

One of the most popular terms to describe the New Military was Nasserite, even though most often even the younger officers—the ones who were supposed to *be* Nasserites—either did not know or much care for the term. When I asked one of the Brazilian majors, for instance, if he considered himself a Nasserite, he looked at me with scarcely veiled hostility and said, "He is a man who has lost three wars. . . ."

"Nasserism is a combination of Puritanism, righteousness and sheer, naked jealousy of the rich," said one American military specialist. "They believe that foreign interests are exploitive. It represents a frustration on the part of the officers that their countries are being overtaken by world events. They are extreme patriots, and their motivation is not ideological but patriotic. They are idealists without ideas. . . ."

Yet Nasserite was only one term to describe the New Military, in whom, actually, qualities were too mixed for any simple characterization. In some instances they could be called fascist; Peru and Argentina particularly had definite corporativist tendencies. Too, they were not at all unlike the Castroites they so despised—both were middle-class military regimes led by revolutionary officers. All believed in the imposition of change from above, stressing human "participation"—but a carefully orchestrated human participation. All to a greater or lesser degree believed in the control of the economy by the state. All were extreme nationalist, anti-foreign and aggressively, often irrationally, egotistical. If it were not for the labels they would have loved each other.

But more interesting even than the qualities of the New Military is the question of why the phenomenon happened. The answer is that it happened indirectly and largely through unexpected circumstances. It was the threat of Castroism, of Marxist military men in beards, which led the military to take over and try to change their own societies and to attempt to transform them—in ways that turned out to be strikingly similar to Castro's.

It is not that there was some military "conspiracy" across the continent—one military did not egg on the other. Certainly they influenced each other, and certainly they were under the same circumstantial influences, for they all attend each other's schools and they all talk to one another. But it was largely a reaction of similarly thinking men of similar class having similar training and similar fears and reacting in the same way. Another example, in effect, of the unity of Latin America.

All this time, through its various military schools, including the Spanish-speaking School of the Americas in Panama, the United States had thought it was training a "democratic military"—officers who would step back from political involvement and let the democrats do it. With this in mind the American officers instituted training in "civic action"—to teach the Latin military to help instead of using their people.

But instead this passion for "nation-building" only contributed to giving these officers a new and profound sense of themselves as the men with the sacred responsibility for transforming their societies. They looked upon their armies as democratic because many of the officers and all of the soldiers were from the lower classes and because most officers had spent some time in the rural marginal areas and therefore knew them. Thus they felt they represented the masses, without the bother of elections. In the army a man could rise from a poor soldier to president, as did President-General Juan Velasco Alvarado, leader of the 1968 revolutionary government in Peru. It was no matter to the officers that the masses of the soldiers were poor Indian recruits earning ten dollars a month with no choice in anything . . . they would train them.

Their new professionalism gave them the power. In

addition the technical know-how they gained in the
United States only caused them to become more politically involved, for professionalization of any armed
forces always means a greater, not a lesser, political
involvement. . . .

What became clear was that there was a strange
convergence of ideologies and forces going on—the
Nasseristic military working with the radical clergy
working with the Castroite New Marxists. What did it
matter, after all, whether you called it the military's
"national statism," the Marxist's "socialism" or the
Catholic's "communitarianism." It all meant basically
the same thing—control of production and land by the
state or in the name of the workers.

These military men were, in truth, men on gray
horses. Men socially drawn from the gray, marginal
areas of their own societies. Men ideologically gray,
for what they believed in they drew from a mixture
of military experience, Marxist collectivism and Catholic radicalism. And across the continent the reaction
to them was very curious. . . .

Many feel that the time is now so late that the
only thing any longer of importance is that the
changes be made . . . however . . . by whomever. "We
cannot wait any longer for reform," Gilberto Freyre
said of Brazil. "We must have it at once. We cannot
wait for the liberal way through parliamentary, legalistic means. People think historically that military rule
means reactionary rule. On the contrary, it may mean
very progressive rule."

Even the Castroites are carefully watching these regimes, although they are watching skeptically. "You
cannot divide Latin America between the civilians and
the militaries," Carlos Rafael Rodríguez, the major
Cuban ideologue told me in a rare interview while he
was visiting Lima in 1969. "Peru and Cuba are close
on many things, but they have considerable differences. I can't say we are putting our hope in these
military regimes. It could be that the dynamics of the
situation could bring the military to a more dynamic
position in terms of national sovereignty. We might be
forced to re-evaluate. . . ."

It might be that these military regimes would simply come and go. It does not look like it.

In Peru, the ruling generals have nationalized U.S. companies and large agricultural holdings, taking more socialist measures than any other country besides Chile. Other military regimes, like Brazil's, have been very favorable to private enterprise and to U.S. companies. It remains to be seen whether Peru stands alone or whether other army groups will follow her example.

Peru's Revolutionary Government
By George W. Grayson

The term "revolution" evokes images of bearded guerrillas hacking their way through snake-infested jungles; Parisian mobs racing tumbrels toward the guillotine; or frenzied peasants setting a torch to the landowner's mansion. Yet in Peru a self-proclaimed "Revolutionary Government of the Armed Forces" is promoting sweeping change without the massive violence and bloodshed that usually accompanies the reshuffling of a pyramidal social order.

General Juan Velasco Alvarado, leader of the October 3, 1968, *golpe de estado,* which ousted President Fernando Belaúnde Terry, heads this regime. It rightfully claims to have accomplished more for its people in four years than all previous governments did during the first 150 years of Peruvian independence. Its importance is not confined to the Inca republic of 14 million inhabitants, for ambitious generals in Bolivia, Ecuador and Panama have copied extensively from the Peruvian model in fashioning "populist" military governments which, because of their commitment to social reform, stand in sharp contrast to the repressive army-controlled regimes in Argentina, Brazil and Paraguay.

Land reform marks the keystone of the Peruvian generals' revolutionary program. When they seized power, rigid stratification characterized the agrarian sector in which half of the nation's population earns a living. Approximately 0.4 per cent of the property holders held 75 per cent of the arable land, which meant that a majority of the peasantry tried to scratch out a living on stamp-sized plots. Thus in 1969 the reform-minded generals decreed the expropriation of abandoned and poorly exploited farms, the abolition of large privately owned estates (*latifundia*) and small properties (*minifundia*) and conversion of massive agro-industrial plantations—such as the sugar estates along the Pacific coast—into worker-run cooperatives. Under this reform, the government has redistributed 8 million acres of land and 1.3 million head of cattle in what has been termed the "most sweeping agrarian reform to be undertaken in South America."

The generals also wish to enlarge the stake of industrial workers in the revolutionary process. Specifically, they have ordered management to allocate each year a certain percentage of its gross earnings—approximately 10 per cent in cash and 15 per cent in stock—to "labor communities," composed of everyone who works in a particular firm. Thus far, the regime has authorized communities in the industrial, mining, fishing, telecommunications, oil and electric power sectors of the economy.

Not only do the workers collectively gain a portion of the equity in the enterprise but, proportional to their ownership, they are entitled to choose voting representatives for the firm's board of directors. Community members will elect delegates to regional and national associations of industrial enterprises which, presumably, will contribute to policy-making in their economic sphere. The government hopes that the new structures modeled along the lines of Yugoslavia's worker-owned factories—will diminish class conflict, enhance worker participation in decision-making, undercut opposition-dominated labor unions, spur production by linking "the human interest of the workers with the authentic, bold and pioneering vocation of the entrepreneur," and reduce turnover of the labor force inasmuch as benefits increase the longer an employee remains with a given community.

In the short run, at least, decisions may flow downward from Lima rather than upward from the grassroots as many Peruvians had anticipated. Indeed, the government has not hesitated to impose policies on independent-minded labor communities deemed to behave too much like "labor unions." Hence, these structures may become the basic element in a hierarchically controlled corporate state.

Also crucial in fostering a new society of "justice, liberty and solidarity" is the education reform promulgated on April 3, 1972. The new educational system contemplates equal opportunities for women, compulsory national service before graduation, student participation in university government and bilingual studies for the 40 per cent of the Peruvians who speak only Quechua, Aymará or other Indian dialects.

For instruction in remote areas, there will be heavy reliance on radio and television, which the government now requires to carry prime time broadcasts on Peruvian culture. Under the General Telecommunications Law enacted in late 1971 and subsequent amendments, all station owners and employees must be Peruvian born; all advertising must emanate from Peru; 60 per cent of programs must have Peruvian content; and all broadcasts should expound "humanist values" and be "socially useful."

Foreign Affairs

Like the hemisphere's other new military governments, the Peruvian regime has fashioned a foreign policy that stresses national dignity and independence, while rejecting domination—or undue influence—from the United States or major Western powers. In pursuit of these goals, it has (1) led the fight for Cuba's reintegration into the inter-American system, (2) demanded sovereignty over 200 miles of offshore waters, (3) resisted perceived United States "intervention" in domestic affairs, and (4) established diplomatic and commercial relations with Communist-bloc states.

Following Cuban aid to Peru during the May, 1970,

earthquake which took the lives of over 50,000 persons in Ancash Province, Peru joined Bolivia in urging that members of the Organization of American States (OAS) consider renewing diplomatic and commercial relations with the pearl of the Antilles; in October, 1971, President Velasco invited a Cuban delegation to attend the Second Ministerial Meeting of the "Group of 77" developing states that convened in Lima: two months later, the Peruvian chief executive warmly welcomed Cuban Premier Fidel Castro when the hirsute Cuban stopped briefly in Peru on his return home from a month-long tour of Chile; and at the April, 1972, session of the OAS General Assembly, the Peruvian delegation again pushed hard for the readmission of Cuba to the 23-member body. When this initiative failed, Peru announced on July 8, 1972, that she would exchange ambassadors with the Havana regime.

Insistence on sovereignty over 200 miles of coastal waters now forms a vital component of Peru's foreign policy. Such a policy seeks to protect valuable natural resources by imposing fines on foreign vessels that fish in coastal waters without a license from the Peruvian government. Also, in extending the nation-state—symbolically, at least—200 miles into the ocean, the generals have fired the spirit of nationalism, so important to the success of populist military governments in Latin America. Peru's leaders, working closely with Ecuador and Chile, have gained acceptance for the 200-mile doctrine among a dozen Latin American states.

Recognizing only 12 miles of territorial waters, the United States Department of State has strenuously opposed the Peruvian policy, which has forced owners of San Diego-based tuna-clippers to pay stiff fines, for which they were eventually reimbursed by the United States government. Consequently, on October 27, 1972, United States President Richard Nixon signed into law legislation that automatically sanctions any country that fines United States boats for fishing in international waters. This law, which, according to Peruvian Foreign Minister Miguel Angel de la Flor

Valle, "introduces new and inadmissible coercive economic measures in inter-American relations," has sparked massive support for the Lima government as labor unions, political parties, student federations, peasant leagues, editorial writers and church groups have vied with each other in denouncing this "insult" to national sovereignty. While stirring Peruvian naval officers to talk about the need for more weapons, the American move has also strengthened Peru's relations with Ecuador and Chile—traditional antagonists of the Lima regime because of long-standing territorial disputes.

The fishing law is only one reason for tension between the United States and Peru. Because the revolutionary generals have not compensated Standard Oil of New Jersey for the International Petroleum Corporation (IPC), expropriated six days after the military seized power, American aid has been sharply reduced. Although Washington's Export-Import Bank has extended credit to permit Peruvian purchases of American-produced aircraft, Congress has restricted United States support for soft loans to Peru in the Inter-American Development Bank—a move which amounts to a legislative veto of support from that financial organization.

Secret talks with the United States on resolving the IPC question collapsed early in 1972, apparently because General Jorge Fernández Maldonado, Peru's militantly nationalistic Minister of Mines and Energy, leaked word to the press of these conversations. Thus relations between the United States and Peru, one of the world's few developing nations committed to social reform with as little repression as possible, now stand at the lowest point since the generals assumed office, a fact evinced by the cool reception accorded former United States Treasury Secretary John B. Connally, Jr., during a visit to Lima in mid-1972.

Peru has also reaffirmed opposition to French atomic blasts in the South Pacific because of the potential radioactive fallout. The foreign ministry has notified Paris that Peru will sever diplomatic ties if additional tests are conducted on the Mururoa atoll.

Meanwhile, relations have improved with the Soviet Union with which Peru's ruling generals exchanged envoys in 1969 as part of a commitment to diplomatic and commercial ties with all countries that can contribute to their developmental goals. The Russians are constructing a fishing port at Paita; their technicians have streamed into Lima; Aeroflot has gained refueling privileges at Lima's Jorge Chávez Airport on its Moscow-Havana-Santiago route; and trade between Peru and the Soviet Union increased 27.5 fold in 1972 ($7 million) as compared with its extremely modest 1970–1971 level ($250,000). Also significant has been the growing cultural and economic intercourse between Peru and Czechoslovakia.

In late 1971, Peru became the third Latin American state after Cuba and Chile to recognize mainland China. In a joint communiqué, the Lima government called Taiwan "an inalienable part of the People's Republic of China," while the Peking regime "recognized the sovereignty of Peru over 200 nautical miles of sea, adjacent to its coast." Shortly after his arrival, the Chinese ambassador to Peru announced his nation's intention to buy 150,000 tons of fish meal from his host country.

Latin America's populist militaries see recognition of Communist states as a means to assert independence of the United States and curry leftist support at home. Peru has carried this strategy about as far as she can, however, for the only politically interesting states that remain unrecognized are North Korea, North Vietnam and East Germany. Though ties with the East Berlin regime may come at any time because of possible trade benefits, opposition within Lima's essentially anti-Marxist military hierarchy blocks recognition of the Pyongyang and Hanoi governments for the immediate future.

While Peru is too small to become a major force, her military government aspires to play the role of a "middle power"—like Canada, Poland or Sweden—in international relations. Peru's tenacious support for the 200-mile doctrine, her advocacy of Cuba's reintegration into hemispheric affairs, her readiness to stand up to the United States and France, and her non-aligned position in the East–West conflict have earned respect throughout the world. The election of a Peruvian as a vice-president of the United Nations General Assembly testifies to the esteem that his country now enjoys within the world community.

Economic Conditions

Unlike most Latin American countries, Peru's economy does not depend on a single crop. This vibrant Andean nation earns foreign exchange from a host of items, including fish meal, minerals, coffee, sugar, cotton and tourism.

Because of a healthy demand for fish meal and copper, Peru's exports totalled nearly $989 million in 1972, compared with $889 million during the previous year; at the same time, the value of imports grew approximately $62 million to reach $845 million in 1972. Owing in large measure to the strength of the export sector, Peru's GNP expanded in both 1971 (7.5 per cent) and 1972 (6 per cent).

Also encouraging is the forecast by Rear Admiral Alberto Jiménez, Minister of Industry and Commerce, that Peru, which now produces 150,000 tons of steel annually, will treble this output by 1974 (500,000) and quadruple it by 1980 (2 million).

Despite these favorable indices, Peru's economic picture darkened in April, 1972, as *anchoveta,* the raw material for the nation's fish meal industry, disappeared from Pacific waters. The absence of these little fish has sparked alarm because in recent years the fish meal industry has generated between 25 per cent and 35 per cent of the country's exports ($200 million to $350 million annually), while providing jobs for about 30,000 people.

What happened to the *anchoveta?* According to the respected British weekly *Latin America,* El Niño, a warm current that originates in the Pacific near Panama and usually flows 300 kilometers or more off the Peruvian coast, suddenly turned inward. Moving closer to shore, it displaced the Humboldt, a cold stream that travels northward from Antarctica, bringing with it rich vegetable plankton that feeds the teeming schools of fish. The Humboldt now runs under El Niño, killing the *anchoveta* that cannot survive at the greater depths.

If past experience is any guide, El Niño will eventually return to its normal course; however, it may take several years for the fish population to replenish itself, and even if fishing should return to normal by February, 1973—and this is not thought possible in Lima—about $150 million in exports have been irretrievably lost. . . .

The fish meal crisis, exacerbated by a sharp fall in agricultural production, places a burden on mining to earn vitally needed foreign exchange. The response to this challenge has been heartening; mining production rose 5 per cent during the first six months of 1972, and mineral exports shot up 33.2 per cent between January and May—an increase attributable to expanded earnings of copper, silver, lead, zinc, oil and its by-products.

Still, output levels remain problematical, because of the large number of work stoppages that have beset the mining sector. In 1971, there were 377 strikes, involving 161,415 workers, with a loss of nearly 11 million man-hours; from January to September, 1972, approximately 300 strikes took place, involving 90,945 workers and the loss of 4.3 million man-hours.

An oil boom has diverted a great deal of attention from the fish meal industry to Peru's Amazonian region where PETROPERÚ, the state oil company, and foreign firms have discovered "black gold." The hope is that the Peruvian fields are part of the same geological structure as the nearby Ecuadorean territory, from which 314,000 barrels of oil have been exported. The generals view a major oil strike as a means to earn foreign exchange, enhance the regime's legitimacy, attract the foreign investors who have heretofore expressed reservations about the government and develop the long-neglected hinterland of their nation which Velasco visited in October, 1972, to emphasize that Amazonia will not be excluded from the nation's development. . . .

Will discovery of oil in the Amazon unleash a flood of foreign investment in Peru? Except for the "devil-may-care" attitude of oil companies, foreign investors—promised security and profits in Brazil, Paraguay, and other military dictatorships—continue to remain cautious with respect to populist militaries such as Peru's. The IPC question still hangs fire; through nationalizations the Peruvian generals have concentrated enormous economic power in the government; labor communities may limit profits and decision-making; foreign interests which hold a more than 49 per cent ownership must fix a deadline for transferring a majority of equity to Peruvians; and now under study is a system of social property—cited by Velasco as the "most decisive step taken by the revolutionary government in four years."

Apparently, the generals intend to reserve to state ownership the country's strategic resources, encourage a private sector "reformed" by labor communities and foster the development of collective, self-managed "social properties," roughly similar to the agro industrial sugar cooperatives and the agrarian co-ops now in operation. In return for state financing—to be carried out by COFIDE, the national development corporation—the new enterprise will pay substantial "rental" for the capital and land which it uses, with all monies earned over these amounts to be distributed to the firm's employees (each of whom is to possess an equal vote in policy matters). Because of the ambiguities surrounding it, investors seem uneasy about the social property concept. It has, however, won vigorous support from Cardinal Juan Landázuri Ricketts, head of Peru's Roman Catholic Church, one of the regime's staunchest backers.

Still, 16 United States banks evidently felt optimistic about the country's prospects when they signed an accord in February, 1972, refinancing Peruvian debts totalling $53.5 million, $23.5 million of which was originally payable in 1972 with the rest due the following year. Peru must now repay the sum in installments over a 54-month period beginning on January 2, 1973. A consortium of European banks has loaned

Peru $38 million to bolster her foreign reserves. Even more striking has been the escalating number of loans, credits, and technical assistance offers tendered by Japan, a nation that clearly believes that fortunes can be made in Peru under the present regime.

Meanwhile, Peru continues to play an active role in the Andean Common Market, a regional economic unit that also embraces Bolivia, Chile, Colombia and Ecuador. Not only have tariffs among these nations been reduced, but plans are now under way to form a multinational Andean group airline, build an Andean region maritime fleet and stimulate tourism as a collective venture. In the distant future, there may even be an Andean currency.

Political Conditions

The discipline that characterizes the new military in Latin America is found in Peru. The 1968 seizure of power sprang neither from a sergeants' revolt nor the plotting of one clique of officers but from a decision of the high command executed through the military's command structure. This same discipline has shielded Velasco's government from worrisome intra-military conflicts during his more than four years in power, and has also steeled his regime from the threat of an opposition-sparked overthrow.

Nonetheless, opponents of the regime have surfaced during recent months. On the right are landowners displaced by the agrarian reform, businessmen whose properties have been expropriated by the government and politicians associated with the American Revolutionary Popular Alliance (APRA) and other parties that dominated the political system before the generals closed Congress and suspended elections. Although under intense government pressure, *El Comercio* and *La Prensa*—Lima's oldest dailies—articulate the conservative viewpoint.

Toward the center-left of the spectrum can be found the publishers of *Sociedad Y Política*, a monthly journal published by young social scientists who intelligently criticize a number of the government's programs.

On the far left are student activists who have launched protests in Trujillo, Huancayo, and Lima, while joining with workers to stage one-day general strikes in such provincial cities of the relatively underdeveloped south as Cuzco, Arequipa, and Puno. An alphabet soup of guerrilla groups—the Trotskyite FIR, VRI, and MIR—has also appeared on the left. The most spectacular confrontation between guerrillas and the government took place in the afforested northern province of Jaén. There military units finally captured 15 of 22 members of a splinter group of the MIR headed by Gonzalo Fernández Gasco, an ex-Aprista who has eluded the military's grasp. . . .

Contemptuous of the old politics that has brought deadlock and drift, new militaries in several Latin American countries have intervened in the name of the people to design a new social order. Yet, imprisoned by their own familiarity with authoritarian methods and wary lest they create unmanageable foes, the generals-turned-politicians recoil from fashioning new political structures that are vital for bargaining with opponents and linking—symbolically, at least— the people to national decision-making. And so it is in Peru, where the President vacillates between rushing in to mediate disputes himself and calling on the riot police to curb student protestors, break up a teachers' strike, or repress a newspaper—an act that has become almost a weekly occurrence in Lima.

Elections would be an obvious way to tie the peo ple to their government. Yet the military has scorned any notion of returning to a political system dominated by self-serving politicos and cynical party alliances. "In five years or so" has been since 1968 the typical response of ruling generals to questions concerning the date of elections. . . .

With the election of Salvador Allende in 1971, Chile became the first country in the hemisphere to choose Marxism by the ballot box. Allende had been trying to win the presidency for a long time; his victory took Chile on the road toward nationalization and state controls. The Allende government was beset by strikes from unions and urban consumer groups, opposition from U.S. corporations nationalized by the Chileans, soaring inflation, food shortages, and economic instability. On September 11, 1973, military forces deposed Allende in a violent coup and said that he had committed suicide rather than surrender to the attackers.

This selection by Joseph Kraft describes how and why the Chilean people chose Allende, how an industrial, democratic nation starts to redefine itself and voluntarily accept a radical alternative to what they have known. Despite Allende's ouster and death, it is doubtful if the forces that Kraft observes will take the country back to a pre-Allende phase. The hard question is whether other countries will adopt Chile's struggle.

Allende in Chile

By Joseph Kraft

In most of the great cities of Latin America, long avenues, straight as the edge of a ruler, run past immaculately perpendicular skyscrapers to plazas in the form of perfect squares: geometry dominates. But Santiago de Chile—partly because of earthquakes, and even more because it grew erratically as a commercial center rather than symmetrically as a city laid out from the beginning as a provincial capital of imperial Spain—is a place with soft edges. Downtown is a profusion of tiny streets in disarray. Homes and public buildings are squat structures done in stones of drab brown or gray, often with graceless columns. Even the obligatory equestrian statue of the founding father—a captain in Pizarro's band named Pedro de Valdivia—bears a distinctly unmartial aspect, since the bold conquistador has no reins to guide his stallion. A far greater local hero, especially among those who call themselves nationalists, is Diego Portales, Minister of the Interior and constitution-giver in the last century, who was neither a soldier nor a landowner but a tobacco merchant. And up to now, at least, the spirit of pliability and business as usual, of accommodation without great fuss, has dominated the reaction in Santiago to the popular-front government of President Salvador Allende, the Marxist physician whose election last September was widely supposed to put this country on the road to being, after Cuba, the second Communist state in the Western Hemisphere.

A good sampling of this spirit may be taken at the Golf Club—as it is known, without more identification, throughout Santiago—where friends took me one Saturday for lunch. On a shady terrace facing the snowy peaks of the Andean *cordillera*, dozens of elegantly dressed members—the men in narrow slacks and Italian sports shirts with long sleeves and open necks, the women in pants suits—were sipping *pisco* sours, eating, and talking of the Allende government. Much of the talk was a retelling of the kind of apocryphal tales the rich and their friends have probably been telling about populist regimes ever since Pericles was replaced by the demagogue Cleon. There was the Minister who asked for a round envelope so he could send a circular letter to the rest of the Cabinet. There was the division of the country into two camps—the weaklings, who fled, and the dimwits, who stayed. There was the trade-union leader who was offered a post by President Allende if he could fit four triangles into a square drawn on a piece of paper. He stared hopelessly at the paper, and then, in a fit of anger, drew a big X mark across the square and thrust it back at the President. "Fine," Dr. Allende is supposed to have said. "You're the Minister of Finance."

Almost everybody at the Golf Club had a personal grievance to air. A lawyer said that the foreign firms he represents are beginning to close down operations. The wife of a broker, who has her luggage packed, ready for a getaway, said her husband went to the Bolsa every day but had nothing to do, because trading there had almost stopped since the election. A young industrial designer reported that all his orders were cancelled after the vote. A visiting member from the Polo Club complained that two polo fields had been set aside for housing projects. But despite these intimations of a deluge to come, hardly anybody was getting out. Indeed, some who left Chile just after the election, on September 4th, had come back. "I suppose that it's too good to last," the wife of the lawyer said. "My sister in New York calls us every day on the phone. She says terrible things will happen and that we must come out. But we're not leaving yet. After all, where else can we live as well as in Chile? . . ."

A premonition of failure among the propertied classes goes to the heart of Chilean politics. The haves have kept what they have by camouflaging themselves in the clothes of the have-nots. Over and over, the right has effaced itself, the better to disarm and then incorporate the left. Three times in the first half of this century—in 1938, in 1942, and in 1946—middle-of-the-road governments took power with Communist support and then turned their backs on their left-wing allies. In the Presidential election of 1964, a left-wing Christian Democrat, Eduardo Frei, won a majority—55.7 per cent of the vote against 38.5 per cent for Dr. Allende, who ran in that election, too, as the Socialist candidate of a popular-front coalition—because conservative voters backed him instead of the candidate on the right put up by the Radical Party. . . .

Actually, the election Dr. Allende won was distinguished precisely in that, for once, the conservatives attempted open opposition instead of relying on their old device of absorbing the left. In an access of mistaken self-confidence, the conservatives backed for the Presidency a man of their own, a grand old man indeed—Jorge Alessandri, seventy-four years old, who was President from 1958 through 1964 and is the son of a former President. With Alessandri preëmpting the conservative electorate, the Christian Democratic candidate, Radomiro Tomic, felt obliged to campaign as a left-winger, and he was able to cut slightly into the vote of Dr. Allende's Unidad Popular, a coalition of the Socialists, the Communists, the Radicals, and some dissident Christian Democrats. In the election of

September 4th, Dr. Allende emerged with 36.2 per cent of the vote—down more than two points from his showing in 1964. The rest of the vote was divided between Alessandri, who took 34.9 per cent, and Tomic, who ran third with 27.8 per cent. At that moment, abundant chances seemed to exist for an undoing of the result by chicanery or strong-arm methods. The Chilean constitution provides that when no candidate has a majority both houses of the National Congress choose the winner. The balance of power in the Congress was held by the Christian Democrats, and since the inauguration was scheduled for November 4th, there were sixty days to shake Chile. But almost immediately after the election, accommodation politics reasserted itself. . . .

With the Christian Democrats going along, the right also made accommodations. Former President Allessandri acknowledged the legitimacy of Dr. Allende's victory in a statement that was delivered three days before the Schneider assassination [a military leader killed around the time of Allende's election]. Alessandri, too, then slipped from sight, surfacing only to deny rumors that he was going to marry Dr. Allende's sister. His most ardent source of support, the big daily *El Mercurio*, underwent a complete transformation. The outspokenly opinionated proprietor, Augustín Edwards, left Chile and took up residence in Greenwich, Connecticut. Control of *El Mercurio* passed to Sonia Edwards, Augustín Edwards' sister and a great friend of Dr. Allende. She curbed the paper's hostility to the government so much at the beginning that a recent meeting of the Communist Central Committee the Party Secretary, Luis Corvalán, felt constrained to warn his comrades against this enemy of the regime, which "today pretends to be its friend."

By all normal standards, the Chilean Communists are a formidable lot. They did most of the work for the Unidad Popular, and they have three Ministers out of fourteen in the Allende Cabinet and a few under-secretaries as well. The Party is the oldest in Latin America, with roots running back to the So-

cialist Labor Party, founded by Luis Emilio Reca-
barren in 1912. The membership is considered the third
largest in the non-Communist world, exceeded only by
those of Italy and France. It is easy to mobilize, being
grouped in labor unions—these are particularly strong
in the copper mines—and hundreds of special local
committees that were set up to campaign in the last
election. The leadership has been tested by adver-
sity—notably in the period between 1948 and 1958,
when the Party was illegal and its chiefs were exiled
to a remote village. The publication of a healthy daily
paper, *El Siglo,* suggests ample finances. Perhaps because so much of the money comes from Moscow, or
possibly because of lessons learned during the bleak
period, the Chilean Communist Party, almost alone
among Communist Parties in the world, seems to have
developed no schisms. The Chilean Communists were
among the first to salute the Soviet invasion of
Czechoslovakia in 1968. In keeping with Soviet
views—and distinct from the emphasis on guerrilla
tactics preached by Mao and Fidel Castro—the
Chilean Party's official line now advocates a takeover
in stages. Violence is approved only as resistance
against middle-class efforts to crush the Party. In an
article published a month ago in an international
Communist magazine, Party Secretary Corvalán
noted, "It is not completely unlikely that in the future
the people may find themselves forced into some kind
of armed confrontation. . . . What we must now do is
to continue cornering the enemies of change, tie their
hands, and put them in straitjackets to prevent civil
war."

Despite their achievements, however, the Chilean
Communists do not give the impression of being particularly self-confident revolutionaries. They have an
obvious anxiety about the perils of compromise with
the system—an anxiety expressed either in too much
protest or in too ready compliance. In his speech to
the Central Committee, Corvalán not only warned his
fellow-Communists against the danger of being deceived by the soft tones of *El Mercurio* but also
warned Communists in the government against the

dangers of "relatively high salaries" and "official automobiles." Yet Corvalán is a senator who has for years participated in the give-and-take of democratic politics. He shares an office with another Communist senator—the Party ideologist Volodia Teitelboim—who is, or affects to be, the very model of orthodox parliamentary behavior.

Teitelboim, a descendant of Jewish immigrants from the Ukraine, is a pink-faced fat man, soft-spoken and elaborately courteous. When I talked with him at the Congress, he was wearing an electric-blue suit, a striped shirt, and a striped tie. He speaks English and French as well as Spanish, and conversation ran easily. When I asked him whether he thought Chile would become the second Cuba in the hemisphere, he said, "The Cuban and Chilean experiences are very different. They achieved independence from Spain at the end of the nineteenth century. We achieved it at the beginning. They had a military dictatorship for years. We have a century and a half of almost uninterrupted parliamentary government. Most of us in the Communist Party have worked in the parliamentary system for thirty years." I asked him about Chile's relations with other Latin-American countries—particularly Argentina and Brazil, which had expressed some misgivings about the Allende regime. He said, "We are not exporters of revolution. We do not imagine ourselves as the liberators of Argentina or Brazil or any other country. We hope for good relations with the United States. We even hope some of the Chileans who fled there will come back." I asked him why the Chilean Communists had been so quick about approving the Soviet occupation of Czechoslovakia. He said, "At first, we were sympathetic to the Czech experiment. But then it got out of control. Foreign powers began to exploit it and to turn it against the Communists. It went sour, and so we approved what the Russians did, just as we approved what they did in Hungary in 1956. But I want you to know that those were not happy pages in our history. They were sad pages."

Inside the Allende government, the Communist

specialty is economics. Communists head the Ministries of Labor, Finance, and Public Works, and the Minister of Economy is a Marxist serving in the Cabinet without party affiliation, Pedro Vuscovic. A diagnosis of Chile's problems given to me by Vuscovic, a boyish-looking academic economist, accords in almost every particular with diagnoses laid out for me by Robert T. Brown, an American economist working for the United Nations in Chile, and by Flavian Levine, a Chilean business executive who has been managing the nation's steel trust. The distinguishing feature of the Chilean economy, as all three men see it, is that demand depends upon a small number of consumers with highly sophisticated tastes. Eight million Chileans, out of a total population of nine million, are estimated to be, in effect, nonconsumers. Many of these are miserably poor people living from hand to mouth in the countryside or in the Chilean version—called *poblaciones callampas,* or mushroom villages—of the shantytowns that have sprung up around every major city in the underdeveloped world. The remaining million, concentrated chiefly in Santiago and ranging from skilled clerical and blue-collar workers, through professional people, to entrepreneurs and landowners, have well-developed appetites for all the latest consumer goods. . . . After an initial burst to satisfy the demand for new products, industry after industry in Chile has tended to stagnate, and when firms are in trouble they cut back production, raise prices, and seek government subsidies. At the time the Allende regime took office, about eighty per cent of all industrial investment in Chile came from government agencies. Inflation was running at roughly thirty-five per cent a year. Industries were operating far below capacity—textile mills at sixty-one per cent, bakeries at fifty per cent, canneries at sixty-five per cent, furniture factories at sixty-one per cent, electronics plants at seventy per cent, shoe factories at sixty per cent. Unemployment was high—about twenty per cent, according to a study by the World Bank. Annual economic growth was very low: with allowance for an annual population increase of 23 per cent (which is conservative), per-capita economic expansion has been at one per cent or less for the last four years.

The remedy prescribed by Vuscovic for this condition is not very different from the pump-priming employed in the United States under Franklin Roosevelt. Vuscovic's aim is to achieve "more dynamic economic growth by a redistribution of income." To that end, the Allende government is stepping up a major public-works and housing program begun by the Frei regime. It has authorized an across-the-board wage raise of about thirty-five per cent—the equivalent of the increase in the cost of living in 1970. Industries are being called on, one by one, to step up production, thus taking on more workers, and to cut prices, thus appealing to more consumers. As an inducement, the government is offering to underwrite expanded production with guaranteed credits at very low rates of interest. To raise the credit, the government—in the one major departure from capitalist practice—is drawing on two sources: it has announced plans to place private banks under nationalized control, and it is planning to take over the chief export firms that earn foreign currency. This means, especially, the copper mines in which the Chilean government now owns a fifty-one-per-cent interest, the remainder being owned by American firms—Anaconda and Kennecott. According to the government plan, compensation for the American investments is to be paid over a period of thirty years after a figure is fixed in negotiations between the companies and the regime.

Nobody knows whether or not this plan can get the economy moving again. If it doesn't, Chile will soon be in severe economic difficulties, and the Communists will be in a good position to exploit the trouble—hence a recent cartoon in *La Prensa* that shows Party Secretary Corvalán eating from a dish labelled "Chilean Economy" and saying "Delicious meal." If the new economic policy does work, much of the credit will go to Dr. Allende and the Socialist Party, for the Socialists have taken the Ministerial posts that are most directly in touch with the homeless and jobless.

It was, typically, not a Communist who took me around to see the poor of Santiago but a Socialist— Eric Schnake, a lawyer and the vice-chairman of the Chamber of Deputies. He drove me late one afternoon to a *población* that had been set up a few months earlier in a hilly field just outside Santiago. Some eight hundred persons, mostly women and children— many of the women having been deserted by their husbands—had camped in the field without authorization. They had been led there by a Socialist labor organizer, and they had named their encampment the Villa Sergio Alvarez after him. Crude shelters had been built from tarpaper, chicken wire, tents, and blankets slung over ropes supported by sticks. Cooking was done over open wood fires. There were no beds and no plumbing. A single faucet connected to a main by the side of the road was the only source of water. Schnake's wife, who does social work in the *población,* had gathered a number of the women together in a mothers' club. She taught them elementary hygiene—"about vaccinations and brushing teeth," she said. She also tried to interest them in knitting and weaving clothes, either to sell or to wear. "Our big trouble is the water," she said as we walked around the encampment. "It is polluted, and almost all the children get sick. In July and August, it will get much worse. There will be rain every day, and many of the houses will be washed out." Her voice broke when she spoke of "the houses," and for a moment I thought she would cry. Instead, she looked straight at me and said bitterly, "This is the Chilean reality. Now you know why we have to take the American copper."

Half a million people out of the three million in Santiago live in such mushroom villages. The unauthorized seizure of lands for encampments has been going on for years. During the election campaign, the Communists and Socialists stimulated seizures all over Chile to embarrass the Frei government, and at one point about a thousand people a day were claiming squatter's rights. The Socialists have given improvement in housing first priority. The Minister of Housing, Carlos Cortés, is a Socialist, and he is responsible for new construction. The Interior Ministry, headed by José Tohá, a former newspaper editor who is also a Socialist, has broken up the police squads once used to protect private landowners against the unauthorized seizures. In his first days in office, Dr. Allende visited one of the *poblaciones*. He told the people there about the government's construction program, and said that once houses were on the way, the seizures could stop. Seizures do still go on, but their number seems to have abated.

Maybe nationalizing the American interest in copper will increase the funds available to the government for improving the lot of the poor, but certainly not by much. The cost to the government, apart from compensation, will probably include a loss of American expertise in management and sales, plus a black mark for the seizure that is apt to scare off future American investment in Chile. Still, the political dividends of taking full control are substantial. The co-existence of native poverty and rich American companies makes it highly advantageous to stand up to the United States and to flirt with Washington's adversaries, and the Allende regime has missed few chances to do either. Real and imagined slights by the United States are regularly exploited. There were harsh words when the American contingent that monitored atomic tests from Easter Island, a remote Chilean possession in the Pacific, was withdrawn brusquely just before Allende's inauguration. When the Washington *Evening Star* and the New York *Daily News* criticized Chilean behavior toward the local branches of two American companies, the government paper, *La Nación*, complained in a front-page banner headline of a "Campaign of Insults Against Chile." Chile has already recognized Castro's government in Havana and Mao's regime in Peking. Delegations from Cuba, mainland China, and North Vietnam were honored guests at the Allende inauguration, and the road from the airport is still plastered with signs of welcome. "Cuba Is No Longer Alone," one says. "Viva el Vietcong," says another. There is even a word of cheer for East Germans in their native tongue: "*Freundschaft mit der D.D.R.*" But, once again, it is the Socialists, rather than the Communists, who reap the political benefits. The Communists are reserved about being associated with Castro, not to mention Mao, and President Allende has forced the pace in drawing Chile closer to Havana and Peking. Allende's daughter Beatriz has spent some time in Cuba, and, at home in Chile, has been closely associated with visiting Cubans who are said to be active in Castro's intelligence service. Clodomiro Almeyda, the Foreign Minister, is, like the President, a Socialist.

The same pattern of Socialists' outflanking Communists on the left shows up in the government's relations with the MIR. In effect, the Miristas are the Chilean brand of the far-out youthful leftists who appeared in many countries during the late sixties. They regard the Communist Party as stodgy and bureaucratic, look kindly on Castro and Mao, and profess to favor the guerrilla tactics associated with Ché Guevara. In Chile, the movement has no more than a few thousand members, most of them concentrated in the universities. Though they have talked of kidnapping in the fashion of the Tupamaro guerrillas in Uruguay, their major action so far has been a spree of bank robberies in the first half of 1970. As a left-wing heresy, the MIR is anathema to the Communists. Party Secretary Corvalán in his report to the Central Committee meeting cited with approval the opinion of another Communist leader that the Miristas were "opportunistic deviationists." Many of the Miristas, including the one I saw with the fancy old car at the university, come from good families with Socialist connections. The Socialists were able to prevail upon the Miristas to cut down on their stickup jobs during the election campaign. When it looked as though a parliamentary trick might be played, the Miristas indicated they would go "into the street" to back up Dr. Allende. They resumed scrapping with the Communists after the inauguration, and in the course of an electoral battle for student officers in the town of Concepción there was an outburst of violence that resulted in the death of a Mirista student at the hands of Communist bullyboys. President Allende happened to be in Concepción at the time, and the day after the killing, the Miristas in Concepción announced that they would again join the Unidad Popular coalition, at least for the purpose of local elections this April.

Shortly after Dr. Allende paid his visit to Concepción, I went to see him in his office at the Palacio de la Moneda. He seemed far shorter in person than I had expected, possibly because pictures reflect the lift given by an upward tilt of the head and a wave in his hair. The President is all motion when he talks, with features doing a kind of dance, hands sawing the air. He has a nervous habit of knocking his knees together. At the outset, he aired some views on how much the dangers of a Communist takeover had been exaggerated in the United States. "We don't hide what we do," he said. "You can go outside and see for yourself. No liberties have been suspended. There is no overwhelming force in the streets. There is no censorship of the press. Everybody said when I came in there would be no more elections. But now all the parties are preparing for the municipal elections in April. And if we had national elections today, more than fifty per cent would vote for the government. . . ."

Should the United States encourage, or oppose, all these revolutionary impulses and developments? Carlos Fuentes, a Mexican novelist, had prepared this paper for a debate that never took place. It is a widely held view of the Latin American left that, whatever happens, the United States should stay out of it.

In the early 1960s, one of the big TV networks arranged a debate between Carlos Fuentes, the well-known young Mexican novelist, and Richard Goodwin, then Assistant Secretary of State for Latin American affairs. The U.S. Embassy in Mexico, however, refused a visa to Señor Fuentes and the debate never took place. Fuentes' text for the debate is presented here.

Words for North America

By Carlos Fuentes

South of your border, my North American friends, lies a continent in revolutionary ferment—a continent that possesses immense wealth and nevertheless lives in a misery and a desolation you have never known and barely imagine. Two hundred million persons live in Latin America. One hundred and forty million of them work virtually as serfs. Seventy million are outside the monetary economy. One hundred million are illiterate. One hundred million suffer from endemic diseases. One hundred and forty million are poorly fed.

Today, these miserable masses have decided to put an end to this situation. Latin America, for centuries nothing more than an object of historical exploitation, has decided to change—into a subject of historical action.

You will ask yourselves: what has caused this Latin American backwardness? Why, if we won political independence more or less at the same time, are North Americans prosperous, free, democratic—and Latin Americans poor, subjugated, unable to govern themselves? You will sigh with relief: now, everything is going to change, thanks to American generosity. The Alliance for Progress will solve all the problems afflicting Latin America. Thanks to those $20 billion, Latin Americans will forget the spectre of revolution so stained with blood and destructive of democracy and human rights, will manage to develop peacefully and, in a short time, will set up democratic societies, twins of the United States.

You are much given to good wishes, to what you call "wishful thinking." You have always believed that what is valid for you is valid for all men in all nations and at all times. You forget the existence of specific historical factors. You fail to realize that in reality there are two worlds, one of rich countries and one of poor countries. You fail to recognize that, of necessity, the poor countries require solutions different from yours. You have had four centuries of uninterrupted development within the capitalistic structure. We have had four centuries of underdevelopment within a feudal structure.

You must understand this key word: *structure*. You had your own origin in the capitalistic revolution, liberal and Protestant. You were born without an anachronistic link. You founded a society that, from its first moment, was identified with the historical reason of the times. You created an economy directed towards the creation of wealth in the social vacuum of Anglo-Saxon America. You did not have to fight against and assimilate the resistance of local cultures. You started from zero, a virgin society, totally equal to modern times, without any feudal ballast. On the contrary, we were founded as an appendix of the falling feudal order of the Middle Ages; we inherited its obsolete structures, absorbed its vices, and converted them into institutions on the outer rim of the revolution in the modern world. If you come from the Reformation, we come from the Counter-Reformation: slavery to work, to religious dogmatism, to *latifundio* (enormous expanses of land under the same landlord), denial of political, economic, or cultural rights for the masses, a customs house closed to modern ideas. Instead of creating our own wealth, we exported it to the Spanish and Portuguese metropolis. When we obtained political independence, we did not obtain economic independence; the structure did not change.

You must understand that the Latin American drama stems from the persistence of those feudal structures over four centuries of misery and stagnation, while you were in the midst of the industrial revolution and were exercising a liberal democracy. You must understand that the only solution for Latin Americans will be to destroy all those structures at once.

But you ask yourselves: is a revolution necessary? Why not abolish those structures through evolution? The answer is simple: because the formulas of free-enterprise capitalism have already had their historical opportunity in Latin America and have proved unable to abolish feudalism.

During the nineteenth century, economic liberalism—laissez faire—was superimposed on the feudal structure in Latin America. Side by side with the landlord class of the colonial period, a new class of entrepreneurs sprang up to deal in the business of exploitation. Those capitalists turned us into single-product countries, exporters of raw materials to the occidental marketplace. The utopia of these entrepreneurs was the following: because of the international division of labor, it was appropriate for some regions to produce raw materials and for others to refine them; such an exchange would produce welfare for everyone. Now we know this is not true; now we know that, in the long run, the price of manufactured goods will always be higher than that of raw materials. Now we know that in a depression of the central economy, those who suffer most are the satellite economies, the producers of raw materials. Between 1929 and 1938, Latin American exports decreased by 70 per cent. In that time, hunger *did* exist in Cuba: 50 per cent of her labor force was unemployed, the national banks failed, the sugar lands were bought at bargain prices by Americans. The myth collapsed. If economies were complementary, as the classical theory states, our standard of living should be equal to yours.

In order to overcome the effects of economic liberalism, many Latin American countries entered another phase after 1930: protectionist capitalism, with the aim of encouraging the internal industrialization of Latin America and making it less dependent on the export of raw materials. But this naive and liberal capitalism was also superimposed on the feudal structure without destroying it. It abandoned to their fate the great masses of peasants and workers, and reserved progress for an urban minority. It ended by crystallizing a dual society in Latin America: the modern capitalistic society of cities and the feudal society of the countryside. The minority society became richer at every turn, face-to-face with a majority society becoming more miserable at every turn. In the last few years, the abyss between the two has done nothing but grow. This is why capitalism has not succeeded in solving the problems of Latin America. It has been unable to destroy the legacy of feudalism. It has been unable to promote true collective development in Latin America.

This is what Latin America is: a collapsed feudal castle with a cardboard capitalistic facade.

This is the panorama of the historical failure of capitalism in Latin America:

Continuous monoproductive dependence. In Brazil, coffee constitutes 74 per cent of the exports; tin in Bolivia, 60 per cent; copper in Chile, 63 per cent; bananas in Costa Rica, 60 per cent; coffee in Colombia, 82 per cent; bananas in Honduras, 75 per cent; coffee in Haiti, 63 per cent; oil in Venezuela, 95 per cent; coffee in Nicaragua, 51 per cent; sugar in the Dominican Republic, 60 per cent.

A *continuous system of "latifundio."* In general, in Latin America, with the exception of Mexico and Cuba, 5 per cent of the population owns half of the land. More than half of all Latin Americans are peasants who work under conditions close to slavery. However, only 24 per cent of the land in Latin America can be cultivated. Of this percentage, enormous expanses are out of active production, either to maintain the earnings of the owners or through pure irrationality. Most Latin American countries must import a good part of their food; only Uruguay and Argentina are relatively self-sufficient. The productivity of agriculture is extremely low in relation to the manpower employed. And international prices of the agricultural products fluctuate and are constantly declining. . . .

We have already spoken about the domination of natural resources: iron ore, copper, tin, coal, lead, zinc, oil. These resources, in your hands, enter your economy: they are not employed in the internal development of our countries. The Alliance does not even speak of that. It does not foresee that the iron and oil of Venezuela may contribute to creation of heavy industry there, that the copper of Chile or the lead of Peru may be motors of national industrialization. At any rate, our industrialization must be light, for transformation, but nothing more.

You are also proprietors of Latin American foreign trade. Sixty per cent of our foreign trade is with you, in accordance with the prices you set. American companies manage 75 per cent of our commercial movement. You impose the conditions and the prices. Last year, the Alliance gave 150 million dollars to Colombia; but in that same year, Colombia lost 450 million dollars because of the decrease in coffee prices.

Ask the great cotton concerns how much they pay for a bale of Mexican cotton, at what price they resell it to the English monopoly in Hong Kong, and how much they charge the Communist government of China, which you detest, for it. The Anderson Clayton in this operation makes five times the amount that the Mexican grower does. And ask the Department of State why it forbids Mexico to sell its excess oranges to Czechoslovakia in exchange for machinery we need, machinery you either do not sell us or sell us for too high a price; ask the Department why the whole crop went rotten on the docks of Tampico while you traded happily with Communist countries and allowed Adenauer's Germany to be the principal Western market of that very same Czechoslovakia.

Investments? Yes, you have invested 10 billion dollars in Latin America. It is a curious thing: we have always received your investments, and we are still poor. You speak about *your* property in Latin America and call us thieves when we expropriate it. But why don't you ask your investors? Ask them how much they invest and how much they take back to the United States in profits. Do you want to know? Between 1950 and 1955, you invested 2 billion dollars, made three and a half billion, and took back to the States one and a half billion. In a single year, 1959, you made 775 million, only reinvested 200 million and sent 575 million back to the United States. In the last 7 years, Latin America lost, because of these shipments of money, $2,679,000,000. You take out too much, leave too little, and even this little is distributed unfairly: where is the real benefit for our economies? Is it just that these profits do nothing, not a single thing, to alleviate the horrible misery, ignorance, and illness of the great majority of the Latin Americans who, with their slavery, made them possible? You, as Americans, tell me if that is just.

And tell me also whether you have not recovered more than your investments, whether it is not right that this squandered wealth should be recovered and directed towards improving the lot of everyone, because it was created by the work of everyone though today it benefits only a dozen corporations. . . .

Sacrificing democracy through revolution? Not if there has never been democracy in Latin America. It has been democracy solely of paper and rhetoric. Sacrificing elections? Not if elections in Latin America have been only a ceremony and a fraud. Sacrificing human rights? Which ones? Those of men who do not eat, do not read, do not write, who live in humiliation and terror? Sacrificing freedom of the press? Not if there is no such thing in Latin America; there is an anti-national corrupt press at the service of the interests of feudalism and the most powerful foreign nation at hand.

No, the problem is different. The revolution would bring to power the popular majority that for centuries has had neither voice nor votes. In the eyes of this majority, the corrupt press, fraudulent elections, submission to foreigners, freedom of enterprise and the human rights of the minority that oppressed the majority are synonyms of those centuries of exploitation, of negation, of not being. This is not what the people are interested in. They are interested in *concrete* democracy: the starting point of their real aspirations. They are interested in destroying the old structure of exploitations; they are interested in creating their own new structures, national, popular, with collective benefits, in the knowledge that many mistakes will be committed and many failures endured, but with the hope that this time they will be working for themselves and for their future and not for a bunch of feudal landlords and foreign enterprises. Of course, this transformation demands great sacrifices and is not easy to bring about: four centuries of insanity weigh against it. But there is no other way. The only available alternative is to bear, forever, the old injustice.

Can't you understand this? Why do you seem so hysterical, so jealous, so angry when a revolution puts into action the liberated energies of the people, and why so indifferent, so calm, so thoughtful when these same people are exploited, tyrannized, and debased by a feudal oligarchy? Why did you not start press campaigns against Somoza, why did you not invade Venezuela while Pérez Jiménez was in power, why did you support Trujillo for 30 years, why have you not declared yourselves against Stroessner? What do you want us to think when you have supported and still support regimes of corruption and crime, but fling yourselves against regimes of honesty and work: against Cuba?

However, it no longer matters what you do or do not do. We already know the path. Open your eyes. Today it is Cuba. Tomorrow. . . . Keep your eyes open. The armies of privilege will be defeated. The old structures will collapse. Land, mines, businesses will be recovered. They will work for the benefit of everyone. There will be difficulties of conversion and organization. But in the long run the economy will be diversified, idle land will be cultivated, illiteracy will be eradicated, the liberated farmer's consumption of goods will increase, national resources will be used for national industrialization, culture will also belong to workers and farmers, and decent houses, hospitals, highways, and schools will be built.

Is this a dream? No, it is not. This is our challenge. Feudalism and superimposed capitalism have failed, in four centuries, to achieve any of this. You said that nationalization of oil was a daydream in Mexico; that within a year the foreign companies would be back because Mexicans were unable to manage such a complex industry. You were right: we *were* unable to do it, we had many difficult moments, just as difficult as those Cuba is now having. But with time, as is happening with Cuba, we created our technicians, our specialized workers, and we succeeded, we surpassed the old companies in efficiency and now we use our oil for our own benefit, rationally. We will not forget this experience: where the Latin American man becomes owner of his land, his industry, his work, he pulls himself out of the ineptitude of past centuries and shows what he can do. This is going to happen, don't you doubt it, in the next few years in Latin America. Nobody learns to swim without diving into the water.

Revolution, yes! Don't be deceived, Americans. Open your eyes. Ask the Peruvian farmer who chews coca and eats rats if he wants fake elections or revolutions. Ask the Chilean miner who crawls through the tunnels of Lota if he believes in free enterprise or in revolution. Ask the northeast Brazilian farmer if he wants capitalism or revolution. Ask the student castrated by the Paraguayan dictator if he wants Stroessner's free press or revolution. Ask the Guatemalan farmer "freed" by Castillo Armas if he wants Alliance for Progress or revolution. Ask the Latin Americans who corrupts the press and the unions, who supports the armies and the oligarchics, who pays miserable salaries, who owns the mines and the oil wells. Ask them who gets the Alliance for Progress money, and ask what they use it for. Ask them if we believe in the free world of Franco, Salazar, Chiang-Kai-shek and Ngo Dinh Diem. Ask them and they will tell you why people spat on Nixon.

Ask the men living in "misery village" in Buenos Aires, in the *favela* of Rio, in the "*callampa* population" of Santiago, if they are afraid of Communism. These beggars, these pariahs, will answer that they are afraid only of their present oppressors, of those who exploit them in the name of capitalism and representative democracy, and that they prefer anything that might mean a change.

Ask these men if they are against Cuba, if they believe the lies they read in the "free press" of our countries, if they do not know that the old American colony of the Caribbean is our hope because there the caste army, the *latifundio*, the administrative corruption, the official cheating are over and everybody works together, with weapons ready, Americans, with weapons ready to defend the Revolution; tell Ydigoras or Somoza to arm their people with the weapons you give them—and then to move forward together despite aggression and boycott.

Ask these men if they are afraid of help from the Soviet Union. Ask them if there is a single Soviet company in Cuba that exploits the Cuban economy for its own gain.

Do you see, Americans? The world has changed. Latin America is no longer your preserve. The world moves ahead. And you are standing on the rim. Are you going to help these inevitable revolutions or are you going to antagonize them with invasions, press campaigns, and economic aggressions? It does not matter. Revolutions are going to progress. The world has changed. You will not be able to put out all the fires in Latin America, Africa, and Asia.

But try to understand. Try to understand that a revolution in Latin America can affect only a handful of Yankee enterprises, but never the concrete welfare you enjoy. Try to understand that our real development, which can be achieved only through revolution, far from hurting you will help you. Do not let yourselves be fooled by this handful of enterprises and investors. Try to understand that the sooner we start our basic development, which can come only through revolution, the more buyers you will have, and we will all be closer to a planned world economy, rational and interdependent. . . .

PART XI.

RELUCTANT NEIGHBORS: THE UNITED STATES AND LATIN AMERICA

Introduction

With the Monroe Doctrine in 1823, the United States committed itself to protect the hemisphere against the invasion of Old World powers from Europe. The threat never completely materialized, though it might have, but the doctrine soon took on another function. It became the justification for the United States to protect Latin America from itself, from the hot-blooded, irrational, passionate swamp of Spanish-speaking affairs. In the U.S. memory, the many military interventions, marine landings, and punitive expeditions that we have unleashed on Latin America are lost as isolated incidents, not even taught in school. But in the Latin American memory, they form an indelible pattern: the war with Mexico for the Texas territory; the San Juan Hill boys who helped liberate Cuba from the Spaniards, only to follow their goodwill with what Cubans considered a degrading military occupation; Pershing's invasion of Mexico to punish Pancho Villa (whom he never found); the forcible creation of Panama for the purpose of building a canal; repeated landings in Venezuela and Central America; the naval arrival at Veracruz because the Mexican president insulted the U.S. flag; the CIA-backed ouster of Arbenz from the Guatemalan presidency in 1954; the marine landing in the Dominican Republic in 1965. These interventions stretch over a period of fifty years, but they are remarkably alike in kind—a quick show of military force, a bloody spanking to teach our neighbors a lesson in democracy and courtesy, and while we are at it, to snatch a little land or power for ourselves. All of our interventions were in some way or another justified through Monroe's piece of paper, which was stretched around various situations and amended to fit the declining threat of Europe. (The Theodore Roosevelt corollary, for instance, expanded the doctrine to allow U.S. intervention even if no direct invasion by a foreign power was involved.) By the time of the Dominican invasion of 1965, the doctrine that had been written to protect the hemisphere from European military invasion was being applied to internal civil wars and revolts (if Communist inspired)— on the theory that communism is always the result of outside agitation. The two views of the original Monroe Doctrine included here (the critique by Argentine leader Roque Saenz Peña and the defense by U.S. diplomat Elihu Root) were written during the last century, but the arguments on both sides have not changed that much.

For all their frequency, U.S. military interventions have been erratically applied, something that mystifies Latin Americans. We send marines to the Dominican Republic but do nothing about the Bolivian revolution of 1952 or the Colombian violence of 1948, which killed thousands of people. We intervene to stop the 1954 election of Arbenz, a leftist in Guatemala, but do not tamper with the election of Salvador Allende, a Chilean Marxist. Some dictators we recognize, others we oppose, others we move to overthrow. Latin Americans find our interventions and meddling in their politics as unpredictable as we find their revolutions. When will the next marine landing occur? It is impossible to say, but the way these things generally happen is illustrated in Tad Szulc's account of the days that led up to President Johnson's decision to send the marines to the Dominican Republic in 1965.

There is, of course, another side to our relationship with Latin America—the money- and aid-giving side; the school-, road-, milk-, machinery-, and expert-giving side. Most of our efforts, like Franklin D. Roosevelt's Good Neighbor Policy, were glorified public-relations campaigns, but one aid program, Kennedy's Alliance for Progress, got the Latin Americans genuinely excited. Part of the attraction was Kennedy himself, a Catholic caudillo, and part was that the Alliance came at a time when people still believed that a little money and a little expertise could bring about rapid changes. There was fantasy in all of it—that the wealthy would somehow voluntarily cede some of their money and power, that U.S. corporations would really permit upheavals that might threaten their interests. The euphoria also hid some more practical flaws: the Alliance money was mostly in loans, which

Latin American countries now have to pay off and which has caused them to fall heavily into debt. In addition, the loan money could not be used as the Latin Americans saw fit; they had to purchase U.S. goods and machinery or hire U.S. technicians with it. This was much more costly and proved that the United States was interested only in development that would not imperil its own balance of payments. All these drawbacks, however, are not as important as the fact that the Alliance was a drop in the bucket; the U.S. companies were taking more money out of the area in profits than the Alliance was pumping back in through loans. And even if this had not been true, there is no assurance that the Alliance would have worked. Jerome Levinson and Juan de Onis describe what the Alliance attempted and why it failed so completely.

The failures of alliances and the constancy of interventions might lead one to believe that the problems with Latin America are all political, that on a personal level we would get along. I don't think so. Moritz Thomsen, in the excerpt from his Peace Corps book, shows how the cultural habits that lead to interventions and paternalism can be created on the most harmless personal level. Sitting across a table from Latin American students, I also found in the tension of the meeting all the hostilities that generate marine landings. During three years in Latin America, I think I felt all the emotions that underlie the benchmarks of U.S. history in the hemisphere—paternalism, arrogance, disdain, violence. The real work of the United States in Latin America is still understanding, and we are still failing at it. The Peace Corps article is the product of one attempt at living in Latin America, and examines the delicate prospects for personal rapport between the two wary neighbors.

The difficulties of friendship stem not only from a language barrier or communications gap but also from the fact that Latin Americans and North Americans are remarkably foreign creatures to one another. Octavio Paz, the Mexican philosopher, writes here about the unfathomable distance between the North American and Latin American minds, between two opposing concepts of the universe and man's place inside it. Paz wrote the comparison in the early 1950's, and for whatever it is worth, the current North American scene seems much more

Latin-Americanized than it did when Paz originally described it. Whether this means there is potential for more understanding across the river, I don't know. Perhaps it means that while we are hoping to be a continual lesson for the Latin Americans, they have become a lesson for us. While we have always seen their future in our machines, money, and democracy, perhaps it is more realistic to find ourselves in a Latin American future of passion, revolution, despair, disbelief in government, romance, and military coups. If any of this is possible, it makes knowing about Latin America a little more important than it was before.

The Monroe Doctrine, formulated in 1823 to dissuade Europeans from intervening in the Western Hemisphere, was invoked many times to justify U.S. interventions in Latin American affairs. In this selection, Argentine political leader Roque Saenz Pena gives his reaction to the doctrine, after it was used to support our intervention in the Cuban revolution of 1898 against Spain. Saenz Peña delivered this address in 1898, but his criticisms are not outdated, and could just as well apply to the Dominican Republic invasion of 1965.

In Opposition to Monroe
By Roque Saenz Peña

The Doctrine of President Monroe, contained in the message of December [1823], was a declaration against intervention; but that declaration contained mental reservations which rendered its objectives doubtful and its effects pernicious; in principle it condemned European interventions, but in fact it did not oppose American interventions, which means that it is not a general, scientific doctrine with unity of concept and principle but rather a national, specific act. It appears to the world as the whim of a strong and invincible power. . . .

That Doctrine in my opinion is the cause and origin of the present perversions of public law. The Mackinley [sic] doctrine is simply the latest chapter in the

Monroe Doctrine and the Polk doctrine; they are not three doctrines, they are three acts sanctifying a single usurpation: the intervention of the United States in the destinies and life of the peoples of the Americas.

When the divine-right governments of Europe were threatening to spread their system over this continent, the declaration of the United States was justified on political grounds, however much justification it may have lacked on juridical grounds: it was an arbitrary act opposing an illegal act. But in the present posture of law, diplomacy, and humanity both the arbitrary and the illegal ought to disappear. No American nation exists nor ever has existed with sufficient political and international capacity to assume to represent the entire continent and to serve as the spokesman for its free peoples; just as there never has existed a single foreign chancellery for the New World, so also there is no single sovereign for the hemisphere.

President Monroe's claims to authority were not only debatable: they were fictitious because no American state had delegated nor alienated its authority to determine its relations with other nations of the world. The warnings which Monroe directed toward Europe were not ratified by the new nations in whose name he spoke and whose destinies he undertook to dispose of; the so-called Doctrine did not emerge from the halls of Congress but remained an internal action without either diplomatic or international ramifications. The essence of that Doctrine in fact was unacceptable not only to Europe, where it evoked protests from Russia and later from Great Britain, but also to the free nations of this continent. To condemn European interventions while at the same time reserving an American right of intervention and to exercise such a right unilaterally and without consultations is not in fact to censure intervention but rather to claim a monopoly of it. . . .

The position of the Latin-American states *vis à vis* a government which has taken over the officious management of the New World in relation to Europe is to ask: From what source did you obtain your solicitorship? Whence came your police authority and your inquisitorial powers over independent states which are no less inviolable than those of Europe? Will we have to search for them in the right of primogeniture, which is an accident of birth rather than law? Will we find them in the right of geographical proximity, which is an accident of nature and not reason?

We will have to conclude finally and emphatically that force creates doctrine, that the army establishes rights.

The Latin-American republics must vindicate, both by honor and title, the generous force of a new doctrine—a doctrine which was consecrated by Bolívar in convoking and organizing the Panama Congress. Bolívar possessed a sure insight into the future and was able to foresee from a distance that [Monroe's] message of December had its Achilles heel. . . .

The theme which Bolívar stressed in convoking that Congress consecrated the doctrine of non-intervention not against Europe but against every foreign power; that was the doctrine in its juridical and universal character; that was the true policy to which the peoples of the Americas aspired in order to become sovereign and free not only in relation to Europe but in relation to all nations. But that redemptive doctrine of free nations which clipped the wings of the eagles of the Capitol provoked the discontent of the Cabinet in Washington to such an extent that the United States was not represented at Panama; one of its delegates arrived late and ill, and the other never arrived because he died on the way. Bolívar proposed not only to establish the true doctrine but also to elevate the stature of these republics by correcting the inert plasticity to which they had been reduced by the message of December 2; he wished to give them political capacity so that they could act of their own accord and strength when deciding their destinies, or speaking in the name of America, or working under the care of the United States. . . .

This defense of the Monroe Doctrine was presented at a law conference in 1914 by ex-secretary of state Elihu

Root. Root had been secretary of war to President McKinley and secretary of state to Theodore Roosevelt; he had ample opportunity to help invoke the doctrine and to fashion our policy toward the rest of the hemisphere. The arguments he puts forth in defense of the doctrine are as applicable as Saenz Peña's opposition.

In Defense of Monroe

By Elihu Root

. . . As the particular occasions which called it forth have slipped back into history, the declaration itself, instead of being handed over to the historian, has grown continually a more vital and insistent rule of conduct for each succeeding generation of Americans. Never for a moment have the responsible and instructed statesmen in charge of the foreign affairs of the United States failed to consider themselves bound to insist upon its policy. Never once has the public opinion of the people of the United States failed to support every just application of it as new occasion has arisen. Almost every President and Secretary of State has restated the Doctrine with vigor and emphasis in the discussion of the diplomatic affairs of his day. The governments of Europe have gradually come to realize that the existence of the policy which Monroe declared is a stubborn and continuing fact to be recognized in their controversies with American countries. We have seen Spain, France, England, Germany, with admirable good sense and good temper, explaining beforehand to the United States that they intended no permanent occupation of territory, in the controversy with Mexico forty years after the declaration, and in the controversy with Venezuela eighty years after. In 1903 the Duke of Devonshire declared "Great Britain accepts the Monroe Doctrine unreservedly." Mr. Hay coupled the Monroe Doctrine and the Golden Rule as cardinal guides of American diplomacy. . . .

. . . It seems fair to assume that a policy with such a history as this has some continuing and substantial reason underlying it; that it is not outworn or meaningless or a purely formal relic of the past, and it seems worthwhile to consider carefully what the Doctrine is and what it is not. . . .

The Doctrine is not international law but it rests upon the right of self-protection and that right is recognized by international law. The right is a necessary corollary of independent sovereignty. It is well understood that the exercise of the right of self-protection may and frequently does extend in its effect beyond the limits of the territorial jurisdiction of the state exercising it. . . . Of course each state must judge for itself when a threatened act will create such a situation. If any state objects to a threatened act and the reasonableness of its objection is not assented to, the efficacy of the objection will depend upon the power behind it.

It is doubtless true that in the adherence of the American people to the original declaration there was a great element of sentiment and sympathy for the people of South America who were struggling for freedom, and it has been a source of great satisfaction to the United States that the course which it took in 1823 concurrently with the action of Great Britain played so great a part in assuring the right of self government to the countries of South America. Yet it is to be observed that in reference to the South American governments, as in all other respects, the international right upon which the declaration expressly rests is not sentiment or sympathy or a claim to dictate what kind of government any other country shall have, but the safety of the United States. It is because the new governments cannot be overthrown by the allied powers "without endangering our peace and happiness" that "the United States cannot behold such interposition in any form with indifference."

We frequently see statements that the Doctrine has been changed or enlarged; that there is a new or different Doctrine since Monroe's time. They are mistaken. There has been no change. One apparent extension of the statement of Monroe was made by President Polk in his messages of 1845 and 1848, when he included the acquisition of territory by a European power through cession as dangerous to the safety of the United States. It was really but stating a corollary to the Doctrine of 1823 and asserting the same right of self-protection against the other American states as well as against Europe. . . .

It is the substance of the thing to which the nation holds and that is and always has been that the safety of the United States demands that American territory shall remain American. . . .

Curiously enough, many incidents and consequences of that independent condition itself which the United States asserted in the Monroe Doctrine have been regarded in some quarters as infringements upon independence resulting from the Monroe Doctrine. Just as the personal rights of each individual free citizen in the state are limited by the equal rights of every other free individual in the same state, so the sovereign rights of each independent state are limited by the equal sovereign rights of every other independent state. These limitations are not impairments of independent sovereignty. They are the necessary conditions to the existence of independent sovereignty. If the Monroe Doctrine had never been declared or thought of, the sovereign rights of each American republic would have been limited by the equal sovereign rights of every other American republic. . . .

It happens, however, that the United States is very much bigger and more powerful than most of the other American republics. And when a very great and powerful state makes demands upon a very small and weak state it is difficult to avoid a feeling that there is an assumption of superior authority involved in the assertion of superior power, even though the demand be based solely upon the right of equal against equal. An examination of the various controversies which the United States has had with other American powers will disclose the fact that in every case the rights asserted were rights not of superiority but of equality. Of course it cannot be claimed that great and powerful states shall forego their just rights against smaller and less powerful states. The responsibilities of sovereignty attach to the weak as well as to the strong, and a claim to exemption from those responsibilities would imply not equality but inferiority. The most that can be said concerning a question between a powerful state and a weak one is that the great state ought to be especially considerate and gentle in the assertion and maintenance of its position; ought always to base its acts not upon a superiority of force, but upon reason and law; and ought to assert no rights against a small state because of its weakness which it would not assert against a great state notwithstanding its power. But in all this the Monroe Doctrine is not concerned at all. . . .

There are indeed special reasons why the United States should perform that duty of equal friendship to the full limit of international custom and international ethics as declared in The Hague Convention, whenever occasion arises in controversy between American and European powers. There is a motive for that in the special sympathy and friendship for the gradually developing republics of the south which the American people have always felt since the days of Monroe and John Quincy Adams and Richard Rush and Henry Clay. There is a motive in the strong desire of our government that no controversy between a European and an American state shall ever come to the point where the United States may be obliged to assert by force the rule of national safety declared by Monroe. And there is a motive in the proper desire of the United States that no friendly nation of Europe or America shall be injured or hindered in the prosecution of its rights in any way or to any extent that can possibly be avoided because that nation respects the rule of safety which Mr. Monroe declared and we maintain. None of these reasons for the exercise of the good offices of equality justifies nor do all of them together justify the United States in infringing upon the independence or ignoring the equal rights of the smallest American state. . . .

How does the United States decide to intervene in a Latin American country? Tad Szulc describes the series of events—and fears—that swept up the U.S. foreign-affairs establishment in 1965, and led them, at great risk, to send marines into the Dominican Republic.

After the events that Szulc describes, an election was held in the Dominican Republic with Joaquin Balaguer, known as a middle-of-the-roader, taking power. The violence subsided, and things stabilized in the Dominican Republic—no real economic or political change, but no revolutions, either. Juan Bosch, ousted by the military in 1963, continued to receive support from the masses through a popularly based political party. Recently, in February, 1973, Balaguer started complaining that Cuban revolutionaries were causing turmoil in the country and he sent the Army out to crush the dissidents. Caamaño Deno, the rebel leader in the 1965 civil war, was identified as the leader of the guerrilla forces and killed. Many Dominicans still hope for the return of Bosch. No true peace has been achieved, and we have not seen the last of revolutionary ferment on the island.

The Dominican Republic Invasion of 1965
By Tad Szulc

In the early evening of Wednesday, April 28, 1965, a flight of khaki-painted helicopters took off from the deck of the U.S.S. *Boxer* and whirred some 10 miles over the Caribbean to the coast of the Dominican Republic.

In twos and threes they landed on the Polo Grounds, immediately west of the Hotel Embajador in Santo Domingo, as dusk began to gather over the capital city. Combat-equipped Marines, jumping out of the choppers as soon as they touched down, could hear explosions and machine-gun fire in the downtown section, a few miles to the east. These were the sounds of the raging civil war in which Dominicans were dying by the hundreds; the established order had utterly collapsed in revolutionary chaos. And as the tough Marines from the Navy's Amphibious Task Force began streaming ashore, the first United States military intervention in the Dominican Republic in nearly 49 years was under way.

In less than a week the initial contingent of 520 Marines, who had landed in Santo Domingo to protect the evacuation of Americans and other foreigners from the war-battered city, had grown to an imposing force of 22,000 men, including a whole Marine brigade and the Army's entire 82nd Airborne Division. Eight thousand additional men aboard 40 warships cruising offshore and an around-the-clock airlift of troop carriers from the United States supported the American expeditionary force in Santo Domingo.

As the month of May began, the United States forces that had at first landed on a humanitarian mission found themselves under orders from Washington to restore peace between the warring factions and, in the words of an official announcement, to "help Dominicans find a democratic solution" to their awesome political problems.

The American intervention in the Dominican Republic was the first instance since 1934—the year the Marines were withdrawn from Haiti—of United States forces, in effect, occupying a Latin-American country or part of one. It was a move that had not been chanced even in the case of Cuba, a Communist-dominated nation honeycombed with Soviet weapons and advisers. It was a move that seemed to flout all of the United States commitments to avoid unilateral intervention. It was a move that appeared to defy all the inter-American treaties signed since the United States renounced its rights of intervention 31 years earlier.

Why, then, had President Johnson ordered the Dominican intervention of 1965, which was from the outset deeply controversial and which has had a considerable effect on the entire fabric of United States relations with Latin America?

To try to understand the situation that brought about this intervention as well as the factors that may have motivated President Johnson, it is necessary to look at the recent political history of the Dominican Republic.

That history begins with the ouster of Juan Bosch in a military coup d'état on September 25, 1963, after he had served for seven months as the country's first constitutional president in 38 years. . . .

The losers in the 1962 elections wasted no time in talking about a coup if "Bosch gets out of hand." Those in the business community and among the wealthy landowners who had opposed Bosch became the nucleus of agitation against him. This is not to say, incidentally, that all or even the majority of businessmen and landowners were anti-Bosch; an important segment of these groups had supported him. . . .

However, the anti-Bosch civilian groups quickly found allies among military officers, particularly the older ones, who had served in Trujillo's armed forces. One of the important things to keep in mind about the Dominican situation is that, despite Trujillo's assassination and the shift to a democratic experiment after 1961, the old dictator's armed forces were never touched—that is, most of the former commanders remained where they were. This is a major reason why the tradition of brutality, dictatorship and corruption did not die with Trujillo.

The right-wing civilians and the Trujillo military came together to form the battering ram that smashed Dominican democracy through the anti-Bosch coup. The immediate charges voiced against Bosch were that he harbored or protected Communists and that corruption was spreading in the country. The latter was a surprising charge, considering the source. . . .

Finally, on September 25, 1963, the military moved and Bosch was ousted and again exiled. The new rulers at first spoke of a "rightist state," then dropped the idea when it became apparent that, contrary to what they had heard from their friends among American military officers, the Kennedy Administration was determined to punish the coup. In fact, diplomatic relations were broken, Alliance for Progress aid was suspended and U.S. technicians were pulled out.

The next step was the creation of a three-man civilian junta—the "Triumvirate"—operating with military support and making vague promises of restoring democracy. . . .

For the next year or so the Dominican Republic lived in a state of comparative calm. The Triumvirate had, for all practical purposes, disappeared. The administration was in the hands of Donald Reid Cabral, a former auto dealer who had been active first in the anti-Trujillo conspiracy and then in the Council of State Government that supervised the elections which gave Bosch his short-lived victory. . . .

But Reid Cabral somehow could never win popularity or establish any rapport with other political forces, and the country grew more and more restive. He announced elections for September, 1965, making it clear not only that he would run for the presidency but that, most likely, he would win.

It was this matter of the elections that sealed his fate and set in motion the preparations for a new revolution. The revolutionary movement was led by a group of younger military officers who had resented Bosch's overthrow and by key members of Bosch's political party. The revolt was actually planned for June 1, 1965, but Reid Cabral became aware of the conspiracy and in mid-April fired seven air-force officers who were among the plotters.

This precipitated the explosion. On the afternoon of Saturday, April 24, a group of civilians captured Radio Santo Domingo, the government's radio and television station, and broadcast announcements that the regime had fallen. Simultaneously the military rebels took control of two army barracks, one in Santo Domingo and one on the outskirts.

Crowds poured out into the streets to celebrate the revolution's apparent victory with shouts of "Bosch!" and "Constitution!" But government forces promptly retook the radio station, and during the evening Reid Cabral announced that the rebellion had been smashed. The government then issued an ultimatum to the rebels holding the two military installations to surrender by 6:00 a.m. of the next day or face attacks by war planes and tanks.

The United States Embassy in Santo Domingo, which had been surprised when the revolt erupted on Saturday, advised the State Department in Washington that matters were well in hand. Ambassador W. Tapley Bennett, Jr., and the head of the economic aid mission and 11 of the 13 members of the United States Military Advisory Assistance Mission were away from the Dominican Republic at the time of the revolution. But the officials at the embassy, most of whose contacts were with the Reid Cabral regime, were convinced that the Saturday rebellion was a minor matter.

How wrong they were, however, became apparent during the night. Shortly before midnight crowds again began pouring into the downtown streets, this time not to celebrate but to clamor for a return to "constitutionality"—the battle cry of the revolutionaries. A telephone campaign was started by students, urging people to come out and demonstrate. Someone went into a firehouse and turned on the siren, adding to the tension. . . .

At dawn of Sunday, April 25, the commanders converged on the Presidential Palace and forced Reid Cabral to resign. He did so promptly, convinced that his ultimatum to the rebels would not be obeyed. Reid Cabral resigned on the understanding that a military junta would be formed to rule the country until elections could be held in some distant future. And this, too, was the understanding of the commanders from the San Isidro Air Force Base across the Ozama River from Santo Domingo where the bulk of the elite forces were stationed. . . .

The pro-Bosch move that Sunday morning was the act that set off what was to be a bloody civil war. The commanders at the San Isidro base, notably Brigadier General Elias Wessin y Wessin, who had led the Bosch ouster coup in 1963, could not accept a restoration of constitutional rule. The lines were drawn. In the afternoon Wessin's aircraft strafed the Presidential Palace in the opening action of the fratricidal conflict. . . .

. . . At the [U.S.] embassy the feeling was that the Bosch movement still had no chance of success. Much of this feeling stemmed, of course, from the embassy's close identification with the Reid Cabral regime and with many of the military commanders who had overthrown Bosch. At the State Department in Washington the judgment was that Bosch's return could mean "Communism in Santo Domingo within six months," though nobody could document this assertion for the record. However, the genesis of what the United States was to do in the Dominican Republic in the next few days was to be found in these initial attitudes and judgments in Santo Domingo and Washington.

In Santo Domingo, meanwhile, matters were not going well for the rebels. Although the provisional government controlled the city, the Wessin forces held the San Isidro base and the approaches to the Ozama River bridge that led into the capital. All day Monday Wessin's P-51 fighters and Gloster Meteor jets strafed and bombed the city and the strategic bridge. The rebels in the streets countered by employing mirrors that reflected the sun's rays in an attempt to momentarily blind the pilots of the diving aircraft. Families of the pilots were detained and brought before television cameras to make appeals to the fliers to desist from the attacks. Others were taken to the bridge as hostages.

As early as Sunday the rebel command had realized that to counter the offensive of the San Isidro forces it must start arming civilians. At first it announced that military veterans could receive arms if they signed a receipt. But within hours it was decided to throw open the doors of city arsenals and army barracks to one and all. Several truckloads of weapons were brought in from the suburban barracks and placed at the downtown Parque Independencia for all to help themselves.

This was a major factor in aggravating the civil war and in influencing the subsequent U.S. decision to intervene. Weapons were now not only in the hands of the pro-Bosch civilians but also in the hands of Communists, Castroites and plain adventurers and thrill-seekers. Bands of *tigres*—hoodlums—were organized along with the fairly disiciplined groups of military and civilian rebels. . . .

Late on Monday the Wessin forces captured the [Ozama] bridge and began entering the city but were repulsed. That same evening the United States decided that a "voluntary" evacuation of Americans should be undertaken because of the growing danger to them from the armed bands. There had, however, been no incident thus far involving Americans.

Embassy officials reported to Washington that it appeared that pro-Communist elements were taking control of the rebellion—mainly because Castro-like broadcasts were being made on radio and television as soldiers and young officers denounced their superiors. Up to then, however, the embassy had had no contact with the rebels except for a visit to the embassy on Sunday afternoon by a group of leaders of the Bosch party, including a former Minister of Agriculture named Silvestre Antonio Guzmán, who was to become highly important in subsequent developments. According to Mr. Guzmán, the delegation was "virtually insulted" by a second secretary of the embassy.

Early Tuesday, April 27, as the ships of the Navy's Amphibious Task Force began moving into position for the evacuation operation, other U.S. forces were being alerted. Several battalions of Marines at Camp Lejeune, North Carolina, were placed on alert. The tough 82nd Airborne Division at Fort Bragg, North Carolina, was told to prepare for a "parachute attack" on the Dominican Republic. Its orders were to secure the San Isidro Air Force Base, the highway leading to the Ozama River bridge and the bridge itself. This indicated that as early as Tuesday morning the Johnson Administration was already thinking in terms of a major military operation.

On Tuesday morning evacuation ships entered the port of Haina, nine miles west of Santo Domingo. Helicopters flew to the Polo Grounds by the Hotel Embajador, in the western section of the city, to help in the evacuation. American and other foreign families began gathering at the hotel early in the morning to be processed by embassy officials and driven to Haina. A few armed Marines, acting as helicopter guards, were at the Polo Grounds.

In mid-morning a band of armed civilians broke into the hotel, apparently searching for a television commentator identified with General Wessin. They forced the Americans to line up against the walls of the cavernous lobby and fired several submachine gun bursts over their heads. This experience, later exaggerated in the reports to Washington, was another major factor in influencing President Johnson to order a full-scale intervention. . . .

During the 1960's, John Kennedy's Alliance for Progress was looked on as the good side of our Latin American policy. The U.S. government committed itself to pumping millions in development loans into Latin American countries, with the hope that this money would improve education, health, and living conditions. The emphasis in the Alliance was on the partnership aspects of the program; the idea of loans (as opposed to direct grants) was that they were not handouts, that the recipient countries would share in the burdens of progress. This selection explains what happened to the Alliance, and why.

The Alliance That Failed

By Jerome Levinson and Juan de Onis

. . . In the last years of the Eisenhower administration, Washington's attitude—avuncular, haughty, and parsimonious, mainly because the exigencies of the Cold War diverted its preoccupation and priorities elsewhere—began to change. The cause was clear. A wave of rebellions had swept out of power a number of military dictators whom the U.S. State Department had previously hailed as champions of anticommunist stability in Latin America. Not the least of these rebellions was Fidel Castro's stunning overthrow of the Cuban dictator Fulgencio Batista in 1959. At precisely that juncture the change in Washington became perceptible. The Eisenhower administration put up $350 million as the initial capital of the new Inter-American Development Bank; Congress authorized a $500 million fund for social investments in Latin America, such as low-cost housing, urban water-supply systems, credits to small farmers, and education; and the United States belatedly joined an international agreement to stabilize coffee prices. It was a good start, generous and positive when compared with the help that had been provided before, but modest and unassuming when compared with what was to come.

The fundamental change began when John F. Kennedy, at the very beginning of his administration, spoke in bold and heady terms of billion-dollar aid for a decade of planned economic development and social reform in the hemisphere. His message proposing the Alliance for Progress was an invigorating mixture of compassion and hope, ambition and urgency, which quickened the hopes of millions throughout Latin America. Reformist political ideas, concepts of economic planning, and a host of other notions that had been confined to the fringes of inter-American discussions suddenly found wide audiences. The result was a striking improvement in the U.S. dialogue with the Latin Americans, particularly those whom the Kennedy administration identified as the agents of democratic change and social reform, and an almost euphoric belief in what they could achieve.

Many of these political leaders, economic planners, and intellectual innovators—described loosely as the "democratic left"—as well as younger, more radical exponents of revolutionary change, had risen to prominence in the Latin American rebellions of the late 1950s. The senior figures of the democratic left, President Rómulo Betancourt of Venezuela and President Alberto Lleras Camargo of Colombia, were essentially New Dealers in political outlook, and they fell in naturally with the New Frontier president in the White House. With these leaders, and the expectation that other modern and moderate political reformers would come forward throughout Latin America, the confident policy-makers in the new administration of President Kennedy formulated in the Alliance for Progress a bold and comprehensive ideology of democratic development. It postulated not only rapid economic growth (the dominant goal of the Marshall Plan) and social reform (which has played a part in southeast Asian development programs), but at the same time the strengthening of representative political democracy.

Cuba's growing allegiance to the Communist bloc helped to accelerate and shape the creation of the Alliance as a democratic alternative to Cuba's revolutionary socialist formula for development in Latin America. As its architects in Washington and throughout Latin America conceived it, support from the United States would enable the democratic left to bring about economic development and fundamental social change within a framework of representative political institutions.

If idealism was a strong element in the Alliance, so were overconfidence and even brashness. It was assumed, for instance, that Latin America's ruling classes would refrain from obstructing the process of democratic development, presumably on the grounds that, as President Kennedy said, "those who make peaceful revolution impossible will make violent revolution inevitable." And the United States would protect the process from Castro-inspired or -supported disruption by providing counterinsurgency training and equipment for the Latin American military and maintaining or establishing CIA stations in each country.

Yet the Charter of Punta del Este, which formally established the Alliance, sought to express the ideology of democratic development in terms of the Latin American reality. The charter enumerated certain objectives, some of them specific, which the Alliance was to achieve by 1970, and which can now be used as yardsticks against which to measure its performance.

The primary objective, on which all others were thought to hinge, was an economic growth rate of "not less than 2.5 percent per capita per year" in each Latin American country. Since the region's population growth rate remained at 3 percent a year (the charter contained no reference to the population question), production of goods and services would have had to increase at a rate of more than 5 percent a year to reach this target. But between 1961 and 1967 the actual average increase per year was only 1.5 percent and only in 1968 did the region as a whole finally reach the target.

The second objective was a more equitable distribution of national income, providing a fairer share of the projected increases to the poorer working class and peasants—the great majorities at the depressed base of the Latin American social structure. According to estimates for nine Latin American countries (including Argentina, Brazil, and Mexico), between 1960 and 1963 the wealthy upper 10 percent of the population received about 42 percent of national income while the poor bottom half received only 14 to 21 percent. A survey taken in 1968 shows little if any change in this structure of gross income inequality. Only Chile seems to have accomplished a significant redistribution of income in favor of the poor. . . .

Still another objective was fuller utilization of the region's natural and human resources in the form of increased industrialization and reduced unemployment. But although industrialization has advanced significantly in most Latin American countries, unemployment has not been reduced. According to estimates by the Economic Commission for Latin America (ECLA), the supply of jobs in relation to the size of the labor force has increased more slowly during this decade than during the 1950s, and unemployment, partly disguised as underemployment, has risen from 18 million persons in 1960 to 25 million now. (The current figure is based on a presumed full-employment labor force of 83 million.) The Latin American economies—even those that are growing quite rapidly—are unable to absorb the growing contingents of young job seekers that enter the labor market each year.

The charter proposed "to raise greatly the level of agricultural productivity and output and to improve related storage, transportation, and marketing services." Advances have been made in the agricultural area, with Latin America's food production increasing by 4 percent annually, a step ahead of population growth, while investment in the modern commercial agricultural sector has been strong. But, according to the Rockefeller Report, "While overall food production is going up, food production per person, due to the population explosion, is estimated at 10 percent less than it was at the end of World War II. And each year there are eight million more mouths to feed."

The charter recommended agrarian reform, including, "where required," the transformation of "unjust structures of land tenure and use." But progress toward a more equitable structure of land tenure and rural income distribution has been very slow. Mexico, Venezuela, and Bolivia have moved ahead with pre-Alliance agrarian reform programs; Chile and Colombia have made real efforts; and Peru has begun to apply what appears on paper to be the most radical agrarian reform law since Cuba's. Other countries, including Brazil, haven't even tried. In the lifetime of the Alliance the number of peasants seeking land has grown more rapidly than the number of family lots provided by division of estates, colonization, and entitling of squatters.

In education the goal was "to eliminate adult illiteracy and by 1970 to assure, as a minimum, access to six years of primary education for each school-age child in Latin America." Unfortunately, the decade has seen no significant increase in adult literacy. To be sure, the percentage of children not enrolled in primary schools did decline from 52 percent to 43 percent between 1960 and 1967. But at the end of 1967 an estimated 27 million school-age children—about three-quarters of a million more than in 1960—were still receiving no formal education.

The health goals were to add five years to life expectancy, to halve the infant mortality rate, and, for this purpose, to provide potable water and sewage-disposal systems for not less than 70 percent of the urban and 50 percent of the rural population. In fact, life expectancy has been extended somewhat, the infant mortality rate has been somewhat reduced, and some water systems have been built, but the specific goals are still remote. . . .

Specifically, the main economic burden of the development programs was to fall upon those in Latin America who could pay for them, through tax reforms "demanding more from those who have most." At the end of the decade, in Latin America as a whole, tax collections, primarily as a result of improved administrative techniques and organization rather than structural reforms, had increased in real terms by 35 percent since 1961. This increase is about the same as the region's cumulative growth of domestic product and thus is far from spectacular.

During the Alliance decade, domestic savings were to provide 80 percent of the capital for necessary investment. In fact, according to the Inter-American Committee on the Alliance for Progress (Comité Interamericana de la Alianza para el Progreso, or CIAP), domestic savings have financed 90 percent, largely because of a shortage of foreign investment. . . .

When the Alliance began, many Latin American countries were deeply in debt and virtually unable to meet their debt payments. A substantial amount of early Alliance lending went to refinance the existing debts. At the same time, the trend in U.S. private investment in the region has been toward Latin American–based manufacturing for local markets, generally increasing the region's imports of raw materials without increasing its exports. Thus Latin America's annual payments of principal and interest on loans, together with profit remittances by foreign investors, have been rising much more rapidly than exports. Any drop in export income or cessation in the inflow of foreign capital now could produce a major crisis, precisely the crisis that the Alliance planners sought to forestall. . . .

But though the Alliance has not come close to most of its explicit objectives and specific targets, it has had some significant results. The decade has given Latin America a new development consciousness, which has permeated large segments of the population (including two of the region's most tradition-oriented institutions, the military and the church). Economic planning, particularly in Brazil, Colombia, and Chile, has reached an impressive level of sophistication, and throughout the hemisphere young, technically trained people are playing major roles in the key public-sector institutions. At the same time, the private sector contains a growing middle level of successful entrepreneurs and an increasing number of efficient industrial managers.

This new sophistication has been accompanied, in many cases, by a profound disillusionment with the Alliance, based in part on failure to reach the charter's targets. Viewed in retrospect, the targets themselves reflect not only the projections of the Latin American development experts but also the optimism with which the Kennedy administration (intentionally, although not cynically) had infused inter-American relations. But hindsight also shows that the problems of development are more difficult, and the political consequences of unfulfilled expectations more disastrous, than the authors of the charter ever anticipated.

The Alliance, defined as the record of inter-American relations in the past decade, provides additional justification for disillusionment. If it has succeeded in preventing any new Castros from coming to power in the hemisphere, it has done so by military means, failing conspicuously to advance the cause of the democratic left. The United States has intervened openly in the Dominican Republic and less obviously in Brazil and Guatemala to assist not the democratic left but the military and civilian forces of conservatism. In disputes between Latin American governments and U.S. corporations, the United States has applied economic pressures against the Latin American governments with a fine disregard for the disputed issues. Loan officials have consistently required that countries seeking financial assistance undertake monetary stabilization programs; they have not required programs of social reform. The U.S. Congress and the executive branch have restricted loan funds to purchases of U.S. goods (particularly those that are not competitively priced) and such other uses as are consistent with a favorable U.S. balance of payments.

These policies have raised serious doubts about both the U.S. commitment to democratic development in Latin America and the Alliance formula for attaining it. They have also given the left and the right in many Latin American countries a common cause: nationalistic opposition to what both regard as a dominating U.S. presence. This opposition has taken forms ranging from restrictions on the acquisition of local banks by U.S. banks to outright expropriation, and has given momentum to at least two successful military coups d'état. . . .

The close of the decade also found strong conservative military dictatorships in power in Argentina and Brazil and a populist military government in Peru, among other countries in the hemisphere that had constitutional civilian governments when the Alliance began and have since lost them. The military governments, whether conservative or populist, maintain that development requires the suspension of democratic participation in public decisions, particularly through political parties. They have explicitly rejected the Alliance proposition that economic growth, social reform, and political democracy are mutually reinforcing aspects of an effective development program.

If the Alliance is defined as policy based on this proposition, the pertinent question becomes not whether it has failed but to what extent it has been attempted.

The spirit in which the U.S. Congress agreed to the creation of the Alliance was less one of compassion for Latin America's needy millions than fear of a spread of Castroism. Even when this fear was at its height, the Congress was less generous in its appropriation of funds than President Kennedy had wished. And as the urgency of the Castro threat diminished, so did the annual Alliance appropriation. At the same time, the priority and cost of the Vietnam War were rising. Preoccupied with Vietnam, the U.S. government has treated Latin America as either a means of shoring up the balance of payments or a potential site for revolutions that might endanger the "national security."

The United States has devoted the largest single

portion of its regional aid during the past decade to the development program of authoritarian Brazil. Such allocation may be consistent with the size and importance of Brazil, but it is inconsistent with the criteria for Alliance lending set forth in the charter. Although U.S. policy-makers have debated this issue at great length, they have usually resolved it by giving greater weight to a country's economic performance than to its political or social conditions in determining loan allocations.

Of course the United States has also supplied assistance to Latin American countries in which constitutional processes, accountability of public officials, electoral contests, and party debates have both contributed to the establishment of social reforms and proved compatible with good economic management. But the priority of economic considerations goes far to explain the difference between aims and achievements under the Alliance for Progress.

These considerations have traditionally dominated U.S. policy in Latin America. The Alliance was designed to break free of them. Its fate raises vital questions about the purposes and consequences of foreign development assistance for both donor and recipient.

The problems that cause misunderstandings between governments are also contained in the day-to-day relationships between North America and Latin America. Moritz Thomsen, a Peace Corps volunteer, describes how he fell into a subtle psychological arrangement with his Ecuadorian friend Alexandro—an arrangement that made him a master and Alexandro a slave.

The Making of an Imperialist

By Moritz Thomsen

. . . This conversation made a couple of complications. Before our secret talk I think he had dreams of raising about twenty-five chickens; afterward he was talking about eighty. Somehow I had to bring him back to earth so that I wouldn't be investing my whole living allowance in tons of corn. I could see another bloody-footed gringo staggering naked down the beach if Alexandro had his way. The other thing I didn't particularly like was the change that took place in our relationship after I offered to help him. The offer had somehow made a *patrón* out of me; I had been catalogued and placed. It was a relationship that almost every poor Latin sought, to be subservient and protected by a powerful father figure. It was the very thing I was trying to destroy. I'd damn well not be Alexandro's daddy.

Yet, to be honest, I have to mention the other side of the coin. I used Alexandro, too. When I had to buy water, for instance, I didn't go out and make my own deal with the kids; I simply told Alexandro, and he scouted around for me. It was the subtle relationship of master and slave, engendered on his part by custom and insecurity, and on mine by laziness and insecurity. . . .

North American visitors to Latin America sometimes complain that the Latins get a misguided impression about the United States from movies—that they think we are all greedy, rich, violent, sex maniacs. Latin Americans say that we have equally exaggerated images of them.

Less Peace Corps, More James Bond
By John Rothchild

Most Americans, whether students, Peace Corps Volunteers, diplomats or tourists, arrive in Latin America as equals. Our political knowledge and our Spanish proficiency may vary. But emotionally, we have all had fairly similar exposures to Cantinflas, Pancho Villa, Ché Guevara, the immigrant Puerto Rican pickpockets of the U.S. cities, and the fat Cisco Kid's Pancho. These are the characters that populate our emotional Latin America.

Latin Americans also have their fantasies about the

United States, and the volunteer often finds his greatest problem not in adapting to the host people, but in adapting to their perceptions of him. All of us who are somewhat like Lord Jim have a vested interest in escaping from the Great Mistake, in finding a brief respite from the World Movers and the Power Brokers back home. Most of us, conscious of our inequality with the world, want to enjoy, at least for 24 months, the myth that we can be equal with humanity. When a *campesino* called me *"patrón,"* I carefully explained to him that I did not want to be a *patrón* (master). He gave me a painful look and then shrugged his shoulders and said: *"Sí, patrón."*

Continued questions about how much my camera costs, why Jackie married Onassis, whether the astronauts brought back the Hong Kong flu, or why I tried to find a comfortable mud hut instead of living in the richest apartment in Riobamba (which I could well afford), are the most painful. It is much easier to suffer poverty than to be told that I am unsuited to live in poverty because I am a rich man. My desire to pay for a two-year indulgence with discomfort, to identify with the powerless, is unattained. And only after this failure did I begin to criticize the society of my hosts, and return to my storybook images of "how things should be in Latin America."

Likewise, the semi-permanent arrival of a gringo into a Latin American town can be a most disquieting thing. After Kirk Douglas in the *Last Sundown*, Marlon Brando in *On the Waterfront*, the Beatles on radio, and Jackie and the astronauts in the papers, seeing an ordinary gringo can be very disillusioning. A study has never been done of Volunteers' effectiveness as dependent on their physical size and beauty, and how they look compared to movie stars; but in Ecuador, many of the Volunteers most successful in integrating themselves are not those who reject the role of the soft-spoken, physically indestructible Gringo God, but those who best conform to the image.

A good illustration of what people want to see in us (if only as a way of rejecting us) is in the images they themselves create of us. In Ecuador, this image has increasingly changed from blurred incredulity to see-ing us as threats: spies or imperialists in revolutionary clothing.

People here have a need to see us as CIA agents, just as we have a need to see them as in need of development. If we are CIA agents, then they will be reassured that there really is something about them worth spying on, and also that the beautiful, destruc-tive world of the movies is real. They also have a need to see us as imperialists. Then, we can be blamed for their own "underdevelopment" and it can be explained why we are here, without having to refer to our painful (for them) altruism. They have a need to see us as elitists. If we are elitists, then by choosing to live here, we are bringing them into our elitism.

The idea that we are here to help is as distasteful as was Lyndon Johnson. Benevolence in Latin America always arrives on a Big White Horse, and the heroes, from Cortés to Kennedy, have always doled out graces from wistful myths like Quetzalcoatl or the Alliance for Progress. Kennedy was loved in Latin America, not primarily because he loved the poor, but because he was rich and beautiful, and secondarily worked for the poor. The idea of *caballero* (dashing gentleman) is central to the way of giving in Latin America.

If the Peace Corps has served any function here, it has been in perpetrating these myths, despite the fact that every Volunteer fights them in some way. Just as our dream of being accepted by the Third World as equals in humanity is shattered every day, and yet we still hold on to it tenaciously, so the movie-picture image of a gringo as *caballero* is also broken by the presence of a Volunteer. But the nationals here, like us, cling to the fiction because the idea of an Amer-ican living as a poor man (Poor Like Me) is repug-nant both to the aristocracy of the rich, who want to feel their society is already equal to that of the United States, and the aristocracy of the poor, who want to believe that there is nothing about their lives that should necessarily be changed.

On a less colorful level, day-to-day relations be-tween nationals and Volunteers are being described in the same terms that Ecuadorians have always used to describe the stereotyped American diplomat. Volunteers were once the exception to such characterizations, but this is less true today.

One Volunteer in Santo Domingo (Ecuador), who worked here almost four years, had a long-time friend with whom he had had contact for his whole stay in Ecuador. A few days before he left, the friend asked him: "Tell me, what really is your purpose here?" Trying to be honest, the Volunteer said: "At times I don't even know." That convinced the long-time friend that the Volunteer was a member of some international spy network. The opportunities to understand were great, but the need to understand was something different. The Ecuadorian in many cases protects his need to understand the gringo as an imperialist spy.

It is hard to condemn this while the world continues to be a stage for our own domestic hang-ups. Only when we are worried about political amorality at home does Latin America's "problem" become seen in the same terms. When we are expanding economically (as in the Post War), the sister nations' problems become economic. And currently, while we are worried about how to get along together at home, we are working toward a non-directive methodology, toward mental and attitudinal change abroad.

After six years of an attempt at being friends, it sometimes seems that Ecuador would like less of the Peace Corps and more of James Bond. It is not just on the intellectual level, where such thinkers as Albert Memmi criticize the "left-wing colonists" and Mon. Ivan Illich of Mexico asks that all American "do-gooders" get out of his country. On the level of the masses, Volunteers trying to shake the international world-mover syndrome have clashed with people who have tried valiantly to remind him of it. While we have not tried to wield power, the people have asked why the country which made it to the moon couldn't save their village. The Volunteer feels a lack of effectiveness. The people do not. They view the problem as a Volunteer's lack of interest (he is really a spy) or lack of drive (he is lazy, doesn't think we are worth it). Increasingly, the Peace Corps is called "Cuerpo de Paseo" (Vacation Corps).

These problems will not be solved by sending more technically-qualified people, or by changing recruiting or training. They may be solved by honest dialogue about our images of each other, and why they don't reach. But most likely, it will probably be that we and they will continue to protect and perfect the image we personally need, by isolating ourselves, by rejecting social realities, by disliking the people's attitudes. There is no doubt that we change in our view of the host country much more than they change their movie view of gringos. But for both Ecuadorians and Volunteers, the process of personal communication and contact is painful and often futile. To paraphrase a Bob Dylan idea: We do not let them live in their dream, and they do not let us live in ours.

Underneath all the images, pretensions, and blunders that we have seen, the mental world of the Latin American is profoundly different from that of the gringo. Octavio Paz is writing about Mexico, but I think what he says also applies to the rest of the Spanish-speaking part of the continent. How can we become good neighbors?

A Mutual Misunderstanding

By Octavio Paz

This is not the moment to analyze our profound sense of solitude, which alternately affirms and denies itself in melancholy and rejoicing, silence and sheer noise, gratuitous crimes and religious fervor. Man is alone everywhere. But the solitude of the Mexican, under the great stone night of the high plateau that is still inhabited by insatiable gods, is very different from that of the North American, who wanders in an abstract world of machines, fellow citizens and moral precepts. In the Valley of Mexico man feels himself suspended between heaven and earth, and he oscillates between contrary powers and forces, and petrified eyes, and devouring mouths. Reality—that is, the world that surrounds us—exists by itself here, has a life of its own, and was not invented by man as it was in the United States. The Mexican feels himself to have been torn from the womb of this reality, which is both creative and destructive, both Mother and Tomb. He has forgotten the word that ties him to all those forces through which life manifests itself. Therefore he shouts or keeps silent, stabs or prays, or falls asleep for a hundred years.

The history of Mexico is the history of a man seeking his parentage, his origins. He has been influenced at one time or another by France, Spain, the United States and the militant indigenists of his own country, and he crosses history like a jade comet, now and then giving off flashes of lightning. What is he pursuing in his eccentric course? He wants to go back beyond the catastrophe he suffered: he wants to be a sun again, to return to the center of that life from which he was separated one day. (Was that day the Conquest? Independence?) Our solitude has the same roots as religious feelings. It is a form of orphanhood, an obscure awareness that we have been torn from the All, and an ardent search: a flight and a return, an effort to re-establish the bonds that unite us with the universe.

Nothing could be further from this feeling than the solitude of the North American. In the United States man does not feel that he has been torn from the center of creation and suspended between hostile forces. He has built his own world and it is built in his own image: it is his mirror. But now he cannot recognize himself in his inhuman objects, nor in his fellows. His creations, like those of an inept sorcerer, no longer obey him. He is alone among his works, lost—to use the phrase by José Gorostiza—in a "wilderness of mirrors."

Some people claim that the only differences between the North American and ourselves are economic. That is, they are rich and we are poor, and while their legacy is Democracy, Capitalism and the Industrial Revolution, ours is the Counterreformation,

Monopoly and Feudalism. But however influential the systems of production may be in the shaping of a culture, I refuse to believe that as soon as we have heavy industry and are free of all economic imperialism, the differences will vanish. (In fact, I look for the opposite to happen, and I consider this possibility one of the greatest virtues of the Revolution of 1910.) But why search history for an answer that only we ourselves can give? If it is we who feel ourselves to be different, what makes us so, and in what do the differences consist? . . .

When I arrived in the United States I was surprised above all by the self-assurance and confidence of the people, by their apparent happiness and apparent adjustment to the world around them. This satisfaction does not stifle criticism, however, and the criticism is valuable and forthright, of a sort not often heard in the countries to the south, where long periods of dictatorship have made us more cautious about expressing our points of view. But it is a criticism that respects the existing systems and never touches the roots. I thought of Ortega y Gasset's distinction between uses and abuses, in his definition of the "revolutionary spirit." The revolutionary is always a radical, that is, he is trying to correct the uses themselves rather than the mere abuses of them. Almost all the criticisms I heard from the lips of North Americans were of the reformist variety: they left the social or cultural structures intact and were only intended to limit or improve this or that procedure. It seemed to me then, and it still does, that the United States is a society that wants to realize its ideals, has no wish to exchange them for others, and is confident of surviving, no matter how dark the future may appear. I am not interested in discussing whether this attitude is justified by reason and reality; I simply want to point out that it exists. It is true that this faith in the natural goodness of life, or in its infinite wealth of possibilities, cannot be found in recent North American literature, which prefers to depict a much more somber world; but I found it in the actions, the words and even the faces of almost everyone I met.

On the other hand, I heard a good deal of talk about American realism and also about American ingenuousness, qualities that would seem to be mutually exclusive. To us a realist is always a pessimist. And an ingenuous person would not remain so for very long if he truly contemplated life realistically. Would it not be more accurate to say that the North American wants to use reality rather than to know it? In some matters—death, for example—he not only has no desire to understand it, he obviously avoids the very idea. . . .

In contrast, one of the most notable traits of the Mexican's character is his willingness to contemplate horror: he is even familiar and complacent in his dealings with it. The bloody Christs in our village churches, the macabre humor in some of our newspaper headlines, our wakes, the custom of eating skull-shaped cakes and candies on the Day of the Dead, are habits inherited from the Indians and the Spaniards and are now an inseparable part of our being. Our cult of death is also a cult of life, in the same way that love is a hunger for life and a longing for death. Our fondness for self-destruction derives not only from our masochistic tendencies but also from a certain variety of religious emotion.

And our differences do not end there. The North Americans are credulous and we are believers; they love fairy tales and detective stories and we love myths and legends. The Mexican tells lies because he delights in fantasy, or because he is desperate, or because he wants to rise above the sordid facts of his life; the North American does not tell lies, but he substitutes social truth for the real truth, which is always disagreeable. We get drunk in order to confess; they get drunk in order to forget. They are optimists and we are nihilists—except that our nihilism is not intellectual but instinctive, and therefore irrefutable. We are suspicious and they are trusting. We are sorrowful and sarcastic and they are happy and full of jokes. North Americans want to understand and we want to contemplate. They are activists and we are quietists; we enjoy our wounds and they enjoy their inventions. They believe in hygiene, health, work and contentment, but perhaps they have never experienced true joy, which is an intoxication, a whirlwind. In the hubbub of a fiesta night our voices explode into brilliant lights, and life and death mingle together, while their vitality becomes a fixed smile that denies old age and death but that changes life to motionless stone.

What is the origin of such contradictory attitudes? It seems to me that North Americans consider the world to be something that can be perfected, and that we consider it to be something that can be redeemed. Like their Puritan ancestors, we believe that sin and death constitute the ultimate basis of human nature, but with the difference that the Puritan identifies purity with health. Therefore he believes in the purifying effects of asceticism, and the consequences are his cult of work for work's sake, his serious approach to life, and his conviction that the body does not exist or at least cannot lose—or find—itself in another body. Every contact is a contamination. Foreign races, ideas, customs, and bodies carry within themselves the germs of perdition and impurity. Social hygiene complements that of the soul and the body. Mexicans, however, both ancient and modern, believe in communion and fiestas: there is no health without contact. Tlazolteotl, the Aztec goddess of filth and fecundity, of earthly and human moods, was also the goddess of steam baths, sexual love and confession.

APPENDIXES

By Michael and Melanie Neidig

Glossary of Foreign Words and Phrases

Abierto. Open.
Adelantado. Provincial governor.
Aguardiente. Liquor.
Alcabala. Sales tax.
Almojarifazgo. Import tax.
A lo divino. From God.
Al palacio del gobierno. To the governor's palace.
Anchoveta. Raw material for the fishmeal industry.
Angelito. Little angel.
Audiencia. Territorial ruling council.
Ayllu. Communal land.
Ayuntamiento. Municipal council.
Bandeirante. Pioneer.
Barriada. City ward, suburb.
Barrio suburbano. "Suburb," slum.
Blanco. White, white person.
Botafogo. Set fire.
Boulevardier. Man-about-town.
Brarcero. Day laborer.
Caballero. Gentleman.
Cabildo. Municipal council.
Cacique. Chief.
Callampa. "Mushroom," slum.
Callejón. Alleyway.
Calmecac. An institution that subjected nobles to fasting and purification exercises.
Calpulli-ejido. Communal land.
Campesino. Peasant.
Campo. Field.
Cantón. Province.

Carioca. Native of Rio de Janeiro.
Casa chica. "Little house," a second, nonlegalized family kept by many Latin American men.
Catinga. Desert plain.
Caudillo. Strongman.
Chalchihuite. Low-grade emerald.
Chalchiuatl. Warm human blood.
Chasqui. Runner, messenger.
Chicha. White-lightning liquor.
Chichería. Bar that sells *chicha.*
Cholo. Mestizo.
Científico. Scientist.
Cocal. Coconut plantation.
Consulado. Consulate.
Corregidor. Magistrate.
Criollo. Creole (a European born in the New World).
Curaca. Governor, potentate.
Dernier cri. Latest fashion.
Diezmo. One-tenth, tithe.
Ejidatario. One who farms public lands.
Ejido. Communal land.
Empleomanía. Mania for public office.
Encomendero. Recipient of land grant.
Encomienda. Royal land grant.
Estancia. Farm, plantation.
Eu fico. I stay.
Favela. Slum area.
Favelado. Slum dweller.
Fazenda. Plantation.
Finca. Farm.
Freundschaft. Friendship.
Gachupine. A Spaniard born in Spain.
Gaucho. Horseman, cowboy.
Giboiuçu. Boa constrictor.
Golpe de estado. Overthrow of the state.
Gringo. Foreigner (pejorative).
Guajiro. Peasant.
Guaso. Cowboy.
Guayacán. Lignum vitae tree.
Guerra florida. Spectacular war.
Hacendado. Landowner, rancher.
Hacienda. Farm, ranch, plantation.
Hidalgo. Nobleman. Someone with the pretense of nobility.

Indio. Indian.
Jodido pero feliz. Screwed but happy.
Ladino. Half-breed.
Latifundio. Large plantation.
Latino. Latin.
Lépero. Wretched, base person.
Ley fuga. A way whereby apprehended persons could be "shot while trying to escape."
Ley lerdo. A system of confiscating Indian lands.
Limeño. Native of Lima.
Llanero. Plainsman.
Llano. Level field, plain.
Macho. Violent, exhibitionist male.
Mi caballada. My herd of tame horses.
Minga. Communal work done by neighbors.
Minifundia. Subsistence land plots.
Mitimaes. Inca institutions that permitted the state to transfer families and whole villages to a faraway region.
Nortista. Northern woman.
Patrón. Bossman.
Pendejo. Coward, fool.
Peninsular. Spanish-born administrator in Latin America.
Pinga. Brandy.
Pisco. Anisette.
Población callampa. "Mushroom" village, slum.
Porteño. Of or from Buenos Aires.
Provincia. Province.
Pueblo. Town.
Quinon. Quinine.
Quinto real. "Royal fifth," natural-resources tax.
Quipu. Colored threads used by ancient Peruvians as a counting device.
Requerimiento. Religious document read to Indians.
Salón. Saloon.
Semana Santa. Holy Week.
Sertão (pl. *sertões*). Hinterland, backland.
Si Dios quiere. If God wills it.
Sindicato. Syndicate, farm union.
Sisa. Food tax.
Socio. Comrade, buddy.
Teule. A god.
Tigre. "Tiger," hoodlum.

Tumulto. Tumult, uprising.
Tunjo. Amulet.
Tupa-Mbae. God's share.
Vecino. Neighbor, neighborhood.
Violencia. Violence. The Columbian civil war in 1948 was
    called the "Violencia."
Ya mismo. Right away.
Zambo. Half-breed (Indian and black).

Conditions and Realities

By John Gerassi

Latin America is bigger and potentially richer than we are. Its borders begin at the Rio Grande and end at the South Pole, more than ten thousand land miles away.

Latin America is made up of twenty sovereign states of French, Spanish, or Portuguese origin. It also includes a series of European and United States colonies (which are called otherwise) and Jamaica and Trinidad-Tobago, which gained independence from England on August 1 and 31, 1962, respectively. Though the latter's economies bear the same characteristics as their Caribbean companions, they are not ethnically or politically part of Latin America. Nor is British Honduras, though it should be. Nevertheless, for purposes of this book, we shall be concerned almost exclusively with the twenty Latin states, with only fleeting glances at the others.

These twenty, according to very optimistic estimates, have an average yearly per capita income of $253. . . .

Such figures, however, hide the fact that the vast majority of the population is far, far poorer. In Peru, for example, more than half the people live outside the money economy altogether, bartering whatever goods they manage to grow. Of the other half, 80 per cent earn $53 a year, while 100 families own 90 per cent of the native (as opposed to foreign) wealth, or $1,334,000,000. Of this total, 80 per cent is in the hands of just 30 families. Meanwhile, 65 per cent of the population is illiterate and 45 per cent has never seen a doctor. In Lima, the capital, whose colonial mansions enveloped by ornate wooden balconies help make it one of the most beautiful cities in the world, half of the 1.3 million inhabitants live in rat-infested slums. One, called El Montón, is built around, over, and in the city dump. There, when I visited it, naked children, some too young to know how to walk, competed with pigs for the few bits of food scraps accidentally discarded by the garbage men.

In Chile, unemployment stays doggedly above 18 per cent. One-third of the 2,000,000 people that live in Santiago, the capital, are crowded in squatters' huts made of earth or stray planks, with no water, no electricity, no transportation facilities, no municipal garbage disposal system, and no medical attention. One of these slum areas, known as *callampas* (mushrooms) because they have the habit of rising overnight, is in the dead center of town, a dime's throw from the fashionable Crillon Hotel. In that slum, called Colocolo, I saw scores of samples of that traditional sign of extreme substandard conditions: toddlers with bulging stomachs (from starches, their only diet) and hairpin legs (from lack of calcium and other minerals).

Such scenes are repeated over and over in every Latin American country. Millions of people barely subsist, while occasional oligarchs exhibit a wealth superior to those who in our country can afford yachts, private planes, and houses in Florida, Virginia, and Hyannis Port. Latin American oligarchs manipulate their respective countries' governments to their advantage. To them, the plight of the masses is just "so much sentimental hogwash."

The masses, however, are rapidly becoming a formidable force to contend with. Together, Latin America's twenty nations have already more than 200 million people. In 1900 their population was barely 62 million (4 per cent of the world). Fifty years later, it had reached 163 million (6.5 per cent). By 1975 it will have jumped to 300 million—more than Soviet Russia's or North America's.

Latin America's yearly rate of population growth was about normal at the beginning of the century (1.8 per cent). Today it is 2.6 per cent, higher than anywhere else in the world; for instance, it is 1.6 per cent in Russia, 0.7 per cent in Europe, 1.8 per cent in Asia, 1.7 per cent in the United States and Canada and, in general, in the world. . . .

Urban centers are constantly gaining in proportion to rural areas. The former will actually surpass the latter within this decade. Already five countries—Argentina, Uruguay, Cuba, Chile, and Venezuela—have more people living in cities than on farms, and these five are among the six with the highest per capita incomes. The populations in Mexico and Colombia are almost at a 50–50 ratio. Panama, El Salvador, Nicaragua, and Peru will soon follow suit.

The percentage of children in Latin America is higher than in any other area of the world—despite a frightening 20 to 35 per cent infant mortality. Slightly more than 32 per cent of Latin Americans are one to nine years old (22 per cent in the United States), and 23 per cent are ten to nineteen years old (17 per cent in the United States). The resulting dependency ratio (unemployable mouths to feed) is also higher than in any other area: 50 per cent of Latin Americans are either under fifteen or over sixty-five, compared to only 26 per cent in the United States. As these proportions increase, dependencies will become more and more of a burden. And as children become adults, a greater and greater demand for jobs will ensue. . . .

The Social and Financial Balance Sheet
By Jerome Levinson and Juan de Onis

Private Investment

Since World War II the United States has provided 75 per cent of foreign private investment in Latin America. But in 1961 U.S. businessmen were undertaking few new ventures in the region. Cuba's seizure of nearly $1 billion in U.S.-owned sugar mills, hotels, banks, nickel mines, factories, and other assets had been a psychological as well as a financial blow. Brazil, Chile, Colombia, and Argentina, suffering from inflation accompanied by high debt payments and low export earnings, generated additional apprehension. During the first few years of the Alliance, although reinvestment of profits by subsidiaries remained relatively steady, new investments were sharply curtailed. But after 1964 with Cuba well isolated from the hemisphere by a collective diplomatic and economic blockade and Brazil under a military regime friendly to the United States, a new mood of optimism arose in the U.S. business community, producing an upsurge of investment in Latin America. . . .

As of 1969, the level of direct U.S. private investment in Latin America was $12 billion. The March 1969 issue of the U.S. Department of Commerce *Survey of Current Business* reports a gradual shift in investment emphasis from Canada and western Europe to Latin America and other countries. With substantial gains in all industries, capital investment in Latin America showed the largest increase of all major areas for 1968, easily surpassing the 16 per cent gain registered in 1967. . . .

The Latin American countries have shown a relatively greater propensity than other developing countries for sustained inflation. The exceptions—Mexico and Venezuela, for instance—have maintained relative price stability during periods of intensive growth. However, these countries enjoy a high level of foreign exchange earnings, sufficient to finance all imports necessary for development, and this income may have contributed to their price stability. More characteristic, however, and more intriguing to economic analysts is the endemic upward spiral of prices accompanied by chronic balance-of-payments problems in Brazil, Chile, Colombia, Argentina, and Uruguay. . . .

Agrarian Reform

Almost a million Latin American families were settled or resettled during the period of 1960–67. . . . An estimated 10 to 14 million families in Latin America remain to be settled or resettled. This figure is increasing faster than the current rate of resettlement. At an average cost of $1,000 per family, close to $15 billion in agricultural credit would be needed now for agrarian reform purposes—a sum approaching total annual gross investment for the entire region.[1]

Education

It is expected that there will be about 69 million children of primary-school age in 1970. This is almost twice the number enrolled in school in 1967. If the present trend of 6 per cent increase in school enrollment annually were

---

[1] U.S. House of Representatives, Subcommittee on Inter-American Affairs of the Committee on Foreign Affairs, *New Directions for the 1970's: Toward a Strategy of Inter-American Development, Hearings,* 91st Cong., 1st sess. (Washington, D.C.: U.S. Government Printing Office, 1969), p. 699.

to continue, enrollment would not reach the level of 69 million children until 1979. By that time, of course, the school-age population would be well above that level, or about 92 million, so there would still be 23 million children not enrolled in school. Not until 1986 would the entire school-age population be enrolled, if present rates of population growth and school expansion continue. . . . If the current rate of increases in school enrollment were to be stepped up from 6 per cent to 9 per cent per year, the entire expected school-age population of 85 million would be enrolled in school in 1977.[2]

Health

Although detailed and up-to-date information on changes in the expectation of life in Latin America since 1960 is scarce, the Pan American Health Organization has been able to estimate that the average future life span increased from 60.2 years to 62.5 years between 1960 and 1966. . . .

Low-cost Housing

The goal of adequate housing for all is obviously desirable, but realistically one which cannot be soon realized. The total need for housing in Latin America has been estimated as being between 15 and 20 million units. This deficit is increasing by at least one million units a year. Squatter settlements continue to mushroom. Given higher priority needs for the use of scarce internal and external resources, the countries of Latin America will not be able to meet the housing need in the foreseeable future. . . . The greatest need for housing is for low-income families. Unfortunately, persons in this income category can make little or no contribution to the cost of their housing, and generally require some form of public subsidy. This raises the hard economic question of the feasibility and desirability of allocating large amounts of capital to low-rent housing.[3]

Employment

Aggravating Latin America's social problems is the inadequacy of productive employment available to a rapidly

[2] *Ibid.,* p. 704.
[3] *Ibid.,* p. 715.

growing labor force. According to ECLA [Economic Council on Latin America] estimates, during the Alliance decade the Latin American population of working age (fifteen to sixty-five) has increased by 2.3 million men and women each year, reaching a total of 136 million people in 1969. Of these, 84 million are "economically active," that is, in the labor market, but ECLA estimates that only about 60 million are fully employed. The remainder are unemployed or underemployed, particularly in the rural areas, where ECLA estimates that 11 million are unemployed in an economically active population of 35 million.

The low rate of absorption of rural manpower is held responsible for an actual slowdown in job openings during the Alliance period; only about 60 per cent of the new job seekers gained employment during the sixties, compared with 62.5 per cent during the 1950s. The percentage of the economically active population engaged in agriculture has declined from 53.4 per cent in 1950 to 47.2 per cent in 1960 and an estimated 42.2 per cent in 1969. Over the same period, the rate of employment in industry, mining, construction, and public services has increased only from 23.5 per cent of the total to 24.8 per cent. The major increase for the period has been in "miscellaneous services," from 13 per cent to 17.3 per cent. It results from the transfer of many job seekers to various marginal forms of livelihood in the urban areas; in short, the displacement of rural poverty to the cities. According to ECLA, the annual per capita income of about two-thirds of the agricultural population, including children and inactive adults, averages less than $90 a year, which implies an annual income per economically active person of approximately $275. Latin America's average per capita annual income is $510.[4]

---

[4] United Nations Economic Commission for Latin America, *Economic Survey of Latin America, 1968*, pt. 1, "Some Aspects of the Latin American Economy Toward the End of the Nineteen-Sixties," E/CN 12/825 (March 1969), pp. 50–60. The figure of $510 for the regional average is based on new ECLA calculations that take into account price-level differential in various countries. The calculation is in constant 1960 dollars, and the dollar level, with adjustment for relative price levels in the United States and Latin America, brings the real value of Latin per capita income higher than before the 1969 calculations.

Income Distribution

If poverty, city slums, migrant workers, welfare, and the "bottom fifth" are symptomatic of severe social ills in the United States, they constitute a crisis of society in Latin America. The United Nations Economic Commission for Latin America (ECLA) calculates that more than half the population of Latin America—130 million people— live on an average annual per capita income of $120. This low level is far higher than that in many parts of the developing world, but Latin American expectations, in this age of trucks, transistors, and television, are not what they were when the rural poor stayed down on the farm and lived out their days in immobile resignation. In contrast, according to ECLA's rough estimates, 60 to 70 per cent of national income in nine representative Latin American countries goes to the upper 30 per cent of the population, and 25 to 30 per cent to the privileged upper 5 per cent.[5] The upper 30 per cent thus enjoy per capita incomes ranging from $500 to $2,500, and have family incomes and standards of living very much like those of the western European countries, while the bottom half of the population lives at or near subsistence level. In between, an insecure 20 to 30 per cent seek desperately to enter the upper group or avoid sliding down to the lower half.

The conventional wisdom has it that the inequalities of income in Latin America are perpetuated by hereditary oligarchies of extraordinary wealth—the "ten families" or "hundred families," depending on the size of the country. This cliché corresponds neither to the political realities, since aristocratic families haven't run Latin American countries for a long time, nor to the complex economic and social conditions of Latin American development. Closer observation suggests that these inequalities are the result of an uneven growth process dominated by external factors, and the reluctance of an extended social sector— the middle groups in particular—to spend a major portion of national income on solving the problems of the huge deprived sector. Many members of the middle class de-

---

[5] United Nations Economic Commission for Latin America, *Some Aspects of the Latin American Economy Toward the End of the 1960's*, E/CN 12/825 (March 1969), p. 23 and Table I–9.

plore the urban shantytowns and the lack of schools for rural children, but they have their own problems and aspirations, such as buying a family automobile.

Trade

In the 1960s, Latin America's balance of trade with the United States continued to deteriorate steadily:

(a) Between 1960 and 1968, U.S. exports of goods to Latin America increased from $3.8 billion to $5.3 billion.

(b) In the same period, U.S. receipts from transportation services and travel by Latin Americans more than doubled, increasing from $580 million to $1.2 billion.

(c) In 1968, the United States posted a record $1.7 billion surplus in its balance of trade on goods and services with Latin America. In the same year, it registered a $1 billion deficit with western Europe including the United Kingdom, and a $1.4 billion deficit with Japan. In other words, U.S. earnings from Latin America made up nearly two-thirds of the U.S. deficit in trade with western Europe and Japan.

(d) On the basis of receipts for U.S. goods and services, Latin America has ranked second only to Canada as a market for the United States during the decade.

(e) Between 1960 and 1968, U.S. imports of Latin American merchandise rose only from $4 billion to $5.2 billion, while total U.S. imports more than doubled, reaching $33 billion in 1968. In that period Latin America's share of United States merchandise imports fell from 27.2 percent to 15.8 percent.

Latin American Gazetteer
By John Rothchild

Argentina

Population (1971 estimate)—23.5 million
Area—1 million square miles
Capital—Buenos Aires
Description—Second-largest country in South America. Four times the size of Texas. Great contrasts of terrain and climate within country. Argentina usually associated with the pampas, the vast plains area that produces cattle—the country's main industry.

Resources and Industries—Argentina is one of the most developed of the Latin American nations. It produces meat, chemicals, textiles, and sugar, and possesses deposits of coal, zinc, lead, sulfur, copper, and petroleum.

Politics—Since the fall of Juan Perón as president and virtual dictator of Argentina in the 1940's, the country has vacillated between unstable democratic governments and military regimes. Perón, who lives in exile but returned to the country in 1973 for the first time in seventeen years, still controls the blue-collar union movements and therefore much of the country's politics. Argentina ended several years' military rule with an election in 1973.

Bahamas

Population (1970 census)—168,000

Area—4,404 square miles

Description—The Bahamas comprise nearly 700 islands, 30 of which are inhabited. They extend from near the Florida coast to Haiti.

Resources and Industries—Main revenue comes from tourism. Islands export salt, crayfish, pulpwood, and cucumbers.

Politics—The islands have, until very recently, been a part of the British possessions. But in 1964, self-rule was granted to the islands, and in 1973 they received full independence.

Bolivia

Population (1971 estimate)—5 million

Area—424,163 square miles

Capital—La Paz

Description—A mountainous, landlocked country, about eight times the size of New York State. Southern portion is dry desert, northern part is a farming area. Indians who make up the majority of the population have more political power than similar groups in other Andean countries.

Resources and Industries—Major industry is mining, especially tin. There is also oil, lead, zinc, gold, and iron. Most people, however, are employed in some kind of agriculture. Has lowest standard of living of all Andean nations—per capita income is about $150 a year.

Politics—In 1952 a leftist revolution took place in Bolivia, but it was beset by fragmentation; during the 1960's, a right-wing backlash occurred. Military government has been the general rule in recent years. Military seems to vacillate between left and right—Ché Guevara was killed in Bolivia, but the U.S.-owned Gulf Oil Corporation was nationalized by the government.

Brazil

Population (1972 estimate)—98 million
Area—3.2 million square miles, larger than the United States without Alaska
Capital—Brazilia
Description—Largest country in Latin America, destined to become its first major industrial superpower. Contains most of the Amazon jungle and river basin. The north is a dry desert plain. Majority of population lives on the coast in large cities like Rio de Janeiro and São Paulo.
Resources and Industries—World's largest coffee producer. Is also known for bananas, cotton, sugar. Brazil manufactures steel, iron ore, manganese, quartz and beryl. Half of the country's work force is rural, but Brazil is the most industrialized country in Latin America. It imports foodstuffs, especially livestock.
Politics—Brazil is ruled by the military. Elections have been promised in recent years, but none have been held thus far. The last few years have seen severe curtailment of civil liberties and freedom of the press. Political dissidents have been exiled, and in some cases tortured. Military rulers say political repression is necessary for rapid economic progress.

Chile

Population (1971 estimate)—8.9 million
Area—286,396 square miles
Capital—Santiago
Description—Long, narrow country running for 2,600 miles along the western tip of South America. Slightly larger than Texas. Mountainous country; most people live in the plains area between the mountains and the coast.
Resources and Industries—Chile is known for its copper

production, mostly run by the United States until the mines were nationalized in 1971 by Marxist president Salvador Allende. The country also produces nitrate, iron, coal, and oil. Major agricultural products include dairy products, wine, rice, wheat, peas, and potatoes. The country has some large steel mills.

Politics—Chile has a recognized tradition of democratic leadership and has not seen military rule for several decades. Most Chileans are descendants of Europeans; the country is full of French-, English-, and German-speaking people, in contrast to the strong Indian-Spanish predominance in other countries. In 1970 Dr. Allende became the first Marxist ever elected president of a country in this hemisphere. His government has nationalized many industries, most notably the copper mines. He has faced severe economic crises and political turmoil, and it is hard to predict Chile's political future.

Colombia

Population (1971 estimate)—21.7 million
Area—455,355 square miles
Capital—Bogotá
Description—Mountainous country, with most of the population living in valleys. Several distinct cultural groups because interchange and travel between areas is difficult. Has fairly extensive coastline on northwestern side of South America; also includes part of Amazon basin.

Resources and Industries—Major agricultural products are coffee, rice, tobacco, cotton, sugar, cocoa, wheat, and bananas. Has large petroleum deposits and some valuable gems. Economy is based on agriculture.

Politics—Long history of change of power between two major political parties—the conservatives and the liberals. The rivalry between these two factions—the former comprising the Church and landowner aristocracy, the latter the industrialists and workers—broke out into bloody civil war in the late 1940's and early 1950's. The result of this *violencia* (violence) has been more than 200,000 deaths. Since that time, a truce has been declared between the factions, and power is automatically alternated between them every four years. A conservative was elected in 1970.

Costa Rica

Population (1971 estimate)—1.8 million
Area—19,575 square miles
Capital—San José
Description—Small country in Central America. Comprises coastal plains and a central mountain chain. Many volcanoes.

Resources and Industries—Major producer of bananas. Also exports coffee and cacao. Small manufacturing and light industry. Economy is predominantly agricultural, with heavy U.S. investments from companies like United Fruit.

Politics—Long history of democratic government. The military has not played a major role in running the country. Known as the most stable of Central American countries.

Cuba

Population (1971 estimate)—8.6 million
Area—44,218 square miles
Capital—Havana
Description—An island, 90 miles south of Key West, Florida. About the size of Pennsylvania. Numerous good harbors. Mountain chains in center of island.

Resources and Industries—Sugar makes up about 85 percent of exports. The United States was once major buyer, but imposed an economic embargo on Cuba after Fidel Castro came to power in the early 1960's. Cuba now trades principally with European and communist countries. Also produces other tropical agricultural products. Castro has attempted to develop industry without much success.

Politics—Fidel Castro engineered a successful revolution to topple dictator Fulgencio Batista in 1959. Before that time, country had been heavily influenced, and often was directly controlled, by U.S. economic interests. Castro turned Cuba into a communist nation, abolished private property, expropriated industries, transformed the educational, political, and social structure of the country. He has ruled as a dictator ever since, with reportedly massive popular support.

Dominican Republic

Population (1971 estimate)—4.1 million
Area—18,816 square miles
Capital—Santo Domingo
Description—Occupies eastern two-thirds of the island of Hispaniola; the rest is taken up by Haiti. Island located in the Greater Antilles, between Cuba and Puerto Rico. There is a central mountain chain.

Resources and Industries—Major agricultural products include sugar, cocoa, tobacco, corn, peanuts, bananas, and livestock. Country has deposits of gold, copper, salt, chalk, and marble, and manufactures rum, sugar, peanut oil, textiles, tobacco and lumber products.

Politics—Turmoil created after the military overthrow of President Juan Bosch in 1962. The United States sent marines and intervened in civil war in 1965. Joaquim Balaguer elected president in 1966, and reelected in 1970. Country still suffering from factionalism and tension from the 1965 civil war, and there is widespread terrorism by political groups and by the police.

Ecuador

Population (1971 estimate)—6.3 million
Area—116,270 square miles
Capital—Quito
Description—Andean country with tremendous mountain spine running down the middle, dividing the tropical coastline and the Amazon-basin region. The area of Ecuador is still questionable, because of an unresolved boundary dispute with Peru.

Resources and Industries—Major exporter of bananas. Also produces fruits, coffee, rice, and cereals. Industries include textiles, chemicals, cement, and balsa wood. A vast oil basin was discovered in Amazon region in late 1960's, and country should begin exporting this year. Has a potentially large fishing industry, if territorial water rights are resolved with the United States.

Politics—See article on Velasco Ibarra, Part IX, 61. In 1972 he was ousted by a military junta, which is currently running the country.

El Salvador

Population (1971 estimate)—3.5 million
Area—8,260 square miles
Capital—San Salvador
Description—Smallest of the Central American countries. Only one without an Atlantic seacoast. Mountainous nation about the size of Massachusetts.
Resources and Industries—Exports coffee, cotton, and sugar. Has developed light industry.
Politics—History marked by unstable governments and boundary disputes. Repeated military clashes with Honduras over the boundary during 1960's; the 1969 war began over a disputed call at a soccer game.

French Guiana

Population (1970 estimate)—51,000
Area—37,740 square miles
Capital—Cayenne
Description—Located on the northern coast of South America. Coastal plains and mountains.
Resources and Industries—Mostly forest, with few cultivated areas. Most important industry is gold. Exports cocoa, bananas, wood, gold, fish, rum, and shrimp.
Politics—A French possession since 1667 except for brief period under British and Brazilian control.

Guatemala

Population (1971 estimate)—5.3 million
Area—42,042 square miles
Capital—Guatemala City
Description—Northernmost country in Central America. About the size of Ohio, containing more people than any other Central American country. Mountainous areas rise abruptly from the plains. Many volcanoes.
Resources and Industries—Primarily an agricultural nation. Produces coffee, sugar, bananas, cotton, and chicle, as well as cattle and wood. Has some light industry, and is exploring potential oil deposits, but foreign exchange depends almost wholly on agricultural export.
Politics—The 1960's saw Guatemala beset with turmoil

and violence. Virtual civil war between leftists and conservative groups spread across the country during the late 1960's. Many people, especially students, were killed. The country is currently run by General Carlos Araña Osorio, a conservative, who has relied on police and military force to stabilize the country.

Guyana (formerly British Guiana)

Population (1971 estimate)—740,000
Area—83,000 square miles
Capital—Georgetown
Description—Small country in the northeastern part of South America. Very hot, poor soil. About the size of Kansas.

Resources and Industries—Sugar, rice, coconut, coffee, citrus fruit, timber, and livestock. Mines bauxite ore, gold, and diamonds: Manufactures rum, clothing, furniture, and some drugs.

Politics—Gained independence from British in 1966. Country has difficult racial problem; the population is 53 percent East Indian, 31 percent blacks of African descent, and about 16 percent mixed European. The East Indians and blacks do not get along, and live in a kind of voluntary segregation.

Haiti

Population (1971 estimate)—4.9 million
Area—10,714 square miles
Capital—Port-au-Prince
Description—Occupies the western third of Hispaniola, sharing the island with the Dominican Republic. Country is mountainous, climate is dry.

Resources and Industries—Coffee is chief product. Also cotton, sugar, bananas, cocoa, tobacco, and rice. Haiti exports wood and rum. Country is usually bankrupt.

Politics—Since the 1950's, country was run by Dr. François Duvalier, who governed through terrorism and voodoo. Duvalier made great use of the Tonton Macoutes, a vicious gestapo group that inhibited political opposition. Supposedly Duvalier had a mystical hold over his people; the country did not progress economically during his rule. Duvalier died in 1971, and was succeeded by his son, Jean-Claude Duvalier, who has also become president for life. He is trying to attract tourism and create better international opinion of his country.

Honduras

Population (1971 estimate)—600,000
Area—43,277 square miles
Capital—Tegucigalpa
Description—Second largest of the Central American republics. About the size of Pennsylvania. Thinly populated and mountainous.

Resources and Industries—Bananas are the chief export. Also produces other tropical agricultural crops. Manufactures textiles and clothing. Trying to develop forest industry.

Politics—Protracted border conflicts with El Salvador, which has a larger population and would like some Honduran land. (See note on El Salvador.) Long history of conflict between liberals and conservatives, but politics not as turbulent here as in some other countries. Honduras now ruled by a constitution ratified in 1965; president is elected for a six-year term.

Mexico

Population (1971 estimate)—50.8 million
Area—758,259 square miles
Capital—Mexico City
Description—Third-largest country in Latin America, joins the United States across the Rio Grande River. Widely varied terrain, including mountains, plateaus, and two extended coastlines.

Resources and Industries—Heavily industrialized. Produces petroleum, gold, copper, lead, zinc, silver, and other minerals. Exports some farm products—tomatoes, cotton, coffee, cane sugar, and cattle. Operates with large foreign investments, especially from the United States.

Politics—One-party system since the 1910 revolution. However, the last few years have seen more rebellion than at any period since the revolution. Student uprisings during the 1968 Olympics in Mexico City were brutally put down—many students were jailed and killed. Government has responded to protests among urban groups and especially among the Indians living in the Yucatán Peninsula with military and police force. There is a growing feeling that the benefits of industry and the revolution have not reached lower levels of society.

Nicaragua

Population (1971 estimate)—1.9 million
Area—53,938 square miles
Capital—Managua
Description—Largest of the Central American nations. Bordered by Honduras on the north and Costa Rica on the south. Mountainous.

Resources and Industries—Mostly agricultural. Bananas, cotton, fruit, coffee, corn, beans, cocoa, and tobacco are produced. Cotton, coffee, and sugar account for 70 per cent of exports. 1973 earthquake that destroyed city of Managua will cause severe economic hardship.

Politics—Early part of century saw Nicaragua ruled by U.S. Marines. In the 1930's the Somoza family came to power. They have held dictatorial sway over the country since that time; three members of the Somoza family ruled in turn until 1972, when Anastasio Somoza, Jr., resigned to allow a three-man government until the elections planned for 1974.

Panama

Population (1971 estimate)—1.4 million
Area—29,208 square miles
Capital—Panama City
Description—A long country joining Central and South America. Primarily mountainous, with heavy forest and jungle region (Darien) separating the two sections of the continent. More than half the population lives in Panama City.

Resources and Industries—Panama depends on revenues paid by the United States for use of the canal. Bananas and petroleum are the largest export items. Also produces various agricultural commodities.

Politics—Generally unstable, with heavy U.S. influence until recently. Now run by a left-wing general, Omar Torrijos, similar to the Peruvian government in its reform attempts and opposition to U.S. policies. Panama is fighting to renegotiate the canal treaty, feeling that it is unfairly compensated.

Paraguay

Population (1972 estimate)—2.5 million
Area—157,047 square miles
Capital—Asunción
Description—One of two landlocked countries in South America (Bolivia is the other). Country possesses lush forests and good agricultural terrain.

Resources and Industries—Exports cattle, cotton, wood products, hides, tea, and vegetable oils. Forty percent of income comes from cattle-raising and forestry.

Politics—Paraguay has suffered two major wars (1864–1870 and 1928–1935) over border disputes with its more powerful neighbors Argentina, Brazil, and Uruguay. Alfredo Stroessner has ruled the country as a strongarm dictator since 1954. Freedoms and civil liberties are curtailed at various times.

Peru

Population (1971 estimate)—14 million
Area—496,222 square miles
Capital—Lima
Description—In the heart of the Andes mountain chain down the western side of South America. Has extensive coastline and owns part of Amazon territory. Travel severely hampered by mountains, and farming is difficult in many areas because of poor soil or lack of irrigation. Peru was the center of the Inca empire; the population is at least one-third Indian.

Resources and Industries—Fishing is a major occupation in Peru. About half its people are employed in agriculture. It possesses copper mines and oil fields, and produces steel.

Politics—See discussion of Manuel Odría in "Four Other Dictators" by Tad Szulc.

Surinam (Dutch Guiana)

Population (1971 estimate)—420,000
Area—62,000 square miles
Capital—Paramaribo
Description—Small country on northern coast of South

America. Swampy plains, hills, and mountains. Population made up of Asiatic peoples of mixed European and African ancestry.

Resources and Industries—Exports bauxite, aluminum, lumber, sugar, rice, citrus, bananas, and shrimp. Has great resources but operates under a trade deficit.

Politics—Granted autonomy from the Netherlands in 1954.

Uruguay

Population (1971 estimate)—2.9 million
Area—72,172 square miles
Capital—Montevideo
Description—Smallest of the South American countries. Very hilly country with some forests.

Resources and Industries—Like its neighbor Argentina, relies on cattle-raising. Economy based on cattle and sheep industry. But about half the population lives in Montevideo and are bureaucrats. Economy beset by inflation in recent years because basic industries cannot support the urban bureaucracies and government agencies.

Politics—Country is very European, looks to France and Great Britain. Not many Indians. Twentieth century began with period of prosperity and progressive politics— the model for moderate socialism. But economy could not support the state, and in 1960's political instability and unrest grew. Uruguay was center of famous urban guerrilla bands, the Tupamaros. Country currently beset by inflation and political turmoil. President is democratically elected.

Rising inflation (estimated at 4,000 percent in the last fifteen years), and increased urban unrest have caused the military to become uneasy and to begin taking over the country. In 1973, President Juan Bordaberry surrendered most of his powers to the military, while remaining president as a figurehead. Uruguay's military seems somewhere between the Peruvians' and Brazilians' in political ideology, but their "soft coup," as it was called, was a significant departure from Uruguay's tradition of democratic politics. Bordaberry also recently shut down the congress, making Uruaguay one more example of Latin America's turn toward dictatorship.

Venezuela

Population (1971 estimate)—10.4 million
Area—352,150 square miles
Capital—Caracas
Description—Located in north of continent; about twice the size of California. Lowlands one of the hottest areas of South America; the plains areas are poor in soil content, but highlands are rich in mineral deposits.

Resources and Industries—Venezuela is known for its petroleum deposits. Third-largest oil exporter in the world. Also produces other minerals, such as iron, nickel, and gold. Largest agricultural crop is coffee. Produces steel, textiles, tobacco products, paper, tires, and shoes. Ninety percent of the foreign exchange is from oil. One of highest standards of living in Latin America.

Politics—1964 started a period of relative stability and democratically elected governments, ending long years of dictators and intermittent military rule. Under Rómulo Betancourt, country was one of the showcases for John Kennedy's Alliance for Progress. Country has gotten increasingly better concessions from the U.S. oil companies that extract the petroleum. Current president is Rafael Caldera, of the Christian Democratic Party, who is carrying on about the same style of government as that introduced by Betancourt. Standard of living is high, but there is a large percentage of unemployment.

United States Military Interventions in Latin America

from the *U.S. Congressional Record*

1822—Cuba. United States naval forces suppressing piracy landed on the northwest coast of Cuba and burned a pirate station.

1823—Cuba. Brief landings in pursuit of pirates occurred April 8 near Escondido; April 16 near Cayo Blanco; July 11 at Siquapa Bay; July 21 at Cape Cruz; and October 23 at Camrioca.

1824—Cuba. In October the U.S.S. *Porpoise* landed bluejackets near Matanzas in pursuit of pirates. This was during the cruise authorized in 1822.

1824—Puerto Rico (Spanish territory). Commodore David Porter with a landing party attacked the town of Fajardo, which had sheltered pirates and insulted American naval officers. He landed with 200 men in November and forced an apology.

1833—Argentina, October 31–November 15. A force was sent ashore at Buenos Aires to protect the interests of the United States and other countries during an insurrection.

1835–36—Peru, December 10, 1835–January 24, 1836; August 31–December 2, 1836. Marines protected American interests in Callao and Lima during an attempted revolution.

1836—Mexico. General Gaines occupied Nacogdoches (Texas), disputed territory, from July to December during the Texan war for independence, under orders to cross the "imaginary boundary line" if an Indian outbreak threatened.

1842—Mexico. Commodore T. A. C. Jones, in command of a squadron that had long been cruising off California, occupied Monterey, California, on October 19, believing war had come. He discovered peace, withdrew, and saluted. A similar incident occurred a week later at San Diego.

1844—Mexico. President Tyler deployed our forces to protect Texas against Mexico, pending Senate approval of a treaty of annexation (later rejected). He defended his action against a Senate resolution of inquiry. This was a demonstration or preparation.

1846–48—Mexico, the Mexican War. President Polk's occupation of disputed territory precipitated it. War was formally declared.

1852–53—Argentina, February 3–12, 1852; September 17, 1852–April (?), 1853. Marines were landed and maintained in Buenos Aires to protect American interests during a revolution.

1853—Nicaragua, March 11–13. To protect American lives and interests during political disturbances.

1854—Nicaragua, July 9–15. San Juan del Norte (Greytown) was destroyed to avenge an insult to the American Minister to Nicaragua.

1855—Uruguay, November 25–29 or 30. United States and European naval forces landed to protect American interests during an attempted revolution in Montevideo.

1856—Panama, Republic of New Grenada, September 19–22. To protect American interests during an insurrection.

1857—Nicaragua, April–May; November–December. To oppose William Walker's attempt to get control of the country. In May, Commander C. H. Davis of the United States Navy, with some Marines, received Walker's surrender and protected his men from the retaliation of native allies who had been fighting Walker. In November and December of the same year, United States vessels *Saratoga,* *Wabash,* and *Fulton* opposed another attempt of William Walker on Nicaragua. Commodore Hiram Paulding's act of landing Marines and compelling the removal of Walker to the United States was tacitly disavowed by Secretary of State Lewis Cass, and Paulding was forced into retirement.

1858—Uruguay, January 2–27. Forces from two United

States warships landed to protect American property during a revolution in Montevideo.

1859—Paraguay. Congress authorized a naval squadron to seek redress for an attack on a naval vessel in the Paraná River during 1855. Apologies were made after a large display of force.

1859—Mexico. Two hundred United States soldiers crossed the Rio Grande in pursuit of the Mexican bandit Cortina.

1860—Colombia, Bay of Panama, September 27–October 8. To protect American interests during a revolution.

1865—Panama, March 9–10. To protect the lives and property of American residents during a revolution.

1866—Mexico. To protect American residents, General Sedgwick and 100 men obtained surrender of Matamoras in November. After three days he was ordered by our government to withdraw. His act was repudiated by the President.

1868—Uruguay, February 7–8; February 19–26. To protect foreign residents and the customhouse during an insurrection at Montevideo.

1868—Colombia, Aspinwall, April 7. To protect passengers and treasure in transit during the absence of local police or troops on the occasion of the death of the President of Colombia.

1870—Mexico, June 17–18. To destroy the pirate ship *Forward*, which had been run aground about 40 miles up the Rio Tecapan.

1873—Colombia, Bay of Panama, May 7–22; September 23–October 9. To protect American interests during hostilities over possession of the government of the State of Panama.

1873—Mexico. United States troops crossed the Mexican border repeatedly in pursuit of cattle and other thieves. There were some reciprocal pursuits by Mexican troops into our border territory. The cases were only technically invasions, if that, although Mexico protested constantly. Notable cases were at Remolina in May, 1873 and at Las Cuevas in 1878. Orders from Washington often supported these excursions. Agreements between Mexico and the United States, the first in 1882, finally legitimized such raids. They continued intermittently, with minor disputes, until 1896.

1876—Mexico, May 18. To police the town of Matamoros temporarily while it was without other government.

1885—Panama, Colón. January 18–19. To guard the valuables in transit over the Panama Railroad and the safes and vaults of the company during revolutionary activity. In March, April, and May in the cities of Colón and Panama, to reestablish freedom of transit during revolutionary activity.

1888—Haiti, December 20. To persuade the Haitian government to give up an American steamer which had been seized on the charge of breach of blockade.

1890—Argentina. A naval party landed to protect our consulate and legation in Buenos Aires.

1891—Haiti. To protect American lives and property on Navassa Island when Negro laborers got out of control.

1891—Chile, August 28–30. To protect the American consulate and the women and children who had taken refuge in it during a revolution in Valparaiso.

1894—Brazil, January. To protect American commerce and shipping at Rio de Janeiro during a Brazilian civil war. No landing was attempted, but there was a display of naval force.

1894—Nicaragua, July 6–August 7. To protect American interests at Bluefields following a revolution.

1895—Colombia, March 8–9. To protect American interests during an attack on the town of Bocas del Toro by a bandit chieftain.

1896—Nicaragua, May 2–4. To protect American interests in Corinto during political unrest.

1898—Nicaragua, February 7–8. To protect American lives and property at San Juan del Sur.

1899—Nicaragua. To protect American interests at San Juan del Norte, February 22–March 5, and at Bluefields a few weeks later in connection with the insurrection of General Juan P. Reyes.

1901—Colombia (State of Panama), November 20–December 4. To protect American property on the isthmus and to keep transit lines open during serious revolutionary disturbances.

1902—Colombia, April 16–23. To protect American lives and property at Bocas del Toro during a civil war.

1902—Colombia (State of Panama), September 17–

November 18. To place armed guards on all trains crossing the isthmus and to keep the railroad line open.

1903—Honduras, March 23–30 or 31. To protect the American consulate and the steamship wharf at Puerto Cortez during a period of revolutionary activity.

1903—Dominican Republic, March 30–April 21. To protect American interests in the city of Santo Domingo during a revolutionary outbreak.

1903–14—Panama. To protect American interests and lives during and following the revolution for independence from Colombia over construction of the Isthmian Canal. With brief intermissions, United States Marines were stationed on the isthmus from November 4, 1903 to January 21, 1914, to guard American interests.

1904—Dominican Republic, January 2–February 11. To protect American interests in Puerto Plata, Sosua, and Santo Domingo City during revolutionary fighting.

1904—Panama, November 17–24. To protect American lives and property at Ancon at the time of a threatened insurrection.

1906–9—Cuba, September 1906–January 23, 1909. Intervention to restore order, protect foreigners, and establish a stable government after serious revolutionary activity.

1907—Honduras, March 18–June 8. To protect American interests during a war between Honduras and Nicaragua. Troops were stationed for a few days or weeks in Trujillo, Ceiba, Puerto Cortez, San Pedro, Laguna, and Choloma.

1910—Nicaragua, February 22. During a civil war, to get information of conditions at Corinto. May 10–September 4, to protect American interests at Bluefields.

1911—Honduras, January 23 and some weeks thereafter. To protect American lives and interests during a civil war in Honduras.

1912—Honduras. Small force landed to prevent seizure by the government of an American-owned railroad at Puerto Cortez. Forces withdrawn after the United States disapproved the action.

1912—Panama. Troops, on request of both political parties, supervised elections outside the Canal Zone.

1912—Cuba, June 5–August 5. To protect American interests in the province of Oriente and in Havana.

1912–25—Nicaragua, August–November 1912. To protect American interests during an attempted revolution.

A small force serving as a legation guard and as a promoter of peace and governmental stability remained until August 5, 1925.

1913—Mexico, September 5–7. A few Marines landed at Ciaris Estero to aid in evacuating American citizens and others from the Yaqui Valley, made dangerous for foreigners by civil strife.

1914—Haiti, January 29–February 9; February 20–21, October 19. To protect American nationals in a time of dangerous unrest.

1914—Dominican Republic, June–July. During a revolutionary movement, United States naval forces, using gunfire, stopped the bombardment of Puerto Plata, and by threat of force maintained Santo Domingo City as a neutral zone.

1914–17—Mexico. The undeclared Mexican-American hostilities following the Dolphin affair and Villa's raids included capture of Vera Cruz and, later, Pershing's expedition into northern Mexico.

1915–34—Haiti, July 28, 1915–August 15, 1934. To maintain order during a period of chronic and threatened insurrection.

1916–24—Dominican Republic, May 1916–September 1924. To maintain order during a period of chronic and threatened insurrection.

1917–33—Cuba. To protect American interests during an insurrection and subsequent unsettled conditions. Most of the United States armed forces left Cuba by August 1919, but two companies remained at Camaguey until February 1933.

1918–19—Mexico. After withdrawal of the Pershing expedition, our troops entered Mexico in pursuit of bandits at least three times in 1918 and six in 1919. In August, 1918 American and Mexican troops fought at Nogales.

1918–20—Panama. For police duty according to treaty stipulations at Chiriqui during election disturbances and subsequent unrest.

1919—Honduras, September 8–12. A landing force was sent ashore to maintain order in a neutral zone during an attempted revolution.

1920—Guatemala, April 9–27. To protect the American Legation and other American interests, such as the cable station, during a period of fighting between unionists and the government of Guatemala.

1921—Panama-Costa Rica. American naval squadrons demonstrated in April on both sides of the isthmus to prevent war between the two countries over a boundary dispute.

1925—Honduras, April 19–21. To protect foreigners at La Ceiba during a political upheaval.

1925—Panama, October 12–23. Strikes and rent riots led to the landing of about 600 American troops to keep order and protect American interests.

1926–33—Nicaragua, May 7–June 5, 1926; August 27, 1926–January 3, 1933. The coup d'etat of General Chamorro aroused revolutionary activities leading to the landing of American Marines to protect the interests of the United States. U.S. forces came and went, but seem not to have left the country entirely until January 3, 1933. Their work included activity against the outlaw leader Sandino in 1928.

1933—Cuba. During a revolution against President Gerardo Machado naval forces demonstrated, but no landing was made.

1940—Newfoundland, Bermuda, St. Lucia, Bahamas, Jamaica, Antigua, Trinidad, and British Guiana. Troops were sent to guard air and naval bases obtained by negotiation with Great Britain. These were sometimes called lend-lease bases.

1941—Dutch Guiana. In November the President ordered American troops to occupy Dutch Guiana, but by agreement with the Netherlands government in exile. Brazil cooperated to protect aluminum ore supply from the bauxite mines in Dutch Guiana.

1957—Haiti, June. Alert, surface patrols during disorders.

1956–58—Cuba, December, 1956–December, 1958. Alert, evacuation, provided presence during Civil War.

1959—Panama, April. Provided presence.

1960—Caribbean, April–December. Alert, air, and surface patrols during tension.

1960—Guatemala-Nicaragua, November. Alert, air, and surface patrols.

1961—Cuba, May. Alert during Bay of Pigs crisis.

1961—Dominican Republic, November–December. Alert, air, and surface patrols.

1962—Cuba, January and July: Alert, provided presence during Guantanamo tension.

1962—Guatemala, March. Alert, provided presence.

1962—Cuba, October–November. Provided presence and intervention during missile crisis showdown with the Soviet Union.

1963—Caribbean. Alert, air, and surface patrols during tensions.

1963—Dominican Republic, September. Alert.

1964—Panama, January–April. Alert, provided presence and evacuation.

1964—Cuba, April–July. Provided presence and surface patrols in Guantanamo tensions.

1964—Panama, May. Provided presence.

1964—Dominican Republic, June–July. Air and surface patrols.

1965—Dominican Republic, April. Intervention and combat operations.

INDEX